A STORY OF SIX RIVERS

# A Story of Six Rivers

## History, Culture and Ecology

PETER COATES

REAKTION BOOKS

*This book is dedicated to the memory of my mother,*
*Lotte Coates (née Petonke) (1922–2008),*
*who also loved flowing water.*

*Published by*
Reaktion Books Ltd
33 Great Sutton Street
London EC1V 0DX, UK

www.reaktionbooks.co.uk

First published 2013
Copyright © Peter Coates 2013

Printed and bound in Great Britain
by TJ International, Padstow, Cornwall

British Library Cataloguing in Publication Data
Coates, Peter A., 1957–
  A story of six rivers : history, culture and ecology.
  1. Rivers. 2. Rivers – Social aspects. 3. Rivers – Economic
  aspects.
  I. Title
  551.4'83–dc23

ISBN 978 1 78023 106 8

# Contents

# Introduction

One of Rome's biggest tourist attractions is Gianlorenzo Bernini's Fountain of the Four Rivers (*Fontana dei Quattro Fiumi*), which has graced Piazza Navona since 1652. The fountain's main ingredients are a marble grotto from which water tumbles into a circular pool, an Egyptian-style granite obelisk and four river deities. Most river deities, from the Nile and Volga to Ireland's Boyne, are female; but there are no goddesses in Piazza Navona. The flowing beards of the gods perched in various postures on the projecting outer edges of the hulking, hollowed-out rock formation evoke the water from the fountain's supply: the Aqua Vergine, a still-functioning ancient Roman aqueduct, funnels water from springs in the marshland thirteen kilometres to the east. Each personified river represents one of the known continents: the Nile (Africa), the Ganges (Asia), the Rio de la Plata (the Americas) and the Danube (Europe).

By the mid-seventeenth century, the deployment of rivers as continental representatives was a familiar 'iconographical device'.[1] Claude Lévi-Strauss remarked that animals are not only "'good to eat'" but also "'good to think'".[2] That rivers are also 'good to think [with]' was demonstrated centuries earlier by Marcus Aurelius. At Carnuntum, a military camp on the Danube's right-hand bank (near today's Austrian border with Slovakia), the Roman emperor over-wintered for three consecutive years during the wars against the Germanic tribes that threatened his empire's northern, Danubian frontier. With plenty of time on his hands, Marcus Aurelius recorded his *Meditations*. One entry invited his readers to 'Consider always this universe as one living being or animal; with one material substance, and one spirit; and how all things are referred to the sense of this spirit . . . and what a connexion and contexture there is among all things.'[3] Turning to the river that flowed past Carnuntum, he reflected that 'Time is a river, or violent torrent of things coming into being; each one, as soon as it has appeared, is swept off and disappears, and is succeeded by another, which is swept away in its turn.'[4] The emperor's meditations not only suggested the links between the passage of time and a river's flow.[5] He also dwelled on how a river exemplified that individual phenomena were in 'regular connexion . . . joined together in the most apposite contexture'.[6] Piazza Navona's dynamic ensemble of river gods embodies Marcus Aurelius's fluvial philosophy. The deities are complemented by the emblematic fauna associated with their respective rivers and continents. A horse splashes into the water from a crevasse beneath the Danube god. The Nile is accompanied by a lion crouching down to drink and a crocodile sports in the drink.

If the use of rivers to symbolize continents was familiar practice, then the choice of this particular quartet has usually been explained with reference to their global pre-eminence: these were the world's four principal rivers.[7] The Nile was the obvious inclusion for Africa, given Rome's longstanding connections with Egypt's river and its acknowledged distinction as its continent's greatest river.[8] And though the Plate is markedly shorter than the Amazon if the name is applied strictly to the 290-kilometre stretch beyond the confluence of the Uruguay and Paraná rivers, which effectively consists of a funnel-shaped estuary (the world's broadest), if measured from the Paraná's source, the Plate is 3,740 kilometres long. Moreover, its basin is second in size only to the Amazon's within South America. The Danube was indisputably the longest river in what was considered Europe at the time (Russia's Volga would not have counted). Regardless of their ranking among the world's leading rivers, however, the selection of the Nile, Ganges and Plate reflects the specific fluvial geography of the missionary enterprises of Pope Innocent x, who commissioned the fountain.

Completing the illustrious quartet is the Ganges, which is by no means Asia's longest river. Just as the Plate provided access to the interior for Jesuit activity in South America, the Ganges was a major conduit for Christianity's penetration of Asia. In his left hand, the semi-reclining Ganges deity bears an oar, presumably to steer the ship of the church. The postures and positions of the four deities reflect their relationships to Christianity. The Nile and Ganges, located on the fountain's eastern side, face away from the spire-like pagan obelisk topped by the insignia of papal power and symbols of the faith (a bronze dove bearing an olive sprig in its beak), perhaps to convey their ignorance of the holy light. In the case of the Nile's shrouded head, it may also indicate that its source remained unknown in the mid-1600s.[9]

Twisting backward and gazing upward, the Danube god enjoys a more comfortable relationship with the symbols of faith above them. But its inclusion may have raised some local eyebrows. The Tiber already symbolized Catholic Europe (as well as Rome) and geographical proximity to Piazza Navona (not to mention the Danube's general absence from contemporary fountain iconography) also seems to give the local river an advantage. Moreover, the twinning of Tiber and Nile was a traditional Roman strategy.[10]

Whether or not it was part of Bernini's original conception, powerful political considerations privileged the Danube.[11] Its basin was a sharply contested religious frontier. The lower river was under Turkish control and Protestantism was ascendant in Austria, Bohemia and Hungary. Though the Treaty of Westphalia (1648) that ended the Thirty Years War had restored these Protestant areas to papal jurisdiction, Innocent was under fire for territorial losses.[12] By including the Danube, he sought to concentrate attention on those aspects of the treaty favourable to Catholicism to boost the morale of formerly Catholic regions and to unite Christendom against the encroaching Turks; Danube holds the papal shield aloft and his surging horse connotes military might.[13] The fountain's iconography lends itself to multiple interpretation. According to the received wisdom, the confection proclaims Catholicism's global authority, heralding a new Roman empire of faith under papal rule.[14] A more ambitious view sees Bernini's design returning the four rivers that flow out of Eden in the Book of Genesis to a single shared source.[15] As Simon Schama observes, the fountain of the four rivers is 'where all the currents of river mythology, Eastern and Western, Egyptian and Roman, pagan and Christian, flowed toward one great sacred stream'.[16]

## Six Rivers

At first, I was also tempted to foreground the notion of a singular, essentialist river. I was also inclined to take a leaf out of Bernini's book and treat the world as my catchment area, dipping into particular streams and watersheds as and when I saw fit. I envisaged the selection of up to twenty rivers representing all continents – some well-known, others not so famous – to be deployed with reference to key themes that would provide the structure: how rivers nurture us and other creatures (river of life), provide us with opportunities (river of riches; river of recreation), confront us with dangers (river of peril) and inform our cultural life (river of inspiration). Each chapter's organizational form would be dendritic. Imitating the shape of a large spreading tree, or a major river's drainage basin, branches (examples) would shoot off from a central thematic trunk. But as I became more deeply immersed, I grew concerned that the thematic approach would damage the character of the rivers in my pool. Chopped into segments featuring in different chapters, the organic integrity and distinctive identity of particular rivers would be swamped. As the nineteenth-century German geographer Carl Ritter observed, rivers 'must be examined singly; they must be studied in their real character and individuality'. Though he added that 'each must have its own monograph', the least I could do was devote a chapter to an individual river.[17] Also keen to root my study in the materiality, or, should I say, the liquidity of rivers, and to convey a strong sense of fluvial place, I then flirted with the idea of confining my coverage to Bernini's four rivers.

This presented fresh problems. I have dipped my feet into the Ganges at Varanasi. Yet I have never set eyes on the Nile or Plate. Mindful that 'rivers are not to be known from books',[18] I did not want to write about rivers I did not know. Of Bernini's four, this left me with the Danube. Finalizing the list of six (four seemed too few) was enjoyable if sometimes exasperating. Hardly a week passed without a new river commending itself or without friends offering suggestions ('You're not including the Avon?'; 'What about the Mississippi?'). Developing watertight criteria was difficult, particularly since I feel the same way about length as Henry David Thoreau. 'I am accustomed to regard the smallest brook with as much interest for the time being as if it were the Orinoco or Mississippi', he recorded in his journal in 1850. 'What is the difference, I would like to know, but mere size? And when a tributary rill empties in, it is like the confluence of famous rivers I have read of. When I cross one on a fence, I love to pause in mid-passage and look down into the water and study its bottom, its little mystery.'[19] Henry Van Dyke, another nineteenth-century American nature writer based in the northeast, also celebrated small rivers, notably the trout streams of the Catskill Mountains in upstate New York: 'I am all for the little rivers. Let those who will, chant in heroic verse the renown of Amazon and Mississippi and Niagara, but my prose shall flow – in praise of Beaverkill and Neversink and Swiftwater.'[20]

Despite the appeal of 'small is beautiful', it was hard to make a case for inclusion of some of the rivers I know best. Like Thoreau's Nut Meadow Brook, near Concord, Massachusetts, they are simply too small and carry purely local or regional meaning. That little rivers possess 'small responsibilities' (Van Dyke's phrase[21]) – they are not expected to carry large ships, power factories or provide big fish – is a bigger problem for a historian than for a nature writer. My favourite 'little river' is an unassuming watercourse that rises in an acid flush atop the Quantock Hills in Somerset. Flowing down Sheppard's Combe and Hodder's Combe, steep valleys thickly wooded with sessile oak, then onward through Holford Glen (whose waterfall was one of Dorothy Wordsworth's favourite haunts when she and her brother lived nearby), the stream enters the Bristol Channel within eight kilometres of its origins. The brook that soaks into the pebbles at Kilve Beach is not navigable and, apart from powering the mill wheels of a silk factory and tannery, has had little commercial import.[22] Holford Brook is probably known to few aside from aficionados of Samuel Taylor Coleridge and the Wordsworth siblings, who spent a highly creative year together in this area (1797–8); the trio was in its element wandering around and tracing tiny streams to their source springs. 'I sought for a subject', reflected Coleridge in a tone reminiscent of Marcus Aurelius,

> that should give equal room and freedom for description, incident, and impassioned reflections on men, nature, and society, yet supply in itself a natural connection to the parts, and unity to the whole. Such a subject I conceived myself to have found in a stream, traced from its source in the hills among the yellow-red moss and conical glass-shaped tufts of bent.

He undertook extensive fieldwork in preparation for an epic poem – to be entitled 'The Brook' – that never made it past the drawing board.[23]

At the same time, I felt that major rivers I knew reasonably well – the Columbia, Colorado, Mississippi, Rhine and Thames – were over-exposed. Bobbing along in the wake of other relatively recent historians and commentators struck me as a dull exercise.[24] I finally settled on six rivers: three from continental Europe, one from Britain, and two from North America: the Danube, Spree, Po, Mersey, Yukon and Los Angeles.

Had Philip Freneau, the prominent American cultural nationalist, ever visited Rome, it is unlikely that he would have been impressed by Bernini's fountain. In 1780, he hailed the Mississippi as 'the prince of rivers, in comparison of whom the *Nile* is but a small rivulet, and the *Danube* a ditch'.[25] Notwithstanding Freneau's dismissive attitude to the old world's natural accomplishments and spread-eagled effort to boost his national river, my first river requires little introduction. The Danube, reputedly hailed by Napoleon Bonaparte as the 'king of rivers', is Europe's longest (excepting Russia's Volga).[26] More importantly, it is the world's most international river. With this one exception, each of my rivers is housed within a single country. One is even contained within a single American state (California). Another crosses just a few smallish English counties. For these, the Danube, which flows through or borders ten countries, provides generous compensation.

Not one of these rivers contained within a single nation state has achieved the uncontested status of 'national riverscape', as defined by Tricia Cusack, who explores the relationship between riverscapes and national identities in nineteenth- and early twentieth-century Europe and the United States from the perspectives of art history and visual culture. She pursues the conversion of particular rivers into national rivers in the United States, England, France, Russia and Ireland through case studies of the Hudson, Thames, Seine, Volga and Shannon.[27] My selection criteria are quite different – as is my primary focus, as an environmental historian, on the river rather than the riverscape as a cultural construction. The appeal of the Spree is partly the appeal of Berlin. But I would rather investigate a river that even many Germans know little about than *the* German river, the Rhine, the Teutonic equivalent of the Thames.[28] The Spree may be an eminently regional river, short even by modest German standards, and does not even carry its name all the way to the North Sea. Yet it played a distinctive role in the Cold War and Berlin provides an instructive example of a growing international phenomenon: the river city's recent rediscovery of urban fluvial identity. I was struck by the Spree's potential, paradoxically, when I visited Berlin for a photo exhibition on the Danube. The Spree, it quickly became clear, is to Berlin what the Seine is to Paris and the Thames is to London.

In 1542, Heinrich Loriti Glareanus's *De geographia* summarized collective knowledge of the earth's physical features. His map of the world only had room for two European rivers: the Danube and the Rhine.[29] And according to Carlile Aylmer Macartney, chief adviser to the British Foreign Office on Eastern Europe during the Second World War, the Danube was of such enormous geographical and historical significance that it rendered 'even the Rhine itself, and much more the rivers of France, Italy or England . . . mere provincials'.[30] Nonetheless, I have included an Italian river. Insofar as Italy is associated with rivers, then the Tiber and Arno are those that commend themselves: 'Can anyone think of Caesar's Rome or Dante's Florence without picturing the Tiber or the Arno?'[31] The most celebrated Italian riverscape is undeniably the view of the Arno from the upper floors of the Uffizi Gallery or the Ponte Vecchio in Florence. Yet neither the Tiber nor the Arno is Italy's longest river, or the most important of modern times.

And it would be hard to describe either as Italy's national river. In contrast, the Po meets the first two of these criteria and has some claim on the third. *Il grande fiume* is sometimes also referred to, affectionately, as *Il Mississippi Italiano* or *Il nostro Old Man River*. I found it far more interesting to write about the *Italian* Mississippi. Besides, *Il grande fiume* possesses truly global significance: the Po valley is one of the world's most favoured agricultural regions, with the Nile a frequent point of reference.[32] Moreover, while there are many things the Po may not be, it is certainly a peerless river of gastronomy. An additional claim to grand status is that the science of river control was born on its banks, or, more accurately put, was grounded in the struggle to keep the river *within* its banks.

The Thames would have been an obvious candidate for inclusion as my British river: the 'mighty King' of British rivers, superior to all others in beauty and importance (according to a commentator in 1801).[33] Instead, I have opted for the shorter, less pastoral and less frequently eulogized river that dominated my boyhood landscape: the Mersey. London and New Orleans spring to mind as cities that exude the special flavour of great river cities. Yet Liverpool enjoys just as intimate and notable fluvial links. Must a river contained within a few English counties or a single American state necessarily be a purely local or little river? Not in the case of Virginia's James, according to Blair Niles, because of its national significance as the birthplace of the nation. In similar style, the Mersey's pivotal position within the history of industrialization has earned it the hyperbolic accolade of 'the river that changed the world' (echoes of William Maitland's eighteenth-century view that the Thames was unequalled 'by any other River in the whole World' because of the importance of its navigation and commerce and the 'incredible Number of People it wholly maintains').[34]

Little more than a century later, it was Liverpool's turn. Second city of the British empire, the future European Capital of Culture (2008) possessed one of the world's most imposing urban riverscapes. The waterfront focused on the 'Three Graces' at the Pier Head – buildings 'as magnificent as their cousins in Shanghai and Chicago'[35] – is the centrepiece of Liverpool 'Maritime Mercantile City', designated a UNESCO World Heritage Site in 2004.[36] A late Victorian enthusiast for industrial progress regaled the river to whose care the 'wealth of nations is entrusted'.[37] 'There is not, probably, a river in the world', mused French geographer Élisée Reclus in the 1880s, 'which sets in motion the wheels of so many mills and carries on its back so many vessels, as does the Mersey'.[38]

Biologically, however, the river paid a stiff price for serving the needs of Britain's most densely populated region and economic powerhouse. If the Duddon, a river in the Lake District, less than a hundred miles away, was 'remote from every taint of sordid industry' (William Wordsworth) in the early 1800s, then the Mersey was deeply stained.[39] Moreover, as rivers in the western world have bounced back in the wake of heavy industry's decline, the Mersey also furnishes a rich case study of a written-off river's unlikely biological comeback. Like the Danube, its rehabilitation has been recognized by the award of Riverfestival's Thiess International Riverprize.[40] This accolade was bestowed on an organization whose focus and clean-up enterprise was basin-wide. The modest dimensions of the Mersey compared to the Po and Danube provides the opportunity to approach a European river within the broad context of its catchment as a whole.

My penultimate river, the Yukon, is by far the most impressive in terms of length and size of watershed (within which several European countries could be hidden). With a catchment that extends over half a million square kilometres, the more than 3,000-kilometre long Yukon is not over-awed in the company of Nile and Amazon. As the Mersey provides the chance to integrate a river fully within its basin – unfeasible for North America's fourth largest – the Yukon supplies the chance to discuss exploration, feats of daring and encounters of a modern imperial nature more readily asso-ciated with rivers in Africa and South America (the point of departure being explorers' own analogies with the Amazon, Congo and Nile).[41] The Yukon is also, by a long shot, the wildest and most untrammelled of my six rivers. In fact, its wildness stands out on any comparative scale; just 21 (12 per cent) of the world's 177 longest rivers flow uninterrupted from source to sea.[42] The Yukon is distinctive too for being a river in a cold zone. Whereas all my other rivers circulate within the temperate zone (regardless of the frigidity of their winters) the Yukon lies within the upper sub-arctic, which means that its flow is frozen for most of the year.

Finally, I thought it would be stimulating to examine a truly obscure river that, despite bisecting another famous city, few people have actually heard of. Though the Los Angeles River was the reason Spanish colonists founded a pueblo outpost on its lower banks in the 1760s – the seed of the eponymous city to which it gave its name – many Los Angelenos remain oblivious to its existence (excepting those who appreciate its value as the world's longest linear canvas for tagging and street art). The Los Angeles river also appealed because of its dramatically altered condition. If the Yukon is one of the least modified of rivers –a 'true wilderness river' according to *National Geographic*[43] – then the Los Angeles is one of the most profoundly reconfigured and disfigured. Since the 1930s, it has been straitjacketed in concrete and is often without substantial liquid content. The river is so extensively metamorphosed that, some would argue, it has lost its status as a river and, hence, its place in local consciousness. And yet, like Berlin and Liverpool, Los Angeles is currently reawakening to its river following a long period of estrangement. Rio L.A.'s plight inspired one of the world's first and still most active grassroots river restoration campaigns.

## Fluvial Power

Rivers symbolize nature's awesome powers. Yet they are also a sinuous blend, the collective product, not just of geology, ecology and climate, but of economics, technology, politics and human imaginings. The lifeblood of communities, they provide habitat and sustenance (river of life). Herodotus characterized ancient Egypt as the 'gift of the Nile' (her floods the tears of the goddess Isis). For Egyptians, it was 'at once their father and their god'.[44] Similarly, London has been dubbed the gift of the Thames. Rivers give us water, fish, hydropower and a means of getting around (even in winter when frozen, in the case of the Spree and Yukon). They have functioned as highways of exploration and arteries of empire. Commerce flows up and down them as well as water. Bernini's deity of the Plate (which, in Spanish, means Silver River) sits next to a bag that spills coins, exemplars of his continent's precious metallic wealth (river of riches). A more realistic way of looking at the material contributions of rivers is to see them as extracted goods rather than spontaneous gifts. The geological significance of a 'working' river is matched by its economic role, more 'servant' than 'god' (to employ the terminology of Reclus[45]). Political-strategic import complements the importance of this labour: rivers connect and divide nations and regions.[46] How we have converted rivers to our needs also exemplifies human control over the rest of the natural world (river of power). Yet rivers illustrate the limits of our authority as well as our unbounded technological prowess and enormous capacity to foul the natural world to within an inch of its life (river of death).

Rivers can impoverish as well as enrich. This dilemma is vividly illu -strated by the long-running dispute between the city states of Padua and Venice over the Brenta, a river fed by alpine snowmelt that frequently burst its banks. As an early nineteenth-century author observed, 'the interests of Padua and Venice were so diverse as to its course that battles were fought for the mere object of demolishing an old dike or constructing a new one'.[47] The first rerouting in 1142 afforded Padua a greater measure of security by moving the river closer to its rival. This presented the Venetian republic with a quandary. On the one hand, the Brenta's arrival in its backyard bestowed considerable commercial advantage by providing a direct link with the flour, gravel, hay, wines and livestock of its hinterland on the mainland. The most precious cargo carried into the city, however, was the Brenta's water itself; the contents of watertight barges slaked the thirst of a city encircled by saltwater. (Returning traffic shipped spices, cloths, oils, soap, glass, books and fish into the interior.) On the debit side, the re-directed river also delivered large quantities of silt to the lagoon, jeopardizing the shipping channels on which the city's prosperity rested. The biggest re-engineering project, the *Taglio Nuovissimo del Brenta*, in the early 1600s, replaced the lower Brenta with a canal that carried the river's flow five miles below Venice.[48]

The dispute between Bologna and Ferrara over the Reno's course provides another glorious northern Italian example of the fluvial dimensions of inter-city rivalry. The Reno, a short but particularly fast-flowing Apennine tributary that joined the Po at Ferrara, was subject to extensive manipulation in the early 1600s. As part of a larger scheme to gain the edge over Venice by tinkering with the Po's main channel, Ferrara diverted the Reno into a marshy area, which aggravated the susceptibility of the Bolognese plain to inundation. Bologna's alternative plan for the Reno, needless to say, damaged Ferrarese interests. A powerful visual insight into this controversy can be gleaned from the best-known work of a prominent Bolognese hydraulic scientist. The frontispiece of Domenico Guglielmini's *Della natura de' fiumi trattato fisico-matematico* (1697) depicts three mythological figures: Achelous, Hercules and Abundance. Achelous was the patron deity of the river of the same name, Greece's longest and largest (now known as the Aspropotamos), which was notoriously flood-prone. A devious and changeable creature, Achelous initially metamorphoses into a snake, which symbolizes a winding river, whereas the guise of a raging bull he later assumes in his fight with Hercules for the hand of Dejanira personifies a roaring river in spate. The horn he loses in the contest stands for a river's subjugation through embankment and canalization. And the prize secured by Hercules, Dejanira, represents the promise of the delta, whose potential can now be realized. Meanwhile, Achelous's lost horn becomes an emblem of abundance: the overflowing horn of plenty (cornucopia) from which the blessed fruits of harvest cascade.[49] In the engraving that forms the frontispiece of Guglielmini's book, Hercules gestures with his left hand to signal the works undertaken to domesticate the wild river. The two towns in the background are believed to be Bologna and Ferrara, which, as the inscription suggests, were are loggerheads over what to do with the Reno.[50]

Whereas some rivers are canalized or encased in concrete, their flow regulated by our requirements rather than nature's laws, others defy efforts to subdue them (river of peril). Devastating floodwaters remain a hazard from the Danube to China's 'River of Tears' (the Yangtze's soubriquet). And rivers can become cleaner as well as dirtier. Especially in urban environments, many rivers are currently enjoying ecological rehabilitation, cleaner today than at any time since the late eighteenth century (river of rebirth).

This reversal in fortunes was apparent during the commemoration in 2009 of the 400th anniversary of Henry Hudson's entry – on his fruitless quest for a short cut to Asia – into the river that bears his name. One of the ways in which the Wave Hill gallery and gardens (located on the banks of the Hudson in New York City's Bronx, overlooking the Palisades) marked the Hudson Quadricentennial was an exploration by contemporary artists of the Native American presence on the tidal river they called the Muhheak-antuck (a Lenape word meaning 'the river that flows both ways'). 'The Muhheakantuck in Focus' departed from a standard meta-narrative of decline. *Please the Waters*, by the Cheyenne Arapaho artist Hock E Aye Vi Edgar Heap of Birds, an outdoor exhibit, consisted of eight aluminium highway-style signs in blue dotted around the lawns. One pair of signs contrasted the estuarine river 'circa 1960' ('Muhheakantuck Knows Dioxin Polychlorinated Biphenyl') with the river 'circa 2005' (Muhheakantuck Knows Hudson Shad, Osprey, Striped Bass, Bald Eagle, Atlantic Sturgeon'). *Harvest*, by Mary Anne Barkhouse, also conveyed cautious optimism: a long table swathed with a river-like flow of blue taffeta, displayed a series of white porcelain sculptures of water lily pads; a porcelain beaver feeds on this symbol of the bountiful river (beaver recently returned to the nearby Bronx River).[51]

As the Wave Hill installations indicate, rivers furnish raw materials for cultural expression as well as providing clean water to drink and to catch fish and to swim in. They course through our imaginations as well as through and over our bodies. Riparian metaphors and expressions saturate our language ('you can't step into the same river'; 'we'll cross that river when we come to it'; 'cry me a river'[52]). Spiritual systems enshrine them (river of reverence). They enthral painters, musicians, song writers, novelists

'Muhheakantuck Knows Hudson Shad, Osprey, Striped Bass, Bald Eagle, Atlantic Sturgeon', by Hock E Aye Vi Edgar Heap of Birds, 2009.

and poets (river of inspiration). 'The power of water over the minds of Poets has been acknowledged from the earliest ages', reflected Wordsworth in the preface to a series of sonnets about his wanderings along the Duddon between its source on Wrynose Fell and its outlet in the Irish Sea after 25 miles.[53]

As well as a source of sustenance, river water is a source of delight and amusement. Bernini's fountain provided diversion as well as supplying drinking water from an artificial underground river. Every Sunday in August (Saturdays too, according to some sources), between 1652 and the 1860s, the four rivers flooded Piazza Navona – which hosted a fruit and vegetable market on Wednesdays – to create a shallow lake. The local populace, young and old, rich and poor, derived enormous pleasure from what they dubbed *Lago di Piazza Navona*. A British guidebook author looked back on this recently terminated practice disapprovingly from a sanitary standpoint:

> Those who kept, or could afford to hire carriages, used to drive backwards and forwards through the water, stirring up the refuse of decayed vegetables below, while the poorer sat around in crowds enjoying the fun. When the sluices were opened, some of the

accumulated refuse of the week was carried off. The remainder, soaked with water, lay and rotted in the sweltering August sun.[54]

Rivers proper (as distinct from Roman aqueducts) provide a more salubrious amenity and supply leisure opportunities on their banks as well as in and on the water (river of recreation). They even furnish companionship. For Van Dyke, a river was 'the most human and companionable of all inanimate things. It has a life, a character, a voice of its own . . . For real company and friendship, there is nothing outside the animal kingdom that is comparable to a river'. The riverside was the perfect place for life's most important things. 'It is by a river that I would choose to make love . . . to confess my faults, and to escape from vain, selfish desires, and to cleanse my mind from all the false and foolish things that mar the joy and peace of living.'[55]

We also take pride in rivers as a source of identity, local, regional and national. As Constance Lindsay Skinner explained in the manifesto for the avowedly populist 'Rivers of America' book series that she launched in 1937, 'we began to be Americans on the rivers . . . The first foreigners on these shores began their transition from Europeans to Americans as River Folk'.[56] This sense of an umbilical connection can also be detected in the Merseysider's belief that all other rivers 'shrink into insignificance' alongside the Mersey (another estuarine river that 'flows both ways').[57] For the ancient Chinese, the Yangtze was 'Great River' or, simply, 'The River'. The aboriginal peoples of the Carrier Nation called British Columbia's Fraser *Tacoutche Tesse*: The Mighty One.[58] All river people think of their river as *the* river. En route to Italy in the autumn of 1838, Lord (Thomas Babington) Macaulay, the historian, poet and Whig politician, paused to reflect on this peculiar form of riparian affection in Lyon as he caught his first glimpse of the 'blue, rushing, healthful-looking', glacier-fed Rhône while strolling along the quayside to his steamer to Avignon. His 25 October diary entry noted 'the singular love and veneration which rivers excite in those who live on their banks; of the feeling of the Hindoos about the Ganges; of the Hebrews about the Jordan; of the Egyptians about the Nile; of the Germans about the Rhine'.[59]

Those who write about rivers also engage in flagrant one-upmanship – a liquid form of ethnocentricity. In his paean to London's river, Peter Ackroyd argues (presumably because he believes that London is the world's greatest city) that the Thames can 'fairly claim to be the most historic (and certainly the most eventful) river in the world'.[60] Simon Winchester is equally convinced that the Yangtze qualifies as the world's most important river, for, 'more than any other river in the world – more even [than] the Nile, which also cradles an entire country and nurtures a civilization – the Yangtze is a mother-river.' Lobbying for one river often involves denigrating others. The Nile and Amazon may be slightly longer; however, for Winchester, their social, economic and cultural importance is 'almost nothing by comparison'.[61]

Promotional exercises of this sort get us nowhere. What is incontrovertible, though, is that the control of a great river through a mega-dam is one of the most emphatic advertisements of collective human prowess, national clout and the muscle of the central state. In June 1956, to demonstrate his potency as a revolutionary leader, Chairman Mao took a highly politicized and carefully orchestrated plunge into the Yangtze. His aim was two-fold: to demonstrate that only the most powerful of men could swim in the most powerful of rivers; and that there was no limit to what could be done to a river. That very evening (supposedly), he dashed off a poem ('Swimming') whose second stanza directly refers to a new great wall, originally proposed by Sun Yat-sen in 1919.

> We will make a stone wall
> against the upper river to the west
> And hold back steamy clouds and rain of Wu peaks.
> Over tall chasms will be a calm lake,
> and if the goddess of these mountains is not dead
> She will marvel at the changed world.[62]

Whether or not Asia's longest river (well over twice the Ganges' length) is also the world's most important river, the recently completed Three Gorges scheme is indisputably the world's biggest dam project. 'Our country must be very strong and prosperous, we can stop the river', remarks an old man, as he watches the waters rise behind the impoundment, in Chinese-Canadian director Yung Chang's elegiac documentary film *Up the Yangtze* (2007), on the eve of the river's transformation by this peerless example of the technological sublime, informed by the ethos of 'high modernism' that transcended national boundaries and political ideologies.[63]

For many environmental historians and environmentalists, how we calm, harness, rearrange and degrade rivers epitomizes human dominion over – and abuse of – the rest of nature. A good deal of recent writing excoriates this record of manipulation and ruination through interventions such as damming, channelization, canalization, water extraction and contamination. This body of work also laments the resultant biological impoverishment, loss of free-flowing wildness and repercussions for adjacent floodplains and riparian lands. In 'Goodbye to a River' (2000), Don Henley laments how a river 'running wild' was put 'in a box' by 'man' who 'must have control'. His song's title is borrowed from a book by a fellow-'river-minded' Texan, John Graves, about the imminent emasculation of a Texas river, the 800-mile Brazos, by a series of dams.[64] Graves dedicated *Goodbye to a River* (1960) to his daughter, Helen, hoping that 'the world she will know will still have a few rivers and other quiet things in it'.

This declensionist narrative of rivers not only diminished but sometimes defunct is encapsulated in the apocalyptic titles of books on the Colorado and Columbia, two of North America's most intensively regulated major rivers: *A River No More*, *All My Rivers Are Gone* and *A River Lost*. *All My Rivers Are Gone* is dedicated to 'The Once and Future Glen Canyon with its Free-Flowing Colorado River', and speaks of a 'crucified' river. The author of *A River Lost*, whose father helped build Grand Coulee Dam in the 1930s, deplores the Columbia's reduction, by the early 1990s, to 'a chain of slow-moving puddles'.[65] This genre of river scholarship rightly exposes how we squander natural capital (the wealth of nature, as Donald Worster calls it, adapting Adam Smith's notion of the wealth of nations).[66] The drawback, though, is that this approach reinforces the divide between the natural and the unnatural; 'a natural and unnatural history' features as subtitle for two books. The front cover of one of these studies presents this dichotomy in stark visual terms: the upper half depicts a tranquil and timeless 'natural' scenario devoid of human input and impact, while the lower half portrays a bustling and denatured urban-industrial Chicago River.[67]

This is a stale conceptual juxtaposition and unhelpful 'before and after' scenario. As well as adopting this 'before the Europeans' approach, ecologist Ellen Wohl introduces the concept of the virtual river: freshwater, say, that looks natural (pristine even) but whose diverse physical form has been heavily modified and which has been stripped of most of its equally diverse ecosystem functions. Yet a narrative based on the 'simplifications of river form and function' is of restricted value to historians.[68] Distinguishing between a river 'in the truest sense' and other rivers is a blunt analytical tool. Treating rivers first and foremost as our victims also limits our potential insight. It is all well and good to dedicate a book to young people 'in the hope that they grow up in a world with respect for rivers'. But crying a river over a river does nobody any good.

In jocular mood, after visiting Cologne and noting 72 distinct 'stenches', Coleridge penned a ditty (1828) about its river's industrial degradation.

> Ye Nymphs that reign o'er sewers and sinks,
> The river Rhine, it is well known,
> Doth wash your city of Cologne;
> But tell me, Nymphs! what power divine
> Shall henceforth wash the river Rhine?[69]

Coleridge also had a clear sense of the contrast between a wild water-course and its muzzled counterpart. His analogy of 1810 for the difference in human discourse between truth and debased truth (vulgarity) was to 'compare a brook in the open air, liable to rainstreams and rills from new-opened fountains' to 'the same running through a mill guarded by sluice-gates and back-water'.[70] This perspective, absolutely fine for a late eighteenth-century romantic poet, is less suitable for a twenty-first-century historian. I am less concerned with what we have done to rivers than with what they have done to us. And I am most interested in what we do *with* rivers. Without being glib or complacent, this account of interactions between people and rivers emphasizes change rather than destruction and the production of new and different rivers rather than non-rivers, lost rivers, silent rivers or dead rivers.[71]

Just as working horses in nineteenth-century cities were 'living machines', fully harnessed rivers are 'organic machines'. As Richard White emphasizes, the Columbia, though transformed by human intervention, retains its 'unmade' attributes: 'It is not dead . . . It lies hidden in aluminium factories and pulp mills, in electric lights and washing machine.' The river has not vanished. Nor has it been killed or raped.[72] To adopt the termin-ology common among the Stoics (articulated in this instance by Marcus Tullius Cicero), first nature remains active within human-fashioned 'second nature': 'We fertilize the soil by irrigation . . . we confine the rivers and straighten or divert their courses . . . In fine, by means of our hands we essay to create as it were a second world of nature within the world of nature.'[73] Even without our intervention, rivers change their morphology. Suspended material hauled to estuaries is dumped on contact with salt-water, extending river mouths out into the sea. Having built its bed, the river runs into the sand. Abandoning its former channel, it then seeks the most direct route to the sea. Rivers are works in progress.

This book deals in variety. Many rivers are shackled and subdued. Others remain wilful and unpredictable. Some are heavily polluted and belong to the category of endangered waterways; all of Bernini's rivers feature on the World Wide Fund for Nature's list of top ten 'rivers at risk' (2007).[74] Others have begun to recover from near-death experience. In 1957, scientists at the Natural History Museum in London announced that the Thames that flowed through the capital was 'biologically dead'; the amount of dissolved oxygen was so low no life could survive. In October 2010, the International Riversymposium awarded the Thames the International Thiess Riverprize for outstanding achievements in recovery.[75] Biodiversity is returning to revitalized rivers across the developed world.

Regardless of their biological condition, we routinely imbue rivers with recognizably human qualities. This habit is particularly entrenched among writers of popular history; lazy, wandering, impatient, ill-tempered, unruly and capricious are standard descriptors (some of these character analyses are gender specific; one American river is 'feminine in its moods and caprices' while another possesses 'devious ways like a woman'). 'If the river could speak' is a favourite gambit and writers of fiction habitually personify rivers.[76] Rudyard Kipling's poem 'The River's Tale', a self-narrated history of the Thames, relates how the 'earliest Cockney' 'trapped my beavers at Westminster', 'caught my salmon' and 'killed my herons off Lambeth Pier'.[77] 'Is it that rivers have', pondered Macaulay in Lyon, seeking to explain their attraction, 'in a greater degree than almost any other inanimate object, the appearance of animation, and something resembling character? They are sometimes slow and dark-looking; sometimes fierce and impetuous; sometimes bright, dancing and almost flippant.' He speculated that rivers mirror national characteristics: 'The attachment of the French for the Rhône may be explained into a very natural sympathy. It is a vehement, rapid stream. It seems cheerful and full of animal spirits, even to petulance.'[78] For Van Dyke, Norwegian rivers are short and vigorous. English rivers move smoothly. And Scottish rivers 'brawl' and 'flash'.[79]

So rivers matter. They play a significant role in human affairs. They are powerful. They can be a city's *raison d'être*. They make a difference to our lives. They capture our attention. Also, making due allowance for literary flourish, they palpably possess character and their own will and direction. But are they also protagonists in a 'wet book of history'?[80] Historical studies of rivers abound, yet they tend to feature as a more or less inert backdrop to the main human action and spectacle; Alan Herbert's *The Thames* (1996), for example, devotes over fifty pages to the port of London during the blitz. Few river writers adopted the policy of Carl Carmer in his 'Rivers of America' book on the Hudson: 'I have tried to keep as near to the stream as I could and to avoid, where I thought it possible, things that happened out of sight of Hudson water.' Nor have they borne in mind, as Henry Canby expressed it, that though the Thames made London, its history is not (just) the history of London.[81] Even studies that ostensibly place rivers centre stage – not least Ackroyd's *Thames: Sacred River* (2007) – are rather dry.[82] Dry in the sense that transcendental and metaphysical meanings overshadow tangible presence.

As Marcus Aurelius and Schama demonstrate, rivers are good to think with. However, this approach can relegate dynamic entities to lifelessness, their role reduced to that of desiccated raw material for human thought. Rivers are very interesting to think with. Yet, like animals, they are even more interesting to live with. Their importance does not end with what they *mean* to us. Taking my cue from Norman Maclean's novella, I am most curious about how they run through and help make the history that we and they co-produce.[83]

The pioneering social historian E. P. Thompson had no doubts about what produces history: 'Men make their own history. They are part agents, part victims: it is precisely this element of agency which distinguishes them from the beasts, which is the human part of man.' If they were mere creatures, like ants, people would simply be 'adjusting their society to upheavals in the terrain'.[84] Since this pronouncement over half a century ago, historians have thoroughly embraced the dispossessed, marginalized, mistreated and victimized – yet still agential – members of the human community. Thanks to the intervention of environmental historians over the past few decades, the debate over agency has moved to a fresh, earthier stage.[85] It would be a particularly stubborn and unimaginative Europe-based historian of strictly intra-human relations – post-conference return flight from North America delayed in April 2010 by the inconvenient eruption of an Icelandic volcano with an unpronounceable name – who did not ponder, while grounded, the role of natural forces.

Nonetheless, some resolutely human-centred historians still maintain that, since consciousness, rationality, intentionality and the exercise of choice (not to mention the facility to record and explain in verbal and/or written form), are faculties that humans alone possess, the very notion of non-human agency is fundamentally flawed.[86] Eyjafjallajökull, in other words, cannot decide whether or not to erupt. Nor did it intend to paralyse air travel, just as Hurricane Katrina did not have it in for New Orleans. To extend it to non-human entities therefore dilutes the concept of agency to the point of meaninglessness.

One response is to question the indispensability of rationality and intentionality to the notion of agency. After all, anyone who surveys the past will be struck by the display of human irrationality and impulsiveness as well as the examples of informed choice between courses of action. What also looms large in the historical record is the evidence of unintended consequences (river-borne silt, for example, was not supposed to back up in reservoirs behind dams; channelization was not supposed to aggravate the danger of flooding; nor was irrigation supposed to increase soil salinity). We can also query the clarity of the distinction, in human behaviour, between instinct and reason. Another way forward is to distinguish between 'thoughtful agency' (Francis Gooding's term for human agency) and a more elastic concept of non-reflective agency that boils down to a capacity to shape outcomes; Chris Philo and Chris Wilbert refer to this as 'the power to act'.[87] In short, actors do not have to be rational, let alone clever – just effective.

When Emil Lengyel remarked that where the youthful Danube was narrow enough to jump across, the river was 'unconscious of its future greatness', he did not intend to spark a debate about fluvial consciousness and agency; this was merely a rhetorical flourish.[88] Yet if possession of will, logic and a sense of direction are deemed essential attributes of agency, then rivers qualify. Though frequently frustrated by human intervention, the purpose of any river (Wordsworth's 'Child of the clouds') is to fulfil its role in the hydrological cycle by pouring its waters into the sea.[89] Moreover, to categorize a river as an inanimate form of nature seems like a flagrant denial of reality. A river has a life and a life history in more than just the scientific sense. In his 'eco-biography' of the Rhine, Mark Cioc presents the river as a character with a 'personality' that appears 'alive to us – restless, temperamental, fickle, sometimes raging, sometimes calm'. Not only are they 'active sculptors of the landscape', rivers do things like burst their banks to 'pour into shops and cellars, wreaking havoc like vandals in the night'.[90]

Historical study of groups such as Native Americans and African American slaves has shifted from the dominant narrative of abject victimhood and largely disempowered recipients of others' actions. It considers how, despite adversity and calculated dehumanization, they exercised a measure of influence over their lives and managed to retain instrumentality (encapsulated in phrases such as 'we are still here' and 'the world the slaves made'). Attention now focuses on resistance as well as phenomena like slave culture. Similarly, notions of animal agency concentrate on the working animal as resistor (with the urban horse even presented – glibly and fancifully, some believe – as a non-human member of the proletariat).[91]

Aside from the river's uncontested status as geological agent, washing mountains down to the sea and building up delta lands, the notion of fluvial agency also seems easiest to grasp in terms of disruption and transgression (note Cioc's example). A river that persists in overflowing its banks in defiance of coercive flood control measures might stand comparison to a slave on a plantation who retains his or her humanity and a non-enslaved identity. A river in this guise can provide its own emphatic answer to those who quibble that it cannot communicate in ways we recognize or leave a record. Inhabitants of a settlement swamped by water, or left high and dry when a river changes course overnight, will laugh at the suggestion that a river cannot make its mark. A force of nature is also a force of history.

An additional perspective on agency, perhaps the most fruitful, seeks to cast off the oppositional mentality, within which either a river or people wield supreme authority or exercise primacy. The social science theorist Bruno Latour and the anthropologist Tim Ingold argue that agency is best treated as an attribute widely distributed among people and non-human nature in the form of associational 'actor-networks'. They offer this hybrid schema as a replacement for the redundant and obfuscating dichotomies of culture and nature as well as for antiquated notions of agency as a human monopoly. As Latour explains – though he has objects in mind rather than natural entities – it is not a choice between a non-human actor dictating an outcome and being a passive element acted on by humans; after all, kettles 'boil' water, locks 'close' doors and knives 'cut' meat. There are many gradations between 'full causality and sheer inexistence', he observes; something non-human can 'authorize, allow, afford, encourage, permit, suggest, influence, block, render possible, forbid'.[92] Recalcitrance is one blatantly obvious way in which a river expresses its will (and thereby triggers human action designed to bolster security). Nevertheless, the river's con-compliance, how it thwarts or triumphs over human intentions and actions, is just one of many modes of expression and exertion. Relations between humans and non-humans are defined by a reciprocity that not only conditions human 'actions' but also moulds human 'intentions'.[93]

Ingold invites us to re-conceive the human being as an 'organism-in-its-environment' rather than as an autonomous ('discrete' and 'bounded') being which faces an external environment composed of non-human elements that 'leaves its basic, internally specified nature unaffected'.[94] Agency, in other words, resides in the linkages and relations within the network rather than in its individual components. By taking a relational approach to the Mersey and its catchment, for instance, we gain a sharper understanding of why the industrial revolution began in that part of the world – and better appreciation of why the subtitle of a book, 'the river that changed the world', is not as preposterous that you might initially think.[95] We can foreground rivers without reviving a discredited environmental determinism, or without substituting an environment-centric narrative for a human-centric narrative. Rivers can also be infused with spirit and character without lapsing into incorrigible personification. We can have a good stab at thinking like a river (a challenge issued by Canadian writer Hugh MacLennan, American environmental historian Donald Worster and American environmentalist David Brower).[96] We can also give voice to rivers. Yet these things can be accomplished without abdication to a quasi-humanized river's voice.[97]

Even if we recoil from the formal grant of agency in a sense most historians will accept, rivers are, incontrovertibly, a key determinant of historical events and processes. Agency is an inelegant word and my preference is for the terminology of authority and power. When a settlement is founded in a particular place because of the advantages a river bestows, this demonstrates fluvial authority. As Canby remarked of rivers, 'more than any other agency of nature, they make the earth usable by man'.[98] And if a river's propensity to spill over prompts the implementation of control measures, then this is a measure of its persuasive power. When a river inspires a poem, the riveting river is the protagonist as well as the poet. In the same way, while necessary to distinguish between a human who wields power and the instrument through which that power is being wielded, the correct answer to the question 'who irrigates the field?', surely, is 'the river and those who divert its water'.[99]

## Liquid History: The View from the River

'Can one think of China without imagining the Yangzi, of ancient Egypt without recalling the Nile?' This rhetorical question posed by Christof

Mauch and Thomas Zeller marks a recent restatement of the conviction, gushing forth from Bernini's fountain, that nations, empires and societies derive their identities from rivers.[100] This fluviocentric approach to the past is encapsulated in the notion of 'liquid history', a charismatic term attributed to John Burns, proud Londoner and citizen of the Thames. After retiring from politics, the former trade unionist, socialist Member of Parliament for Battersea (1892–1918) and Liberal Party cabinet minister busied himself studying London's history. For Burns, his native city without the Thames was as unimaginable as Egypt without the Nile.

A definitive version of events (and date) proves elusive. But the impetus appears to have been supplied by an uppity visiting American who sang the praises of the Mississippi and spoke disparagingly of the (puny) Thames. In a guide to the Thames (1910), Geraldine Mitton (an equally proud Londoner) reported the occasion as follows:

> When the American wondered what all the fuss was about, and 'guessed' that any one of his home rivers could swallow the Thames and never know it, the Englishman replied, he 'guessed' it depended at which end the process began: if at the mouth, the American river would probably get no farther than the 'greatest city the world has ever known' before succumbing to indigestion![101]

Under American provocation, Burns apparently also retorted: 'I have seen the Mississippi. That is muddy water. I have seen the Saint Lawrence. That is crystal water. But the Thames is liquid history.'[102]

Burns' evocative term (certainly in use by 1911 and common currency by the 1930s, though often unattributed) resurfaced (1960) in the title of a book about a far more prosaic subject: the history of the Port of London Authority.[103] It cropped up again in 2003 in the title of a popular history of the river.[104] This book also taps into the sparkling potential of 'liquid history', yet seeks to invest the concept with real physical meaning. After all, according to one version, what Burns said to the unappreciative American was 'we do not call it a river, we call it liquid history'.[105]

This environmental history calls a river a river. It makes the river a leading participant, if not overwhelming protagonist. Emphasis on the materiality of the environment, which scholars in the arts and humanities have tended to bury under layers of socio-cultural construction, mirrors the perspective of a photography exhibit about the Danube that toured the river's major cities between 2006 and 2008. What is unusual and striking

Regensburg, Germany, from Andreas Müller-Pohle, 'The Danube River Project', 2007.

Budapest, Hungary, from Andreas Müller-Pohle, 'The Danube River Project', 2007.

TOC 3.46 - CONDUCTIVITY 370 - NITRATE 7.21 - PHOSPHATE 0.15 - POTASSIUM 2.08 - CADMIUM 0.09 - MERCURY 0.01 - LEAD 0.17

Ingolstadt, Germany, from Andreas Müller-Pohle, 'The Danube River Project', 2007.

about the photos taken by Andreas Müller-Pohle (who lives in Berlin and based his pilot project on the Spree) is their perspective.[106] The vantage point of the river photographer is usually that of the bank or a bridge. Similarly, Tom Fort's *Downstream*, a paean to a thoroughly ordinary, 'deeply unfashionable' English river, the Trent, takes the perspective of a river-lover looking down from a bridge ('down there' among the weeds; 'down there' in the silt) to 'investigate what lies beneath'.[107] Müller-Pohle's pictures, by contrast, were either shot at or below water level. Looking up at the underside of a bridge, we feel pulled in. The Danube is defined by its water, which is sometimes still, but more typically an energetic, boisterous, ever-changing medium.

Müller-Pohle stepped into the water and took underwater shots with a camera housed in a watertight box, against which the water slaps. Three-quarters of some photos are underwater, providing real depth. The river occupies the foreground and riverside buildings are firmly in the background. 'The space between the lens and housing holds the water at bay', explains Roman Schmidt, 'although we are in its midst'.[108] Not only does the viewer feel drawn into the river; it sometimes feels like the water is falling toward us. In one photograph, the neo-gothic Hungarian parliament building on the embankment in Budapest seems about to be engulfed by a tidal wave. As the Bulgarian cultural anthropologist Ivaylo Ditchev reflects in the companion book: 'Nature is close, immediate, insolent, unpredictably blocking the view at various degrees.' The 'heavy materiality' of water is the leading protagonist.[109] This approach parallels what David Blackbourn has called 'real' space and landscape and a 'sharply physical sense of place' in a study of the taming of rivers and the draining of wet-lands in Germany.[110]

People are conspicuously absent from Müller-Pohle's photographs. One shot (Ingolstadt) contains a largely submerged lower leg and foot and another features two calves. That is the closest we get to an overt (bodily) human presence. Yet every photo contains evidence of human activity. At each location, Müller-Pohle took a water sample. This 'blood test' provided information, displayed as a data bar at the bottom of each photo, about concentrations of nitrates, phosphate, potassium, cadmium, mercury and lead, as well as the water's TOC (total organic carbon) value and its conduct-ivity (total load of dissolved ionic compounds). Not even near its source in southwest Germany is the Danube without its burden of contaminants. Immersion in rivers, whose plashy character has been restored, promotes a perspective that dislodges people from their hallowed and entrenched position within the study of the past. But this bottom-up point of view does not submerge, let alone drown the human element.

# ONE

# *Danube*

The Danube flows through or past ten countries: Germany, Austria, Slovakia, Hungary, Croatia, Serbia, Romania, Bulgaria, Ukraine and, briefly, Moldova (the river's northern bank forms the border with Ukraine). Four capitals reside on its banks: Vienna, Bratislava, Budapest and Belgrade. The Danubian basin encompasses the territories of a further nine nations: Albania, Bosnia-Herzegovina, Czech Republic, Italy, Macedonia, Montenegro, Poland, Slovenia and Switzerland.[1] This superlative internationalism, reflecting an east-west orientation unusual among major European rivers, is encapsulated in the title of Goran Rebić's German-language film: *Donau, Dunaj, Duna, Dunav, Dunarea* (2003). The river's name in the languages of the various Danubian lands (German, Slovakian/Polish, Hungarian, Serbian/Croatian/Bulgarian and Romanian, respectively) is inscribed on the prow of Captain Franz's vessel, which plies between Regensburg and Budapest with its multi-ethnic crew (Serb, Hungarian, Romanian and Ukrainian).

## Dividing Danube

In his guide to a river that the steamship had recently opened up to tourists, Richard Claridge, an early nineteenth-century exponent of hydropathy, explained that, though shorter than the Volga, the Danube was nonetheless 'the first river' of Europe because of its location at the continent's heart.[2] And so, as the Merseyside-born travel writer Walter Jerrold emphasized, to write the Danube's history was to 're-tell' a substantial part of continental Europe's history.[3] Since then, and especially over the past quarter-century, as new nations emerged, the Danube has become even more international. 'No river in the world', Claridge announced, 'is more intimately associated with interesting historical facts'.[4] The connection with not just interesting but momentous historical facts derives from its long-standing role as divider as well as linker of peoples.[5] The Danube valley, Carlile Aylmer Macartney stressed, was a stranger to stability. Responsible for devising a post-war regional settlement, he warned that

> Even the normal questions which confront those who draw frontiers in any part of the world – Should this village or that railway line be assigned to State A or to its neighbour, State B? – are exceptionally numerous and complicated on the Danube, where nationalities are intermingled to such an extraordinary degree, and where . . . claims often seem diametrically opposed.[6]

The often grave consequences of acutely contested claims were at the forefront of an American article about the new Europe emerging from the former Soviet Bloc. The Danube, the correspondent observed, was unparalleled among rivers in terms of the quantity of 'savagery and brutality' it had flowed past.[7] In the first century AD, it formed the frontier between the Roman imperium and the German tribes beyond. A thousand years later, as Hitler consolidated his power, Emil Lengyel, a Hungarian-American author – playing off the axiomatic association (since Johann Strauss) of the river with the colour blue – split the Danube into three coloured sections: brown denoted the fascist 'brownshirt' Danube of Germany and Austria; green signified the rural, Hungarian stretch; and red denoted the prevalence of bloody conflict along the Yugoslavian and Romanian stretch. But the entire river was red in practice in view of the copious quantities of blood shed during more or less incessant warfare as a string of empires – Roman, Ottoman, Napoleonic and Habsburg – rose and fell along its banks.[8]

The latest imperial power, the Third Reich, co-opted the river itself. The use by Hungarian nationalist collaborators with the Nazis of 'great national rivers' such as the Danube for dumping bodies 'constituted a cleansing of these unwanted elements from the national body politic'.[9] Novi Sad in Serbia was a key site in the fluvial topography of terror. In January 1942, Hungarian fascists invading the town (which had been Hungarian until transferred to the new state of Yugoslavia in 1920) herded unsuspecting Jews and Serbs down to the river. Here, 4,000 of them (according to some estimates) were shot en masse at the Strand public beach and their bodies tossed into the water. Aleksandar Tišma, a Serbo-Croat/Hungarian writer, tells the victims' story in a novel set in Novi Sad in the early 1950s. *The Book of Blam* (1972) focuses on the guilt-ridden and regretful Miroslav Blam, the only surviving member of a Jewish family, who is haunted by those who 'died in the Danube'. 'Usually

coloured blue', the Danube temporarily assumes the hue of Lengyel's river
of blood. Novi Sad's nurturing 'womb', the city's *raison d'être*, now operates
as a watery grave.[10] Downriver in Budapest, the river also served Hungarian
fascists as unwitting collaborator and liquid dumping ground. In the
winter of 1944–5, the Arrow Cross regime's militiamen marched thousands
of local Jews to Danube Promenade in Pest, across from Buda Castle.
At the river's edge, they removed their shoes (the most valuable item of
clothing) and were tied together in pairs. After one of each pair was shot,
both were shoved in. The handful that survived were dubbed 'Danubians'.
The memorial to the more than 3,000 victims is an even less conventional
piece than the three gaunt figures (1971) that commemorate the victims in
Novi Sad. About 300 metres south of the Parliament building resides the
artwork *Shoes on the Danube Promenade*. The creation of a Hungarian
sculptor (Gyula Pauer) and filmmaker (Can Togay), the installation (unveiled on 16 April 2005) features sixty pairs of authentically modelled iron
shoes, as worn by men, women and children at the time, arranged in a row
over a 40-metre stretch of waterfront.[11]

Notwithstanding harrowing events such as these, a Czech engineer
employed by the International Danube Commission, whose remit was to
maintain and improve navigability, predicted a happy future for the river.[12]
Otto Popper was confident that when the Allies liberated the Danubian
countries, the river would, at long last, 'fulfil its destiny and develop into a
free link between free, happy, and peaceful nations'.[13] Despite these hopes,
the river's lower half languished under Soviet rule between 1945 and 1989:
the Iron Curtain crossed at Bratislava, and the river separated Austria from
Hungary and Yugoslavia. And when Yugoslavia disintegrated into civil war
in the 1990s, the river resumed its role as watery grave for civilian victims
(in Croatia).[14] Today, the Danube separates Hungary and Slovakia, Croatia
and Serbia, Serbia and Romania, and Romania and Bulgaria. With many
of these countries now included in an enlarged European Union, however,
much of the Danube basin resides under a single political unit for the first
time since the Roman era.

## Delivering Danube

Alongside its role as border (and receptacle for victims of tyranny), the
Danube has provided Europe's main internal highway for the flow of goods
and peoples. The Bavarian city of Ulm is the highest point of navigation for

sizeable (100-ton) boats. In the late sixteenth century, a new kind of cargo vessel emerged alongside the traditional raft that carried wine, ore and salt downriver: long, flat-bottomed rowing boats known as *Ulmer Schachteln*.[15] From Regensburg, 225 kilometres downriver from Ulm, the Danube is navigable by steamships with a low draught of up to 1,500 tons. Hartmann Schedel's authoritative *Schedel'sche Weltkronik* (1493) carries illustrations of Ulm and Regensburg, the river in the foreground bustling with boats and rafts that shipped western European goods to the Black Sea and Asia.[16] Larger boats, however, found it difficult to surmount the barrier of the Iron Gate (today's border between Serbia and Romania), where the turbulent river slices through central Europe's most imposing mountain barrier. With industrialization, the river's commercial value to Germany waned: by 1900, the Rhine, Elbe and Oder carried more German freight. Meanwhile, lower river settlements such as Vidin (Bulgaria) and Calafat (Romania) grew rich by connecting their grain growing hinterlands with upriver industrial cities. The Danube flowed 'in the wrong direction' – a more meaningful commercial highway for the lower countries, with their preponderance of bulky, low-cost agrarian goods.[17]

The lower Danube's turn-of-the-twentieth-century mercantile bustle is evoked in the memoirs of the Bulgarian-born novelist Elias Canetti. The son of a Jewish grain merchant, Canetti lived in Ruse (Ruschuk) until he

Elias Canetti's home town of Ruse (Ruschuk), by W. H. Bartlett, from William Beattie, *The Danube: Its History, Scenery and Topography* (1844).

was six (1905–11). In the first volume of his memoirs, the future Nobel Prize-winner recalled growing up in Bulgaria's most affluent and cosmo-politan city. With its profusion of consulates, neo-baroque and neo-rococo architecture, and rich stew of itinerant and displaced peoples united by riparian commerce, Ruse sounds like a smaller version of Liverpool. On its streets, Bulgarians, Turks, Greeks, Albanians, Armenians, Romanians, Gypsies, two types of Jew (Sephardim – like Canetti – and Ashkenazim) and the occasional Russian rubbed shoulders. On a typical day, in the early 1900s, you could hear seven or eight languages spoken. And the river that drew these peoples to Ruse and sustained them (not least by supplying the city with much of its domestic water) was the staple topic of conversation. In this regular port of call for grain ships, Canetti remembered the boy-hood pleasure of running his fingers through open sacks of millet, rice and barley in the family store. The river connected Ruse to the world beyond; when someone took the boat to Vienna, they were travelling to 'Europe', which began where the Ottoman Empire once ended.[18]

Despite the Danube's enormous political, military and commercial significance, the river itself remains an insubstantial presence in the out-pourings and accolades of scholars and travellers. Puzzling over the 'Blue' Danube's 'curiously neglected' status, relative to the Rhine's reputation, despite its 'almost incomparable' greater all-round fascination, Jerrold com-municated the river's value in terms of legendary and historical features and the scenic attributes of the picturesque.[19] Yet the river, as distinct from its dramatic gorges, is nonetheless curiously negected. Jerrold notes the current's speed at Regensburg, where the water is channelled between the piers of the twelfth-century stone bridge. Otherwise, he is mostly interested in the illustrious battles that the Danube has hosted: the river is primarily a 'scene' for human events.[20]

A reviewer hailed Claudio Magris' book on the Danube as a masterful blend of history, literature, cultural criticism and 'intelligent' tourism.[21] Again, though, the river gets lost in a maze of digression, drowned by the culture and literature of *Mitteleuropa*. Magris' tendency to disregard the river's own identity is highlighted in his coverage of the obsessive Austrian hydraulic engineer Ernst Neweklowsky, Director of River Works at Linz, who devoted his life (1882–1963) to the river. It is 'impossible to deny the advantage', comments Magris, that Neweklowsky with his river possesses 'over the believers in other cults', because 'various gods, religious and secular, so often disappoint'. Whereas other gods may fail us, Magris reassures his readers that the Danube is there before your eyes; it does not vanish, nor does it make any promises it cannot keep; it does not let you down, but flows on loyally and open to scrutiny. It knows nothing of the hazards of theology, the perversions of ideology, the pangs of despised love. It is simply there, tangible and truth-telling.[22]

This notion of a simple and unchanging (eternal) river is matched by the concept of a helpless and inert river. Lengyel notes that the Danube was silent, powerless to prevent the dreadful turn of events that brought on the First World War: 'Slowly the river rolled down its appointed way, unable to warn, an unwilling witness to impending doom . . . If the river had a voice, it would have cried out when the wise men of the West [at the Paris peace conference] cut to pieces the bleeding body of its valley.'[23] Compounding this neglect of the river's ability to make a mark is the view that the river *as nature* – the prelude to history as distinct from the setting for history – is a tedious, ahistorical subject: 'To the old Romans whose dull task it was to make a beginning to its history', reflected the German geographer and travel writer, Johann Georg Kohl, 'how uninteresting must have appeared this Danube, which was to us invested with all the charms of a long eventful history!'[24]

Bernard Granville Baker, who travelled downstream in the early 1900s, took a refreshingly different (if heavily anthropomorphic) view. The British soldier turned travel writer was fortunate to encounter a calm human world in the Danubian domain, with no hint of the impending storm of world war.[25] Baker introduces 'my friend Danube' to the reader as a companion of great stature who, 'like all the truly great . . . is modest'. That humans have toiled diligently for centuries to render rivers 'subservient' by altering their physical features in no way detracts from their animism and personalities. For Baker, the river bears solemn witness to the course of human events and serves as the repository of memory: 'Dost remember, brother Danube, how I flung corpses down across the marshes?' The river is all seeing, all knowing and all remembering.

Baker also humanizes the river as a willing servant, who knows that he is appreciated, and appears sad when he can no longer be of service (in Ulm, for example, where the linen industry, once so heavily reliant on river water, is now moribund). To ascertain the river's opinion, Baker instructs, follow it from source to sea. Tracing a river from origins to outlet was a well-established narrative trope, equivalent to the human journey from childhood to adulthood. His reasons for flattering the Danube as the 'aristocrat of rivers' illustrate the often irresistible tendency to bestow personhood (if not social ranking) on rivers. Unlike the Rhine and Rhône, the Danube does not have to struggle to emerge from an alpine fastness. Born in a 'cradle' in a palace garden, in its 'infancy' it continues to enjoy a life of ease and grace. Yet whether a river of nobility or of peasantry, the Danube knows he must serve man's needs.

At the same time, the river retains a primordial spirit. Baker interprets intermittent flooding as an assertive act punctuating the normal condition of 'bondage' (a reference to channelization).[26] Today's reader may dismiss this approach as another stale and clouding example of the literary device of personification. Yet Baker's rapport with the river demonstrates a firm grasp of its authority. The charge of anthropomorphism notwithstanding, creative writers have usually possessed a keener sense of the Danube as protagonist than historians or even travel writers. George Meredith's poem 'The Nuptials of Attila' (1887) conveys a potent sense of fluvial place. The early thirteenth-century *Nibelungenlied*, based on ancient oral legend, is usually associated with the Rhineland because Richard Wagner's operatic version foregrounds the Rhine. Yet the epic poem features the Danube in equal measure; not surprisingly, since it was written for Wolfger, bishop of the Danubian city of Passau (its unknown author probably hailed from the Danube Valley between Passau and Vienna).[27]

The fifth-century story pivots on a west-east axis stretching from Worms on the Rhine (the Burgundian capital) to the Danubian city of Esztergorm (in today's Hungary), the seat of Attila, king of the Huns. The *Nibelungenlied* relates how, in 454, Attila (Etzel) spent his wedding night near Hainburg, an Austrian river town close to the Slovakian border, which partly occupies the Roman site of Carnuntum. Meredith's poem opens with Attila camped here for his marriage feast, taking a break from his customary business of wholesale savagery (a leitmotif of Hunnish exploits being the streaking red of rivers with victims' blood). Throughout the poem, the Danube is a brooding symbol of the 'huge, wild, primitive forces, of nature and of man'.[28]

## Disputed Danube

The strife that has been the leitmotif of Danubian history begins at the source, even if no blood has been shed over it. Identifying where a river starts can be a complicated business if there are tributaries. Is it the source of the tributary furthest from the river's mouth? Or the source stream with the highest altitude? Alternatively, is it the start of the source stream with the heaviest flow? Usually, little more than local pride is at stake, and the search for precision a mere exercise in pedantry. Sometimes, though, this absence of clarity can be a matter of considerable political consequence.[29] And in the Danube's source region, tourist revenue is at stake.

Since at least 1500, cartographers and chroniclers have located the official *Donauquelle* at Donaueschingen in Baden-Württemberg. What originates here, at 678 metres above sea level, in the grounds of the Prince of Fürstenberg's palace, is the Danube brook (*Donaubächlein*), one of many springs that bubble up from the local limestone strata and supply Donaueschingen's drinking water (also the Fürstenberg brewery, which, by the 1860s, was Baden-Württemberg's biggest).[30] The *Donaubach* once flowed into the Brigach, one of the Danube's source streams, at a point two kilometres from the palace grounds. Then, in 1828, the Fürstenbergs channelled the water into an underground canal that flowed into the Brigach after just 90 metres. At the source, steps led down into the basin and, according to tradition, visitors drank there (some even jumped in or poured in an oblatory cup of wine). In 1875, Fürstenberg family architect Adolf Weinbrenner replaced the simple railed enclosure around the brook's source with an elaborate encircling marble wall.[31]

Local sculptor Adolf Heer's marble statue ('*Mutter Baar unde die Junge Donau*') was installed at the rear of the enclosure in 1896. Standing next to the seated 'Mother Baar' is the infant river in the shape of a young girl. Representing the Baar plateau, the region between the southern Black Forest and the Swabian Alb, she points eastward toward her daughter's destination, the Black Sea, which, the plaque explains, lies 2,840 kilometres distant.[32] The erection of a neo-classical temple over the discharge of the underground stream into the Brigach (1912; funded by Kaiser Wilhelm II) completed the statuary in the palace gardens.

Since 1987, behind the spring enclosure, on the wall of the parish church, each Danubian nation with the exception of Moldova has erected a plaque inscribed with suitably grandiloquent statements.[33] The inscription on the plaque of Romania, which occupies more river than any other country, including much of its outflow, reads: 'Romania, age-old Europe's guard, watches the Danube Delta.' The inscription on Ukraine's reads: 'Your water carries the memories and hopes of millions of Europeans.' Austria's plaque (the most recent) presents the river as symbol of the new Europe, contrasting the continent's divided state in 1989 with its unity twenty years later.

Danuvius reclining in
a pastoral setting, 1726,
engraving.

Since the early nineteenth century, various commentators have
questioned the claim of the *Donauquelle*. One sceptic who demoted it
to the status of *Schlossquelle* was Poultney Bigelow, member of an Anglo-
American trio that paddled downriver in the 1880s in cruising canoes
(fifteen feet long, with two masts and sails). He suggested that the source
had been 'arbitrarily' designated by the construction of an ornamental
basin. When Bigelow proposed to a local citizen that the real source actually lay higher up in the Black Forest, the person reacted with indignation
and impatience: '*Gott in Himmel!* Here lives the prince; here is his palace;
here is the official statement cut in the stone. What more do you want?'
This silenced Bigelow, though, remaining in mischievous mood, he

> could not help feeling that if an enterprising promoter could
> secure some other prince, get up a stock company, hire a spring
> further up, build a summer hotel, call the place 'Danube High
> Spring' or 'Danube Source Original,' carve it in stone, and make
> the rival prince hold court at the summer hotel, in three seasons
> Donaueschingen would be bankrupt.[34]

Donaueschingen claims legitimacy from ancient Greek and Roman evidence. For the rulers of Allemania, locating the Danube's source was a far from trivial pursuit. The Greek historiographer Herodotus (fifth century BC) provided the earliest known description of the river the Greeks called Istros. Beyond locating the source in Allemania, however, he omitted further details. But Tacitus recorded that the Roman general Tiberius visited the source during field manoeuvres from his base at Lake Constance in 15 BC.[35] Donaueschingen has seized on Pliny the Elder's observation that the source resided close to a river to refute the allegation that it randomly designated the source for its own ends. In a study for the local tourist board, Ernst Zimmermann insists that the Brigach is the nearby river identified by Pliny (whose visit is well documented).[36] Donaueschingen's claim received its clearest endorsement to date in Hartmann Schedel's *Schedel'sche Weltkronik* (1493): 'the *Thonaw* most renowned river in Europe, arises from the edge of the Black Forest at the village of Donaueschingen, from where it flows toward the Orient'.[37] In *Cosmographia* (1544), Sebastian Münster, a cartographer, theologician and cosmographer at the University of Basel, restated Donaueschingen's claim on *Fons Danubi*. In the most authoritative study of Germany to date, the dispassionate Münster (from Mainz on the Rhine) included a detailed map of the area in the immediate vicinity of the source, which, there is good reason to believe, was based on a personal visit.[38] To clinch its case, Donaueschingen cites archaeological discoveries in the 1970s of a large early Roman camp just four kilometres from the *Donauquelle*, on the route of a major Roman road with its southern terminus in Switzerland.

Nonetheless, the possibility that the Danube was fed by waters beyond Fürstenberg Park had already occurred to inquisitive Romans. Tacitus, who probably did not visit the area, identified a mountain from which the Danube sprang, which he named Abnoba (a Celtic forest and river goddess, worshipped in the Black Forest and surrounding areas, whose name translates as 'misty stream').[39] In the sixteenth century, the dispute expanded to encompass the relative merits of the two rivers that meet in Donaueschingen: the Breg and Brigach.[40] Thereafter, the controversy was sucked into the larger rivalry between Donaueschingen and Furtwangen, a town 35 kilometres distant, near the Breg's headwaters.[41] Though he dismissed it as a 'pretty little quarrel', Jerrold (who resided in Hampton-on-Thames) tried to give British readers a sense of the rivalry between Donaueschingen, Furtwangen and a third place, St Georgen, the town nearest the source of the Brigach, by alluding to Britain's most celebrated

Moritz von Löhr's Danuvius outside the Albertina Museum, Vienna, erected in 1869. The river's depiction at Donaueschingen as a child – and a female child at that – is the great exception. Statues of muscular, bearded men with flowing robes – typified by Danuvius in sculptor Johann Meixner's neo-Baroque fountain and rooted in ancient Roman depictions – are the norm.

source dispute, over the Thames, between two places in Gloucestershire, Thames Head (the incumbent) and Seven Springs (the upstart).[42]

At the source of the Brigach, water emanates from under a stone slab on the Heinzmann family property. This locale remains a destination for pilgrims: sixty-five had already visited by 11 a.m. on the day a *National Geographic* reporter visited in 2002.[43] Yet on multiple grounds, the Breg has a stronger claim, firmly established in the 1840s.[44] It is slightly longer than the Brigach (48 versus 43 kilometres), possesses a larger flow, a much bigger watershed (291 sq kilometres versus 195), and rises at a higher altitude (1,078 versus 921 metres). Of the numerous springs in the Kolmenhof area, one near the *Martinskapelle*, barely a hundred metres down the eastern slope of the European watershed, has been singled out for the supreme honour. Irma Öhrlein, a geologist, and her geographer husband, Ludwig, who own the land hosting the *Martinskapelle*, conducted experiments with dye involving 600 measurements that, to their satisfaction, established their spring as the Danube's source on 17 July 1954.[45]

*42*

Fully aware, though, that Donaueschingen was not about to relinquish its claim without a fight, Furtwangen's representatives tactfully sought formal recognition of the Breg's source as an additional source. Distinguishing between source and origin eventually allowed the warring parties to arrive at an uneasy compromise and declare a truce of sorts in the late 1950s. Donaueschingen's spring retained its ennobling status as official *Quelle* (the sign for the town on the A81 Autobahn depicts Heer's sculpture and points to 'Donauquelle und Fürstenschloss'). Meanwhile, Furtwangen's Breg spring achieved recognition as the *Ursprung* (origin). A stone marker near the resort hotel of Höhengasthof Kolmenhof, erected by the Öhrleins (and vindicating Bigelow), intones: 'Here is the origin of the main source river of the Danube, the Breg, at 1,078 metres above sea level, 2,888 kilo-metres from its mouth and 100 metres from the watershed between the Black Sea and the North Sea' (the difference from the distance specified at the *Donauquelle* [2,840] accounted for by addition of the Breg).[46] The 'real' Danube (as one late nineteenth-century American visitor explained) begins on the eastern edge of Donaueschingen at the Breg's confluence with the Brigach.[47] Adding to the confusion, the stone marker at this auspicious spot (photographed by Müller-Pohle) registers the distance to the Black Sea as 2,775 kilometres.

Other potential sources have also been identified and promoted, if less vigorously and persuasively. Eduard Suess, President of the Vienna Academy of Sciences, advanced a theory based on the Danube's disappearance after just twenty kilometres (Danube Sinkhole). The bed of the fledgling river is often dry as the flow disappears underground into limestone caves. In 1911, a year of particularly low rainfall, locals walked along the riverbed for a kilometre between Immendingen and Tuttlingen without getting wet feet. This arid condition, which can last for up to half the year, was recorded annually between the 1880s and 1910s.[48] Making a mockery of the European Watershed between Danube and Rhine, the water within this complex karst hydrogeology reappears twelve kilometres to the south of the Aach.[49] The Aach, which begins here, flows down to Lake Constance, and thence into the Rhine (which, by comparison, enjoys a gloriously unproblematic source). In deference to the Aach, Suess identified the Danube's source as a permanent stream at Friedigen, where water resumes its flow in the Danube's channel after receiving two tributaries.[50]

An all-round Swiss scholar also muddied the waters by registering another candidate. In the early 1700s, Johann Jacob Scheuchzer promoted the alpine headwaters of the 500-kilometre Inn – the highest point in the entire Danube watershed (4,049 metres) – as the Danube's real source.[51] An ardent nationalist, he further pointed out that where it enters the Danube (Passau, Bavaria), the broader (if not so deep) Inn contributes more water than the Danube already carries. Yet the Inn is considered a tributary because the Danube is longer up to this point, has drained a surface area twice the size, and has a more consistent flow.

Regardless of where precisely it rises, it has been customary since classical antiquity to split the Danube into two more or less equal sections: the upper (western) and lower (eastern) river. Strabo distinguished between an upper Danuvius and a lower Istros (Ister). The Iron Gate ('the cataracts'), which checked the westward expansion of Greek colonists, who travelled upstream as early as the seventh century BC, divided the two sections.[52] In the second century AD, the Roman geographer Ptolemy introduced a further distinction within the lower section. His Ister did not begin until Axiopolis (present-day Cernavodă) just above Braila, the highest point that sea-going vessels could reach at that time; the final 161-kilometre section was the Maritime Danube.[53]

The volume of water the Danube debouches is so large that a mid-nineteenth century proponent of a delta canal reckoned its outflow remained noticeable 80 kilometres out into the Black Sea.[54] And according to a British traveller who sailed past in the late 1790s, you could dip a bucket into the water three leagues (nine nautical miles) from its mouth and it was 'almost sweet'; at one league it was 'perfectly fit for use on board'.[55] Nonetheless, the Danube's flow and discharge (whose impact is magnified by the shallowness of the Black Sea) are far less consistent than those of other major European rivers. Reflecting the wider range of climatic zones within its basin, its level is subject to greater fluctuations than, say, the Rhine's. Flow is low in autumn and winter, and high in spring and early summer.[56] In the autumn of 2003, unprecedented low water (record-keeping began in 1888) halted hydrofoil traffic between Vienna and Budapest, and the prows of Hitler's remnant Danube Fleet (scuttled in 1944) poked up near the Serbian port of Prehovo.[57] Yet little over a year earlier (August 2002), the river had experienced record-setting floods.


## Dangerous Danube

Springtime flooding has been a regular feature of life for Danubian peoples – and a particularly severe problem in areas where major tributaries enter.

Alfred Parsons, 'The Start' of the Danube at Donaueschingen, from F. D. Millet, *The Danube: From the Black Forest to the Black Sea* (1892).

As well as snowmelt, a common cause of early spring inundations along the entire river was the ice dam (*Eisstoss*), a phenomenon that resembled a pile of broken concrete. The ice dam (ice drift mountain) that accumulated in the winter of 1928–9, for example, eventually stretched from southern Hungary to northern Austria (Melk).[58] Budapest was particularly vulnerable because, unlike Vienna, the river resides at the heart of the Hungarian capital. The particularly harsh winter of 1837–8 aggravated the impact of the melting dam the following spring. The ice that had shut down the river since early January eventually built up to a metre thickness and created a gargantuan *Eisstoss* below the city.

When break-up eventually arrived on 8–9 March, backed-up ice-filled water eventually overflowed on the evening of 13 March. The two-metre-high breakwater made of sand and timber could not protect the flatlands of Pest. The disaster was still a major talking point when Kohl visited a few years later. Attributing malevolent powers and a wicked temper to the river, he conjured up an 'angry flood [that] despised the weak obstacles which human hands raised to oppose it'. Floodwater pushed up from under floorboards that hydraulic pressure shot into the air; rising water lifted large pieces of furniture from lower to upper floors.[59] Within five hours, parts of Pest were under 27 feet of water. After 72 hours, the overflow peaked at a record 29 feet above the average river level.[60] When the waters began to subside on the third day, as the ice dam started to melt, Pest was a scene of devastation. Writing about the 'acme of misery' on 15 March, Julia Pardoe, a British poet, historian and travel writer who visited the following year, also evoked a wrathful, abusive river: 'Pesth will probably never number in her annals so dark a day again – she might perhaps not be enabled to survive such another; – the mad river, as that day dawned, rioted in ruin.'[61]

In addition to Germanic folklore, Meredith's 'Nuptials of Attila' perhaps also drew on accounts of the flood of 1838.

> When the pitch of frost subsides,
> Danube with a shout of power
> Loosens his imprisoned tides:
> Wide around the frightened plains
> Shake to hear his riven chains,
> Dreadfuller than heaven in wrath,
> As he makes himself a path.[62]

Heavy rescue barges shrugged off their moorings, careered around and cannoned off buildings. After the floodwaters had completely subsided (18 March), death toll figures varied dramatically. According to Pardoe, a 'comparatively trifling' number died: 200. But another British visitor (writing within a few years of the event, and quoting a German source), recorded that, in Pest, 1,000 perished. Estimates of damage also varied widely; conservative figures, based on a housing stock of about 4,250, were 2,281 destroyed and about 1,000 damaged.[63] The 'silent gradual influence of water', reflected a sombre Kohl (who cited 3,000 destroyed dwellings), 'had in three days wrought more mischief than a hundred days of bombardment would have done'.[64]

An international appeal raised money to help finance a massive new foundation for houses in Pest and to strengthen the river banks. One contributor was the 26-year-old Hungarian composer and pianist Franz Liszt, who had not been back home since he left as a boy of ten in 1823. But when he read about the disaster in a German newspaper, allegedly while drinking his morning coffee in Piazza San Marco, Venice, one of the most vulnerable spots in another flood-prone city, he was 'badly shaken'.[65] The flood precipitated not only an unanticipated re-identification with his homeland (not to mention a golden opportunity for self-promotion in Vienna, the venue for his charity concerts).[66] It engendered admiration for unbridled fluvial power: 'I was suddenly transported back to the past . . .

46

A magnificent landscape emerged before my eyes . . . it was the Danube rushing over the reefs!'[67]

The Danube's human users interpreted the notion of a free and unregulated river, articulated here by Liszt, in two different ways. In a commercial sense, it meant freedom of navigation and the unrestrained movement of goods, unimpeded by political barriers and and constraints on trade such as tolls. Yet an unregulated river also denoted a free-flowing river bristling with non-human impediments to navigation such as rapids, shifting channels and fluctuating levels. During the First World War, a German geographer hailed the Danube as Central Europe's 'nature-given highway'.[68] And on encountering the Danube for only the second time, in rural Austria, during his solo walk from Hook of Holland to Constantinople in 1933–4, the eighteen-year-old British wanderer Patrick Leigh Fermor was struck by the river's 'overpowering impression of urgency and force'.[69] To establish a river of riches, however, a river that reflects human power, fluvial power must be checked and redeployed. Deepening, shortening and straightening channels, embanking shores and eliminating seasonal variations in depth, liberates a wilful and truculent entity's potential as a navigable waterway.[70] A river becomes an artery of transportation and highway of commerce: a *Wasserstrasse*.

Smooth passage on the uppermost navigable section depended on adequate water and flat-bottomed craft. Long-distance transit to Vienna from Ulm and other German river towns began in the late seventeenth and early eighteenth centuries. *Ordinari*, wooden rafts up to 35 metres long and 7 metres wide, provided regular weekly service to 'Emperor Town' for passengers, freight and mail. Some *Ordinari*, called *Zillen*, relied on horse power – particularly on the return leg, and in the Wachau gorge – while others (*Platten*) were oar-powered and often chopped up to sell as wood on reaching their destination.[71]

Various stretches of the upper and middle river presented their own challenges to the navigators and operators of these vessels, as well as during the early years of steam. The Danube's unstable flow was aggravated by an alternating pattern of multiple, intricately braided channels in the lowland stretches and the narrow gorges of more hilly sections. The terrors of the whirlpools known as the 'Strudel' and 'Wirbel' awaited shipping in Austria's Wachau. Even scarier rapids and eddies lay in store in the Iron Gate.

First up was the Strudel, a set of rapids that loomed large in the left-hand channel where Wörther Insel divided the river. Unfortunates who fell overboard were written off as propitiatory offerings to Celtic and Teutonic gods. Those who succumbed to the whirlpool included *Jodelen*, drivers of the teams of up to fifty horses and oxen that towed lashed-together fleets of barges and boats upstream.[72] Again, nobody tried to assist the hapless hawsiers because, explained British tourist James Robinson Planché (1828), the Spirit of the Waters 'demanded victims'.[73] Wörther Insel was topped by a ruined watch tower crowned with a twelve-foot cross, 'to which, in the moment of danger', explained British tourist William Beattie, 'the ancient boatmen were wont to address their prayers for deliverance'.[74]

A kilometre and a half below the Strudel lurked the even more fearsome Wirbel. The diabolical effect was produced by the Hausstein, a large rock 150 metres long and 50 metres wide, that thrust six metres above the regular water level and cleaved the river into the main channel to the left, containing the Wirbel, and a narrower channel only navigable by small vessels (the *Lüng*). This right-hand channel rejoined the main branch at a right angle, fomenting a series of large boiling circles. Each maelstrom had a 50–60-metre circumference; and at the centre of each was a basin up to two metres deep. According to local legend, the whirlpools were bottomless and anything that landed in them was sucked in for good (in fact, most bodies were eventually spat out).[75] The key to a safe passage was to speed through at maximum velocity.

This natural peril was exacerbated by the menace posed by extortionists and robbers, who exacted tribute and/or plundered boats in distress. As soon as Planché's vessel had negotiated the Wirbel, a boat from the village of St Nikola pulled up alongside and a man held out a box containing the figurine of St Nicholas so the passengers could cough up 'voluntary contributions' in return for the protection the patron saint of sailors had extended during their transit through this watery hell. Unscrupulous boatmen also talked up the danger to raise the price of freighting and collect tips from relieved passengers after getting them through without incident. Planché reported a ceremony held on the Vienna-bound *Ordinari* that plied this stretch of river. The steersman circulated on deck with a water-filled wooden scoop and those who had just passed through the Strudel and Wirbel for the first time either paid tribute or faced a dousing.[76]

Cursed by boatmen and the source of consternation for routine passengers, these turbulent stretches were serenaded by the travellers who filled the passenger lists in growing numbers from the 1820s.[77] Imbued with the romantic ethos of delicious terror, those who took a pleasure cruise to Vienna regarded these whirlpools as the river's unrivalled scenic highlights ('highly picturesque . . . even sublime').[78] Planché, a veteran of

W. H. Bartlett, 'The Strudel', from Beattie, *The Danube* (1844).

W. H. Bartlett, 'The Wirbel and Hausstein', from Beattie, *The Danube* (1844).

Alfred Parsons, 'The Kazan Defile', from Millet, *The Danube* (1892).

The Iron Gate that divides Romania and Serbia, from Walter Jerrold, *The Danube* (1911).

the Rhine, was in the vanguard of Danube tourism. By the late 1820s, the
seasoned traveller considered rivers such as the Thames, the Seine and
the Rhine rather tame, if not insipid. Yet the Danube offered a voyage into
the relatively unknown. A reviewer of Planché's pioneering account (1828)
opined that, whereas the British voyager (armchair as well as actual) was
as familiar with the Rhine, Seine and Po as with his own Thames, the
Danube was as little known as Siberia's Irtis or Obi.[79] After descending
from Ratisbon (Regensburg) to Vienna in the autumn of 1827, he hailed
the 'celebrated' Strudel and Wirbel as the river's 'Scylla and Charybdis'.[80]
But when the arrival of steamboats on the Danube encouraged increasing
numbers of foreigners to travel downstream as a leisure pursuit – with
obligatory post-trip survival tales – the passage through the Strudel and
Wirbel was already considerably more placid. In the early 1890s, Bigelow's
canoe party breezed through both rocky patches 'without knowing it': all
bark and no bite.[81]

## Disciplined Danube

Empress Maria Theresa's Navigation Board had already made the first
efforts to extract the Strudel's teeth in the late 1770s. With gunpowder,
engineers blasted out 30 cubic fathoms of rock. As is so often the case,
though, solving one problem only served to create another. The removal of
so much rock from the riverbed altered the current's direction so dramatic -
ally that vessels now shot down directly onto the *Wildriss*, a midstream
rock. The remedy was to widen and deepen the channel on the Wörther
Insel side so it could carry the main flow. Work continued intermittently,
weather permitting, for eight years.[82] Still, as the accounts of Planché,
Beattie and others indicate (allowing for exaggeration), the whirlpools
continued to alarm (and to thrill) in the first half of the nineteenth century.
Beattie was convinced that if the Hausstein was blasted to smithereens,
the Wirbel would be disposed of once and for all.[83] This policy was imple
mented in stages soon thereafter. A plaque on the left-bank cliffs reads:
'Kaiser Franz Josef freed shipping from the dangers of the Donau-Wirbel
by blowing up the island of Hausstein 1853–1866'.

The next (and last) hair-raising stretch of river was the Iron Gate
(also known as the Kazan gorge; *kazan* in Turkish means 'hissing kettle').
Slamming into a spur of the Transylvanian Alps, the river has carved a
path betweeen the southern Carpathians and the northwestern Balkan

Ada Kaleh (Turkeninsel) and the Iron Gate of the Danube, Tatra, Austro-Hungary, *c.* 1890–1900. When the gorge was dammed in the early 1970s, the mosque, bazaar, Mahmut Pasha's house and the graveyard were removed and re-erected downstream on Simian Island. The community itself relocated to Dobruja, a Romanian territory with a Turkish minority, or emigrated to Turkey.

Mountains. The result is a 120-kilometre long defile whose limestone cliffs rise 450 to 600 metres above the river. At its most slender, near Dubova, it is just 120 metres wide. This defile was not just the most difficult stretch to navigate. Bigelow also hailed it as 'one of the grandest bits of scenery in the world'.[84]

Though sometimes applied to the entire string of gorges, the name Iron Gate is often restricted to the lowest and most spectacular canyon, Great Cazane (*Veliki Kazan*). The wider the gorge, the lower the water depth. The channel is broadest and shallowest (6.5 metres) where the strata is hard granites or crystalline schists. In calcareous zones or their contact area with harder formations, the defile is narrowest and the water deepest (45 metres) as the 'iron-bound' river squeezes between almost vertical walls. However, 'Iron Gate' may refer to the riverbed rocks that explain the difficulty of passage, and their ferruginous hue, rather than indicate the gorge itself.[85] Ridges of serrated rock resembling the bars of an iron gate stretch for 2,200 metres, over which the fall is five metres and velocity of flow (pre-regulation) at least three metres per second.[86] However, the most persuasive explanation for the name remains the most obvious: before rectification works, this stretch of river was considered impassable by larger vessels, upstream and downstream progress blocked as if by a sturdy gate. The 'rocky spikes' 'literally' tore the water 'into shreds'.[87] Exposed at low water, they triggered comparison with a monstrous creature's 'gaping jaws'.[88] Bigelow, who claimed to be the first to canoe through without mishap, rated them more difficult than the rapids of Canada's St Lawrence.[89]

Prior to the 1830s, rough and shallow water conditions required goods and passenger transfer to smaller, oared vessels, and complete cessation of travel when the level was too low.[90] The coincidence of lowest water, in autumn, with the grain-shipping season for Romania and Bulgaria, exacerbated navigational difficulties; for up to three months of the year, the Iron Gate was effectively non-navigable (individual rocks were named after ships that came to grief ).[91] In the autumn of 1834, on behalf of the Vienna-based, state-owned Danube Steamship Company (*Donau-Dampfschiffahrt Gesellschaft*; 1829), Stephen Széchenyi (sponsor of the first permanent bridge between Buda and Pest), visited the area to report and recommend solutions. The Turks, he believed, had done nothing to ameliorate the rocky water-road as it served them as a shield against intrusion. Széchenyi foresaw a daunting and prohibitively expensive remedial task, calculating that 180 blasts of powder would be needed to blow up just one and a half cubic metres of rock, equivalent to 60 days' work for one man.[92] The Steamship Company undertook the first improvement work in 1834, blasting a channel through solid rock along the right-hand (Serbian) bank to ensure a minimum depth of three metres.

These adjustments enabled steamships to negotiate the gorge at normal water levels without unloading and reloading. More ambitious works were financed by a major international loan, in accordance with the Treaty of Berlin (1878), which authorized a tax on ships passing through the gate to fund engineering works.[93] Blasting began in September 1890, drawing on the experience of the regulation of the Mississippi, Rhine and St Lawrence as well as the construction of the Suez and Panama canals. The initial plan was simply to dynamite away the underwater rock and to remove the debris with dredgers. But the fierce current interfered with precision blasting and riverbed slate gummed up boreholes. As a remedy, the two proposed channels were sealed off and drained, which allowed work to go ahead, quarry-like, in a dry 'valley bottom'. By late September 1896, the workforce of 9,000 wielding the latest American, British and French technology – rock breakers, shovel excavators, bucket dredgers, steel and diamond-tipped rotary drilling rigs, and underwater drilling machines – had produced a fresh riverbed consisting of two 80-metre wide canals of 2.5 and 2 kilometres, walled off from the main river.[94]

Nonetheless, problems for navigation persisted. Travelling upstream in low water season in October 1910, Jerrold's steamer ran aground and perched on the rocks for a few hours before being towed off at a second attempt.[95] Moreover, taming one troublesome aspect of the river rendered another drawback even less tractable. Canalization boosted the current's speed to five metres per second – too powerful for upstream traffic to make headway unassisted. A thousand horsepower tug took an hour to tow a 650-ton barge upstream through the 2-kilometre channel.[96]

Looking beyond navigational improvements, shortly after the Second World War, an American geographer suggested the application of the ethos and methods of the Tennessee Valley Authority (TVA) to realize the Danube Basin's full potential for power generation, flood control and extraction of natural resources. George Kiss, who had travelled the river extensively on barges, steamers and skiffs, pondered the relatively modest success – though underway for a century – of efforts to calm the river to benefit shipping and to rein in its tendency to overflow for the sake of floodplain residents. The limited achievements reflected their discon-nected and uncoordinated nature. Effective and lasting 'taming' could only flow from a joined-up, supranational strategy. A Danube Valley Authority, Kiss ventured, with the optimism typical of a post-1945 technocrat, might 'bring a modicum of peace and prosperity to one of the stormiest corners of the planet'.[97]

When it came, the impetus for more effective subjugation of river resistance in the Iron Gate was not a TVA-style international initiative. The drive was a by-product of Romania's desire to reduce reliance on Soviet energy supplies and to build good relations with Tito's autonomous Yugoslavia. A Romanian-Yugoslavian hydro-project (1964–72) raised the Danube's level by 35 metres in the 150-kilometre impoundment behind the Portile de Fier (Iron Gate) Dam at the gorge's lower end. Six villages with a combined population of 17,000 were inundated. Also submerged was the fortress island of Ada Kaleh, which Bigelow described as a 'perfect bit of Moslem life separated from all the world by the rushing Danube at the junction of three states'. The reservoir also threatened other, more ancient features of the riverscape that had attracted the attention of nineteenth-century travellers, whose interest was not confined to monumental scenery: the remains of the Roman Emperor Trajan's bridge and road, which (as an American visitor remarked in the 1890s) once supported cities 'as important in their way as Liverpool and New York are today'.[98]

Rivers can provide a protective barrier. Yet those who seek to expand their domains must also cross them. Compared to most other large European rivers outside Russia, the Danube has few bridges. The reference point in the 1840s for Kohl was the 'little' Thames, with its generous apportionment of nearly 50 bridges; in contrast, down from Ulm, there were fewer than twelve (and all but one was on the upper river). Kohl, author of a recent pioneering study of urban geography and modern transportation, explained that the Danube's width, swift flow, irregular course and tendency to flood were major inhibiting factors.[99] He also noted that, prior to Széchenyi's bridge – at the time of writing, under construction between Pest and Buda – the only permanent structure that had ever spanned the middle or lower river was Trajan's bridge.

Roman soldiers were accomplished swimmers. But this did not dispense with their need for bridges, in pontoon or more durable form. To consolidate Trajan's hold on the land of the Dacians, who occupied the left bank, Apollodoros of Damascus designed and built the middle and lower Danube's first permanent bridge in AD 103–05, to the east of the Iron Gates, just below the entrance to Djerdap Gorge, near today's cities of

In a frieze at the bottom of Trajan's Column, Danuvius, the god of the Danube, watches Roman legionnaires crossing a pontoon bridge into Dacia, AD 113.

Drobeta-Turnu Severin (Romania) and Kladovo (Serbia). This remarkable
feat of engineering – according to most accounts, the largest military
engineering work of its era – may even have entailed the river's temporary
diversion.[100] The Danube here is nearly a kilometre wide and, by general
consensus, flowed fast, though it was also reliably deep. The wooden
superstructure rested on around twenty enormous piers constructed from
brick, stone, mortar and pozzolana cement; at each end was a massive
stone abutment.

Yet Trajan's bridge did not outlast Roman control of Dacia. According
to the historian, Cassius Dio, Trajan's successor, Hadrian, after relinquish-
ing Dacia, dismantled it to foil barbarian raids across the river into
Moesia.[101] 'It is a certain fact', remarked an early Victorian authority, that
the bridge 'stood firm enough till Hadrian destroyed it'.[102] Natural collapse
in the wake of severe flooding cannot be ruled out, however. Whatever the
cause, the imposing piers were still there in 1856, when record low water
permitted an unprecedented inspection.[103] Serbian archaeologist-diver
Gordana Karović – who conducted the first underwater investigations
using sonar technology (September 2003) – surmised that the current had
swept away the four pier stumps apparently lost between the 1930s and
1980s.[104] Today, the only visible remains are the first pillar on either side
and the abutment on the left-hand (Romanian) bank.

A companion internal improvement that assisted the conquest of
Dacia was a partially suspended high road that Trajan's legions imposed
along the right-hand (Serbian) bank. Some sections of *Via Trajana* were
cut or hacked out. Others exploited a broad ledge that juts out above the
river. But where the canyon walls were sheer, the military track consisted
of planks overhanging the river, laid across large beams rammed into
square holes drilled deep into the rock face.[105] Whereas Trajan's bridge
was depicted on his column in Rome (the frieze also features the river god,
Danuvius, as guardian of the Roman fleet), a commemorative tablet was
chiselled out on location (present-day Kladovo) to mark his road's completion (103).[106] The oblong *Tabula Trajana* consists of a scroll supported by
flying genii, flanked by dolphins and crowned by an eagle. The engraver
worked directly above the road at a spot where the carriageway benefited
from a broad ledge.

Over the centuries, the *Tabula Trajana* has been damaged by the camp-
fires of boatmen who overnighted on the ledge (in the 1870s, the surviving
sections were still used as a towpath by mules and horses dragging grain
barges to Budapest and Vienna).[107] These scorch marks put the finishing

Inscription on the Via Trajana (Trajan's Tablet).

touches to the inscription's gradual obliteration. As late nineteenth-century English-speaking voyagers were inclined to regard the road and bridge as a victory over the natural savagery represented by the gorge as well as the Dacians, they interpreted this decay as the non-human world's sweet revenge: 'Nature', remarked the late nineteenth-century American artist, sculptor and classicist Francis Davis Millet, 'has not forgiven Trajan the desecration of this, one of her sublimest works, and in the lapse of cen-turies she has gradually eaten away the hard rock tablet, threatening it with utter destruction, in spite of the projecting stone above it, until solid masonry supports have been erected to hold the shattered inscription in its place'.[108] As the waters rose behind the Iron Gate Dam in the early 1970s, Trajan's tablet was relocated.[109]

Prior to the dam that pacified the Iron Gate, navigational hazards ꞏꞏꞏꞏꞏꞏꞏꞏꞏ ꞏꞏ ꞏꞏꞏꞏꞏ ꞏꞏꞏ ꞏꞏꞏꞏꞏꞏꞏ ꞏꞏꞏꞏ ꞏꞏꞏ ꞏꞏꞏ ꞏꞏꞏꞏ ꞏꞏꞏ ꞏꞏꞏꞏ ꞏꞏꞏꞏꞏꞏꞏꞏꞏ ꞏꞏ Ulm rendered costly upriver carriage of bulky commodities.[110] However, despatching grain westward was not the only option. In the early 1800s, when western European demand for lower Danubian wheat, barley and maize was high, navigational control of the lower river and its outlet was a major source of friction in Russian relations with Austria-Hungary and Britain. Under the Treaty of Adrianople (1829), which transferred the Turkish principalities of Wallachia and Moldavia (formerly Dacia) to

Russia, the entire delta came under Russian control. To boost the grain trade in its newly acquired Black Sea port of Odessa, Russia allied itself to the river's uncooperative attributes to thwart Austrian and British commerce.

Sandbars stymied upstream ships bound for Galatz and Brăila to buy grain. Russia not only refused to improve navigation but discontinued a Turkish strategy that ensured sufficient depth for safe passage: attachment of an iron rake to ships quitting the river, which stirred up sand and mud that the current could wash out to sea.[111] The nature of the river itself encouraged the Austrian and British search for another route. Entering the home strait at Cernavodă, a town no more than 70 kilometres from the sea as the crow flies, the Danube turns northward abruptly, away from the easterly course followed for hundreds of kilometres, and then fans out into a labyrinthine delta. Cutting a route due east from Cernavodă to the coast at Constanţa would shave off nearly 200 kilometres. By-passing the delta would eliminate the need for marine vessels to slog up to Galaţi or Brăila, the terminus for river barges and trans-shipment point for sea-going craft.

David Urquhart, secretary to the British Embassy to the Ottoman Empire in the 1850s, emphasized the obstacle to commerce this penultimate stretch of river presented. After the river's northward lurch, it inexplicably lost itself in 'useless wanderings' that carried it away 'from the direction of its usefulness'. The river had conspired with Russian machinations to thwart its own (unappreciated) destiny. By taking a wrong turn, the Danube had deprived itself of its rightful role as co-agent of British interests. Urquhart's objective was to 'set free the king of rivers'. A canal of just 70 kilometres would effectively grant a coastline to landlocked Serbia, Hungary and Transylvania, opening the 'floodgates of fertility on the heaven-blessed and man-cursed Dacian plains'.[112]

Despite the river's almost unnatural deviation, the commercial outlook for Britain improved markedly after the Crimean War. The Treaty of Paris (1856) internationalized the river by bestowing 'free' status upon it. The body responsible for establishing and maintaining unrestricted navigation, physically as well as politically, was the seven-country European Danube Commission.[113] The Commission's authority extended from Brăila to Sulina (Kilometre Zero), the port at the mouth of the river's main delta channel. The Commission's engineers set about improving navigation along the Maritime Danube by straightening, shortening and dredging the river as well as installing revetments (retaining walls to combat erosion).

W. H. Bartlett, 'Sulina at the Mouth of the Danube', from Beattie, *The Danube* (1844).

The Commission also had its work cut out in the delta, where mid-nineteenth-century shipping faced the choice of three channels – each one unsatisfactory. The Kilia arm was the deepest and enjoyed the largest flow. But its entrance banks were particularly treacherous. The St George arm, the shallowest and most winding, was the least viable for ocean-going vessels. The Sulina arm was deeper, but not enough to support maritime craft, and carried a small volume of water; and Sulina itself was buried in the delta's depths.[114] Nonetheless, the Commission's long-serving chief engineer, Charles Hartley, established it as the main artery.

On the eve of assuming his duties in 1856, as Hartley later recalled, the channel was 'wild' and 'open', littered with wrecks. Hulls and masts thrusting up from submerged sandbanks provided the sole clues to the shipping lane's whereabouts. The banks were discernible only by 'clusters of wretched hovels built on piles' and quays and narrow strands fringed by tall reeds readily flooded when the level rose a few centimetres. About 2,000 vessels a year landed their cargo in the Sulina 'roadstead' during the early 1850s, and mishaps were common before the Commission commenced operations. In the worst single incident, in the winter of 1855, 24 sailing ships and 60 lighters ran aground in a gale, with the combined loss of over 300 lives.[115] When Hartley stepped down from his post (1907), the Sulina channel was 1,585 metres long, 7.5 metres deep, 91 metres wide between the guiding piers, and 183 metres wide until the open sea was attained. From these corrective measures flowed a massive (five-fold) increase in freight from 1861 to 1902.[116]

Whether in its uncorrected condition, or more recent, relatively redeemed and domesticated guise, the Maritime Danube attracted little attention from Britons and Americans whose relationship with the river was recreational (rather than scientific). And when they did record their impressions, they were rarely positive. Edmund Spencer typically described the Danube, where it deteriorated into a swamp, as 'a desolation of desolation'.[117] On the other hand, he and his compatriots always commented on Vienna's and Budapest's riverscapes.

However, this usually involved an invidious comparison between the river's two greatest cities. The river at Vienna generated as little enthusiasm as the delta. Jerrold found the approach 'disappointing' and reckoned this stretch was 'one of the least attractive' parts of the entire river. Millet also felt short-changed: Vienna presented 'an unsightly water-front to the Danube navigator'.[118] There was little evidence of the grand imperial city, which was separated from the river by a scruffy industrial area and the open ground of the Prater (Vienna's largest park, occupying an island between the river and a former arm now known as the Danube Canal). Vienna's imposing buildings were all set well back. Yet those unmoved by Vienna's fluvial setting were invariably enchanted by Budapest's.[119] Visitors noted the dignifying role of the river and its integral position within the cityscape; the parliament buildings and Franz Josef Quay sat on the left-hand, Pest bank while the royal palace on the Blocksberg graced the opposite, Buda bank.[120]

Adolf Hitler was equally impressed by Budapest's superior relationship to the Danube. Albert Speer, official Nazi architect, recalled that Hitler wanted to transform his home town (Linz) into a showcase 'Führer' city. Linz would be an improvement on Vienna, which was 'orientated all wrong . . . since it merely turned its back to the Danube'. Hitler wanted Linz to become a German Budapest.[121] However, detractors from Jerrold to Hitler showed little grasp of why Vienna was disassociated from the Danube (nor of Budapest's vulnerability to high water). An earlier river traveller, however, had recognized the need to respond to the threat of inundation. Impatient with the dominant pictorial perspective, Kohl (1854) implored artists to stop deluging viewers with so-called 'romantic' and 'picturesque' images that perpetuated the myth of the 'beautiful' natural Danube. Kohl sought an honest portrayal that included the aftermath of distressing floods (such as broken bridges) and contemporary features of river life like shipwrecks and ice dams.[122] A keen modernizer, Kohl wanted visual

images to advance the campaign for a strictly trained river that (in Reclus'
terms) was more servant than god.

In spate, when the Danube is at its most dynamic, driftwood blocks
channels, banks erode and fresh channels open up. New sand and gravel
bars appear in the wider, shallower channels. A navigable channel becomes
non-navigable and the impassable becomes passable. Smaller channels meta-
morphose into lakes and lakes return to open water. Ever contrary and unsat-
isfied, observed Kohl, the 'wild river-god tosses about in his procrustean
bed, which he finds now too narrow, and now too spacious'.[123] Intractable
and restless but also bountiful and amenable, the Viennese feared and valued
the river in equal measure. Since the thirteenth century, it had tended to
shift course in a northeasterly direction, away from the city. A relief as regards
vulnerability to flooding, this was less desirable for trade and communica-
tions.[124] The trick was to keep the Danube close, but at arm's length. For the
river provided a plentiful local source of fish as well as a conduit for meat from
livestock grazed on the Hungarian plain (*Puszta*). Goods also arrived along
the *Donaustrasse* from the west on rafts, notably lumber from the forested
slopes of the Danube's tributaries in the Tatra mountains and the Alps.[125]

In the Middle Ages, flooding regularly prompted abandonment of
bankside or adjacent villages. In 1501, the worst flash flood in Vienna's
history swamped the growing city.[126] As a major city took soggy root in
the floodplain, the proactive strategy of confronting the river replaced
the reactive/adaptive strategy of flight and relocation. The arrival of the
Habsburg dynasty and the need to fortify the new imperial capital against
Ottoman assault sharpened efforts to 'correct' the river. Yet keeping the
Danube in check was massively expensive. In 1662, river regulation in the
Vienna region cost as much as maintaining the Habsburg household.[127]
The modern era's first major river training works were undertaken at the
close of the sixteenth century, with canalization over a 17.3-kilometre
stretch of the branch of the river nearest the city.

This arm, subsequently designated the *Donaukanal* in 1686, could
not, by itself, provide the security that an increasingly risk averse (rather
than risk accommodating) city demanded.[128] Drastic inundation after
the sudden release of meltwater behind an *Eisstoss* in the spring of 1830
drowned a hundred Viennese. Ice dams also wrecked wooden bridges.
More substantial bridges were not an option, however, due to the chaotic
channel regime. As late as the 1860s, the river's morphology in Vienna's
vicinity consisted of a bewildering skein of main and subsidiary branches,
the principal channel's location shifting routinely.

The Danube Regulation Commission (*Donauregulierungskommission*) initiated a massive public works project to alleviate the capital's vulnerability in 1867. The Commission's instructions (from Kaiser Franz Joseph) were to replace the meandering channelscape with an arrow-straight, embanked riverbed. At the festive inauguration of the *Durchstich* on 14 May 1870, through a telescope, from a gloriette erected near the military swimming school in the Prater, the Kaiser surveyed the future river marked out with flags. He then made the first ceremonial cut (*Spatenstich*) before handing the project over to the French contractor (Castor, Couvreux and Hersent) chosen for the grand make-over, not least because it had just dug the Suez Canal (1859–69). Thousands of attendees consulted the engineering plans on display, poured over the artistic vision of a future city with four monumental bridges spanning the 'blue channel' that would actualize the link between the imperial capital and the empire's principal *Wasserstrasse*, and marvelled at the state of the art exhibition of excavation equipment.[129] On 15 April 1875, the temporary *Rollerdam* was breached and water started to flow into the thirteen-kilometre-long and 280-metre-wide manufactured riverbed – a spectacle witnessed by thousands. Within three hours, the level had risen to nearly half the new channel's depth; after four days, it was full. Suess, a local geology professor, was integral to project planning and implementation and had the honour of breaching the *Rollerdam*. This eminent Viennese scientist (who, toward the end of his life, would propose an alternative source for the Danube) recorded that a steamer passed through the *Neue Donau* without incident on 18 April. The Kaiser returned for the new river's formal opening at the end of May; his ship, the *Ariadne*, steamed upriver at the head of a fifteen-boat flotilla.[130] Having canoed down the river more than a decade after the re-configuration works, Millet delivered a positive verdict: the Danube was now 'thoroughly well-behaved and well-regulated'.[131] In addition, the first stable bridges could now be constructed.

The sweetest victory that humans can experience, pronounced the mayor of Vienna in his toast to the 250 guests at the banquet celebrating the official opening of the new riverbed, was the victory over the elements.[132] From an engineering standpoint, however, flaws remained. Concentrating three channels into one increased the current's force and erosive power. Moreover, the refashioned main current did not oblige by flowing in a straight line. Vacillation encouraged sandbank build-up, which inconvenienced a city still dependent on waterborne traffic. Rectification works (1898) deepened a 180-metre section of main channel over toward the right bank.[133] Nonetheless, commerce on the New Danube doubled between 1877 and 1880.[134] Further modifications to the *Donaukanal* at this time bolstered protection against flooding and *Eisstoss*.[135] The most notable device was a floating barrage installed across the canal entrance at Nussdorf, when required, in the form of a blocking ship, itself superseded in the 1890s by a movable iron floodgate. The abutments to Otto Wagner's *Nussdorfer Wehr und Schleuse*, a fine example of *Jugendstil*, were adorned with a magnificent pair of bronze lions that face upriver, as if responsible for keeping the ice at bay themselves. Rudolf Weyr's beasts exude imperial pomp and potency, emblems of the unruly river's domestication (at last).[136]

Though these measures cut flooding incidence, districts between the *Donaukanal* and the new Danube were still susceptible – with particularly high water in July 1954. A second major flood control project was finally implemented between 1972 and 1987. Regulation works undertaken a century earlier had created a half-kilometre-wide flood zone to the east of the new Danube. Another Danube of sorts, parallel to and within a stone's throw of the main river, was now carved out within this *Inundationsgebiet*, effectively replacing it by serving as a 21-kilometre relief canal *(Entlast-ungsgerinne)*. Aiming to deliver total security, the new system was designed to accommodate the all-time high flow of 14,000 cubic centimetres per second (measured in 1501).[137]

## Delightful Danube: Vienna's Watery Retreat

Through these improvement works, the Viennese Danube had literally acquired multiple identities. Moving eastward from the city centre, the first Danube was the *Donaukanal*.[138] The second Danube was the new river. The third (and most recent) Danube was the relief (discharge) canal, which, to confuse matters, was dubbed the *Neue Donau*. Yet there was also a fourth Danube (third in chronological order) lying further to the east: the Old Danube. During canalization in the 1870s, stretches of the former main channel were plugged with freshly excavated materials. Not all of the channel was filled in, though. Nor did all the water from the unfilled sections drain away.[139] Protecting the city from the old river, paradoxically, allowed the city to come closer to the Danube in its former guise. A portion of the *Alte Donau* became a lake-like loop, eight kilometres long, half a kilometre wide and up to seven metres deep. Complete with bays and islands, the *Alte Donau* was sealed off from the new river. Its shorelines

Satellite image of Vienna, showing four Danubes: the Danube Canal, Danube, New Danube and Old Danube.

became desirable locations for rustic cabins and gardens to which the Viennese retreated on summer evenings and weekends – not least to bathe.

This freshly created recreational riverscape compensated in part for modernization's obliteration of bathing sites at Kaiserwasser. Though the original *Frey-bad* (1810) was re-located to the Danube's north bank, where it remained until 1914, the city government established the first public bathing area (*Kommunalbad*) on the old Danube in 1876, with a visitor capacity of 1,200.[140] However, the river swimming locale that became the most popular was the *Gänsehäufel*. The 'pile of the geese' denoted a heap of sand in the former main channel. On this artificial island (*Schotterinsel*), the locals raised geese, the river providing watery defence akin to a moat.

64

After reengineering, the defunct channel containing Goose Island effectively became a lake.

The *Gänsehäufel's* first human occupant was Florian Berndl, who, from 1900, rented a 5,000 cubic metre patch from the Danube Regulation Commission. Though his ostensible purpose was to grow willows, what Berndl really wanted was a retreat where he and his coterie could luxuriate unfettered in a naturist paradise (other river swimming clubs were fenced in and enforced a strict bathingsuit code).[141] Yet by 1905, the municipal authority had converted Berndl's nudist commune into a public lido inoffensive to conventional morals. Baker, who visited shortly afterwards, noted that the geese were gone from the place 'where geese disport themselves', replaced by 'mixed' bathing in the 'cool, swift stream'.[142] By the summer of 1909, the 4,000-capacity island drew a seasonal total of 300,000 visitors.[143]

Though three of the five bathing ships (*Strombäder* or *Schiffbäder*) moored in the *Donaukanal* since the early 1800s survived into the interwar period, the centre of gravity shifted decisively to the *Alte Donau*, where a rash of swimming clubs broke out in the wake of Goose Island's success.[144] The old river offered free outdoor relief for denizens of the burgeoning city's overcrowded working-class neighbourhoods and outer suburbs, where rickets, tuberculosis and Spanish flu thrived in cramped dwellings, aggravated by poor nutrition and sunlight deprivation in dingy, gardenless

Bathing at the *Gänsehäufel* family bathing station in the Old Danube, Vienna, 1920s.

apartments.[145] Encampments of unemployed youth (havens for unsupervised outdoor activity) also sprang up along the Danube.[146] The Austrian Social Democratic Party that governed post-imperial 'Red Vienna' (*Rotes Wien*) between 1919 and 1934 promoted river bathing as an integral component of public health policy.[147] Identifying swimming in the *Alte Donau* as a preventative medicine that equipped the post-war 'new person' with a 'new body', city fathers encouraged heavier use of *Gänsehäufel*. To bring the island closer to the city, they built the first concrete bridge in 1927. Between 1918 and 1945, 6 million bathers came, cementing the island's reputation as Europe's largest inland beach.[148]

During the Second World War, the Allies – having mistaken the changing cabins for barracks – carpet-bombed the island.[149] This erasure of infrastructure more or less returned the island to the condition in which Berndl found it in 1900. One hundred and thirty bomb craters were counted at the onset of the 30 million Schilling reconstruction project (1948). That the island's rehabilitation was completed before the reconstruction of the badly damaged state opera house and national theatre (*Burgtheater*) speaks volumes about river bathing's value to the local citizenry.[150] Today, in summer, the former island of geese receives 30,000 daily visitors (the maximum capacity established in 1950), yet still contains habitat for species such as the European beaver. And Berndl would be gratified to know that a naturist section (*Freikörperkultur:* FKK) was formally established in 1981. In 1993, the island secured historic monument status.[151]

Walking to the island from the subway station in Donaucity one sweltering July day in 2009, I was left in no doubt that I was entering the company of a world-class river. The names of some of the greatest rivers are etched into the white stone of the last office building before the path leads down to the Old Danube's sunbathing meadows. In turn, you pass the Danube, Nile, Amazon, Yangtze, Mississippi and, finally (and perhaps most surprisingly), Australia's Murray. At the first public swimming area, a sign identifies a majestic old willow, 'patriarch' of the forest, a survivor of the wetland woods (*Auwald*) that predated the improvement works of the 1870s.

Like these previous works, the re-ordering of the river in the 1970s was a high modernist project. But the socio-cultural climate was radically different in terms of environmental sensibilities. A central feature of the newly dawned age of ecological consciousness was the more intensive scrutiny of large engineering projects. Concerns were voiced over the indirect impact on the Lobau, Vienna's 'water forest' to the east, of lowering the floodplain's watertable.[152] Other elements of Viennese society did not want the mega-project's direct consumption of a landscape to be compounded by inappropriate development on *Donauinsel*, another fresh feature of the riverscape.

*Donauinsel* was an almost incidental by-product of this latest flood protection scheme. Sandwiched between the Danube of the 1870s and the new relief canal, the ribbon island had been fashioned from 30 million cubic metres of excavated materials dumped onto the floodplain. Completed in 1984, *Donauinsel* is long and narrow: over 21 kilometres in length but just 210 metres at its widest. Project proponents had given little thought to its potential uses and elements in the press ridiculed the fatuous '*Spaghettiinsel*'. Initial proposals for what to put on the sliver of an island included multiple soccer pitches, a golf course and a new main railway station.

The environmentally aware, however, regarded *Donauinsel* as an opportunity to mend the city's fraught and somewhat distant relationship with the Danube. These advocates of low-profile, discreet recreational provision responsive to the larger context of a relatively natural floodplain environment eventually came to the fore.[153] For despite the automatic

View of Danube City / Donaucity, Vienna, from the New Danube, 2009.

association in many visitors' minds between Vienna and the Danube (thanks to Strauss's waltz), the city's rapport with the river was not comparable to Budapest's.[154] *Donauinsel* quickly assumed a recreational significance compatible with its watery environs that matched that of the *Alte Donau* (fine tuning incorporated gravel banks, side channels and shallow water areas).[155] *Die Insel* (as it is often referred to) is a car-free space that provides the opportunity (as interpretative signs indicate) to 'Holiday in the middle of Vienna' (*Urlaub mitten in Wien*). The island shifts the city eastward, embedding the notion of a city on the river rather than a city next to the river. A more high-profile statement of the closer relationship is Danube City (Donaucity), a high-rise development within the former flood zone that houses, among other transnational organizations, the International Commission for the Protection of the Danube River (ICPDR).

## Distressed Danube

Established in 1998 by the Danubian states to implement the Danube River Protection Convention (1994) for transboundary water management throughout the river's basin, ICPDR differs from previous international commissions for the river in its avowedly ecological remit.[156] That the Danube now requires protection from people as much as people have traditionally required protection from the river is painfully clear. The river's human diversity was once matched by its piscine diversity, which includes the endangered huchen, a uniquely Danubian (entirely freshwater) variety of salmon.[157] Manipulation of morphology and flow regime and degradation of water quality has impoverished species richness. Since the reconfiguration of Vienna's fluvial backyard, a fifth of fish species found locally have become extinct through habitat loss – elimination of meanders, sloping banks, islets, inlets and gravel beds – aggravated by pollution.[158]

Relaxing in a riverside inn at Persenbeug, between Linz and Vienna, en route to Constantinople in the winter of 1934, Fermor met an erudite local. The minor nobleman was as concerned for the river's future as he was about the fate of titled folk like himself: 'Everything is going to vanish! They talk of building power-dams across the Danube and I tremble whenever I think of it! They'll make the wildest river in Europe as tame as a municipal waterworks.'[159] The dam proposal Fermor's acquaintance had in mind was Ybbs-Persenbeug, the first hydroelectric project on the Austrian

Danube, initially mooted in the 1920s and eventually completed in 1959.[160]
Easily the most controversial project, however, was authorized in 1977.
A Czechoslovakian-Hungarian scheme to increase peak-time electricity
generation and improve navigation, it envisaged two hydro stations and
dams, at Gabčíkovo, Czechoslovakia, and Nagymaros, Hungary.[161] Work
on the Hungarian half, begun in 1985, ran into opposition that coalesced
into a citizens' protest group, the Danube Circle. The stretch the dam
builders targeted was the scenic Danube Bend, where the river executes
a dramatic 90-degree southward turn. 'The Knee' – which nineteenth-
century British and American travellers judged to be immeasurably superior to the Rhine Gorge – was a favourite destination for recreationists from
Budapest, 50 kilometres downstream. But the defence of a river that was
diverted into a plastic-lined canal was also grounded in historical and
ecological values. Above the proposed site, on the north bank, loomed the
ruins of Visegrad, a thirteenth-century castle where the Hungarian court
resided during the Renaissance.[162]

A founder of the Danube Circle reflected that this was the first occasion since the uprising of 1956 that a 'feeling of identity appeared in people
that *this* is a part of our nature; a part of our land'.[163] At the same time, a
more visceral link was established between the river's interests and spirit
and those of the Hungarian people. The Circle's logo showed a blue zigzag
line cut in half by a white strip representing the dam that sliced through
the water's natural flow.[164] Empathy ran deep because they identified with
the river as a fellow victim of manipulative policies and coercive control.
'It offended me', recalled a scientist and Danube Circle co-founder, 'the
idea of twisting the river out of its natural course'.[165] Following sustained
pressure from the Circle, the Hungarian government held dam construction to stricter environmental accountability (1988). Within twelve months
(May 1989), a body advising the post-communist government recommended unilateral abandonment of a relic of the communist era's discredited 'command economy'.[166] 'There were two ways to protest in Hungary in
the 1980s', explained the director of a Budapest policy research and con-
sulting firm. 'One was protesting the dam; the other was to deface one of
those big statues of Communist heroes that used to be all over the place'.[167]

Undeterred, Czechoslovakia steamed ahead with its half of the project,
reconfigured as 'Variant C'. This entailed construction of a third dam, upstream from Gabčíkovo, and diversion of 80 per cent of the river's flow
(October 1992) into a 40-kilometre parallel concrete side channel (power
canal). This move unleashed all manner of ecological mayhem onto the

surviving stretch of river-bed. The chronically inadequate water supply was evident in a steep drop in the watertable, the drying up of oxbow lakes, and the dessication of floodplain forests.[168] The project (completed in 1995 by the new nation of Slovakia, which emerged [1993] after the 'velvet divorce' from the Czech Republic) benefited navigation and produced more electricity to sell to Austria. It did nothing, however, to ease the perennial threat of inundation. In April 2006, Serbia, Hungary, Romania and Bulgaria experienced the worst floods on record.[169] Channel straightening, dyking and wetland reclamation (polderization) had not only failed to contain floods but exacerbated their force.[170]

Large-scale polderization, begun in the 1950s, accelerated under the dictatorship of Nicolae Ceausescu. Between 1983 and his overthrow (1989), the regime converted 15 per cent of delta wetlands into a quarter of a million acres of rice paddies and maize fields. Aside from being an economic flop – the drained lands were marginal and salty – measures to protect crops caused an enormous buildup of water behind defences with no safe outlet.[171] Completion of the first and second Iron Gate dams (1972 and 1984) exacerbated wetland loss by halving the amount of sediment reaching the delta (meanwhile, silt back-up occupies 10 per cent of reservoir capacity behind the first dam).[172] Delta shrinkage permits greater ingress of salt water into freshwater lakes and ponds, reducing the capability for pollutant sequestration and detoxification and intensifying beach erosion at Black Sea resorts.[173]

For decades, Romanian ecologists had recommended two basic remedial actions. First, to accommodate the river's need to relieve the pressure of excess water by setting aside low-lying receptor areas. Second, to protect and expand reed beds and marshland vital for cleansing water before it enters the Black Sea (an ecosystem 'service' comparable to the human kidney's function). 'We are paying the price of the works made against nature', conceded Romania's prime minister, Calin Popescu-Tariceanu, during the flood crisis of 2006, which highlighted the signal failure of nineteenth- and twentieth-century approaches to deliver immunity.[174]

An international body had implemented the first compensatory measure hot on the heels of communism's collapse. The Danube Delta Biosphere Reserve, established under UNESCO's Natural World Heritage Site programme (1990), encompasses 580,000 hectares of the Romanian delta, 9 per cent of which enjoys strict protection.[175] An early beneficiary was Babina Island, where 2,100 hectares were drained in 1985. Breaching the island's dykes in 1994 reconnected former wetlands to the river's hydrological system. Re-flooding (a low cost strategy) could not restore the water regime that prevailed before the first dyke was raised in the delta (which, at certain seasons, would have completely submerged Babina). Yet within a few years, signs of large-scale regeneration were already abundant. The island's previous function as fish habitat and spawning ground (for sturgeon, mullet and Black Sea herring) had been reinstated; in tandem, otter and mink were also returning. In 1996, the project received the World Wide Fund for Nature International's 'Conservation Merit Award'.[176]

Protection of surviving marshland oases complemented wetland rehabilitation. The wetland of Kopacki Rit, located where Drava meets Danube, contains the largest remnant of Danubian floodplain forest. An area that an American advocate of modernization dismissed as a 'bewildering maze of oxbow lakes, cutoffs and marshes' constituted prime habitat for black storks, white-tailed eagles, otters, wild boar and other creatures of watery lowland whose living space has shrunk elsewhere in Europe.[177] In 1999, by tripartite agreement, Serbia, Croatia and Hungary set up an international nature reserve of a quarter-million acres. Kopacki Rit Nature Park and Danube/Drava National Park remain littered with mines planted during the recent Balkan conflicts, but revivification continues apace in these pioneering sites for trans-national Danubian conservation strategies. A key tool is the re-introduction of beavers to assist with the restoration of floodplain dynamics.

The Danube's grave ecological condition received further high-profile attention in October 1999. A few months after the cessation of NATO bombing in Serbia, a nine-day symposium moved down the river from Passau (Bavaria). 'A River of Life: Down the Danube to the Black Sea' was the third in a series of voyaging symposia commissioned (under the auspices of the Athens-based organization 'Religion, Science and the Environment') to reflect on the state of the world's seas and rivers. Discussions aboard the *Delphin Queen* among ecological scientists, religious leaders and environmental activists ranged from the legalities and practicalities of restoring the river's natural flow to cultural matters such as the river's role in European identity formation. The trip began with an early morning (optional) multi-faith blessing of the river on the banks near the monastery of Niederaltaich. As part of the ceremony, a fleet of miniature boats bearing candles, one for each river nation, was released into the current.[178] The 125 delegates stepped ashore at various points. They visited the former concentration camp at Mauthausen, inspected the Gabčíkovo dam and power station, and contemplated the contorted girders and smashed concrete of the stricken bridges at Novi Sad (those photographed by Müller-Pohle) that blocked further downstream progress. In Novi Sad, a service was also held at the memorial to the victims of Hungarian fascism. After reboarding a boat (*Delta Star*) beyond the obstacles, participants negotiated the Iron Gate. Finally, they toured the delta in small boats, inspecting the Babina restoration project.

The driving force behind the Danube symposium was His All Holiness, The Ecumenical Patriarch Bartholomew, leader of the Orthodox Christian Church. The Danube, the 'Green Patriarch' warned, was losing its status as a 'river of life'.[179] From the delta, Bartholomew wrote to Romano Prodi, President of the European Commission, the symposium's co-sponsor. As well as reflecting on the outcome of the voyage, he urged EU support for the task of setting 'this great river free' by building a new bridge at Novi Sad and clearing the debris and shattered bridges, which snuffed out traffic between the lower and upper rivers. Bartholomew emphasized the Danube's role as Europe's river, a status that EU entry for all Danubian nations would enshrine.[180]

The European Union's stake in a greener future Danube deepened the following year. In accordance with the EU's Water Framework Directive (WFD) of 2000, ICPDR publishes annual surveys of the Danube's ecological status.[181] The second of the 'WFD Roof Reports' (2004) pooled data from the basin's thirteen nations, which indicated that only a few stretches enjoyed a decent condition. Seventy-one per cent of water samples contained DDT levels well in excess of safe limits. Defunct but not decontaminated factories and mines leached heavy metals. Fifty-seven per cent of water samples submitted exceeded limits for lead and copper and 4 per cent registered above for cadmium. Various cities on the middle and lower river still discharged unacceptable quantities of untreated or partially treated human waste. Sturgeon and sterlet were gone from the upper and middle river. Successive dams block access to these anadromous species' breeding grounds and sterilize the water by trapping sediments behind impoundments.[182]

Resignation to a terminally degraded condition militated against the river's revival, according to Janos Zlinsky, a senior scientist at the Regional Environmental Centre for Central and Eastern Europe (Szentendre, Hun - gary): 'I think now some countries are saying, "This river's gone to the dogs anyway, so let's just use it as an industrial highway."'[183] Ecologically and hydromorphologically, there are two Danubes, reflecting recent political and economic divides. 'Roof reports' indicate that the upper river in Germany and Austria is heavily constrained by dams, canals and concrete embankments (a dam or other impoundment interrupts the flow on average every 16 kilometres). Yet water quality is superior to that of the lower/middle stretches. Though less engineered, the sections in the former Soviet bloc bear a heavier burden of pollutants.[184]

Over the short term, NATO's 78-day bombing campaign worsened the problem of industrial pollution on the middle Danube. At Pancevo, upstream from Belgrade, stricken fertilizer and petrochemical plants spilled ammonia and mercury into the river and a refinery disgorged crude oil.[185] At the same time, the fall of communism and war brought unintended ecological benefits. Patches of former wetland re-hydrated and self-restored as flood defences fell into disrepair.[186] The problem of eutrophication in the delta – nutrient-rich runoff from fertilizer plants and large animal-raising operations causes algal blooms that deplete oxygen – abated with the post-communism crisis in the agricultural sector.[187] Meanwhile, water quality improved as outmoded factories shut down. Air strikes disabled other manufacturing plants while some were paralysed by disruption of navigation and EU sanctions.

The single most infamous event in Danubian ecological history, however, was post-communism. And it stemmed from mining. The incident also served as a reminder of the need to think like a watershed rather than just like a river and to develop basin-wide solutions. The collapse of an earthen dyke holding back a toxic waste lagoon at Baia Mare, northwestern Romania, on 30 January 2000, triggered an international disaster. A hundred thousand cubic metres of water saturated with cyanide, copper, zinc, lead and other heavy metal by-products from a private-cum-state (Australian-Romanian) gold mine, were released into three streams. One of these watercourses, the Someş, feeds Hungary's second largest river, the Tisza, which the 40-kilometre long poisonous plume reached five days later. The Tisza, in turn, discharges into the Danube, where the noxious brew arrived after another seven days. Three weeks from the initial accident, the slick discharged into the sea.[188]

Dead fish and fish-eating mammals and birds (including the endangered white-tailed eagle) were reported along the Tisza and the Danube as far downstream as Belgrade.[189] Fishing on the Tisza was suspended for four-and-a-half months. Bathing was banned. Hungarian towns whose public water systems were based on treated water extracted from the river shipped in bottled and bagged water until the plume had passed. No human deaths were recorded. Nor were serious health problems noted by the international task force appointed to investigate and recommend how to avoid similar incidents.[190] Nonetheless, unofficial reports were awash with pronouncements of the death of the river and associated ecosystems. Two weeks after the disaster struck, Jozsef Feiler, representing Friends of the Earth, pronounced: 'Everything down to bacteria is dead. There's more life in a sewage channel than this river now. Nothing is alive. Zero.'[191] Residents of Szeged and Szolnok, the Tisza's two main cities, performed the ritual they conducted for drowned loved ones. They cast flowers onto the water from bridges and lit candles on the banks. In the spill's immediate aftermath, scientists estimated that it would take between ten and twenty years for significant biological life to return.

A ray of hope appeared on the tenth anniversary of the Danube River Protection Convention (29 June 2004): the establishment of Danube Day – an annual, basin-wide event to foster 'Danube solidarity' among its 85 million residents. The consortium of international and transnational organizations, governmental and non-governmental, that collectively care for the river selected a logo for Danube Day that is far more upbeat than that adopted by the Danube Circle twenty years earlier. Two blue swirls of water chase each other's tails in a circular motion as 'symbol of water movement and the connection of people'.[192]

## Blue Danube

At one of the funeral ceremonies for the personified Tisza, a speaker announced that 'waters have no nationality, fishes bear no passports'.[193] In ecological terms, this statement makes perfect sense, providing an object lesson in dependence and interdependence. Less than 10 per cent of the water in Hungary's rivers originates within Hungary; the rest derives from Romania, Ukraine, Slovakia and Austria. Nature's supra-nationalism is also clear with regard to the biological ramifications of pollution; toxins flow freely across political boundaries too: a recipe for national environmental insecurity. Within the context of nature's cultural capital and the emblematic role of environmental features, however, this assertion of universal dependence and internationalism makes far less sense. 'Rivers are not just rivers', reflected Ronnie Lipschutz with reference to the river-inspired Hungarian environmental consciousness of the 1980s, 'they are a signifier of place and a source of identity, both large and small'.[194]

The sense of self that communities acquire from rivers often depends on comparison. Since the early 1800s, the Danube has rarely been characterized without reference to the Rhine. Magris' juxtaposition of the mongrelized Danube, multi-ethnic and multi-national, Slavonic and Asiatic as well as Germanic, against the purified Rhine, nationalized and Germanic, falls within a well-worn groove.[195] For many commentators, the position the Rhine occupies within German consciousness is peerless among relationships between rivers and nations. Lewis Spence's account of the sagas and legends of the storied Rhine began with a disquisition on the emotional power of various major European rivers within their respective national contexts.

> The Englishman has only a mitigated pride in the Thames as a
> great commercial asset or, its metropolitan borders once passed,
> a river of peculiarly restful character; the Frenchman evinces no
> very great enthusiasm toward the Seine; and if there are many
> Spanish songs about the 'chainless Guadalquivir,' the dons have
> been content to retain its Arabic name. But what German heart
> does not thrill at the name of the Rhine? What German cheek does
> not flush at the sound of that mighty thunder-hymn [*Die Wacht*
> *am Rhein*] which tells of his determination to preserve the river
> of his fathers at the cost of his best blood?

The Rhine, Spence concluded, 'commands a reverence and affection which is not given by any other modern nation to its greatest and most characteristic river'.[196] If the Rhine has been appropriated as *the* German river (its Swiss entrance and Dutch exit are trivial geographical details), then is the Danube simply the European river par excellence? Or has it been subject to competing claims?

With the notable exceptions of the nineteenth-century German poet Friedrich Hölderlin and the twentieth-century German philosopher Martin Heidegger, few scholars have pondered the Danube's contribution to German identity. And though Hungarians care deeply about their Danube, the Tisza exercises an equal hold over national consciousness. Though the territorial reconfigurations of 1920 (Treaty of Trianon) transferred its source region to Romania, the Tisza remains mostly Hungarian, flowing through the centre of the national landscape, the *Puszta*.[197] 'Blond river', the Tisza's nickname, refers to its sandy colour, but also reflects the (male?) Hungarian belief that it is more attractive than the better-known

Danube. The friendly rivalry between the two rivers' human constituencies extends to the culinary sphere. As Ida Miró Kiss, a prominent Hungarian environmentalist, reflected in 2000: 'Szeged fishermen's soup and Upper Tisza fishermen's soup were often in competition with each other, but both were considered better than Danube fish soup.'[198]

For Lengyel, the Austrian claim on the Danube's symbolic ecology was the strongest: 'it is their national river and the biggest'.[199] And with more than a little help from Johann Strauss, the world knows the Danube not just as an indelibly blue river but as an irrevocably Austrian river. On 15 February 1867, Strauss's new waltz, *An der schönen blauen Donau*, composed for the Vienna Men's Choral Society, received its first performance on the banks of the *Donaukanal*, in the ballroom of the Dianabad. Lyrics by Josef Weyl, the Choral Society's poet, accompanied the musical score. He borrowed the title from the opening lines of Karl Isidor Beck's love poem '*An der Donau*': 'By the beautiful blue Danube/Lies my Village, peaceful and fine/Blessed with world-famous wines'.[200]

Weyl's lyrics omit all reference to riverside features and river-associated events. They are also devoid of any mention of the river itself. The libretto is all about drinking and dancing to forget your woes. The context for this mood of resigned levity was the national morale boost required after recent military defeat by Prussia.[201] Yet the German novelist Heinrich Eduard Jacob has identified a deeper, non-visual relationship with the river beneath the surface of the waltz (though he concedes that 'perhaps one must be a swimmer to realize this'). From the first note

> comes the rippling sound generated by the play of the waters on the river's bottom . . . It appears as the basic tone in the introduction and continues for twenty-two bars. The melody is as it were under water. Then it comes to the surface and the body of the river becomes one with the body of the swimmer.

According to Jacob, Strauss incorporated the two basic movements of the river that flows down toward Vienna: the current's basic forward thrust and the 'waltzing movement' of small waves and whirlpools ('every swimmer knows it').[202]

Whether or not listeners were passionate swimmers, the work became a sensational hit across Europe after Strauss delivered it – minus the lyrics – at the Paris International Exposition (28 May 1867).[203] The words that nearly everyone seems to know – though the instrumental version is more

Cover of Johann Strauss II,
*An der schönen blauen Donau*
(Leipzig, 1900).

frequently performed – were composed by Franz von Gernerth in 1890. In complete contrast to Weyl's original lyrics, they are entirely about the river, beginning with '*Donau, so blau*'. The river portrayed in what has become the unofficial Austrian national anthem is selectively benign: 'through vale and field you flow so calm . . . a picture of peace for all time'. There is no allusion to the volatile river that wrought havoc prior to the recent rectification works.[204]

According to legend, Strauss composed the waltz while reclining on the riverbank. Another local story maintains that Strauss coloured the river blue because, when he was a boy, his mother washed his blue suit in the river and the dye ran out.[205] Indisputable, though, is that Beck, Strauss, Weyl and Gernerth got the colour wrong. Though an extract from Beck's poem prefaces his account, the only 'blue Danube' that Millet and his party found was in the river's quiet side branches. Jerrold recalled that it was yellowish green at Regensburg, and wonders how on earth, in view of the resolutely green and grey colouring, it ever acquired its 'reputation for blueness'. (In fact, he already knows the answer: 'Strauss's waltz has impressed the "blue" Danube on our minds most persistently.'[206]) The author of an article in Vienna's main newspaper, marking the official opening of the New Danube in May 1875, doubtless provoked by the sound of the band playing Strauss's waltz as a send-off for the Kaiser's mini-fleet, addressed the slippery business of the blue Danube head on. Even bathed in brilliant spring sunshine, nowhere was the river blue. The blue Danube, a fond conceit for poets and painters, had had its day. This day was the moment for the everyday working river, clad in its ordinary labourer's garb, to supersede the mythic blue Danube and assert its more prosaic but honest credentials.[207]

The most detailed data on colour reside among the extensive hydrological records that Anton Bruszkay, a Habsburg court counsellor, compiled in the early 1900s and the *Wiener Hydrographische Central-Bureau* published from 1903. Each morning, between seven and eight, over a number of years, Bruszkay looked at the river where it flowed through Mautern (a small town about 80 kilometres upstream from Vienna), where he resided. His records for one of those years contain the following statistics: brown (11 days); loam yellow (46); dirty green (59); light green (45); grass green (5); steel green (69); emerald green (46); and dark green (64).[208] Yet regardless of Bruszkay's meticulous data-gathering – or the title of Jules Verne's novel of 1895, *Le Beau Danube Jaune* (*Beautiful Yellow Danube*) or that of the movie version (*The Red Danube*, 1949) of Bruce Marshall's Cold War novel set in Soviet-occupied Vienna about the repatriation of Russian refugees to the Soviet Union (*Vespers in Vienna* [1947])[209] – the Danube remains forever Straussian blue. Standing on the quayside (1934) in Orsova, where ships from Vienna docked after emerging from the Iron Gate, Fermor listened to a pilot call out to the assembled crowd as the *Saturnus* steamed into view: 'You wait! When they weigh anchor, they put on [the ship's gramophone] *The Blue Danube*.'[210] The river and its fictive blue became so inseparable from the waltz that the concept has been adopted even for books that have absolutely nothing to do with the river.[211]

## From Danube to Ister: Poet, Philosopher and Filmmakers

In view of these vacuous nods to a clichéd river, it is telling that the most influential disquisition on the Danube's cultural and intellectual import was colour-blind (as distinct from colourless): a poem by Hölderlin. A more esoteric event in 2004 than the establishment of Danube Day was the release of *The Ister*, a three-hour, self-funded, prize-winning debut 'cine-video essay'. Five years in the making and shot with a hand-held camera by two young Australians, David Barison and Daniel Ross, the relationship between the material and metaphysical Danubes and the river present and past resides at its heart. *The Ister* was inspired by the forthcoming 200th anniversary of Hölderlin's poem of the same name (1803). Yet an equally strong and more direct source of inspiration was the three-part lecture series that Martin Heidegger dedicated to Hölderlin's poem in 1942.

Born in a small town on the Neckar, Hölderlin spent most of his life in its valley, where he wrote a series of river poems, each bearing a river's name. Like many poets, he regarded a river's course as an allegory for the stages of a human life. An emblem of temporality, it comes from the past and flows into the future. He also saw the river as a symbol for the passage of a day. The Main, for instance, flows from morning (the source) to evening (confluence with the Rhine).[212] In his Neckar poem, Hölderlin imagines the river bearing him down to the Rhine. Though there is more on ancient Greek lands with their pomegranates than about the Neckar, he closes with a declaration of loyalty to his home stream with its 'amiable meadows and bankside willows'.[213]

Hölderlin's Danube poem was unfinished and untitled. The title his editor chose a century later, 'The Ister', derives from the German rendering of the ancient Greco-Roman name for the lower river: *Istros*.[214] In his 'hymn' to the Ister (by which he meant an ode to the gods), Hölderlin reflected that 'rivers make arable the land' and water us and our livestock.[215] But this particular river's greatest gift was cerebral: it evoked the intellectual heritage of ancient Greece that had travelled up the river. To underline German culture's Greek origins, Hölderlin bestowed the lower river's Greek name on the entire river and reversed the Danube's flow so that it ran from east to west. For in the east – code for the classical Greek world – resided Western culture's origins.

Yet almost this river seems
To travel backwards and
I think it must come from the East.[216]

In his lectures on Hölderlin's poem at the University of Freiburg, Heidegger ruminated on the meaning of poetry, the human dwelling place, the poetic essence of rivers, the nature of technology and its impact on culture and the natural environment. Yet he also chewed over a topic particularly close to Hölderlin's heart – the relationship between ancient Greece and contemporary Germany. Heidegger, who was born, raised and buried in Messkirch, a small town about twenty kilometres south of the Danube, often saw eye to eye with Hölderlin regarding rivers, and the Ister in particular. He, too, believed that a river, possessed of its own spirit, goes its own way in obedience to its own dictates. A river belongs to 'the waters'. And what a river does is easily knowable: it flows.[217]

And yet, like Hölderlin, he also wondered whether this was its full or highest meaning. He agreed that rivers, having distinct origins but bound immediately for other places, helped us understand the tension between the foreign and the native: 'the Ister is that river in which the foreign is already present as a guest at its source, that river in whose flowing there constantly speaks the dialogue between one's own and the foreign' (the homely and the unhomely). Crucially, rivers play a key role in our 'coming to be at home' (*Das Heimischwerden im Eigenen*).[218] The Ister 'whiles by the source and is reluctant to abandon its locale because it dwells near the origin. And it dwells near the origin because it has returned home to its locality from its journeying to foreign parts.'[219] The river comes from somewhere else and goes somewhere else. At the same time, it 'determines the dwelling place of human beings upon the earth'.[220]

Heidegger diverged markedly from Hölderlin, however, in his attitude to the transformation of nature and the benefits of technological advance. Hölderlin regarded environmental manipulation as a constructive process.

> But the rock needs incisions
> And the earth needs furrows,
> Would be desolate else, unabiding.[221]

He believed that technology allowed us to take what we needed from the natural world. It made us human, and, not least, permitted us to write and produce books. But during the intervening century and a half, the mystic river alive with natural divinity and haunt of ancient gods had been dredged, channelled, embanked and straightened. Heidegger railed against the onslaught of runaway innovation. Intrinsically malevolent twentieth-century technology, informed by dubious modernist values, had betrayed the essence of rivers and stripped away their poetic splendour.

One of Heidegger's major preoccupations was the imposition of 'un - reasonable' demands on nature through technological apparatus qualita-tively different from earlier technologies (the 'hopeless frenzy of unchained technology' that united the USA and USSR).[222] In the midst of the Soviet blockade of West Berlin (December 1949), he infamously declared that 'agriculture is now a motorized food industry, the same thing in its essence as the production of corpses in the gas chambers and [the] extermination camps, the same thing as blockades and the reduction of countries to famine, the same thing as the manufacture of hydrogen bombs'[223]). More to the point, in another lecture that year ('The Enfram-ing'), Heidegger foreshadowed discussion during the past quarter-century of the 'death' of rivers. Citing Hölderlin's poem 'The Rhine', he contrasted 'The Rhine' as a modern technological creation (the *power* works) with 'The Rhine' as Hölderlin's poetic inspiration (the *art*-work).[224] Heidegger's specific example was an unnamed hydroelectric plant and dam.[225] Apparently unconcerned about its ecological impact (there is no mention of interference with migratory fish runs), he zeroed in on the dam's impact on the idea of the river's autonomy, self-sufficiency and dignity.[226] For, unlike inoffensive structures such as an old wooden bridge, it had altered the Rhine's fundamental essence and purpose: a river has become a mere supplier of power. The dam's 'monstrousness' enslaved the river, so that 'even the Rhine itself appears to be something at our command'. And, as if anticipating the objections of recent historians like Richard White, Heidegger issued a defence: 'But, it will be replied, the Rhine is still a river in the landscape, is it not?' He conceded that the river was still there, but dismissed this presence as largely meaningless, a hollowed-out identity, a debased and denatured entity existing 'in no other way than as an object on call for inspection by a tour group ordered there by the vacation industry'.[227]

Heidegger's and Hölderlin's philosophical and poetic musings feature directly in Barison's and Ross's own river meditation. Their videofilm opens with lengthy quotations from Heidegger's lectures and Hölderlin's poem. They engage at the outset with Heidegger's dialectic between the 'Home' (*heimisch*) and the 'Foreign' (*unheimisch*). The gurgling water of the source (embodiment of 'Home') supplies the opening footage. But after a few shots of misty romantic gorges on the upper river, the scene shifts to the mouth ('The Foreign'). From the sea, in homage to Hölderlin's reversal of its flow – but also recognizing that, exceptionally for a river, the measurement of the Danube's length begins at its mouth – the filmmakers take us on a 2,840-kilometre journey. Travelling upstream from Kilometer Zero at Sulina, the dominant vantage point is the stern of a boat, and the river is the churned-up water flowing eastward in the boat's wake at an accelerated rate. Yet the source remains their lodestar. From Sulina, the distance to the source is specified at each location. And when the film goes beyond the official source at Donaueschingen, upward to the river's 'origin' at the source of the Breg, the distance is indicated in negative figures (Furtwangen – 48 kilometres).

Three people whose work involves the river feature as interviewees: a Romanian archaeologist in charge of a dig at the ancient colony of Histria, near the delta, where the Greeks grew wheat; a Serbian engineer, who recounts NATO's destruction of Novi Sad's bridges, as well as progress with debris clearance and reinstallation of permanent structures; and a German botanist studying riverside wetlands in Bavaria. The main human characters, however, are three French philosophers and a German filmmaker. The first philosopher, Bernard Stiegler, is particularly interested in the dialogue between technology and human existence. The other two, Jean-Luc Nancy and Philippe Lacoue-Labarthe, tackle Heidegger's relationship with the Third Reich. The final armchair river guide is Hans-Jürgen Syberberg, best known for his seven-hour *Hitler: A Film from Germany* (1977).

Though these four men were filmed in their home environments, the film (despite various detours) never ceases to be a visual hymn to the river. Part two of the cine-essay, dedicated to the German Danube, ditches the more or less orderly progression upriver.[228] We are taken to Heidegger's Black Forest cabin (50 kilometres from the source), where he wrote his best-known book, *Being and Time* (1927), to Messkirch, and the lecture theatre where, as rector of Freiburg University, he gave his inaugural address (1933).[229] In the fifth and final section – prefaced by Hölderlin's enigmatic statement 'Yet what that one does, the river, Nobody knows'[230] – the film returns us to the 'historically recognized' source at Donaueschingen, zooms in on the plaque that reads 'Bis zum Meer 2840 kilometer', and winds up at Kolmenhof, origin of the Breg. This pilgrimage to the disputed sources is accompanied by a wry caption recommending a 'position of strict neutrality' to those planning to 'enjoy the hospitality of Donaueschingen and Furtwangen'.

The Danube is a large enough river to float the big themes of culture, memory, technology, war, home, politics, ecology and nature that the filmmakers raise in its company. A few picturesque scenes of the natural world in repose are included: cows grazing alongside white sand beaches near the delta; the slender infant stream running through mountain meadows. But this is no nature film. The river's historical geography and environmental history is firmly ascendant. Moreover, past and present entwine. Boys clamber up the residual stump of Trajan's bridge.[231] Other

'The Walhalla with View of the Danube Valley, Ratisbon (Regensburg), Bavaria, Germany', *c.* 1890–1900. Perched on a hill above the river near Donaustauf, this monument, whose image appears repeatedly in *The Ister* (2004), is an almost exact replica of the Parthenon. It was built in 1830–42 for King Ludwig I of Bavaria, a leading Grecophile. Walhalla houses the busts and plaques of over 200 illustrious Germans of the past two millennia. Hölderlin, however, is neither among the original cast nor one of those since added.

disabled, if much less ancient, bridges feature regularly in the river's middle section: a bridge at Dunaföldvar, Hungary, attacked by Soviet forces quelling insurrection in November 1956, and those that were casualties of Balkan conflict in the 1990s. At the Iron Gate dam and hydroelectric plant (operative since 1972), Stiegler asks whether a dam should have been built on 'Hölderlin's River' and Syberberg confronts Heidegger's dichotomy between the river as '*power* works' and '*art*-work' to re-emphasize the end of the 'poetic power' of rivers in which Hölderlin believed so passionately. 'The rivers', Syberberg runs, 'are no longer poetic.' They are just dirty.

For the first and only time, one of the filmmakers intrudes, to request clarification. What Syberberg means is that a river's personal and mystical impact is obliterated by its role as the 'machine' of 'daily life'. A river once had the god-like capacity to inspire a monumental work of art: Syberberg mentions Hölderlin and Richard Wagner (presumably in connection with *Das Rheingold*). Then he makes a larger point that chimes with his broader critique of German cultural decline; the unnatural debasement of the land

83

The Hall of Liberation (Befreiungshalle, photographed *c.* 1890–1900), which crowns a cliff at Kelheim, Bavaria, features in the Barison and Ross film *The Ister* (2004). Work on this Greco-Roman style round temple began on the day Walhalla was unveiled. Completed in 1863, it commemorates the German Confederation's liberation from Napoleonic rule (1814).

of mighty poets and thinkers. The Danube has become like the 'new' Germany in which he lives. Reunification did not restore the majesty of the old Germany (Europe's 'home' through possession of the river's source), which has become a 'good friend' to all nations but embarrassingly 'weak'.[232]

If the possession of prowess and poetic power entails the capacity to endanger human life, then Syberberg is wrong. For casualties of the most recent bouts of devastating floods (April 2006 and June 2010), the suggestion that the Danube might have become weak, friendly and unthreatening (never mind whether its essence has been as comprehensively submerged as the Iron Gate and Ada Kaleh) is surely a joke in poor taste. Whether or not it amounts to a clear and present danger, the Danube constitutes a vital presence. It would be a mistake to conclude that the documentary's most enduring fluvial feature is the ceaseless flow of intellectual babble. We do not have to choose between a natural Danube and a cultural-historical Danube (or between a Green Danube, bloodstained Danube or Blue Danube). The documentary's epilogue is a recording of Heidegger reading Hölderlin's poem. Yet the final footage – also the first image shown and one that crops up randomly – is of a mallard duck. Not that this duck is where you would expect it to be, bobbing along on the river. As Heidegger finishes the poem, over the closing credits, it waddles off under grey skies in a downstream direction along a wet riverside pavement in Regensburg. Meanwhile, the brisk current sweeps the river toward the Black Sea, and ancient Greece.

# *Spree*

elicia Mary Frances Skene first clapped eyes on the Danube in 1845. She was returning to Britain with her family from Athens, where her father, a diplomat, had been stationed. Skene was in no doubt that she had entered the presence of an awesome river – a river in whose league the Rhine, Rhône and Hölderlin's Neckar simply sank out of sight. Her steamer to Linz paused for half an hour at a Bulgarian village, where the captain encouraged passengers to stroll to the top of a low hill, where they could enjoy a magnificent view of the river. Looking down from the ruins of a Turkish castle, the future novelist and philanthropist was struck by the river's universalism:

> Here was indeed the Danube at last, which till then, seen in detail, and most unfavourably, in its swollen and irregular state, we had never comprehended as the great, the stupendous, the noble river which it is. Springing in the very heart of that Europe, of which it is the great artery . . . it came, turning its mighty stream through the green meadows which it fertilized, and rushing deep and wide, as though it had gathered all the rivers of the earth to its bosom.[1]

The Danube had lived up to its reputation – eminently worthy of Bernini's Fountain of the Four Rivers. It is also the longest river in Germany. The Spree, by contrast, is undisputedly minor: the longest river contained entirely within Germany is the Oder. Under 400 kilometres in length – less than half of which is navigable – and with a drainage basin of only 10,104 square kilometres, incorporating not many more than twenty (often tiny) tributaries, the Spree is a very modest river.

The choice of the Spree for this series of fluvial biographies partly reflects the desire to avoid re-telling familiar tales of some of the biggest and best-known rivers. But there are more positive reasons for its inclusion. The Spree has been chosen as an example of a river that is a tributary. This subsidiary status is complicated (as many disgruntled Berliners note)

Looking up the Spree from its confluence with the Havel, 2011.

The *Havel* heads up the Spree at its confluence with the Havel, 2011.

by the oddity that the Havel, to which it commits its water at nearby
Spandau, is not only narrower at this point but also carries less than half
its volume, and is supported by a catchment area two-thirds smaller (3,714
square kilometres versus 10,104).[2]

More importantly, the Spree enjoys a special relationship with a city.
Various rivers experience this close rapport – the Thames is London's river
first and foremost and the Seine belongs to Paris rather than to France.
'Wuppertal lies on the Wupper; Berlin on the Spree', reflects filmmaker
Tom Tykwer, who directed the internationally successful movie *Run Lola
Run* (1998). Tykwer, a Wuppertaler who became a Berliner, believes that
'cities without rivers are unthinkable'.[3] We more readily associate with
rivers cities that have an estuarine connection, such as Liverpool and
London and, in Germany, Hamburg. Nonetheless, it makes sense to
examine the intimate identification between a city and a river with reference to the major European capital city with the most turbulent and
poignant recent history, and which is also, currently, Europe's most talked-
about capital. For if it is known at all, the Spree is known as the river that
flows through Berlin, where, according to Karl Marx (quoting Heinrich
Heine), its dirty water 'washes souls and dilutes the tea'.[4]

In a more serious vein, Berlin poet Erdmann Wircker, in a poem of
1706 praising Frederick William I's ennoblement of the Prussian capital's
cultural life, dubbed Berlin 'Athens on the Spree' (*Spree-Athen*).[5] But this
did not imply reverence for the river. The prominent Berliner Walter
Rathenau was as unimpressed by the river as he was by the city's attempt
to align itself with Athenian splendour. The Spree offered him no natural
compensation for the absence of beautiful architecture. 'A city does not
necessarily need beautiful buildings', reflected the writer, industrialist and
future Weimar Republic foreign minister. But when it also had to make
do 'without scenic beauty, without a liberating view of the sea, without
a broad, flowing river', then that city was obliged to provide an imposing
streetscape. Unfortunately, Berlin possessed nothing to compare with
the *Strassenlandschaft* of Trafalgar Square or the Place de la Concorde.
Rathenau felt that his native city's public buildings bore no connection
to their locale, drawing the analogy between a plant in a pot and a plant
rooted in the open soil. If Berlin was relocated to the banks of the Neva or
Danube, it would make no difference. The city would seem just as *heimisch*
(homely) – or *unheimisch* (unhomely) – as it did on the Spree. He also
envied Londoners and Parisians the therapeutic and distinctive riverscapes
of the Thames Embankment and the Seine.[6]

Rathenau's jaundiced view of the decline from *Spree-Athen* to '*Parvenupolis*' has not prevailed among the majority of Berliners. The river is surprisingly broad as it flows through the city that, as Berliners since the 1870s have fondly recalled, is located *am grünen Strand der Spree*: on the green shores of the Spree.[7] In fact, the shores of Berlin occupy 12 per cent of the river's total length, not inconsiderable in itself but even more considerable in terms of the momentousness of this 12 per cent: far more than 12 per cent of the river's human history has transpired along this stretch. And because the Spree is Berlin's river, it assumed a geopolitical significance during the Cold War completely disproportionate to its scale or previous reputation. When the division of Berlin was a microcosm of Germany's division, the river served on the front line in East-West confrontation. The fluvial dimension of Berlin's topography of terror serves as a particularly acute example of the role of rivers as borders.

As Werner Bergengruen grasped in his historical novel, *Am Himmel wie auf Erden* (1940), Berlin is first and foremost a place of water. His point of departure is a legendary flood described in a chronicle of 1524 in which the Elector of Brandenburg, Joachim I, abandons his castle by the Spree and heads for the hills, convinced that Berlin will go under and be wiped out. The scenario of the first chapter, '*Wasserland*', is the watery mosaic of the Spree, a maze of branch channels interspersed with wooded marshland: a frogland, fishland and swampland. But the river is a giver as well as a taker of human life. The place that Bergengruen juxtaposes to Berlin, those who found no use for its natural condition, and the notion of the threatening river, is the Spreewald, whose Wendish inhabitants revere and contentedly co-exist with the nurturing river.[8]

If Germans associate the Spree with somewhere other than Berlin, then it is the Spreewald. A waterland of 484 square kilometres – roughly half Berlin's size – the Spreewald carefully cultivates its personality and has a deeply rooted reputation as one of Germany's most distinctive regions. This characteristic stamp derives from the river, which loses direction completely within the region and becomes all-pervasive. Despite the conspicuous absence of the sublime and monumental features of alpine peaks, gorges and steep-sided valleys, a quiet beauty unparalleled within Germany was increasingly identified. The Spreewald was a prime example of what Siegfried Passarge meant by *Landschaft* – a concept that encompassed environment, flora, fauna and *Kulturlandschaft* as well as the visual appearance.[9] Advice in 1920 to Americans planning a trip to Germany on how to transmit their experiences to friends and family afterwards specified a Sunday walk in the Spreewald as an example of a topic for a 'little talk in your reading club at home'. And in the late 1920s, the University of Berlin's courses for foreign teachers of German language, history and culture included an excursion to the Spreewald, 'where there are boats instead of trolley cars and the women wear wonderful embroidered costumes'.[10] This woody fenland forms a fitting counterpoint to the city just over an hour to the north. However, the foil is not wholesale, for various threads connect them, not least the Spree's role as a recreational resource, both within the city and in the Spreewald, a long-standing destination for Berliners.


## Source and Course

The Spree has ambiguous origins in various streams rising in the Lusatian Mountains that form the borderlands between Germany and the Czech Republic. Its origins are also rather inauspicious. As the historian and jurist Johann Benedict Carpzov remarked in his exhaustive early eighteenth-century study of Lusatia, the Spree springs lack the vigour and volume of other river sources, announcing themselves to the world in far gentler and more unassuming fashion, like the dispersed spray of a soft, silent rain; that the German word for spray is *sprüh* prompted speculation that the river's name reflects the nature of its spring.[11]

The encasement and memorialization of all three main contenders for the accolade of supreme source has ratcheted up the tripartite rivalry. What is now the best known of the trio, the Walddorfer Quelle, near Kottmar, is the highest at 480 metres. The local *Humboldt-Verein* first advanced its case in the late nineteenth century. A memorial, commemorating members of the local hiking club, the *Verband Lusatia,* who fell in the First World War, enclosed the source in 1921. The rustic, semi-circular stone wall that forms the memorial (extensively renovated in 1957) offers a stark contrast to the elaborate structure erected at the rival Ebersbach source in 1895, after General Field Marshal von Moltke established that it was the 'true' source in 1887. The 'Spreeborn-Pavilion' (at 387 metres) is decorated with the crests of sixteen towns along the river, from Ebersbach to Berlin. The third source (the lowest, and just a few kilometres south of the Walddorfer Quelle) is located in a small town whose website logo proclaims 'Spreequellstadt Neugersdorf'. In the eighteenth century, its claim went relatively unchallenged; Frederick the Great not only paid his respects to the origins of *Spree-Athen* en route to Bohemia in 1778, but donated 50 thaler to enclose *Spreeborn* (a structure that survived until 1848). The Neugersdorf spring (extensively restored in 1996) was re-encased in 1888 within a simple, square stone basin framed by a sturdy wrought iron fence on what was then the edge of Neugersdorf, but now abuts the town's *Freibad*.[12] Unlike the intense bipolar rivalry over the Danube's origins, however, a spirit of peaceful co-existence hangs over the Spree's source region. A hiking trail triangulates all three candidates, and, as the local tourist authority points out in exemplary non-partisan style, each source enjoys a particular distinction: Kottmar's is the highest, Neugersdorf's has the greatest volume of water, and Ebersbach's is the prettiest.[13]

The young Spree flows north past Bautzen. After passing Cottbus, it divides into a network of channels that form the Spreewald, whose principal settlement is Lübbenau. Re-emerging from this marshy wooded region as a single channel at Lübben, it advances toward Berlin. Before entering the city, half its flow is diverted by a combination of the Müggelsee waterworks and the canal that connects to the river Oder to the east.[14] After winding slowly for 45 kilometres through Berlin, the Spree extinguishes itself in the Havel.

## Stadt Spree and Swim Spree

The Spree is Berlin's lifeblood (*Lebensader*).[15] The future capital of Prussia and Germany sprang up as an entrepôt at the intersection between trade routes linking east and west and north and south.[16] Here, on the island formed where the river splits into a main (eastern) branch and side (western) channel, the settlement of Cölln was founded around 1230. The sister settlement of Berlin (today's Nikolaiviertel) was established on the main channel's eastern bank in 1244. The two settlements eventually joined up and Cölln was incorporated into Berlin in 1307.[17] From the Baltic, via the port of Stettin, the river Oder, and an overland leg from Oderberg, dried fish and salted herring were shipped via Berlin to Leipzig in Saxony. Rye, wool and oak harvested from Berlin's Brandenburg hinterland moved northward to Hamburg along the Spree, Havel and Elbe.[18] The growing city's reliance on the Spree matched Vienna's dependence on the Danube. In the Middle Ages, as elsewhere, the river provided power for mills as well as water and a commercial highway.[19] The construction of a link with the

Oder (1662–9) and the circumvention of the meandering city river by
the 10.6-kilometre Landwehrkanal (1845–50) enhanced Berlin's position.
Add the canalization of the Spree within the city to these improvements
and Berlin became, by the late nineteenth century, Germany's second
largest inland port (*Binnenhafen*), and the final destination for shipping
from Hamburg.[20]

Though river traffic declined somewhat after the rail link to Hamburg
opened in 1846, water remained the most cost-effective method of transportation for heavy goods with a low bulk to value ratio. Building materials
for the city's burgeoning industrial areas, such as Kreuzberg, arrived by river.
Between 1900 and 1910, approximately 3 million stone blocks arrived
annually along the Spree (and Havel) from the quarries of Brandenburg, as
well as sand, wood, cement and mortar – not to mention foodstuffs such
as flour, rice, pepper, salt, horseradish, gherkins and fruit – giving rise to
the saying 'Berlin was built from a boat' (*Berlin ist aus dem Kahn gebaut*).[21]
The river was far from pretty – in fact, its condition was scandalous – but
it was incredibly useful.[22] Many of the city's most prominent buildings
were subsequently built on its banks: Schloss Charlottenburg and Schloss
Bellevue; the Reichstag; the cathedral; the cluster of world-class galleries
and museums on Museum Island, a UNESCO World Heritage Site (since
1999) that lies between the Spree and the Kupfergraben (Spree Canal); the
city palace (Stadtschloss), residence of Prussia's kings; and the building that
replaced it, the Palast der Republik, which served as the GDR's parliament
(1976–90).

Berlin's growth imbued the river with another, unforeseen, quality-of-
life value. In the 1820s, like many other ballooning industrial cities, Berlin
offered little open space within its confines. Expansive public squares were
absent. Riverside strolls along broad quaysides were unavailable; houses
ran right down to the water's edge. Berlin lacked lungs.[23] Only the river
itself represented unused potential for outdoor recreation. Yet in the
eighteenth century, immersion in the Spree was not only discouraged;
it was forbidden. The authorities had multiple objections. They believed
that bathing and swimming were dangerous to life and limb in view of the
density of boat traffic. Even if there had been no boats plying back and
forth, the city fathers would have been opposed. Bathing and swimming
were considered dangerous. This was not because of the effluent from the
many laundries and slaughterhouses (*Wursthöfe*) clustered on the river (a
British correspondent commented that 'the slaughtermen placidly cleaned
the entrails of the defunct animals in the Spree, while seated on a floating

washing-bench'[24]). The problem for them was the risk of drowning. To cap it all, bathing and swimming were regarded as undesirable as well as dangerous. From their vantage point as guardian of public morals, the city fathers viewed these pursuits as a threat to public decency.[25] The police tried (usually in vain) to deter the growing number of persistent offenders by confiscating clothing, immediate arrest and, sometimes, the administering of a sound thrashing.[26]

Local medics vigorously supported the cause. Christoph Wilhelm Hufeland, in particular, propounded the benefits of open-air immersion in cold water. The powerful voice of the Prussian military (an almost ubiquitous presence in the city) supplemented his lobbying. The generals advocated exercise in the form of gymnastics, fencing and swimming as a vital tool of military preparedness. Berlin's military authorities identified swimming (as distinct from bathing) as a means to (covertly) improve the fitness levels of young male Berliners in preparation for an uprising against the Napoleonic occupation (the city fell in 1806). Responding to pressure from medics and the intervention of King Frederick William III (acting on his generals' advice), Berlin's city fathers reluctantly lifted the bathing ban along certain stretches of the inner city river. In his 'Schwimmhütte' (1811), near the site of the future Reichstag, military officer Friedrich Friesen trained young Berliners for the liberation struggle.[27]

The first 'swimming bathhouse' (*Badehaus*) avowedly for civilians was established some years earlier in 1803 by Hufeland's colleague Georg Adolf Welper, Berlin's City Physician (*Stadtphysikus*). The site lay between Langen Brücke and den Mühlen (on the site of the future National Gallery), a stretch of river that reputedly enjoyed the cleanest water of the entire urban Spree.[28] Built in classical Greek style and bearing the inscription 'in balneis salus' (bathing heals), *Welpersches Badeschiff* consisted of three floating sections; the first was for men, the second for women and the basement catered to the great unwashed. Regardless of social status, access was restricted to those of 'impeccable reputation'. A bathing ship moored to posts rather than a bathhouse, the *Welpersche Badeschiff* differed from a swimming pool by having no bottom, providing direct access to the river's water, if not to the river itself.[29]

By 1811, the Prussian interior ministry had arrived at a broader appreciation of the river's value, decreeing that 'swimming is the best form of exercise, and should become the most widely practised'.[30] The next stage was to provide for public swimming. Again, the military took the lead. General Ernst von Pfuel instigated organized, mass swimming instruction.

The former commander of the Prussian sector of occupied Paris (1815) and future Prussian Minister for War, Pfuel was a global pioneer in swimming instruction for soldiers. Often credited as the inventor of the breaststroke (based on his observation of frogs), at a time when doggy paddle was the default stroke, he founded a swimming facility on the river in 1817 while serving as a teacher at Berlin's nearby military academy. A square structure raised on stilts rather than a floating entity moored to the bank, the 'Pfuelschen Schwimmanstalt' was a swimming station rather than a swimming ship. And to minimize attention from potentially disapproving passers-by, it was entirely enclosed.[31]

In the evenings, Pfuel's bathing station welcomed civilians.[32] Here, at Berlin's first public swimming facility, young male Berliners – self-styled *Frösche* (frogs) – received free lessons.[33] Swimming was not restricted to the precincts of the station itself; the entire river in this vicinity was deployed. Boys who completed the return trip across the open river without floundering received a diploma. Between 1817 and 1867, 68,616 Berliners learnt to swim thanks to Pfuel.[34] He also organized regular swimming festivals that attracted large crowds. The most spectacular event was staged to mark the facility's 25th anniversary (3 August 1842), when early-morning swimmers turned out in fetching frog and fish costumes.[35] A measure of the swimming station's contribution to city life was a reference to swimming cadets in one of Heine's later poems (early 1850s) and the scale of the 50th anniversary celebrations in 1867. A fanciful engraving by H. Scherenberg depicts a series of highly decorative floats and boats, to one of which (among others) a fully clothed, top-hatted gentleman swims. Meanwhile, a Neptune-like man cruises past in a boat towed by swimmers.[36]

'Almost every German can swim', remarked an Englishman who rowed up the river Main in the early 1850s. He meant this literally. For swimming was 'by no means an unusual accomplishment for ladies'.[37] Again, Berlin was firmly located in the national and international vanguard. The rectangular Lutzesche Schwimm- und Badeanstalt was founded in 1831 at Moabiter bridge near Schloss Bellevue in the Tiergarten by Andreas Lutze, who had come to Berlin specifically to work as a swimming instructor. He and his wife, Amalie, who operated the facility, had moved from Halle, a town on the river Saale renowned for its salt springs and mines (salt miners were one of the few categories of people who washed with water at this time).[38] Fanny Hensel, the composer, whose grandfather, David Itzig, owned a mansion overlooking the Spree, was a leading devotee. 'My greatest pleasure is to swim in the Spree every day [at Lutzesche's]', she wrote to her younger brother and fellow composer, Felix Mendelssohn, during the divine summer of 1834.[39]

Hensel's passion for swimming was widely shared by fellow Berliners. Helmut Gruber remarks that the 'virtual swimming mania' among inter-war Viennese workers was a phenomenon 'virtually absent in the larger cities of other countries'.[40] Yet the widespread enthusiasm for swimming in the new German capital rivalled that of its Austrian counterpart. An elderly Berlin novelist who boasted of having been born literally on the banks of the Spree in the heart of the original settlement recalled how, as a schoolgirl in the early 1850s (before she learnt to swim at the age of eighteen), she regularly frequented Pfuel's bathing station twice a week during summer to refresh herself in the Spree's cool waves. Germany's first swimming association (*Tichyschen Frösche*) was founded at a Spree bathing station in 1840.[41] Moreover, the steam-powered ships that appeared regularly on the Spree from the late 1840s were closely linked to swimming.[42] In 1848, bathing station owner A. Maass introduced a service to bring bathers from the Inselbrücke to his establishment at Schlesisches Tor. The timetable allowed for 45 and 60 minutes at the swimming station in the morning and afternoon respectively. This marked the origins of organized recreational boating on the Spree.[43]

The Spree's first public pool (free, but men only) was established in 1855. After a left of centre majority took charge of the city council in 1862, one outcome was the first public river pool for women (1865). By 1885, though, the capacity of the Spree's eight public pools had been out-stripped; in summer, many patrons were turned away. [44] The first unisex facility was installed in the early 1890s, though changing and bathing sectors remained segregated. The swimming pontoon (*badeprahme*) at Cuvrystrasse, Kreutzberg (1896), adopted a similar arrangement. This *badeprahme*, constructed of pine and cedar, was the most elaborate to date. In 1897 it was showcased at the international exposition in Brussels as part of the hygiene display. By 1905, Berlin boasted fifteen public river baths with a total of eighteen basins – ten for men, seven for women and one that alternated.[45] And yet this was still not enough to satisfy demand on hot days.

The city's population growth and industrial expansion that raised the river's recreational value also compromised its ability to deliver the congenial conditions on which that value depended. The decline in water quality was already noted in the mid-nineteenth century. The poet

Friedrich Rückert, who held a professorial post in Berlin between 1841 and 1848, speculated that the Spree was reluctant to enter Berlin, because it arrived as pure and clean as a swan (*Schwan*) only to re-emerge as filthy as a swine (*Schwein*).[46]

As late as 1920, a swimming competition (*Wettschwimmen*) was still being held along a four-kilometre stretch of downtown river: '*Quer durch Berlin*' (in which 27 women participated).[47] But river swimming's heyday was over. A magistrate's order shut down most bathing stations on 20 May 1925.[48] The Spree's horribly polluted condition, which reflected Berlin's status as continental Europe's greatest manufacturing centre, drove mass closure. Mark Twain, who spent a few months in Berlin during the spring of 1892, characterized it as 'the German Chicago'. Between 1800 and 1871 (when it became the capital of a united Germany), Berlin's population swelled from 170,000 to 826,000. Subsequent growth produced a city of 1.5 million inhabitants by the early 1890s that was unrecognizable from the place Twain knew from what he had read:

> The site it stands on has traditions and a history, but the city itself has no traditions and no history. It is a new city; the newest I have ever seen. Chicago would seem venerable beside it . . . The main mass of the city looks as if it had been built last week.[49]

Twain was struck most by the new Berlin's spaciousness and awesomely straight and wide streets (he never mentioned the river that winds through the centre). Taking his cue from Twain, Rathenau bemoaned the replacement of the so-called 'Athens on the Spree' (*Spreeathen*) by 'Chicago on the Spree' (*Spreechicago*).[50] Nor was the Spree any cleaner than Chicago's own eponymous river. As Élisée Reclus noted, where it entered the city, the Spree was a 'respectable river'. During its journey through the city, however, it was slowly but surely transformed into an open sewer. The compiler of the 1908 edition of the Baedeker guide to Berlin also registered this transformation. He recommended a steamboat ride to appreciate just how much the Spree's banks had become dominated by a procession of tile-, cable- and dye-manufacturing plants. In addition to industrial poisons, domestic wastewater also flowed freely toward the river's 'so-called' 'green shores'.[51] So many chemical gases rose off the river that it was flammable – like Cleveland, Ohio's notorious Cuyahoga.[52] Young Berliners allegedly set fire to the surface to watch the flames dance on the water. As the population climbed to over 3.5 million and water quality plunged, the bathing stations themselves were also showing their age. Echoing city public health officials, the renowned Berlin cartoonist Heinrich Zille pointed out that the few that remained open after 1925 were cramped and decaying boxes, depriving patrons of light, air, sun and space.[53] Regardless of their state of repair, these structures quickly vanished from the riverscape. The Pfuel-strasse in Kreuzberg is the only trace on the urban landscape of the pioneer-ing facility that survived until the 1930s.

The river remained a *Lebensader* during the interwar period. Yet its very usefulness seemed to preclude the development of a dignified relation-ship with the river and its banks commensurate with its central position in the city's economic life. As the paucity of grand riverside buildings suggested to an advocate of a more beautiful Berlin in the 1930s, the Spree had failed to become the city's grand lady; instead, she remained an impoverished maiden (and nearly become a Cinderella).[54]

## Shooting Spree

Swimming in the Spree in central Berlin did not disappear completely after the bathing stations threw in the towel. During the Cold War, howe-ver, swimmers were a distinct breed: East Germans who literally swam for their lives. Upriver from the Reichstag, for a kilometre, the northwesterly flowing river divided the two Berlins. In this district, known as the *Spreebogen* (Spree Arc), new government buildings have sprung up since reunited Germany's capital reverted to Berlin, notably the *Kanzleramt* (Chancellery) and *Bundestag* (Parliament). The choice of location for the *Regierungsviertel* (Government Quarter) was no coinci-dence. Architect Axel Schultes wanted to supplant this marker of the city's division between 1961 and 1989 with a symbol of reunification: two covered bridges span the river.[55]

The Berlin Wall also paralleled the Spree along a second stretch. This section ran from the Schillingbrücke near the Ostbahnhof to the Ober-baumbrücke in the city's southeastern area. The wall's course then ran due south across the Oberbaumbrücke that connects Friedrichshain with Kreuzberg. After West Berlin and the German Democratic Republic signed the first of four permit agreements in December 1963, the Oberbaumbrücke was one of the city's eight internal checkpoints for travel from west to east.

During the wall's 28-year existence, GDR citizens tried various exit strategies. Some dug tunnels; some crawled through sewer pipes; one

Ice floes at the Spree Bend, Regierungsviertel, January 2009.

Looking east toward Museum Island, with the neo-Baroque Bode Museum (1904) in the foreground and the Fernsehturm (1969) at Alexanderplatz in the distance, January 2009.

person tried to float across in a homemade gas balloon. One group tackled the river itself. A resourceful crew hijacked an excursion steamer after getting their captain and chief engineer drunk and trussing them up, making it across under a hail of bullets from GDR patrol boats.[56] A handful adopted a more elementary strategy of crossing the river. Just as their counterparts in other Soviet Bloc countries regarded the Danube between Yugoslavia and Austria as the Iron Curtain's weakest link, some East Germans saw swimming the Spree (and other watercourses such as the Teltow Canal) as their best option. An early scene in Gerd Conradt's documentary film, *Die Spree: Sinfonie eines Flusses* (2007), consists of archival footage of a swimmer's successful escape (the majority of successful crossings occurred during the first few months when the new arrangements were still porous).

Where precisely does the boundary fall within a river that forms a political border? In the case of the Savannah, which has divided South Carolina and Georgia since the 1780s, this delicate matter remained unresolved until the Supreme Court ruled in 1922 that the divide ran straight down the middle.[57] By contrast, a wholly partisan boundary separated the two Berlins. The GDR owned the entire river; the frontier was the left-hand, western bank. With reference to Andreas Senk, a six-year-old West Berliner who tumbled into the river by accident in September 1966, Hans-Hermann Hertle reflected: 'The banks belonged to West Berlin but the water belonged to East Berlin, so he, in practical terms, fell across the border.'[58] Floodlights from the eastern side illuminated the surface after dark, with border guards and patrol boats alert to the smallest splash or ripple.[59]

One of the lucky ones was Ingrid Pitt (born Ingoushka Petrov in Warsaw), a concentration camp survivor who eventually achieved global fame as an actress in Hammer horror films such as *Countess Dracula* (1971). In her autobiography of 1999, Pitt recounted her astonishing escape shortly after the wall was raised. On the night of her debut at Bertolt Brecht's Berliner Ensemble, the Volkspolizei came looking for her (she was too outspoken in her criticism of the regime) and she fled the theatre. Still wearing the costume of Kattrin, the mute in *Mother Courage*, she plunged into riverside bushes to evade capture. Inadvertently, she rolled into the icy winter waters. Initially, the wide, thick skirts of her costume functioned as a life jacket, keeping her afloat. Once soaked, though, it became a liability that she struggled to shake off. Drifting into the main current, she eluded her pursuers' torchlights and eventually attained the West Berlin bank, where a group of American GIs fished her out (one of them became her first husband).[60]

Others in East Germany entered the river with greater intent and more careful planning than Pitt. Diving clubs in East Berlin experienced a surge in membership after the border shut on 13 August 1961. From April 1962 onwards, GDR police interrogated all diving club members.[61] To further deter potential escapees, the regime outlawed the sale of diving suits and sub-aqua equipment in East Berlin (undeterred, some would-be escapees made their own), punctuated the river-bed with metal spikes and strung up barbed wire underwater.

The precise number who died in their quest for freedom remains a matter for debate. Some place the figure at over 200, but the most reliable tally is probably that compiled by the Centre for Contemporary Historical Research at Potsdam (*Zentrum für Zeithistorische Forschung Potsdam*): (at least) 136, the majority shot by border guards.[62] At the eastern end of the Spree Bend is a monument (*Gedenkstätte*) to those who died in flight. Enshrining the practice of West Berliners, who erected a makeshift white cross to mark the spot where an escapee was shot, eight white crosses are set in the railings (an additional one is hollow). Six of the solid crosses bear the name of a particular individual and their date of death, and the seventh is dedicated to the unknown victims.

The first of the young men (the vast majority of victims were male) to whom a cross has been dedicated is Günther Litfin, the wall's first victim, shot while swimming across the Humboldt Harbour adjacent to the Spree (24 January 1961). The second victim memorialized is Udo Düllick, a 25-year-old engineer, drowned under fire after jumping in near the Oberbaumbrücke, where the river is 150 metres wide (5 October 1961). A powerful swimmer, he kept ducking under the water to elude the hail of bullets and nearly made it to safety in Kreuzberg. It was initially believed that he sank after being hit, but the biopsy found no bullet wounds; he probably died of exhaustion.[63] The third named individual is Hans Räwel, a trainee pastry chef aged 22. Another good swimmer who entered the river near the Oberbaumbrücke, he, too, almost made it. He sank early on the icy morning of New Year's Day, 1963, after being gunned down at short range from a patrol boat, within 35 metres of the western bank; the official cause of death his mother received was death by drowning.[64] The fourth remembered person is Klaus Schröter, an electrical engineer aged 24. In the early hours of 4 November 1963, he cycled down to the Marshall Bridge, where he cut the barbed wire to access steps down to the water. He

Memorial to Klaus Schröter, shot in the head while swimming across the river on
4 November 1963, Spree Bend.

pulled on a diving suit and jumped in, heading for the Kronprinzenbrücke.
But guards in a nearby watchtower had already spotted him and killed him
with a shot to the head before he could make any appreciable progress.[65]

Other victims of the river swim included Werner Probst, a 25-year-old
truck driver and Stasi informer who made it over on 14 October 1961 but
suffered fatal gunshot injuries while climbing up ladder steps onto the
western bank; he collapsed onto the quay, was retrieved by GDR river police
and pronounced dead on arrival at the eastern bank.[66] Another 'border
violator' (in official GDR terminology) was Ingo Krüger, a 21-year-old cook
who wanted to reunite with his family. A seasoned sport diver, he took
a taxi to Schiffbauerdamm, wearing a diving suit under his coat. Shortly
before midnight on 10 December 1961, he entered the water under Fried -
richstrasse railway station and headed upriver, intended to climb out at
the Reichstagufer, just inside West Berlin. He soon drowned, perhaps due
to equipment failure, but most likely from hypothermia; GDR customs
officials fished his body out of the river near the Marshall Bridge.[67] One
of the final victims of the attempted water crossing was eighteen-year-old

Bernd Lehmann, who left his clothes and documents on the bank in Treptow and swam for Kreuzberg via Osthafen (28 May 1968). Five days later, his body was discovered near the Osthafen, tangled in the underwater barbed wire.

The divided and dividing river also claimed five accidental child victims between 1966 and 1975. Andreas Senk, mentioned above, drowned near the Oberbaumbrücke on 13 September 1966. Inadvertently pushed into the river by a playmate at the Gröbenufer in Kreuzberg, the unsuspecting six-year-old was on GDR territory as soon as he hit the water. But the mishap was either unnoticed or not taken seriously by the watchtower guard 200 metres away on the bridge. Nor did the patrol boat react. A few hours later, members of the West Berlin fire department pulled out Senk's body.[68] The same fate befell a further four children at the Kreuzberger Gröbenufer between 1972 and 1975. Eight-year-old Cengaver Katranci drowned here on 30 October 1972. He had gone to feed the swans with a friend, but lost his balance and tumbled into the chilly water. A fisherman whose instinct was to jump in checked himself with the sobering awareness that he risked being shot at if he entered the water. When the West Berlin fire brigade's divers showed up, GDR border guards barred them from intervening. More than an hour after the accident, GDR divers recovered Katranci's body, which they took across to East Berlin.[69]

Giuseppe Savoca, a six-year-old Italian citizen, drowned on 15 June 1974, also while playing at the Gröbenufer. A toy tumbled into the water and, as he tried to coax it out with a stick, stretched ever further out over the water's edge and eventually toppled in. Just 60 metres away on the Oberbaumbrücke, a guard was watching everything through binoculars. Again, GDR officials took no action beyond fishing out his body over an hour later, despite efforts by a passer-by on the West Berlin side to alert them. This became a familiar incident, followed by a regular pattern of events. Cetin Mert, who died on his fifth birthday (11 May 1975), also tumbled in trying to recover a ball at the Gröbenufer.[70] As previously, West Berlin police and fire brigade divers show up promptly, but GDR border guards, despite monitoring everything, did nothing.[71] Since Mert was the fourth child in three years to die here, the West Berlin authorities raised a mesh wire fence to block access to the embankment and erected large warning signs in German and Turkish (protective measures that, according to the GDR, should have been enacted long ago).[72] Since June 1973, the two Germanys had been in negotiation over rescue measures in the event of accidental infringements of the border. For the GDR, however, agreement was conditional on the formal Allied recognition of Berlin's internal sector boundaries as national state boundaries, which threatened the city's 'Four-Power' status. Negotiations stalled on these grounds for over two years. The West Berlin city senate and GDR regime finally reached an agreement on 29 October 1975, according to which those who fell in from the West German side could also be rescued from that side.[73]

## Spreewald: Rural River

A far cry from these harrowing events, yet barely 100 kilometres southeast of Berlin, lies the Spreewald. In this other fluvial world, the river dissipates into a maze of more than 200 smaller branches (*fliesse*), whose total length (1,300 kilometres) is almost five times that of the entire river.[74] About 13,000 years ago, at the end of the most recent ice age, the Spreewald emerged as a thickly wooded wetland, its *fliesse* overhung with an *urwald* canopy of weeping willow, poplar, birch and black alder (so many black alder populated its banks, according to the late fifth-/early sixth-century Roman scholar Anicius Manlius Severinus Boethius, that water and fish both assumed a black hue[75]). The Sorbs (also known as Wends), a Slavic tribe hailing from a region north of the Carpathians, first settled the area between the sixth and eighth centuries.[76] However, the high water table and constant threat of inundation that defined this bayou environment inhibited cultivation. Incrementally, the *fliesse* of the river that the Sorbs named *Sprjewja* were reclaimed. Farming, hitherto restricted to oats, rye, barley, millet and buckwheat cultivation on higher, sandier ground that pine trees previously covered, moved down to occupy the moister, humus-rich moorland soils formed by the accretion of silt deposited by regular flooding. Drainage of bottomlands permitted more extensive cultivation of lucrative crops – previously confined to raised beds in kitchen gardens – such as gherkins, horseradish, potatoes and onions.[77]

For centuries, the Spreewald was more or less impregnable, and boats were the main form of transit within the roadless region's mosaic of meadows, woodland and water. For much of the year, the Sorbs' traditional flat-bottomed punt (*Kahn*) – a craft usually carved out of a single oak – transported everything: schoolchildren, wedding guests, churchgoers, funeral-attendees, coffins, gherkin cucumbers, pumpkins, manure, live-stock and the mail.[78] Heavy commodities such as logs were towed through the water. In winter, hauliers on skates pulled sleds laden with lumber, hay

H. Lüders, 'The Arrival of a Funeral Punt Bearing a Coffin in Lübbenau', the main town in the Spreewald, 1869.

and firewood.[79] Isolated and insulated by their watery environment, the Sorbs retained their language, dress and customs as late as the 1920s. One of these rituals was to take the blessing of the water at sunrise on Good Friday. Those who washed in *Osterwasser* (Easter water) extracted from a *fliesse*, preferably at the point of extraction – and without uttering a word – were guaranteed beauty for life. To make doubly sure, some beauty-seekers dunked themselves completely. The less scrupulous carried the water home in a bottle.[80]

The work of the renowned Sorbian poet Mato Kosyk, who produced his first major body of work before emigrating to the United States in the early 1880s, is deeply immersed in the liquid landscape (*Blota*) of his youth. 'A Spreewald Boy' ('*Ein Spreewaldjunge*'), published in his first collection (1882), demonstrated Kosyk's intimate knowledge of the environment of his idyllic boyhood near the village of Werben, which he spent hopping over sidearms and punting down *fliesse*. In 'Childhood's Pure Bliss' (1878), he recalled the happiness he found in the marshes (ironically, his thirty years as a Lutheran pastor in America were spent in the semi-arid lands of Nebraska and Oklahoma, places that remained forever foreign to him).[81]

Kosyk's beloved *Blota* had not changed much by the time he retired to his farm in Oklahoma in 1913. The village of Lehde, at the heart of the

Spreewald, was still only accessible by boat (or sled in winter) when the compiler of Baedeker's guide visited in the early 1900s.[82] But the region was on the cusp of profound transformation. A two-kilometre raised path was forged between Lübbenau and Lehde in 1929.[83] The first roads penetrated in the 1930s. (Highway construction, alongside the 1937 ban on the Sorbian language and other cultural suppression measures, was part of the Nazi effort to forcibly Germanize this tightly-knit ethnic minority, whose numbers stood around 150,000 at the end of the First World War. For the Sorbs in Bergengruen's *Am Himmel wie auf Erden*, the prospect of catastrophic flooding from the Spree that confronts Berlin embodies revenge against the oppressive, displacing Germans.)[84] At the same time, some patches of land survived in an unimproved condition; in 1938, the Nazi regime set up the area's first formal nature reserve (230 hectares). In 1991, UNESCO established a biosphere reserve at its core. Just over 48,000 hectares in extent, the reserve incorporates 1,300 kilometres of waterways and 50,000 residents, who are mostly descended from the original Sorb colonists.[85]

The Spree cannot compete with the Po in the department of gastronomic attraction. Since 1999, however, it can boast one foodstuff that has been dignified with the European Union's badge of Protected Geographical Indication (PGI; *Geschützte Geographische Angabe*): the Spreewald gherkin (*Spreewälder Gurke*).[86] Fluvial-infused terroir is a vital ingredient on the banks of the Po and Spree alike, conducive to flavour as well as growth. The gherkin cucumber (*Cucumis sativus*), the variety suitable for pickling, probably arrived with the final waves of Sorb immigration in the eighth century.[87] But the *Spreewälder Gurke* achieved wider renown as the Spreewald's signature food thanks to Flemish weavers. Imported by the ruler of Saxony in 1580 to set up a cloth industry, they noted the local soil's suitability for intensive and extensive raising of gherkin cucumbers and shifted to this more profitable pursuit.[88] Growing conditions were – and remain – ideal for the humidity-loving, water-rich vegetable (fluid content: 97 per cent). High wintertime water enriches the soil with alluvium (controlled flooding to a depth of a quarter of a metre facilitates even distribution of silt), proximity to water makes for easy summertime irrigation, and the damp air is conducive to growth.[89]

Lübbenau emerged as the Spreewald's urban hub by becoming Berlin's 'cucumber barrel' (*Gurkenkammer*) in the early 1700s.[90] In the nineteenth century (first by punt up the Spree; then, from 1866, by rail), local producers supplied Berlin's soaring population with a vital winter vegetable that kept well after several weeks of fermentation in wooden barrels. (The popular expression *Sauregurkenzeit* denoted a period of quiet or inactivity, during which everyone was busy preserving gherkins for winter consumption.[91]) Gherkin connoisseurs across the world revere the hand-pickled *Spreewälder Gurke*. In the vanguard of the recent rediscovery of German traditional regional foods, the Spreewald's leitmotif gained a high international profile when it featured in the film *Goodbye, Lenin!* (2003) as a symbol of the good old days of the GDR.

After 1989, with the collapse of agriculture in the former East Germany, this crunchy, savoury delicacy was ever harder to obtain. In Wolfgang Becker's quirky film, Christiane, the mother of the main protagonist, Alex, finally awakens from the eight-month coma she fell into after suffering a heart attack shortly before the Wall's fall (November 1989). A staunch Communist, she returns home to convalesce at a time when Westernization and the onslaught of free market economics are in full swing. Alex is determined to protect his bed-confined mother from further, potentially life-threatening shock by deluding her into thinking that everything is exactly as it was before her illness: in short, that the rapidly evaporating worker's paradise is still alive and kicking. So, when she requests a Spreewald pickle, he hurries off to a grocery store in search of the genuine article. The bemused shopkeeper expresses astonishment at his detachment from reality; the shelves are brimming with pickled gherkins, but they are all from Holland. (The best Alex can do is decant Dutch gherkins into an old jar that once contained the real thing.) Before securing PGI status, gherkins from other parts of Germany, as well as from Holland, Poland and Hungary, were being passed off as *Spreewälder Gurken*.

Under EU protection, local production is rising and the gherkin remains a crisp and firm regional badge: in Conradt's filmic homage, *Die Spree*, Manfred Werban, the first warden of the Spreewald Biosphere Reserve (1991–2000), is pictured crunching on a freshly pickled specimen. A big draw in rustic Lehde is the *Gurkenmuseum*, located in a former production plant. The visitor's first duty is to sample some of the 150 different methods of preparing freshly pickled gherkins devised over the centuries. Other highlights of the world's only gherkin museum are the enormous (3.5 ton capacity), century-old oak and beech fermentation barrels and the photographs of a succession of women crowned as Gherkin Queen (*Gurkenkönigin*). The coveted crown is awarded annually during the third weekend in July to the local woman who prepares the tastiest gherkins.

The edible delights of the Spree were not the only attributes of the area that Berliners consumed. By the late 1700s, they were discovering the attractions of riverside communities on the swelling city's fringes. Stralau (opposite Treptow) was a favourite destination for day trippers, who arrived in punts and gondolas (steamers from the 1830s onwards) and feasted on eel and cucumber salad at the restaurants that sprang up.[92] But as the city encroached on its immediate rural hinterland, excursionists looked further afield. The railway that made it easier to satisfy the Berliner's appetite for gherkins also brought the Spreewald closer to the urban excursionist. The region's most influential early tourist was undoubtedly the novelist and poet Theodor Fontane. In 1898, he recalled how, as a young Berliner, he had spent many happy hours on summer evenings gazing out at lights dancing on the surface of the misty twilight river from the window of his uncle's sitting room on the Burgstrasse, near the Mühlendamm.[93] In middle age, when countryside rambles (as far afield as Scotland) were among his favourite pursuits, Fontane's interest in his local river extended to its rural reaches.

For three days in early August 1859, Fontane and three Berlin-based friends punted around the Spreewald.[94] His account became a well-known visitor guide. Fontane saw the Spreewald as a perfect rural counterpart to Venice, complete with gondoliers. He hailed Lehde, a jigsaw of 28 islands, as the 'Venice of the Spreewald', describing it as the lagoon city in miniature, a throwback to what La Serenissima was like 1,500 years ago, when the first settlers arrived seeking refuge in the marshlands. The culinary delicacies of what he hailed as a veritable Eldorado for epicures also loomed large in the renowned gormand's account. He praised the local horseradish and celery, but the gherkin took pride of place in Lübbenau (the '*Vaterland der sauren Gurken*') and noted that one merchant had sold 800 'schock' a week the previous year, which, though nothing special by the standards of Liverpool or Hamburg, was an impressive trading figure for a small town. He also reflected that the gherkin was a key attribute of Berlin and the Spree Goddess.[95] Following closely in Fontane's wake, the marketing efforts of guidebooks and, more recently, the local tourist authority, have capitalized on this imaginative connection with the watery woodlands of the 'Green Venice'.[96]

With the full onslaught of industrialization in Berlin, and the river's attendant metamorphosis from swan to swine, Berliners increasingly frequented the rural river to the south of the city, where it was still friendly and light (rather than alienating and dark). Further afield, they also sought out the Spreewald's 'charming rural scenery'. And though the river between Berlin and Köpenick was also heavily used for rambling and recreational boating (*Wanderruderei*) by the 1920s, when the *Wandervogel* movement was at its height, the Spreewald's status as a destination for Berliners was also firmly entrenched.[97] One of the two places of 'special interest' recommended for study by those who sought to re-establish German and Germany as legitimate subjects for instruction in American high schools after the First World War was the Spreewald ('the great swamp near the Oder', not least because of the presence of the curious 'lost tribe', the Sorbs, 'slaves still to some ancient superstitions').[98] The region retained its appeal during the communist era, when GDR factory workers descended en masse for vacations sponsored by government trade unions (Dresden lies the same distance to the south as Berlin to the north). During the 1980s, the area routinely received a million annual holidaymakers from a total population of 17 million.[99] Since reunification, visitors flock in ever greater numbers, as 'Wessies' re-connect with a region effectively erased from their consciousness.[100]

The gherkin's future as a distinctive regional product is secure. The Spreewald's flora and fauna have also been afforded a measure of protection. The biosphere reserve was established to shelter rare fauna such as sea eagles, otters, beaver, dragonflies, black stork and butterflies, and flora such as orchids, marsh gentian, Siberian iris and waterlilies. Their well-being improves with the retreat of pesticides and chemical fertilizers; two-thirds of farmland within the biosphere is now free from chemical taint.

When the historian Gordon Craig visited in 1994 to retrace Fontane's footsteps, he felt that little had changed since 1859 and that the novelist 'would have no trouble recognizing' its features.[101] Natural systems are never static, though, and some aspects of the Spreewald's ecosystems remain under threat. Many smallholdings, too small to be worked with tractor and plough, continue to be cultivated with a spade and remain accessible only by boat. Yet some farmed areas are returning to forest: along the path from Lübbenau to Lehde, and beyond to Leipe, trees have replaced fields of cucumber and horseradish. Yet this re-wilding process is not necessarily in the interests of certain bird species, such as becassine and hoopoe, which are creatures of the open field. Some environmentalists want to halt mowing, but in an unmowed meadow, white storks cannot find frogs.[102] The abandonment of traditional cultivation practices can harm biodiversity.

The region's most precious resource and defining feature – water – also faces an uncertain future. During the communist era, the lower Lausitz was a major site for the opencast mining of lignite, a low-grade (brown) coal that literally consumed the terrain and displaced villages. The legacy is a 'lunar landscape' of deep canyons, spoil heaps and crevasses (*Grossräschen*).The implications for the Spree's hydrological regime are enormous.[103] Not only has the river frequently been re-routed. To access coal strata up to 60 metres underground, the depth miners reached in the 1970s, they pumped out groundwater and diverted it into the nearby Spree. Water required to dig out the coal was then also discharged into the Spree, raising the level considerably. In the heyday of pumping, water flowed at an average of 30–36 cubic metres per second, that is, at middle highwater level, so riverside fields were frequently flooded. To speed the passage of excess water, *fliesse* were re-engineered.

Now that most mining operations have shut down, and groundwater is simply accumulating in the mines, flow has fallen to seven cubic metres per second, which constitutes low water. This water deficit is aggravated by the demand placed on Spree water to dilute the heavy acidity of the ground-water refilling the gouged-out holes. The reduction in the river's flow since the 1970s has altered conditions of biological life. Paradoxically, lignite mining benefited the river. Low water effectively brings flow to a standstill, not just to the detriment of fish and aquatic plants, but also the riparian forest zone and associated fauna. Aquatic life in today's Spree is more characteristic of a pond than a river. The rate of flow through Berlin is also slow. In the early twentieth century, travelling at a rate of seventeen kilometres a day, water took three days to clear the city. Nowadays, depending on the season, the journey from the Müggelsee to Spandau varies from the laborious to the excruciatingly slow: between eight days and a couple of weeks; some days, the flow is a scarcely discernible eighteen metres per hour.[104] Autumn leaves scarcely move downstream, even near the confluence with the Havel – though the tame conditions are easier for tourist boats to navigate. Sometimes parts of the river even flow backwards.

## Spree Bridge and Spree Symphony

Berlin's Spree also flows through interesting times. Twenty years after the Wall's fall, river access remains hotly contested in two parts of town (Friedrichshain and Kreuzberg) immediately adjacent to the freshly reconstituted city centre (*Mitte*). One of the two stretches of river that once separated East and West, which adds up to 3.7 kilometres of waterfront, has become a prime target for real estate developers and urban rejuvenation. In the 1990s, the first area to attract the attention of a group of investors and developers known as Mediaspree was the strip of no-man's land on the north bank in Friedrichshain sandwiched between the river and a railway line.[105] This zone was readily accessible due to the Ostbahnhof's proximity. And property prices on terrain previously occupied by the wall or defunct factories, warehouses and other industrial buildings were low relative to those in former West Berlin. Prominent among the renovations and conversions pioneered by media and telecommunications companies on the former GDR bank (many of the structures are listed) are MTV's Central European headquarters (2004) in a refurbished warehouse, and Universal Music's German headquarters (2002) in the *Eierkühlhaus* adjacent to the Oberbaumbrücke (a refrigerated warehouse for eggs, built in the Bauhaus style in the late 1920s).

The focus of entities such as the Anschutz Entertainment Group has now shifted across to the Kreuzberg bank.[106] A gritty nineteenth-century industrial area, Kreuzberg found itself on the eastern fringes of the American sector during the Cold War. Between the 1950s and 1980s, an influx of students, immigrants, artists, squatters and counter-culturalists, enticed by the area's low rents, transformed it into the city's epicentre of 'alternative' lifestyles. After *Die Wende*, Kreuzberg was suddenly reinserted into central Berlin and earmarked for an array of mixed office, retail and residential complexes. Many local residents are unimpressed, fearing the erasure of their neighbourhood's unorthodox character by the intrusion of high rents, high-rises and big corporations that view the waterfront as *tabula rasa*. On the other side of the river, paralleling the East Side Gallery, is the Spreepark, which in summer becomes an urban beach complete with imported sand and deckchairs. But protest groups such as *Mediaspree versenken* (Sink Mediaspree) and 'Flood Media Spree!' fear further erosion of public access to the riverfront. Rallying (since 2008) around the slogan '*Spreeufer für alle!*' (Spree Riverfront for Everyone!), opponents seek a buffer zone to prevent encroachment of commercial premises and private apartments within 50 metres of the riverbank – a fluvial littoral they want reserved for footpaths, bicycle lanes, 'green zones' and other 'community space'.[107]

The alternative vision to Mediaspree is Spree 2011, a project launched in 2007 by Ralf Steeg, a landscape engineer and environmental planner.[108]

A visit to Bern in the 1980s inspired Steeg's ambition to return the river
to ecological health by 2011. For some river restorers, the litmus test of
cleanliness is fishability; for others, like Steeg, it is swimmability. And the
Swiss capital is the undisputed European mecca of urban river swimming.
The Aare, which flows through the centre of town, is very different
from the Spree: fast-flowing and deep blue-green in hue (being partially
glacier-fed).[109] Back in Berlin, Steeg gazed out over the Spree from the
Gröbenufer – scene of tragic Cold War accidents – and pondered what
was needed to bring home the Bernese experience.[110]

The Spree is much cleaner now than it was during the division of
Germany, thanks to the demise of heavy industry, here, as on rivers like the
Mersey. Yet household waste persists as a serious source of contamination.
Much of Berlin is still served by nineteenth-century 'combination' drains
that carry both storm water and domestic waste to purification plants.
During heavy rains, the capacity of sewage works is exceeded. When this
happens, excess water, contaminated with nitrogen and phosphorus – not
to mention cadmium and lead from automobile exhaust and zinc from
lampposts, benches and gutters – flows straight into the river. Cocaine
residue is another lurid ingredient in the cocktail of contaminants.[111]

Steeg wants to install overflow tanks moored on large pontoons along a
four-kilometre stretch of river to intercept wastewater. Construction on the
pilot project at Osthafen (a 1,000-square metre pontoon with a 1-million
litre storage capacity) began in the spring of 2009.[112] Steeg wants Berliners,
like their Bernese counterparts, 'to jump into a river to cool off'.[113] Within
the context of Berlin's venerable river bathing culture, Spree 2011 is a
restoration strategy rather than a radical new departure, though Steeg
envisages a river cleaner than it was during river bathing's late nineteenth-
and early twentieth-century heyday. Berliners not only want to go to the
river; they would also like to get *into* the river.

The post-reunification development along the Spree most acceptable
to locals resides on the south bank between Treptow and Kreuzberg, in
the former East Berlin. The most imaginative feature of Arena Berlin, an
event venue that occupies an enormous omnibus depot built during the
First World War, is *Badeschiff Spreebrücke* (Bathing Ship Spree Bridge).
Designed by Berlin artist Susanne Lorenz, *Badeschiff* is a converted cargo
barge built in the 1960s that transported sand and gravel around the city
for thirty years.[114] In 1995, the decommissioned barge was moored at the
derelict bus station's waterfront, close to where the wall turned south and
crossed the river. The flat-bottomed container vessel had the perfect

dimensions for an open-air swimming pool: 2 metres deep and 25 metres long. Lined and filled with 400,000 litres, the rim sits 70 centimetres above the river's surface. Originally intended to change location every year, the *Badeschiff* found a permanent anchorage here in 2005, just a stone's throw from Lohmühlen Island.[115] Lorenz also initially anticipated that the *Badeschiff* would be a summer phenomenon. Yet since autumn 2005, it has been open year-round.[116]

Despite the striking visual contrast between the Spree's dull, steel-coloured water and the pool's sparkling azure blue, the purpose of *Badeschiff Spreebrücke* is to amplify local fluvial awareness. Tykwer has compared Berlin's relationship with the Spree to New York City's rapport with the Hudson: for both cities, bridges are the focal point rather than the river they cross.[117] The *Badeschiff* seeks to re-engineer this association. A sign at the entrance informs that the pool forms a 'living bridge' to the river. Another sign (echoes of the late 1700s) warns that jumping into the river itself is prohibited (and not recommended). But you can make direct physical contact with it simply by reaching over the pool's rim and dipping a hand into the water. Many visitors assume that the *Badeschiff* is yet another example of the avant-garde in Europe's coolest capital. In fact, it is simultaneously innovative and revivalist. Spree 2011 regards the

*Winter Badeschiff*, Berlin, 2009.

*Badeschiff* as a way to highlight a once clean river's lost innocence. And it marks a conscious resurrection of the city's bathing culture (the entrance sign also points out that, in 1900, fifteen private bathing ships dotted the riverbanks).

There has been no attempt, though, to mimic the design of the original *Welpersche Badeschiff* (1802).[118] The style is minimalist and the faithful recreation of the original design, with its bottomless bottom immersing bathers directly in the river, was not an option. Though the Spree itself is not yet clean enough to swim in, it is now at least possible to swim *on* the river, which, as Falk Walter, *Badeschiff*'s director, explains, provides a foretaste of what it will be like to swim *in* a clean future river. However visionary, the *Badeschiff* is intended to become obsolete.[119]

Walter (an interviewee in Conradt's film) learned to swim in the river at Cottbus during the GDR era (blithely disregarding its polluted condition). Like Conradt, he feels that after a long period of indifference and neglect the city is slowly returning to the river. Conradt's film is an expression of Tykwer's belief that 'film and river are friends, flowing in time and space'.[120] His subtitle – *Sinfonie eines Flusses* – is a nod to Walter Ruttmann's avant garde modernist documentary about the river's city: *Berlin: die Sinfonie der Grossstadt* (1927). Yet this was more than just a gesture on Conradt's part. The city itself in all its glorious, reified (and brutalist) modernity was the main protagonist of Ruttmann's seminal silent film about a day in the life of Berlin – which is by no means the same thing as a film about a day in the life of a Berliner.[121] The opening shots are sombre panoramas of a train arriving in the slumbering city at dawn and the film ends with a night-time firework display. The time and space between dawn and dark is populated with restless, Futurist-influenced shots of highly aestheticized machinery in motion, frenetic traffic, and bustling factories, which possess a quality of autonomy and purposefulness that the Berliners depicted lack (one of the most vital images is the strangely animalistic shot of the front end of the train to Potsdam). Ruttmann's style dehumanizes Berliners, rendering them ant like and anonymous (tantamount to the department store mannequins that feature in acts one and two). There are no scenes of quiet domesticity or interior intimacy; we see only the exterior of dwellings. And in one memorable sequence, the legs of workers are conflated with those of cattle herded into a courtyard. Non-human nature is confined to a fleeting shot of the river, a few trees, the occasional dog and cat and a group of riders in a park. What Berlin was for Ruttmann – the main protagonist in constant flow – the river is for Conradt. However, his perspective on the river is less frenetic than Ruttmann's city and his view of people is far more humane than Ruttmann's.

*Sinfonie eines Flusses* is most fully appreciated with reference to Berlin's pivotal role in the tension between town and country that has loomed large in German cultural politics since the late nineteenth century. For advocates of rural life and values, especially the *völkisch* element, Berlin was the ultimate 'soulless' city that had severed contact with the soil, a process that culminated during the Weimar Republic, when *Spreechicago* became some-thing even worse: *Spreebabylon*.[122] For Wilhelm Stapel, editor of *Deutsches Volkstum*, late 1920s Berlin was an un-German place. Juxtaposing the denatured city and the German land, he proclaimed that the 'spirit (*Geist*) of the German Folk revolts against the spirit of Berlin. Today's battle cry rings out: "The Resistance of the Landscape against Berlin"'.[123]

Others simply ignored the city's natural features. Walter Benjamin, the prominent interwar literary critic and cultural commentator, demonstrated virtually no awareness of the river in his recollections of city living.[124] The favourite haunts of the Berlin flaneur were the elegant boulevards of Unter den Linden and the Kurfürstendamm.[125] Another renowned chronicler of Berlin during the 1920s who overlooked the river was Joseph Roth. The foremost German journalist of the decade, who perfected the genre known as the *feuilleton* (a short prose essay based on personal observation, usually of the ordinary and everyday), he wrote about a walk to the outskirts of Berlin. In this account, '*Spatziergang*', 'nature' is a place beyond the urban environment that poets and painters seek out and to which those in need of recreation and recuperation flee; the only place and time in the city he sees nature lovers is at railway stations on Sunday mornings, heading out of the city. He overlooks the possibility that the river might qualify as *die Natur* or provide an antidote to the city that is 'large and grey and grim' (*gross und grau und grausam*).[126] On the rare occasions he mentioned the Spree, it was only because he had to cross to reach a gallery on Museum Island. Or because a thief in flight falls off a bridge and drowns.[127]

Moving beyond the standard critique of 'asphalt culture' and stale juxtaposition of sacred country and profane city, Conradt sought to reunite Berlin with its rural environs through the mechanism of the river. This approach was anticipated during the dark days of the Second World War, when the city tried to bolster the spirits of its soldiers in far-off foreign fields by sending *Heimatsgrüsse an die Front*. In one contribution (entitled 'When the Spree was still "green"'), Eberhard Faden put it bluntly: '*Ohne die Spree kein Berlin*' (without the Spree, no Berlin).[128]

114

The message in Conradt's film's companion book is identical: without the Spree, Berlin would not exist. Since Berliners drink from the river (if indirectly), when they cry, their tears are Spree water: 'We are the Spree.'[129] Initially, Conradt wanted to let the river speak for itself. But the funders considered this proposition too bizarre. And so the documentary includes the voices of various river people as the Spree flows from source to Berlin: fishermen (lured by large Wels catfish, if not quite as big as the Po's), recreational rowers and a river researcher; a manager of the company that operates the Bautzen-Burk reservoir and dam; the official responsible for monitoring water quality in Berlin; and Werban, former biosphere reserve superintendent, who emphasizes how much Berlin relies on the Spreewald's wetland filtration system for high-quality potable water.[130]

Karsten Gundermann's soundtrack (performed by the Dresden Philharmonic) also follows the river's course, beginning with Slavonic tones, continuing with Sorbic music in the Spreewald, and closing with Prussian martial music in Berlin. Having spent seven years making his film, Conradt is understandably upset that four out of five Berliners apparently do not know where their river rises. Berliners' comparative lack of affinity with their river perplexes him. When he first became interested in making a film, he was astonished to find that his would be the first about the Spree. According to Rainer Milzkott, public relations manager for urbanPR, the orientation of Berlin's cathedral speaks volumes about the lack of intimacy between city and river: the rear faces the river – a feature that many other major downtown buildings share.[131] Even those Berliners who appreciate the opportunity it provides for boating excursions, laments Heinz Götze, are woefully ignorant of the river. They know about the source of the Nile and that Paris sits on the Seine, but young or old alike have no clue where the Spree rises.[132]

Seeking to explain this lack of knowledge, Conradt draws attention to the manifestly unjust situation that, when Spree joins Havel, it becomes the Havel, despite the disparity in size. (And since the Havel, when it enters the Elbe, is also patently the longer river, Hamburg, in his view, is still on the Spree.) Another, more plausible explanation for Berliners' lack of awareness of the rest of the river can be found in a work of fiction. Roth may have neglected the river in his prose works, but he included it in his pioneering 'documentary' novel, *Die Flucht ohne Ende* (*Flight without End*; 1927). The storyline follows the trans-European journey of Franz Tunda, an Austrian officer in the First World War, following his flight from a Russian prisoner of war camp. En route to his hometown, Vienna, Tunda hangs out in Berlin, which strikes him as a singular place, existing out-side Germany; a sealed-off, self-contained city state. He marvels that this 'capital of itself' (*die Hauptstadt ihrer selbst*) not only has its own animal kingdom (the zoo), its own plant kingdom (the botanical garden) and its own harbour (Osthafen). It also possessed its own sea in the shape of the Spree (*ihr Fluss ist ein Meer*).[133] The ignorance of Berliners does not apply to their part of the river; it applies to the non-urban river. How many Londoners know (or care) where the Thames rises? How many Liverpudlians know (or care) where the Mersey begins?

## Sprea

Like so many rivers, the Spree has a resident deity. In this instance, the deity is female. As Berlin cultivated its credentials as *Spree-Athen*, Sprea assumed a prominent role. She was the lead character in a musical play by Karl Wilhelm Ramler, performed in Berlin on 24 January 1775 to mark the birthday of the King of Prussia (Frederick the Great). The setting is a pine forest on the banks of the river and the cast includes the gods of the Oder and Vistula. Fellow river nymph Pregolla, nymph of the river Pregel, announces that Sprea is 'proud of your city'.[134] Sprea not only watched over a river whose water was allegedly holier and packed with more *Wunderkraft* than the waters of the Nile and Ganges.[135] In the 1860s, she lent her name to a river steamboat. But the strongest evidence of the high regard in which Berliners held their river in the late nineteenth-century heyday of river bathing is the commission to create 'Sprea' that the Magistrats of Berlin awarded, after fierce competition involving 109 entrants, to the Berlin-based German-Danish sculptor Jeremias Christensen in 1895. Sprea sits on a mussel shell with her right arm gently around the city's better known symbol, the Berlin bear (*Berliner Bär*). Just as the river dispenses water to the city, the grateful (and much smaller bear) laps up Spree water from the shell. In her right hand she holds a white water lily (*nymphaea alba*) – a characteristic flower of the river.

The original location of the 3-metre high, 8-ton statue (unveiled on 21 March 1899) was the entrance to the municipal chambers (*Magistratssitzungssaal*) on the first floor of the 'Rote' Rathaus, which lies near the river. Badly damaged in the Second World War (though Sprea escaped unscathed), the town hall became part of East Berlin. When the town hall's restoration began in 1951, the river goddess was

Sprea, the Spree Goddess, with the Berlin bear, illustration, 1940. The illustration is based on Jeremias Christensen's statue in the Berliner Rathaus.

Jeremias Christensen's *Sprea*, relocated to Tierpark Berlin-Friedrichsfelde in the 1950s.

initially relocated to Jüdenstrasse (*Mitte*), then to a peninsula in a lake at Berlin-Friedrichsfelde zoological park (*Tierpark*) (1955).[136] Sprea languished there in obscurity among the trees, five kilometres from the river, until shortly before Reunification.

Horst Vollrath rediscovered her while researching his book *Wiedersehen am Strand der Spree: Ein Fluss und seine Geschichte* (1990), and launched a campaign to rescue her from this insular backwater, hidden by vegetation, near the llama enclosure, and restore her to a more appropriate and dignified spot. His book included a plea for forgiveness: 'Dear Goddess of the Spree! Forgive these faithless Berliners for keeping you so well hidden [at the zoo]'. For Vollrath, she was yearning for a place from where she could see her river and 'stretch out [her] protective hand towards it'.[137] Spandau signalled its desire to receive the scrubbed and renovated statue and install her in a fitting spot to mark the town's 800th anniversary in 1997. The position that Spandau's city fathers had in mind was atop a 3-metre stand at the Spandau Citadel, just north of where the Spree joins the Havel.

But Spandau was not the only interested party. The Märkisches Museum, the museum of Berlin, located in the harbour area of the city's historic core, just a few metres from the river, mounted a rival bid. Though the Spree barely merits a mention in the museum's visual chronicle of the city, it insisted that Sprea rightfully belonged to Berlin. In 2001, the press reported that Sprea would move from the zoo to a temporary home in the museum's inner yard (*Innenhof*), and that, after restoration, she might find a permanent home in the museum restaurant. This outcome suited the historic preservationists, who insisted that another outdoor location – whether in the centre of Berlin or on the outskirts – would be highly detrimental to Sprea's fabric. Nearly half a century of exposure to the ravages of wind and rain, under a canopy of trees, had extensively damaged a statue designed for indoor display. The moss encrusted marble had lost its lustre and begun to crack under the assault of acid rain. A cafe may be a safer location than outdoors at Spandau Citadel – or the *Tierpark* where she still stands. But for a river goddess, this seems like a banal and undignified fate.[138]

# THREE

# *Po*

The ancient Greeks, who knew the lower Danube as the Istros, were just as familiar with the lower Po, which they called the Eridanus; in classical myth, the Po was in fact a continuation of the Istros (while the Rhône, in turn, extended the Po). *Eridanus* probably derived from *danu*, Proto-Indo-European for 'river', which features in river names across Europe, not least the Danube itself, and the Don in Scotland and Russia. A somewhat generic name, Eridanus has been associated with other rivers too. In early Greek texts, Eridanus was a northwest European (Celtic) river.[1] Palaeogeographers also identify it as a river that flowed between Lapland and the North Sea during the early Pleistocene, disappearing as recently as 700,000 years ago during the first ice age, after which the Baltic Sea replaced its main course and the North Sea took over its vast delta region. The Eridanus has also been linked to the Nile, Ganges, Rhône, Ebro, Elbe and Vistula.[2] The river it is most regularly associated with, however, is the Po (*Padus* in Latin).[3]

As the Eridanus, the Po was instrumental in Greek tragedy. The Fall of Phaeton (*La caduta di Fetonte*) began when his father, Helios (Apollo), reluctantly lent him his chariot of the sun (*quadriga*) for the day. But the son of the sun was a reckless and inexperienced driver. Unable to keep a firm grip on the reins, he deviated from the recommended route across the universe and his borrowed chariot careered out of control. Phaeton swooped so close to the earth that much of Africa turned into desert, and the Danube, Rhine, Rhône and Tiber dried up (while 'frightened Nile ran off, and under ground, Conceal'd his head'). Then, soaring up too high, Phaeton threatened to set the sky ablaze and freeze the earth. To avert an all-consuming cosmological catastrophe, Zeus (Jupiter) smote his godson's runaway chariot and its petrified learner driver with a thunderbolt and the hapless charioteer dropped into the waiting Eridanus.[4]

Elements of this myth may have been incorporated into Bernini's Fountain of the Four Rivers, through the deity of the Plate, who strikes a startled posture (left arm and right leg extended), and appears to be

Michelangelo's 'Caduta di Fetonte' (Fall of Phaeton), 1533.

'Ridanus a finiſtro pede profectus orioñis z per/
ueniens vſq3 ad piſtrice : rurſus oiffundiſ vſq3 ad
leporis pedes z protinus ad antarcticum tendit cir
culum. huius figurationem circu us byemalis oiui
dit ab eo loco quo prope coniungitur ceto: hic ſcor/
pione z ſagictario exorto occidere: Exoriri aute cũ geminis z can/
cro videtur. habet aute ſtellas in prima curuatura tres. Ju ſecun
da tres. Jtem in tertia vſq3 ad nouiſſimã ſeptem. Omnino e ſtel/
larum numero tredecim.

The Eridanus constella-
tion, river and river god,
woodcut engraving from
Hyginus's edition of the
1st-century BC *Poeticon
Astronomicon* (Poetic
Astronomy, 1482).
Hyginus identified them
with the Nile rather than
the Po.

Eridanus flumen

shielding his eyes from a blinding light.[5] Thanks to Ovid, however, whose
version of the story was the most influential, Eridanus and Po became more
or less synonymous: 'Phaeton, with flaming hair, Shot . . . like a falling star
. . . Till on the Po his blasted corps was hurl'd, Far from his country, in the
western world'. Phaeton's watching sisters on the river bank, the Heliades
(dryads), were so traumatized that the merciful gods turned them into
poplar trees and their tears into drops of amber (electra). Meanwhile, the
river god, Eridanus, emerged to retrieve Phaeton's body and 'bathes his
steaming face'.[6]

Then, as now, poplars (*pioppi*) lined the Po. Yet amber is the fossil-
ized resin of pine not poplar; and there was no known source of amber in
Italy at that time.[7] And though some authorities identified a river mouth
directly south of Venice, terminus of a trade route bringing amber from
the northern Baltic region, Strabo and Herodotus were inclined to locate
the Eridanus in Greece.[8] Nonetheless, in the third century BC, Apollonius

The god of the Po reclines as part of Umberto Baglioni's *Fontane del Po e della Dora* in Turin's Piazza Comitato di Liberazione Nazionale.

Rhodius recorded that Jason's Argonauts, who reputedly sailed up the Eridanus after stealing the Golden Fleece (having entered the river from the Istros), could still smell Phaeton's smouldering corpse, which made them sick. 'Even now', Apollonius observed (offering an imaginative explanation of the river's notorious fogs), 'it belcheth up heavy steam clouds from the smouldering wound'.[9]

A further complication in the identification between mythical and actual rivers derives from the blurring of the distinction between the earthly Eridanus and a heavenly river.[10] The two-stream Eridanus was the stellar constellation of the river of fire (the galaxy's longest; also known as 'Stream of Ocean' and 'Stream of Tears'), named for the trail of fire that marked Phaeton's precipitous descent (the Milky Way).[11] According to Nonnos of Panopolis, the early fifth-century Greek epic poet, Zeus, to console Helios, casterized (placed among the stars) the 'fire-scorched' 'Celtic' river that swallowed up Phaeton ('in the starry circle rolls the meandering stream of burning Eridanos').[12] The terrestrial river *Padus* mingled with the extra-terrestrial starry stream 'fed by melting snows at the rising of the Dog Star [that is, in the dog days of summer]', explained Isidore of Seville in the seventh century, 'and with the addition of thirty other streams it empties into the Adriatic Sea near Ravenna'.[13]

Just as Eridanus once caught the falling Phaeton, today, the god of the Po maintains a watchful eye over Turin, the Po's first major city and Italy's industrial centre. Giuseppe Momo's design for Piazza Comitato di Liberazione Nazionale centred on reclining figures representing the Po and its 125-kilometre tributary, the Dora Riparia, at whose confluence the Romans founded Turin. Umberto Baglioni's *Fontane del Po e della Dora* (erected 1939; restored 2005), consists of a bearded male symbolizing the Po and a female figure personifying the Dora. The small handful of wheat ears Po holds in his left hand (Dora's right hand cradles an apple) symbolizes the river's bounty. With its rich load of nourishing silt, the Po is Italy's Nile.[14] Just as crop yields in the Spreewald were among Germany's highest courtesy of the silt spread out by the Spree, the high productivity of the Po Valley (*Val Padana*) was the gift of the Po.

Yet *Val Padana* is not just Italy's most productive agricultural region. It has also been the peninsula's commercial powerhouse for centuries, flowing through or near some of Italy's oldest cities (Pavia, Piacenza, Cremona, Mantova and Ferrara).[15] Po Valley cities such as these, as well as Turin and Milan, comprise one of relatively few close European approximations to the network of megalopolises first identified in the northeastern United States. The Po basin's population now stands at 16 million – almost a third of the nation's total.[16] The Po is also, therefore, Italy's most heavily transformed river (*maggiormente antropizzato*), morphologically and ecologically. Flood defence and irrigation works that the Etruscans began in the sixth century BC were resumed by the Romans, who drained marshes, embanked the main river and cut feeder canals to water crops. An intensive and highly commercialized form of farming was already installed on the eve of unification (1860).[17]

The Po's national political significance, though not commensurate to its economic stature, is nonetheless substantial. For three politicians in the vanguard of the *Risorgimento* the river was a rallying point for the new Italy declared in Rome in February 1849. A few weeks after they were appointed triumvirs of the short-lived Italian republic, Giuseppe Mazzini, Aurelio Saffi and Carlo Armellini (none of whom had direct connections with the river) proclaimed it *Il fiume nazionale*. Though this turned out to be an inconsequential gesture (French forces overthrew the republic in June 1849), this act articulated the Po's meaning for a unified Italy. At the time, the Po divided the Papal States from Austrian-occupied upper (*alta*) Italy: Lombardy and Veneto. The representative for Ferrara (which resided on the river's southern, Papal bank) argued in legislative chamber

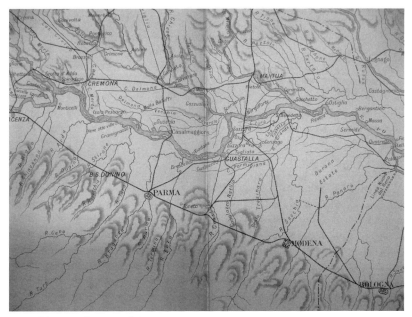

Map of the Po Valley east of Cremona, 1902.

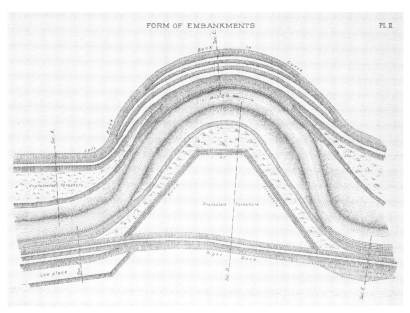

Embankments on the Po, 1902.

Po

debate that the Po's upkeep should be a responsibility of the new national government. For the river's contribution to Italian life was not confined to the provinces it traversed. Representative Costabili wanted to elevate the Po to the status of Rome's Tiber: 'If the Tiber was the river of Kings, then the Po was the King of Rivers'.[18] Not only did northern Italians feel more affinity with the Po. It was also a more fitting symbol for a modern democratic republic than the Tiber, as well as a symbol of their freedom struggle.

At the same time, the Po exudes a strongly regional flavour befitting its transitional position between Central Europe and the Mediterranean. Many residents of *Val Padana* derive their sense of place from a symbolic harnessing of the river. Most strikingly, within present-day Italy's volatile political environment, the Po provides the separatist Northern League (*Lega Nord*) with a liquid source of bioregional identity – the Po as anti-national river.

The Po's cultural contribution is also considerable, proving it worthy of the moniker *il grande fiume*.[19] Occupying a powerful place within twentieth-century Italian literature and film, the river demonstrates the conviction of the director, Giuseppe De Santis, that, though landscape is insignificant 'when deprived of the presence of man', 'the reverse is just as true'.[20] The bond between the river and its people *(il rapporto uomofiume)* that drew many post-war directors to the Po is hardly unique among human-river relations. Nor did the film-makers pretend that the river which exerted such a pull on their hearts and minds was the only river capable of eliciting such a powerful response. 'Actually, this is a commonplace phenomenon in many places which are intersected by large rivers', reflected Michelangelo Antonioni. 'It is as if it were the destiny of such lands to terminate in a river.'[21] Nonetheless, in the 1940s and 1950s the Po exercised a particularly tenacious hold over those intrigued by this long and intimate partnership between people and rivers.[22]

The Po also illuminates other indispensable themes of liquid history. At 650 kilometres, it just about squeezes onto the list of Europe's twenty longest rivers (though only if Russia west of the Urals is excluded). Of greater consequence, though, is that the Po offers a vivid example of how a river is imbued with promise and peril in equal measure. One of Europe's richest agricultural areas, *Val Padana* has also suffered some of Europe's worst floods. Italy is particularly flood-prone.[23] And within Italy, the Po Valley is especially vulnerable. As those who live with the river say: *Al Po al dà 'e'l tos* – the Po gives and the Po takes away.[24]

125

The desire to maximize value (wanted water) while minimizing danger (unwanted water) sums up the worldwide, age-old effort to regulate rivers. The science and technology of river regulation was pioneered on the Po – a memorable example of Cicero's second nature. Bolton King noted in the early twentieth century that 'Italy is the historic country of irrigation, and, especially in the Po valley, it has been carried to a high pitch of perfection'. Another British geographer ventured further: the Po Valley exhibited the 'most remarkable irrigation in Europe' (yielding what a nineteenth-century American agriculturalist hailed as one of the richest and most densely popu-lated regions 'the world has ever seen').[25] The Po's global significance does not end, though, with its status as the cradle of hydraulic engineering. The icing on the Po's cake is its reputation as a river of gastronomy. Some of Italy's most renowned foods – gorgonzola, parmesan (*Parmigiano Reggiano*) and Parma ham (*prosciutto crudo di Parma*) – are rooted in its valley.

## Source and Course

The Po rises at 2,022 metres at Pian del Re on the northern slopes of Monte Viso, an isolated pyramid peak close to the French border that dominates the Cottian Alps in the province of Piedmont. Unlike the sources of the Danube and Spree, the location is uncontested, though that undisputed source has recently become politically highly charged. The initial direction of flow is northeastward. From Turin, though, it maintains a steady easterly course to the Adriatic. The Po quickly sheds the characteristics of a mountain river (*torrente montano*). *Val Padana* (which nineteenth-century geographers dubbed the Italian Netherlands) begins after just 30 kilometres. From Casalgrasso, 240 metres above sea level, the plain (*pianura*) stretches for 530 kilometres, averaging 200 kilometres in width – Italy's only extensive plain. The tidal river begins 90 kilometres from the sea at Pontelagoscuro, the port of Ferrara. Yet what is truly impressive about the Po, geographically speaking, is the size of its catch-ment area (*bacino fluviale*), which, at 71,057 square kilometres, encom-passes 141 tributaries and occupies roughly a quarter of Italy (the next largest, the Tiber's, covers just 17,200 square kilometres).[26]

The basin's hydrological regime consists of two low water periods: winter (peaking in January) and summer (August peak). These are matched by two periods of high water: late autumn (November peak) and late spring (June peak).[27] The dramatically fluctuating water levels of the Po and its tributaries frequently inconvenienced travellers. W. E. Frye, a major in the British army, passed through the valley on his way from Turin to Bologna in the spring of 1816. As well as surveying the meanderings of 'that King of Rivers' ('as the Italian poets term it') in repose from the top of the palace of the Dukes of Ferrara (whose courtyard was nonetheless nine feet below the level of the river in spate), Frye had a more direct encounter.[28] He experienced the vagaries of flow in the *seguaci del Po* (tributaries; literally, disciples of the Po). Between Castel Guelfo and Parma the 'very troublesome' Taro crossed his path:

> which at times is nearly dry and at other times, so deep as to render it hazardous for a carriage to pass, and it is at all times requisite to send on a man to ford and sound it before a carriage passes. This river fills a variety of separate beds, as it meanders very much, and it extends to such a breadth in its *debordements*, as to render it impossible to construct a bridge long enough to be of any use.[29]

It was the dry season, so he had an uneventful crossing. In November 1839, however, high water prevented the composer Fanny Hensel, en route from Venice to Florence, from crossing the main river.[30]

## Productive Po

'Of all the rivers of Europe', A. C. Ramsay reflected in 1872, 'perhaps few have a more interesting history than the Po'.[31] As director-general of Britain's Geological Survey, he was referring primarily to its geological history. Yet his remark holds water more generally. The Po is not an artery of commerce comparable to the Rhine and Danube (small craft can navigate 480 kilometres upstream, but acute seasonal variations in flow hamper larger vessels). But *Pianura Padana* (in the valley is also known) proceeded on the auspicious combination on a large scale of suitable climate, soil and relief – as well as a reliable water supply. This convergence of qualities is exceptional in an upland dominated country (rare, indeed, across the Mediterranean basin). Silt washed down from the mountains by its tributaries since the Pliocene (5 million years ago, *Pianura Padana* was part of the Adriatic, which lapped up against the foothills of Alps and Apennines) has built up alluvial deposits several hundred metres thick.[32] Travelling

The low-lying bottomlands (*golene*) between the river (almost hidden behind the row of trees in the distance) and the embankment (*argine*) at Zibello, April 2009.

along a poplar-lined road that ran above field level, near Piacenza, Frye praised the 'rich meadow country', the 'immense quantity of cattle grazing' and the opulence of the farmhouses.[33]

A wealth of dependable tributaries (literally paying liquid tribute) renders largely unnecessary the storage of water to mitigate summer drought. Alpine glaciers and snow combine with deep sub-alpine lakes (Como, Garda, Iseo and Maggiore) to ensure a year-round supply. Northern tributaries (some of which emerge from these natural reservoirs) represent a winning mix of so-called summer and winter rivers: the former, which emanate from the mountains, experience their greatest flow in summer due to their sources' high elevation; the latter are at maximum volume in winter because they are pre-alpine and derive their water from rainfall on the slopes.

This abundance of water represents a double-edged sword. All rivers are dynamic entities but northern Italy's are particularly wont to move around. Communities face a a delicate balancing act: how to reap the advantages without undue exposure to risk. 'We confine rivers, we straighten their course, we divert them altogether', explained the Roman orator Marcus Tullius Cicero in the first century BC.[34] And in *The Prince*, doubtless with his own unsuccessful early sixteenth-century effort to re-direct the Arno for Florentine benefit and to disadvantage Pisa in mind, Niccolò Machiavelli likened Fortune (determinant of half of human affairs) to 'one of those destructive rivers that, when they become enraged, flood the plains, ruin the trees and buildings, raising the earth from one spot and dropping it onto another'. He also compared the need to marshall defences against Fortune's adversities with the imperative to 'take precautions' against wanton fluvial power by raising dykes and dams.[35]

Among the many quotations inscribed on the marble wall of Madonna del Po, a tiny chapel situated between the levee and the river at Zibello, is a quotation from Virgil's *Georgics* (1.535–8).

> Monarch of rivers, raging far and wide,
> Eridanus pours forth his torrent tide,
> Down the wide deluge whirls th' uprooted wood,
> And swells with herds and stalls th' incumber'd flood.

Virgil's early nineteenth-century translator noted that 'matted' huts were spaced along the river at one to two hundred metre intervals, manned by 'Guardia di Po', 'ready to assist with their tools at a moment's warning, in case of a breach'.[36] Po valley villages and towns such as Zibello lie at a discreet and respectful distance from the often invisible river. The protection afforded by a grassy earthen embankment (levee and dyke are synonyms; the Italian term is *argine*) is reinforced by a buffer zone of bottomlands (*golene*) that stretch between *argine* and Po. In Guarda Ferrarese, the houses huddle behind the church that faces the river, cheek-by-jowl with the *argine*. Novelist Riccardo Bacchelli thought it was protecting the villagers 'from the encroaching river, like a hen covering its chicks'.[37]

Total security has not been achievable for the people of the *bassa*. The main channel's drastic vacillations have caused villages (and cemeteries) to disappear or relocate. Bankside erosion destroyed some settlements; others suddenly found themselves on the opposite bank. Ermanno Cavazzoni's novel *Poema dei lunatici* (1987), set in the Po Valley near Padua, captures this standing threat of inundation and perpetual state of flux. When the narrator, Ivo Savini (a fraudulent inspector of wells), meets the local prefect, he vents his frustration at how hard it is to map the area accurately. Savini muses that transparent paper or sheets of glass would be more suitable for maps and atlases of the mercurial Po than regular paper because these materials would reveal the palimpsest: previous configurations underlying the latest configuration. He finally decides on water for his atlas: like the river on the land, the water on the map could shift and reshape, just as the ink could assume life and flow.[38]

Cartographers have pinned down the Po's geomorphological evolution over the last few centuries by scrutinizing a section between the entries of the Sesia and Adda. Researchers reconstructed the Po's shifting channel by drawing on three types of data: recent aerial photographs (1980) facilitated mapping of terrace scarps, abandoned channels and bars; printed materials such as documents and maps (available since 1588) enabled them to date abandoned channels (Ramsay's 'ancient abberations'); and examination of natural events shaping morphological evolution and landform patterns revealed geological and neotectonic impacts. Maps based on these data sets display the dramatic channel swings over the past three centuries.[39]

Since 1700, human agency has increasingly shaped fluvial morphology. Hard labour is required to reap the river's rewards and keep disadvantages at bay. 'A continual struggle is engaged in between the forces of man and those of nature', noted Egypt's Inspector of Irrigation, who toured northern Italy in the summer of 1899.[40] Armouring a winding river like the Po posed a particular challenge because erosion is endemic to concave bends; straightening was necessary as a concomitant form of redress.

Hydro-engineering works on the Po provide a compelling European example of the operations of a hydraulic society (a concept Karl Wittfogel advanced in 1957 with reference to ancient Chinese practices). A major body of law and complex state apparatus emerged to govern possession and distribution of Po Valley water, covering intake and outtake, the operation of embankments, dams and sluices, and the coordination of regulatory efforts from one end of the basin to the other. Wittfogel suggested that the political and administrative system best suited to an elaborate system of hydraulic control is a highly centralized authoritarian regime able to impose its authority basin-wide and armed with ample financial and technological resources, not to mention vast manpower reserves it can mobilize in coordinated fashion. This kind of authority was absent from the Po Valley after the fragmentation of power following Rome's demise. A California-based geographer and scientist who conducted an extensive survey of irrigation works beyond the United States in the early 1870s reported that post-Roman governing bodies lacked the political authority as well as the conception of water as a public resource to ensure that activities in one part of the basin were connected to and supportive of efforts in other locales.[41]

Roman hydraulic society's collapse reshaped economy and river. As the infrastructure of regulation deteriorated, fields and villages were abandoned; without a sophisticated water control system, arable farming centred on wheat production was hard to sustain. The river reoccupied its floodplain and reconstituted its marshes. The frequency of floods (*alluvioni*) along the lower and middle river (encouraged by deforestation in the Apennines) discouraged the re-emergence of substantial settlements. Early medieval villages and farms retreated to a safer distance and developed diverse economies adapted to the renatured fluvial regime. Casting off reliance on arable crops and vineyards, a mixed and flexible economy incorporating fishing, waterfowl hunting, water meadow grazing and the harvesting of reeds emerged that capitalized on existing fluvial assets. Rather than being regarded as an aberration in an orderly world, the watery environments were 'normalized'.[42]

The painstaking process of rebuilding Roman *argini* began in the eleventh century. Six hundred years later, the Po Valley resumed its role as the epicentre of advances in river control. The practical work of confining the unruly river and its tributaries underpinned the great leap forward in the 'science of waters' that encompassed the mechanics of fluids, fluvial hydraulics and fluvial geomorphology. The growing cadre of hydraulic scholars (the University of Bologna established a chair of hydrometry in 1694) applied its knowledge by training water managers in Bologna and Venice.[43]

Venetian hydraulic manipulators (whose predecessors had remade the Brenta) converted the ancient Po delta into its modern (lobate) form: a large protuberance into the Adriatic. The main channels near Ferrara, which had a penchant for northeastward migration at the best of times, swung close to the Venetian lagoon in the mid-1300s, a problem exacerbated in the late 1590s when the Po di Tramontana became the main branch. The new course was much too close for Venetian comfort. Venice worried that silt infill would seal off the openings (*porti*) in the chain of sandbanks (*lidi*) that separated the lagoon from the open waters of the upper Adriatic (Gulf of Venice) – the worst case scenario being the lagoon's eventual degeneration into marshland – jeopardizing Venetian insularity and hegemony. The decisive act in creating the 'active' delta and leaving behind the 'fossil' delta was the Porto Viro Cut (*Taglio di Porto Viro*) – excavated through sand dunes with shovels – which diverted the main channel southeastward into a fresh bed 5 kilometres long and 12 metres deep between 1600 and 1604.[44]

By the 1720s, through the translation of key texts (Benedetto Castelli's *Della misura dell'acque correnti* [1628], for example, which was informed by local field studies) and the relocation of engineers, the Po Valley was exporting its expertise to Holland's lower Rhine. The river subsequently maintained this vanguard status. British irrigation engineers in late nineteenth-century India looked to the Po for guidance.[45] And it comes as no surprise that the leading proponent of government sponsored reclamation in the American West visited the 'school of irrigation for the rest of the world'. The Department of Agriculture's Chief of Irrigation Investigations, Elwood Mead, spent two months on location in the summer of 1903. Irrigation delivered two crops in one season; wheat harvested in July was followed by a supplementary crop of maize, beans, cabbage or alfalfa. South of Milan, irrigation nurtured the winter water meadows (*marcite)* that raised clover and rye grass to feed cattle.[46]

Whereas some branches of agriculture required reclamation (*opere di bonifica*), others exploited the watery world. Rice was first planted in the swampy Lomellina region of the western Po in the fifteenth century and also grown in delta marshland unsuitable for other crops. But the heartland was the 'quadrilateral of rice', with its four corners in the Lombardian provinces of Pavia, Novara, Vercelli and Milan.[47] Such was the reputation of this region's rice that Thomas Jefferson, who was American ambassador

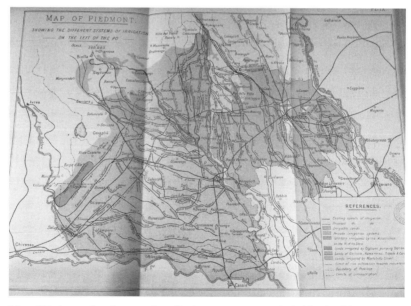

Map of Piedmont showing complex of irrigation systems on the left bank of the Po.

to Paris at the time, visited in April 1787. He departed with bulging coat pockets (the export of peerless Vercelli rice in the husk was illegal).[48]

Lombard paddies (*risaie*) were drained and harvested in September. After drying out over the winter, they were tilled in April, and then flooded with water supplied by the Po's 'winter' tributaries. The seeds were steeped in water before sowing in May to encourage germination and the *risaie* were soaked from irrigation canals (*la canalizzazione dei corsi d'acqua*) to protect seedlings from often low night-time temperatures in spring. The most arduous phase of labour was hand weeding in May to prevent the seedlings from being choked out.[49] Young women (*le mondine*) were shipped in for this gruelling task.[50] In his memoir, *The Farm on the Po* (1920), though he does not mention the leeches that clung to their bare legs, Mario Borsa described them as 'up to their knees in water and mud . . . in long rows of twenty or thirty, bent over their work, moving their hands to the accompaniment of languid, insipid, monotonous songs'.[51] When the gang lines, inching backwards, reached the bottom of a field, the overseer high up on his platform instructed those in mid-row to stand aside to allow the seething masses of cornered frogs an escape route.

Seed planting machines and selective weedkillers replaced *le mondine* in the 1960s.[52] Yet thanks to a 1949 neo-realist film starring Italy's answer to Jane Russell and Rita Hayworth, these seasonal workers have become the upper river's best-known group of people. Giuseppe De Santis's *Riso amaro* ('Bitter Rice') depicted an old agrarian order on the brink of take-over by a modern agro-industrial regime (not to mention American popular culture).[53] Filmed on location near Vercelli in July 1947, the action spans the 40-day planting and weeding season. The producer drew on the local migratory workforce for an 800-strong army of extras.[54] But the lead was an eighteen-year-old former Miss Italy, Silvana Mangano, in her debut role as Silvana Melega, the voluptuous, gum-chewing, boogie-woogie dancing *mondina*.

The fifth most commercially successful Italian film of 1949 (and Oscar-nominated for best cinematography) *Riso Amaro* combined lush cinematography with documentary-style social commentary. The subject matter was natural terrain for the most engaged Communist among postwar Italian film directors. Yet the film also contained a powerful erotic charge that outraged Vatican and leftists alike. The Communist paper, *L'Unità*, protested that Mangano's bare legs, tight shorts and clinging sweater – compounded by the flesh of her co-workers standing thigh-to-thigh, knee-deep in water – were not calculated to raise political consciousness one iota.[55]

Despite these distractions, De Santis remained firmly focused on class war between the landless and the landed.[56] Yet there was another struggle he engaged with, if less overtly: the ambivalent relationship with the river of humans as a species (rather than subdivided into groups). Finely attuned to the dramatic possibilities of landscape, especially its 'primordial' qualities, he insisted that it was difficult to understand human behaviour divorced from its environmental context.[57] And the river itself, though lurking unseen, exerts a powerful indirect influence. The dominant motif is water – whether still, flowing or churning. Christopher Wagstaff categorizes the film's depiction of landscape as 'classical, Virgilian', as distinct from the romantic attraction to landscape as the 'threatening sublime'.[58] Yet water serves as a secret weapon to advance individual interests against those of the group. Melega betrays her class (and sisterhood) by conspiring with a no-good petty thief-cum-easy charmer (Walter) to steal the portion of the harvest paid as wages. As his henchmen drive away the rice during the end of harvest festivities, she creates a distraction by opening the gates to flood the paddies, a disaster her compatriots discover and rush off to avert.

Further east, where wheat replaced rice, the miller replaced the *mondina* as the emblematic human figure. Few mills on the lower Po were land-based; fixed terrestrial locations quickly become redundant when the main stream altered course. In the absence of stable banks, some were placed on boats. But most mills floated on the river; with prows dipping into the current, they resembled anchored ships. This arrangement not only obviated the need to cut a millrace to divert water to the wheels but facilitated adjustment to the current's shifts and changing water levels, enabling around the clock operation. (Nonetheless, floodwaters could tear mills from their moorings and hurtle them downstream; sometimes they slammed into bridges or wedged under arches.) The lower Po's signature 'wheels of bread' (*la Ruote del Pan*[59]) inspired an epic work by an author who grew up in the Po Valley city of Bologna. Riccardo Bacchelli's three-volume historical novel *Il Mulino del Po* (1938) is a family drama that tracks three generations of the Scacerni family across a century.[60] A tormented American reviewer observed that 'the story goes on with as slow a pace as the Po as it slacks down to the sea'.[61] Once hailed as the Italian equivalent of *War and Peace*, *The Mill on the Po* is now generally acknowledged to possess greater historical and geographical merit than literary value.

The action begins in Russia in November 1812 and ends with the Battle of Vittorio Veneto in October 1918, when the Allies broke across the Piave to invade Austrian territory. Though the opening scene unfolds far from the Po, the characters import the skills they have honed on its banks. A vanguard of pontoniers from an Italian corps of Napoleon's army are tasked with bridging the 'hostile' river Vop during the retreat from Moscow. As he works, a soldier from this company of military engineers – Lazzaro Scacerni, the central character – sings folk songs sung back home in his native Po Valley by peasant girls who feed cattle on leaves plucked from trees on the hottest days of summer.[62]

Since the Vop proves too stiff a challenge for the pontoniers, the company must swim across. Scacerni (aged just sixteen) tries to carry his captain on his shoulders. But his passenger dies en route. The dying captain, Mazzacorati, who has accumulated a small fortune in stolen church jewels, appoints Scacerni heir to his ill-gotten gains. The boy deserts and returns to Ariano in the delta, where he spent his childhood as the son of a ferryman and fisherman hunting and fishing in Mesola's riparian woodlands.[63] Reclaiming Mazzacorati's fortune from a money-lender in Ferrara, he buys a mill on the Po, which he moors near Guarda Ferrarese. Aside from Scacerni, the mill and river are the novel's main characters.

The screen adaptation by Alberto Lattuada (1949) illustrates the anti-pastoral and anti-picturesque cultural enterprise of neo-realism that was drawn to the lower Po like no other Italian region.[64] The social turbulence that marks this populist melodrama set in the late nineteenth century mirrors the convulsions that rent Italian society after 1945. The chief human characters are Berta, daughter of the mill-owning family of Lazzaro Scacerni, and her fiancé, a well-to-do farmer. Yet the millers have their grievances (high taxes) and the Scacerni family's deteriorating circumstances reduce Berta to the level of servant to relatives of her fiancé's landowning family. The film exposes the plight of landless day labourers in the wheatfields of the Po Valley's great estates, who go on strike alongside the millers.[65] When the police manhandle Berta, her brother intervenes, mistakenly slaying her fiancé, whose body is slung into the Po. The river people believed that a drowned person's soul can only come to rest if a loved one retrieves the body as soon as it surfaces. That evening, the Scacernis accompany an old man of the river to a bend where bodies often resurface. An otherwise unflattering American reviewer reckoned that the film's redeeming feature was the cinematography of Aldo Tonti, who created 'the panorama of river country and farms that is spread upon the screen in vast profusion'.[66]

In turn, the communities of this neck of the river country have spread Bacchelli's novel profusely across their riverscape. The abundance of intimate local detail that he included has enhanced the reputation of the small town of Ro, just downriver from Guarda Ferrarese. Ro proclaims its location within '*Le Terra del Mulino del Po*' (though the movie was filmed in Crespino, in the delta province of Rovigo). Near the town bridge is a reconstructed floating mill in full working order. Dating from the early 1900s, when they were still common – there are none today – it forms the centrepiece of a riverside 'theme' park. Oasi Mulino del Po, which houses nine hectares of increasingly rare riparian woodland, hosts demonstrations of the ancient art of milling and bread making.[67] The Ferrara region to which Ro belongs is known as the 'breadbasket of Italy'. Particularly renowned are its crusty wheat rolls, *Coppia Ferrarese*, which, like the Spreewald gherkin, now enjoy (since 2001) coveted Protected Geographical Indication (PGI) status (*Indicazione Geografica Protetta*). The distinctive taste of these starfish-shaped rolls (whose ingredients and production process are governed by a thirteenth-century statute) derives from humidity and high-quality flour (as well as the olive oil and lard). As Bacchelli crowed, 'there is no better flour for making bread than that evenly and gently ground by the turn of a wheel in the water'.[68]

## Palatable Po

Bread from Ferrara is just the start of the feast spread out along the pastoral Po. To the west, also in the region of Emilia-Romagna (province of Parma), the riverine villages between Busseto and Boretto are connected by one of Italy's many routes that promote regional gastronomic tourism (*Le Strade dei vini e dei sapori*). The sign for *La Strada del Cula - tello di Zibello* features a pear-shaped haunch of cured ham known as *Culatello*, a round of Parmesan (*Parmigiano Reggiano*), and a bottle of *Fortana del Taro*. The backdrop is a stretch of bright blue river, fringed by a beach and strip of riparian woodland, on which floats a traditional wooden boat (*pirogue*), which, like the Danube's *Ulmer Schachtel*, is flat-bottomed to cope with low water and can be paddled or punted.[69]

*Parmigiano Reggiano* – awarded the EU's Protected Designation of Origin (PDO; *Denominazione di Origine Protetta* [DOP]) status in 1996 – needs no introduction.[70] *Fortana del Taro* is a light, gently sparkling (*frizzante*) wine, the valley's oldest variety. A variation on the Po Valley's

Sign for *Le Strade dei Vini e dei Sapori*
(*La Strada del Culatello di Zibello*),
Zibello, April 2009.

characteristic pale red Lambrusco, a wine designed to be consumed young
(the spring after harvest) – and carrying the protected status of *Indicazione
Geografica Tipica* (IGT) – it traditionally accompanies *Culatello di Zibello*.
Breed of pig, production method and fluvial terroir combine to yield this
sweeter, more delicate version of *prosciutto di Parma* (*culo* is slang for
buttock, hence little buttock). The nearby Po generates a distinctive micro-
climate defined by high year-round humidity. Add the extremes of stifling
summer heat and extreme winter cold. Mix in the dense fogs that hang
over the river in autumn and winter. The result is the ideal environment
for aging the 'Lamborghini of cured ham'.[71] Dampness rising off the river
floats on the breeze to cellars that, according to the regulations attached to
DOP status (1996), must be located in one of eight villages hugging the
river.[72] (Zibello is one of them, another is Polesine Parmense, whose
name, loosely translated, means the village that the river has destroyed
many times.) Moist air circulation around the hams hung from the rafters
is regulated by nothing more complicated than windows – a far cry from
mass production's automated humidity and temperature controls.

Trips down the Po revolve around food rather than scenery. Topo -
graphic splendours such as the Danube's Wachau and Iron Gate – and
picturesque waterlands like the Spreewald – are singularly absent. Frye,

who boarded a Venice-bound barge at Pontelagoscuro, commented on the wholesale absence of scenic enticement. The lower river was wide and the land beyond utterly flat. There was literally nothing to see, with houses and farms prudently located at a remove.[73] Locals, however, were more attuned to the riverscape's more subtle landscape values, which, allied to the delectable cuisine the river shaped, offered sublime compensation for the lack of overt visual charm. In the mid-1950s, Mario Soldati, a 50-year-old novelist and filmmaker from Turin, took a gastronomical tour from source to mouth. Soldati's sensitivity to landscape as an authentic rather than stylized entity had impressed the future director of *Riso amaro*. De Santis praised Soldati's 1941 screen adaptation of Antonio Fogazzaro's novel, *Piccolo mondo antico* (1895) in which landscape (in this instance, the pre-alpine lakes of Lombardy) was 'neither rarified nor picturesque, but . . . corresponded to the humanity of the characters either as an emotive element or as a clue to their feelings'.[74]

In 1954, Soldati had directed *La Donna del fiume* ('The Woman of the River'), set on the lower Po, replete with mudbanks, reeds, flat lagoon waters, the reed cutter's equally flat wooden boat (*battana*) and the huts (*casoni*) of the fishermen who caught eels in the lagoons in the autumn. The story pivots on the romantic entanglements of Nives Mongolini, a young peasant woman (played by Sophia Loren) who works in an eel-canning factory. Made pregnant by a trawlerman, she leaves the delta, but returns two years later and scythes reeds in muddy Wellington boots and Mangano-style hotpants to support her son.

The film's co-director, Florestano Vancini (from Ferrara), recalled that Soldati, 'who was only familiar with the Turin Po, basically a city river, really had to immerse himself into the rural, naturalistic Po valley'.[75] Regardless of how much effort was actually required on Soldati's part, his acute sensitivity to the correspondence between people and place suffused the series based on his gastronomical trip that ran on the RAI television channel between December 1957 and March 1958. Each of the twelve half-hour weekly episodes of *Viaggio lungo la valle del Po alla ricerca dei cibi genuini* ('A Journey through the Po Valley in Search of Real Food') was devoted to a different place on the river. A forefather of the Slow Food movement founded in 1986, Soldati went in search of disappearing dishes such as Vercelli's signature meal, *la panissa* (rice with beans and sausage in broth). He was equally interested in recording time-honoured food production methods and traditional fluvial communities and ecologies. Soldati's bittersweet series revealed the intimacy between food, people and place on the Po at the dawn of the chemicalized agro-industry that Heidegger lambasted.

On the 50th anniversary in the autumn of 2007, a group of students and scientists reprised Soldati's tour. *Alla ricerca del Grande Fiume* ('In Search of the Great River') was the brainchild of Carlo Petrini, founder of Slow Food and president of Slow Food International. One hundred and eighty students from the University of Gastronomic Sciences, near Bra, in the Piedmontese region of Cuneo (within the Po watershed) were involved in the project, which took the form of a 25-day examination of the river's condition and culture.[76] The undertaking bore some resemblance to the Greek Orthodox Patriarch's voyaging symposium down the Danube in 1999. Travelling by boat and bicycle (on riverside paths), the expedition conducted a comprehensive health check. Participants examined water, sediment, flora, fauna and morphology and collected daily ecotoxological data. The team also assessed the valley's cultural, social and economic condition. Assisted by a film crew, they interviewed local farmworkers, fishermen and scientists, recording their equivocal interactions with a river that nurtures and threatens. Field trips included a farm raising *radiccio di chioggia* (red chicory), which thrives on sandy delta soil (PGI status since 2008).[77] Invited to sum up the Po in three words, one student replied: 'big,' 'long' and 'dear'.

This river trip was not the only commemorative event. Giuseppe Bertolucci – brother of Bernardo, whose 1976 film *Novecento* ('1900') showcased the Po valley's representative riverscape of canalized watercourses, irrigation ditches and *argini*, visually complemented by severe lines of poplars – directed a documentary in 2009 to mark the 50th anni - versary of Soldati's series. In *Un paese chiamato Po* ('A Land Called the Po'), Bertolucci explained that a journey down the Po is also a journey through Italian cinema, the river having attracted Antonioni, Pupi Avati (whose films were inspired by the legends of the delta), Federico Fellini and Ermanno Olmi. Presented and narrated by Edmondo Berselli, the five-episode documentary delved into the river's economic, political, cultural and social landscapes, visiting its cities and villages, and its rural and industrial zones. Beginning at the beginning in Monte Viso, the episodes moved down to Turin, and on to Pavia, Cremona and Piacenza. Next, it focused on Busetto and Brescello, the territory of Giovanni Guareschi's river-infused short stories, followed by Ferrara and its vicinity, which is just as indelibly associated with Antonioni and Olmi. The final episode came to rest in the delta and the coastal lagoons of Comacchio. Seeking out the *genius loci*, the documentary featured a string of river people. Interviewees over the age of sixty regularly recalled that when they were children they swam in the Po and drank straight from the river.

## Pictured Po

The first director to feel the pull of the river that flowed through his home-town of Ferrara was Antonioni, for whom the relationship between people and river was visceral and almost magical:

> It is not ridiculous to say that the people of the Po Valley are in love with the Po. In fact, the river is surrounded by a halo of instinctive attraction . . . and, to a certain extent, the Po can be regarded as the despot of its valley. The people of the valley 'feel' the Po. How this feeling comes to reification, we do not know. We only know that it is 'in the air' and is felt as a subtle bewitchment.

Though 'a long time ago, the river used to look more serenely romantic: a thick vegetation, numerous fishermen's cabins, floating mills . . . and bridges made of barges', the close identification between river and people was not predicated on a primordial river of static and timeless quality: 'Neither for men nor for things did the years pass in vain.' Change, specifi-cally the dynamic forces of industrialization and modernity, was in the nature of things: 'and for the river too came the time to awaken.' The river people accepted this as necessary progress: 'Yet, in the midst of this destruction of their old world, the population had no regrets.'[78] Nor does the river bear any resentment; far from fading into the background, it emerges from the background to become a full and active participant in bustling, technologically revolutionized modern life.

Antonioni had been impressed by *The River* (1938), American film-maker Pare Lorentz's acclaimed short documentary about the Missis-sippi.[79] Yet he distanced himself from what he saw as 'the trite formulas of "what was, is what is" and "the eternal river"'. He wanted to capture the spirit of place while celebrating progress: 'I would like a film with the Po as the central character, in which the spirit of the river would provide the interest of the film; that is to say, a film which is the sum total of its moral and psychological elements, rather than a heap of its folkloric, exterior, decorative elements.'[80] The river regulates the social, economic, gastro-nomic and cultural conditions of human life in its basin – and this protag-onism and authenticity of spirit is not eroded by the arrival of modernity or its impact on the river.

*Gente del Po*, the neo-realistic documentary expression of Antonioni's views, was mostly shot in the delta in the winter of 1942–3. The ten-minute film eventually released in 1947 depicts disjointed fragments of working river life and uncoordinated, banal glimpses of human stories, connected by the thread of a river of labour.[81] The opening scene shows a bustling flour mill, where workers load sacks onto steam barges. Women cook on board the barges, wash clothes in the river, and beat carpets hang-ing from the windows of riverbank houses. A young couple meets on the bank. Boats pass through locks. A cyclist rides up and over a levee. Reeds flutter, a storm approaches, waves wash in at the river's mouth. And we are left gazing out to sea.

The Po is grey and (according to the voice-over) 'flat as asphalt'.[82] It appears to be just there, a dreary, barely moving, unblinking, uninvolved presence. Seymour Benjamin Chatman feels that the river's 'indifference to human fate is signalled by its juxtaposition with human situations of different emotional charge'; for him, it is the 'same old river'.[83] Yet to ask whether the river is really the protagonist that Antonioni intended, or if *Gente del Po* is more about the river's people is redundant. That the river has shaped its people is the film's unspoken yet incontrovertible message.

The river that features in Luchino Visconti's first film, *Ossessione* ('Obsession', 1943), shot across the river from where Antonioni was working on *Gente del Po,* is the same river in more than just in a technical sense. The long opening shot features the dusty, blindingly white road from Ferrara to Polesella that parallels the dreary river. Rural California is the setting for *The Postman Always Rings Twice* (1934), James M. Cain's crime novel about the volatile relationship between a drifter and a woman with an older husband, on which *Ossessione* is based; and the subsequent (authorized) US screen version (1946) was filmed in coastal southern California. But the environmental reference point for the unauthorized Italian film version of the story appears to be the American Great Plains rather than California (or the Mississippi).[84] The horizons are wide, the views uninterrupted, the river broad and placid; this is big sky country.[85]

The Po delta (Porto Tolle) and Adriatic shores, locale for the last scenes, were also the setting for the final episode of Roberto Rossellini's *Paisà* ('Paisan', 1946), which, through six stories set in six places, collectively depicts the American liberation of Italy in 1943–4. Rossellini originally intended an alpine setting for the final episode. However, prompted by fond childhood memories of his aunt's estate in the delta, he switched the location. In the opening scene, a partisan killed by a German gunboat crew floats toward the camera and is fished out of the river; in the closing scene, dead partisans are tossed into the river (a scene that was actually filmed on the Tiber, near Fiumicino). In Wagstaff's reading, the episode centres on the contest for 'survival in an extreme and hostile environment', and demonstrates the deployment of place as 'antagonist' that 'dwarfs' the 'fragile human presence with its "sublime monotony"'.[86]

Yet there is more affinity between people and place than this approach to a landscape of alienation suggests. This impression of the Po as a forlorn environment that supplies a fitting backdrop to human dejection, a kindred spirit rather than an antagonist, is suggested by *Il Grido* ('The Shout'). Antonioni's plaintive film (1957) narrates the trials of Aldo, an itinerant from the Polesine who has worked in a sugar beet refinery.[87] Again, the Po's contribution does not reside in beauty conventionally defined: the defining features are mud, fog, flatlands and leafless poplars that fringe the ribbon-like roads and pierce the blank sky. This is bleakness taken to new heights. Antonioni returned to the delta for his first colour film, *Il Deserto rosso* ('Red Desert', 1964).[88] Once more, it demonstrates his deep infatuation with the Po region, even if the river features as a grim, lifeless, inauspicious grey slick thoroughly in tune with the colour-drained, damp and wintry, smoke-belching industrial landscape hosted by the foggy delta region and the enormous, recently constructed petrochemical complex on the Candiano Canal, on Ravenna's northern fringe. Capturing the desired environmental ambience was not easy, however. Assistant director Flavio Niccolini expressed his frustration with the lack of meteorological cooperation during filming. His diary entry for 15 October 1963 read: 'Weather: Sunny. And we need to shoot under clouds, fog, gray.' And on 11 November, increasingly impatient, he commented sardonically that 'the majority of difficulties with this *Red Desert* are sun-related'.[89]

A much sunnier river courses through the veins of one of Italy's most popular twentieth-century writers, Giovanni Guareschi. Geographically, his stories (many of them based on his maternal grandmother's tales of the river people) are located in *Val Padana*, somewhere east of Piacenza, where, for Guareschi (born near Busseto, the birthplace of Verdi), the Po proper began.[90] Politically, these stories were set between December 1946

and December 1947, when many Po valley communities elected communists to public office. The incessant feuding, in an unnamed river village,
between the parish priest, Don Camillo, and his arch-rival, Peponne, the
local communist mayor, was the mainstay of almost 350 hugely successful
short stories Guareschi published in the late 1940s and '50s.[91]

The ever-present river sometimes assumed a central role in the alterca-
tions between priest and politician. The Po has traditionally served its
landlocked residents – including priests, if we are to believe Guareschi – as
a surrogate sea (*il nostro mare*). One particularly insufferable August afternoon ('On the River Bank'), Don Camillo decides that it is no mortal sin
for a man of the cloth to bathe in 'the great river' that lies 'motionless and
silent . . . not so much a river as a cemetery of dead waters'. With the heat
rising off the fields of hemp and buckwheat, he strips down to his under-
garments in a secluded spot and flings himself into the motionless waters.
Then, though it is siesta-time and the world seems deserted, the clothes he
carefully stashed in a thicket of acacias are pinched as part of a politically
motivated prank. To prevent himself becoming the laughing stock of the
communist crowd that has gathered at the top of the bank, he returns to
the river and takes refuge among the reeds on a mid-river islet.[92]

In the preface to the first collection (1948) of *Don Camillo* stories,
Guareschi described the scene of the two big men's hilarious skirmishes as
'almost any village on that stretch of plain'. But though the settlement itself
was indistinct, the place was unmistakable: 'In the Little World between
the river and the mountains, many things can happen that cannot happen
anywhere else. Here, the deep, eternal breathing of the river freshens the
air, for both the living and the dead, and even the dogs, have souls.'[93]
Whether communists had souls was another matter (Guareschi was
staunchly anti-communist). Yet seemingly irreconcilable ideological and
political differences between priest and communist mask a profound if
grudging mutual affection.

In the same way, the people of the Po were locked in an intimate
relationship with the river based on a complex and contradictory mix
of affection, appreciation, respect, indignation and fear. One of the most
respectful locals was Guareschi, for whom the Po was Italy's only 'respectable' river – by which he did not mean a river that could hold its head up
high in international company but a river that traverses a plain ('water was
created to stay horizontal and only when it is perfectly horizontal does it
preserve its natural dignity'). He characterized it as a quiet river with a flat
surface; a soothing place conducive to tranquil contemplation. His chosen

counterpoint was the brash and agitated Niagara with its ostentatious falls – a circus freak of a river that resembled a performer walking on his hands.[94] 'I want to go down', he reflected, 'and sit as I always do on the bank of the great river and chew a stalk of grass and think "it is better here on the river bank".[95]

Though the river bank and the village in the stories is unnamed, a small town at the heart of Guareschi's river country soon became the place most closely associated with them. In the summer of 1951, searching for a location exuding the right atmosphere, the Italian film producer, French director and Guareschi happened on Brescello, which provided the main set for the five film adaptations produced between 1951 and 1965.[96] The many staunch communists among Brescello's 2,000 residents were not amused at the prospect of becoming a film set for the tales of such an adamant anti-communist. But they eventually succumbed to Guareschi's charm offensive and supplied most of the extras. Guareschi, in turn, was annoyed that the local communists enjoyed the films so much.[97] River scenes formed the backdrop to the opening credits. The camera moved slowly up the river, across the fields, and over the town, descending into the central piazza.

In this small corner of the world, Guareschi reflected, the 'landscape never changes . . . the climate is always the same'.[98] Yet this was only partly true. The Po may not have been a show-off like Niagara. But it did not lack eye-catching dynamism. *Alluvioni* were a constant threat (worsened by the denudation of woodland in the catchment).[99] The first film adaptation (*Little World*) was released early in 1952, shortly after the Po burst its banks in one of the worst floods on record (November 1951). The opening scene is based on the story called 'The Procession' (*Il Processione*), whose starting point is the ancient tradition of propitiation: rivers that river people depend on but which also threaten their security and livelihoods need to be rendered well disposed. The annual blessing of the Po ('in order that it should refrain from excesses and behave decently') entails removing the crucifix from above the altar and carrying it down to the bankside. The local communists boycott the time-honoured *benedizione delle fiume* because Don Camillo bars them from bringing along their own sacred object, the red flag (*Bandiera rossa*). Faced with a boycott and the threat of disruption (not to mention the timidity of his flock, who desert en masse), a defiant Don Camillo sets off for the river alone bearing the cross, after the impatient Lord inquires: 'Are we going now? . . . The river must be looking beautiful in this sunshine and I shall really enjoy seeing it.'

On reaching the bank, the priest is surrounded by the communist citizenry who, having gone through the motions of mounting a roadblock, eventually join him (minus their flag and in suitably reverential mood). Don Camillo then delivers a sharp rebuke. He tells them that, if the few decent homes left in the godless village could float like Noah's ark, he would entreat the Lord to make the river overflow its banks and drown the filthy, communist-infested place. Since this cannot be arranged, Don Camillo prays that He delivers them from the evils of floods and showers prosperity on the local countryside.[100]

But even the Lord cannot always protect the villagers (whether righteous or unrighteous) from floods. The second collection of stories, *Don Camillo and the Prodigal Son* (1953), concludes with various tall tales of high water.[101] In 'When the Rains Came', the 'mighty Po', swollen with days and nights of relentless rain, pushes harder and harder against the embankment. The villagers are particularly concerned about the vulnerability of a dyke bombed in the war which had only recently been fixed and not had time to bed down. Old-timers associate the impending trouble with Don Camillo's absence; when the irascible and pugnacious priest was rusticated to a remote mountain village – a snowy alpine exile he detests – he took with him the altar crucifix that protects the villagers against the river's wrath. When the priest returns, to demonstrate his faith in the Lord and his confidence in the engineers who inspected the dodgy dyke, and to reassure the fearful villagers that it will hold, he goes down and sits on it (where the mayor joins his vigil).[102]

The second film, *Il Ritorno di Don Camillo* ('Return of Don Camillo', 1953) also culminates in an almighty springtime flood. The action begins when Peppone coerces a conservative vintner into donating a patch of vineyard to the village, ostensibly to build a protective dam. The mayor's real objective, though, is to redistribute the land to the local peasantry. The bishop agrees to restore the desperately homesick Don Camillo to his river people only because Peppone needs him to settle the dispute with the landowner. When the village is swamped after days of incessant rain, the entire population is evacuated to the main embankment. While they are perched here in safety on a Sunday morning, surrounded by the worldly goods they have salvaged, the doughty priest, who stands waist-deep in the water that fills his church, tolls the bell at 10 a.m. and then conducts Mass in front of an absent congregation (a sequence based on the stories 'The Bell' and 'Everyone at His Post'). Don Camillo offers the consoling reminder that this is not the first time the river has invaded their homes, and that, as before, the bellicose waters will eventually calm down and 'return to their rightful place'. Meanwhile, the sun will reappear, the work of reconstruction begin afresh, and life return to normal.[103] In the film, spiritual leader and communist chief cooperate to save the place and people they both love. Guareschi's flood stories published in 1953 took their cue from the inundation of November/December 1951, a flood of biblical proportions, after which devoted readers from other countries mailed him parcels containing blankets and clothing 'For the people of Don Camillo and Peppone'.[104]

## Political Po

In 'The Procession' – which also provides the opening sequence of the most recent film adaptation (1983), shot in Pomponesco, a village across the river from Brescello – Don Camillo objected to the politicization of a religious event. But in the real world, the most striking effort to appropriate the river's spirit for secular ends has been made by a political force at the other end of the spectrum to Peppone's communists: the Northern League (*Lega Nord*). For much of its history, the Po has divided rather than united. In Roman times, *Val Padana* corresponded to Cisalpine Gaul, which the river subdivided into Cispadane Gaul (South of the Po) and Transpadane Gaul (North of the Po). In the nineteenth century, prior to unification, the Po separated the papal states from the Austro-Hungarian empire and Venetian republic to the north. Most recently, the Po and its valley generate the boundaries between the aspirational secessionist nation of Padania and the rest of Italy.

Since its establishment in 1991, *Lega Nord* has tried to erect a collective political and cultural group identity on a firm environmental base. Yet the precise territorial parameters of this particular ethnoscape remain elusive.[105] Conceptions of Padania both narrow and expansive have been promulgated. The original and stricter conception is firmly bioregional. Corresponding exactly to Padania's Latin meaning – the Po Valley, *la pianura padana*[106] – its envisaged territory resurrects Cisalpine Gaul. However, the broader (and vaguer) construction stretches as far south as Florence – encroaching on the watershed of the Arno. Umberto Bossi, the Northern League's founder and first leader (1992–2012), is a strict constructionist (though not himself a son of the Po). Overturning Mazzini, Bossi disassociates the river from Italy by referring to 1,100 years of 'autonomous history of the Po Valley area'. Devoid of historical-cultural authenticity, this attempt to naturalize and territorialize the fictive entity of Padania provides not just a spectacular example of political misappropriation. It also supplies a particularly intriguing example of the unwitting instrumentality of nature.

The mythological Po is back with a vengeance as *Lega Nord* seeks to supplant universalized ancient myth with its own rigidly regionalist lore. The League did not embark on a procession to the river in the manner of the devout believers of Don Camillo country. Nonethelesss, they indulged in a *benedizione delle fiume* of their own. A three-day procession ('Independence March') down the Po ended with a declaration of Padanian independence in Venice on 15 September 1996.[107] The procession began on 13 September, when Bossi undertook a pilgrimage to the source to mark the birth of his new nation. (A small black granite slab inscribed with the date and 'Padania-Po' commemorates the event, an act of fluvio-jingoism repeated annually.) As he filled a flask made of Murano glass with chilly alpine water, Bossi reminded the party faithful and assembled press corps that 'water is the source of all things, of life, of Padania'.[108] This fluvial essence of Padania played an integral part in the imminent birth of a nation. The sacred water was carried downstream like an ampulla (an ancient Roman vessel for transporting sacred substances), by boat, hot-air balloon, car, helicopter and catamaran. The procession's purpose was to bond northern Italians together with the river's powerful, if liquid glue.[109] Shortly before Bossi's declaration of independence, a young girl poured the water from the Po's source into the Venetian lagoon.[110]

These liquid rituals mimicking the hydrological cycle demonstrate how a separatist movement, as a basic precondition of a shared sense of nationhood, strives to establish a nation as a 'psycho-geographic fact'.[111] The procession's surreal quality attracted a high degree of coverage in the British press, especially in Scotland, one reporter describing Bossi's journey down the Po as 'quasi-mystical'.[112] Not all advocates of greater autonomy for northern Italy were comfortable, however, with the procession's reverence for the river and its 'blood and soil' temper (not to mention the sinister echoes of Mussolini's 'March on Rome' of 1922). Irene Pivetti, expelled from the League the day before Bossi's pilgrimage to the source for criticizing his leadership and the politics of secession, commented that 'this mystical worship of the God Po is offensive to me as a Catholic' (though this had not posed a problem for Don Camillo).[113] For a member of the Young Padanian Movement (*Movimento Giovani Padani*), the youth wing of *Lega Nord* (who lived far from the river, in Bergamo, but within its catchment), independence meant 'being free to love our land with its mountains, its rivers, with its immense Plain and its fog! It means being moved by the sight of the Mighty River Po.'[114]

The Declaration of Independence and Sovereignty of Padania, signed on the river's 'sacred shores', was firmly rooted in the basin's fertile soil and fecund water (and, it could be argued, its nebulous quality was in keeping with the Po's fabled *nebbia*). Padania was first and foremost a 'natural' community:

> We, the Peoples of Padania, gathered together along the great river Po from Emilia and Friuli, from Liguria, Lombardia, and the Marche, from Piemonte, Romagna, and Sudtirol-Alto Adige, from Toscana, Trentino, and Umbria, from Valle d'Aosta, the Veneto, and Venezia Giulia, united today, affirm and declare . . . Since time immemorial, we live, we build, we work, we protect, we love these lands handed down to us by our forebears, bathed and quenched by the waters of our great rivers . . . These lands are united by the ties which run as deep as the enduring cycles of the seasons revolving about them, as strong as the spirit of freedom of the Peoples that inhabit them.[115]

The Po's own role in this arch example of the political theatre of the eco-absurd was unclear. According to a British journalist, though 'truly a mighty river' (unlike the much less physically impressive Thames, Seine or Tiber), the Po was an innocent bystander to the farce it was hosting (and inadvertently inspiring).[116] We cannot fathom what the river thinks about Padania any more than Hölderlin could figure out what the Ister knew and wanted. But it was not entirely compliant. Bossi's plan to arrive at Cremona by boat was cancelled, ostensibly due to low water levels.[117]

The Northern League's passionate cooptation of the Po clearly shows, though, that despite the spate of references to the Po as the mighty river over the past half-century, it has not acquired a secure position within the territorialized ethnoscape of Italian national consciousness comparable to that occupied by the Thames or Rhine within their English and German counterparts. It 'seems as if [the Po] had never existed for the Italians', mused Luciano Ghelfi. The reason for this failure to beome the locus of group identity, he suspected, is that the Po has never ceased to threaten those who live in its valley.[118]

## Perilous Po

Gianni Brera, the journalist who described himself as a legitimate son of the Po and coined the term Padania in the 1960s, summed up the mixture of emotions with which Italians approach their Old Man River in a memorable phrase: 'this old drunken and malicious father'.[119] Generations of wary, fearful children have been unable to curb their elderly father's drinking habits and nasty streak. Since the 1600s, engineers have thought they knew what to do. They literally straightened Old Man River to get him back on the straight and narrow. According to their calculations, increasing the channel's slope and speed by smoothing out the bends would reduce discharge and therefore the risk of overflow. Yet it often transpired that the cure was worse than the disease.

Concentrating a river's flow makes it behave, in Erla Zwingle's arresting phrase, like a bobsleigh run.[120] When confinement within levees accompanies channelization, the danger of spillage is further heightened by shrunken floodplain storage capacity. Even when canalization eases the threat on an upper river, this transfers vulnerability to the lower reaches, where, in the case of the Po, it is already acutest. When heavy flows from steeply inclined Alpine and Apennine tributaries coincide in the middle Po, the lower Po is exposed to perfect flood conditions.[121] Moreover, as the *argini* that divorce the river from its floodplain trap the silt, the bed rises. Constrained by rising *argini* (the standard solution, from lower Po to lower Mississippi, is to build them up ever higher), the Po flows well above its floodplain (whose elevation has not even remained stationary, since reclaimed lands subside). In the 1870s, Ramsay recorded, 'the full-flooded river often runs higher than the tops of the houses'.[122] Today, the embankment at Guarda Ferrarese, for instance, is ten metres higher than the surrounding farmland (sinkage, aggravated by groundwater extraction, also potentially compromises the embankment's structural stability). From Ferrara onwards, the Po is a 'perched river' with an inoperative flood plain.[123]

Rushed along to the sea instead of being deposited en route, the heavy silt load fuelled a process of delta expansion that lasted well into the twentieth century. In the Middle Ages, Ravenna was a port with an important naval facility at Classe (Classis). By the late 1890s, Classe was marooned eight kilometres inland.[124] Two thousand years ago, Adria was on the coast; by 1300, it was stranded nine kilometres inland (22 kilometres by the 1870s). Between the thirteenth and seventeenth centuries, the delta aggrandized at an average annual rate of 30 metres; from 1600 to 1800, yearly growth was over 70 metres.[125] Visiting the 'perfect plain' around Ferrara in May 1816, Frye observed that the valley was 'liable to the most dreadful inundations', with flocks, herds and farmhouses – 'and sometimes whole villages' – brushed away by the raging waters.[126] He quoted Po valley poet Ludovico Ariosto's description of the river in flood in his epic romance *Orlando Furioso* (1516):

> Even with that rage wherewith the stream that reigns,
> The king of rivers – when he breaks his mound,
> And makes himself a way through Mantuan plains –
> The greasy furrows and glad harvests, round,
> And, with the sheepcotes, flock, and dogs and swains
> Bears off, in his o'erwhelming waters drowned;
> Over the elm's high top the fishes glide,
> Where fowls erewhile their nimble pinions plied.[127]

The prospect of fish swimming where fowl flew is evoked in a semi-autobiographical novel that includes a detailed account of early-twentieth-century agricultural life on a farm (Ronco) close to the river between Pavia and Cremona. *La Cascina sul Po* (1920) by Mario Borsa features a boy who grew up along the Po, but leaves for Milan and then London. Eventually, he returns, 35 years later, with his son, after service in the First World War.[128] The embankment divides two starkly contrasting landscapes. On the one side, heath, marsh and pollarded willows stretch down to the river. On the other lies the cultivated plain, with its farms and fields of millet, maize, wheat, flax and rice split up by regular rows of squat, hulking mulberry trees. These fields are interspersed with plantations of poplar, alder, oak and elm. Once extracted from the river, water is converted from a hazardous substance into a benign commodity: 'busy night and day, bearing everywhere nourishment, life, and verdure, it was the great, good, untiring housekeeper'.[129]

At the book's heart is a blow-by-blow account of a late autumn flood. Water barrels down from swollen tributaries like the Ticino. The heads of poplar trees stick out of the water. The large rectangular vat (*navassa*) for treading grapes doubles as an emergency raft for cattle. And troops from the barracks of military engineers in Piacenza and Pavia finally come to the rescue.[130] The popular mind usually associates the breaching of flood defences (Borsa compares the sound to a cannonade) with the overtopping of an embankment. Yet Borsa's narrative highlights a sometimes greater danger. 'Not always', he points out, 'does the river assail and beat down its banks fairly. More often it takes them treacherously by surprise, seeping in below by invisible and unsuspected ways.' Notwithstanding the use of earth with maximum impermeability to build embankments, lengthy floods generate subsurface leakage that travels horizontally; an excessively saturated levee eventually collapses. The prospect of flooding pitted community against community. A village could save its own neck by puncturing the embankment downriver on the other side, sacrificing another community and its crops in the process (hence the proverb '*Vita mia, morte tua*').[131]

In the dining room of Borsa's Ronco farmhouse, plates nailed to the wall record the crest of the waters lapping within the room in 1807, 1812, 1839, 1848, 1857 (the highest level, at 1.6 metres), 1868 and 1872 (a very wet year across Europe). But the most devastating flood in the Po's recorded history afflicted the lower river in mid-November 1951. The cause of *la rotta biblica* was simple: prolonged heavy autumn rainfall throughout the basin. After 214 milimetres fell in a week, three stretches of levee were overtopped over a combined length of 736 metres.[132] The region worst affected was the Polesine – a strip of land 100 kilometres long and 19 kilometres wide that is sandwiched between the lower courses of the Po and Adige, corresponding to today's province of Rovigo. In places, the river rose ten metres, and water spread across two-thirds of the Polesine, whose Venetian name means 'destroyed by the Po'. The 'dreary sea', wrote an American reporter, was 'fetid with carcasses of drowned animals, floating debris and uprooted coffins from cemeteries'. (The *Life* article also reported an alleged communist smear campaign that US atomic tests were responsible for the excessive rainfall.) Nearly 6,000 houses and almost 9,000 farms were destroyed. At least a hundred *polesane* drowned and a further 170,000 were rendered homeless; an additional 150,000 were evacuated (American and British amphibian planes and helicopters, as well as rowboats, rescued 30,000 from the town of Adria). The casualties extended to 13,000 livestock and 100,000 tons of ruined wheat.[133]

The anguish and ordeal – which had a mythological precedent of sorts as the main square in Crespino (Piazza Fetonte) is dedicated to Phaeton, who, according to local legend, fell into the river hereabouts – was commemorated in a lengthy piece of free verse. Roberto Cervo witnessed the events that cemented the area's dubious distinction as northern Italy's most impoverished region. With a nod to *Riso amaro*, he entitled his poem

*Polesine amaro* (1953).[134] The flood of 1951 delivered a heavy blow from which the area never really recovered.[135]

For Cesare Zavattini, the pioneering *neorealismo* screenwriter from the lower river village of Luzzara, a flood was a tyrannical force. Inundation, he reflected with reference to the calamity of 1951, reduces people to 'slaves of nature' (*schiavi della natura*).[136] At his suggestion, the American photographer, Paul Strand, spent eight weeks in Luzzara in 1953 (divided between the spring and autumn), visually documenting its inhabitants (population: 10,000). Strand felt no less passionately about the imprint of place on people than the era's Italian film directors and scriptwriters, always seeking out the ancient alliance between people and place that imparted a special personality to each environment and moulded its human character.[137] And it was precisely the ordinariness and plainness of Luzzara and its Po Valley environs that appealed to him: 'a flat, flat land of fields and vines and little undistinguished villages, which have no traces

The flood in the Polesine ('Alluvione del Polesine'), November 1951.

Paul Strand, 'The River Po, Luzzara, Italy, 1953', photograph.

of historical or present charm or the faintest picturesqueness'.[138] Many of Strand's photographs depict people. But they are not just photographed in Luzzara. They appear out of town with water, poplars, boats and willow branches (*fascine*) cut to reinforce embankments. Nor is the river ever free of human imprint. As Zavattini observed, even in a picture without people (such as 'The River Po, Luzzara, Italy, 1953'), 'the landscape itself breathes the evidence of human effort – the boats lined up in the foreground two by two'.[139] What Zavattini tended to overlook, though, in his voluminous writings on the Po and *il Gente del Po* was the degree to which humans were complicit in their own enslavement to the brute force of watery nature through their very efforts to emancipate themselves.[140]

## Poisoned Po

As well as reflecting the input of human labour in Zavattini's terms, the river exhales the less endearing evidence of human endeavour in the heavy burden of contaminants it carries. In Casa dei Pontieri, the Museum of the Pontoneers, near Boretto, hangs a photograph of a boy swimming in the river in 1950. The swimmer is the museum's founder, Romana Gialdini, son of the Po's last master pontoon bridge builder.[141] It is doubtful whether river people would want to bathe or swim in the Po and its associated waterways today, as they were accustomed to do in the 1940s (as reflected on screen by *le mondine* and in fiction by Don Camillo).[142] Swimmers were still a common sight at urban river beaches such as Ponticello, Cremona, in the 1970s. But bathing has been prohibited along the entire Po since the early 1990s.[143] The water may be pure where *Lega Nord* draws its inspiration (unlike the Danube at Donaueschingen). But a half-way point report scientists released (October 2007) on the trip down the Po to commemorate Soldati's journey soberingly detected contamination just 50 kilometres from the source.[144] And once the Po entered Lombardy, its health went downhill as rapidly as the river's gradient.

The river has paid a heavy price for supporting Italy's urban-industrial heartland. *Val Padana* houses 27 per cent of the nation's population, provides 46 per cent of its jobs, contains 37 per cent of industrial capacity and consumes 48 per cent of total electrical energy.[145] More than half the sum total of pollutants derive from industrial production and domestic effluents contribute a further 15 per cent.[146] When factories shut down for a few weeks during the August holiday season, water quality improves noticeably.[147] Air standards also benefit from the temporary summer respite. One of Europe's hottest air pollution hotspots, the valley's haze is often visible from outer space.[148] A picture taken by an astronaut from NASA's Johnson Space Center in September 2006, looking southwest at a tilted angle, depicted northern and central Italy with the Adriatic in the foreground and the Mediterranean islands of Corsica and Sardinia in the distance. Skies were clear over the Adriatic, the Alps and parts of central Italy; light white clouds obscured much of the Mediterranean. Yet over the Po Valley hung a thick pall of smog, trapped by stagnant air and effectively contained by high atmospheric pressure in the mountains enveloping it on three sides.

The agribusiness that occupies 3 million hectares of the valley reduces air and water quality too. The tremendous quantities of dung that 3.5 million pigs and more than 3 million cows (over half Italy's total) generate contribute a third of the river's total pollutants. Between 1968 and 1980, the Po's load of phosphorus and nitrogen doubled. Nutrients like these (which also contain high concentrations of pharmaceutical residues such as veterinary antibiotics[149]) inflame eutrophication, encouraging the expanding biomass of the lotus plant. As well as choking out native aquatic flora,

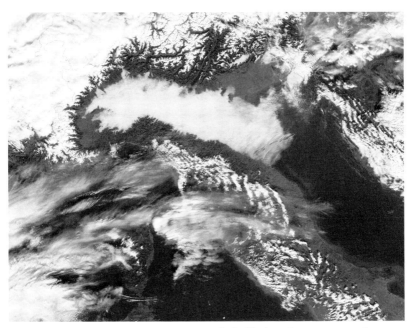

This NASA image taken on 4 January 2003 reveals the blanket of smog covering the Po Valley.

this invasive non-native hampers water flow. Since the Po contributes roughly half the total input of freshwater to the shallow and confined northern Adriatic, its own water quality has enormous implications for the Adriatic's. Stimulated by the river's heavy nutrient load, algae has proliferated near some of Italy's busiest coastal resorts, coating beaches with slime (and depriving fish of oxygen).[150] Though this tourist horror story was picked up internationally, the biggest splash made by the polluted Po was rather more bizarre. The world's media reported research findings in 2005 that the river carried high levels of a cocaine residue contained in the user's urine (benzoylecgonine, a cocaine metabolite) – the first evidence of an illicit drug's presence in a major river.[151]

Not all contaminants are human derived. Saltwater ingress is a centuries-old problem, triggered by strong southeasterly winds that hurl the Adriatic upriver. Yet human activity intensifies salinization. Drilling for methane in the delta between the 1930s and '60s lowered the water table, opening the floodgates to seawater, which wrecked rice paddies. Saltwater's depredations have also worsened with the delta's retreat since the 1940s. During the eighteenth and nineteenth centuries, the delta accreted steadily, peaking in the 1930s and 1940s. Since then, retreat has replaced progradation as the construction of dams and barriers and river-bed excavation for sand and gravel has reduced the silt load.[152] Over-extraction of freshwater and rising sea levels brought by climate change aggravate salt wedge intrusion. Tides now regularly penetrate 20 kilometres upriver, compared to just two kilometres in 1960, reducing the availability of water to irrigate increasingly saline delta farmlands.[153]

On the riverbank, little remains of the original riparian forest of ash, white willow, black alder, white poplar, black (Lombardy) poplar and oak.[154] Ninety per cent of the floodplain is planted with rice, cereals, grass, fruit trees and, not least, plantations of poplar harvested for cellulose.[155] The plantation staple, *Populus euroamericanus*, a fast-growing hybrid, was specially developed for the Po Valley in the eighteenth century and is harvested in eight-year cycles.[156] Unlike native trees with their extensive root systems, they offer little resistance to surging floodwaters, which rip them out and wedge them against bridges in snarled log jams.

This consciousness of an ecologically diminished river informed a Bernardo Bertolucci film in the 1960s. In a BBC interview of 2003, he explained how he turned to the river time and again, getting wrapped up in the mystique of his native bio-region, which he had come to think of as an epic waterscape of Mississippian proportions.[157] Toward the end of *Prima della rivoluzione* (*Before the Revolution*, 1964), mostly filmed in and around Bertolucci's hometown of Parma, the main characters, Gina and Fabrizio, go down to the river. On the shore of a pond (*stagnio*), they meet a friend of Gina's. Puck is a country gentleman in a tweed jacket and Wellington boots whose land is about to be repossessed by the bank that now owns it. Out of the blue, he delivers a startling, proto-ecological lament for a dying river, which Bilge Ebri describes as a 'lushly scored ode to the environment'.[158] Facing the river, which is partly obscured by poplars, but whose presence 'you can always feel', Puck bids a Chekhovian farewell to the passing of the old order and the river that makes him who he is. As a man punts through the mist in a traditional boat, Puck announces the end of life as he, the boatman and the river know it. There will be no more fishing for perch and carp. No more ducks and flocks of wild geese will fly overhead. There will be no more call for his fowling piece. The boatman might as well sink his pirogue. In their place will come men with noisy machines and excavators (an intrusive force conjured up, somewhat oddly, by footage of flood conditions, the river-side trees standing in the water like pencils). The time has come to say good-bye to the river and to learn to forget the river. These are the sentiments of John Graves's *Goodbye to a River*, transposed from Texas to Emilia-Romagna.

Puck's requiem also informs the first of Ermanno Olmi's two films about the Po: *Lungo il fiume* ('Down the River', 1992). But the river portrayed in this 81-minute documentary (1992) for RAI television is far from one-dimensional. *Lungo il fiume* is an inclusive portrait of the Po in all seasons, moods and guises: from a mountain stream tumbling over boulders to a broad glassy expanse near the Adriatic; from foggy church towers to summer sunbathers on sandy river beaches; from logging scenes in poplar plantations, aerial spraying of orchards and derelict industrial sites to deer bounding through delta woodlands and long-legged birds pecking in the mud; from ruined village buildings to slick industrialized agriculture; and from wooden pirogues and the gentle dip of oars in the calm water to gargantuan modern barges that generate a churning wake. The opening scene depicts a teacher aboard an excursion boat lecturing a party of primary schoolchildren on how to treat the earth kindly. Footage of children snacking and the boat chugging briskly downriver are interspersed with images of foaming pollution.

If *Lungo il fiume* cracked the mould firmly established by *Gente del Po* by depicting the river in a much more benign, sometimes idyllic mode, then *Centochiodi* ('One Hundred Nails', 2007) breaks it completely. *Centochiodi*, the most recent film about the Po, and Olmi's final production, was shot during the spring and summer in and around the villages of Bagnolo San Vito, San Benedetto Po and San Giacomo Po in the province of Mantua.[159] The central human character is a malcontented professor of the philosophy of religion at the University of Bologna, who expresses his malaise by perpetrating a symbolic crucifixion: he nails a hundred precious theology books (incunabula) to the library floor. With strong echoes of Mark Twain's Huckleberry Finn – Olmi demonstrates that *Il Mississippi italiano* is not a throwaway soubriquet – *il professore* (Israeli actor Raz Degan) then lights out for the territory (as Huck would say). Having abandoned his BMW convertible (!) midway on a bridge, he fakes suicide by tossing his jacket and wallet off the bridge. *Il professore* then takes up residence in a dilapidated, overgrown riverside cottage (*baracca*) tucked beneath the embankment.[160] Local villagers (who affectionately call him Jesus Christ due to the strong physical resemblance) not only welcome (and quasi-deify) him but help rebuild the stone dwelling.

Though *il professore* does not build a raft and float down the peaceful Po, the river is the essential ingredient of his new, more earthly life, providing a place of escape (if not forever). His first encounter is with a placid river slipping past gracefully with the sheen of the evening sun on its surface. In other scenes, moonlight plays on the water and gaily lit river boats with dancing couples on deck slide by; children turn cartwheels on the river beach to which the villagers decamp on a hot afternoon; fishermen land enormous catfish; and villagers cut reeds from the shoreline to rethatch the cottage roof. Though it rains on occasion, it is mostly sunny.

Yet the film depicts the Po as a flawed and thoroughly contemporary river as well as a calm and timeless counterpoint to the city, modernity and denatured intellectualism. A tug pushes a huge container barge past the fugitive's cottage; a helicopter whirs overhead; deafening dirt bikers intrude on the serenity of the sandy beach; and a bulldozer scoops up its sand. Olmi leaves the viewer to speculate about the source of the Christ-like lapsed scholar's drinking water and he certainly never bathes in the river. But drinking straight from the Po is clearly not an option for those who wish to pursue the simple life on its banks. Not only is the water too contaminated for human consumption. The aquatic life the river does support consists increasingly of invasive non-native species, notably the European (Wels) catfish (*Silurus glanis*), which thrives in water conditions that indigenous fish cannot tolerate.[161]

The campaign to remediate the Po's degraded condition was launched in 1980, when *Amici del Po* (Friends of the Po) was established in Villa-franca, Piedmont. This grassroots organization, whose symbol is the vanished otter (*lontra*), is dedicated to the enjoyment of the river through water sports, the revival of traditional watercraft, and the pursuit of cultural and recreational activities.[162] *Amici del Po* promotes awareness of the river's ecological condition by getting local residents into kayaks, canoes, rafts and punts, and hosting parades with illuminated boats. The Friends launched an annual promotional campaign, '*un Po per tutti*', in 2000. In June 2002, this fluvial festival consisted of a hundred coordinated events: boat trips, regattas, cycle rides along the levees, exhibitions of traditional fishing boats and (of course) the serving up of venerable local dishes (*sapori tipici locali*) such as frogs fried in batter (*rane fritte*) and *torta di riso*.[163]

Italy's leading environmental organization, Legambiente, initiated a campaign in July 2005 to secure a better future for Italy's most valuable river. Underlying *Operazione Po* is support for a governing authority with basin-wide decision-making powers and an eco-compatible agriculture (*agricoltura eco-compatibile*).[164] At the official launch of the Soldati-inspired 'In Search of the Great River' project (5 May 2007), Italy's minister for the environment, Alfonso Pecoraro Scanio, hailed the Po as 'a national resource' and a 'precious river'. He reminded Italians that other nations' actions to resurrect their national rivers put Italy to shame: 'The English have cleaned up the Thames and the French have cleaned up the Loire.'[165] The ecological recovery of the Thames since the nadir of the 1950s has been remarkable. Still, the most notable British fluvial renaissance is that of the Mersey, a more truly industrial and momentous modern river than the so-called 'monarch of the British rivers' and 'King of Island Rivers'.[166]

FOUR

# *Mersey*

In *A Treatise, Concerning the Causes of the Magnificence and Greatness of Cities* (1606), Giovanni Botero, the Jesuit priest, thinker and diplomat, observed that 'forasmuch as the commodities and profits are such and so great which the water bringeth to advance the greatnesse of a Cittie, of consequent those citties must be the fairest and the richest that have the most store of navigable Rivers'. His examples of rivers that 'runne the longest course, especially through the richest and most merchantable Regions', were the Po, Scheldt, Loire, Seine, Danube and Rhine.[1]

Two and a half centuries later, in a book about Liverpool's rise to 'commercial greatness', Thomas Baines, the editor of the *Liverpool Times*, referred expansively to the role of rivers in creating great commercial cities and regions at their mouths: the Nile's contribution to Alexandria's eminence; the Rhône's gift to Marseilles; the Rhine's role as 'chief creator' of the mercantile riches of the Netherlands; the Venetian debt to the Po; Antwerp's reliance on the Scheldt and the Meuse; the way the Elbe had 'sustained' Hamburg; how the Thames was London's 'true creator', and, not least, the 'unparalleled advantages' that New Orleans derived from its location at the mouth of the Mississippi.[2]

Less than a century later, Lewis Mumford, the American historian of technology and cities, reemphasized that liquid capital underpins human achievement. With the exception of a handful of maritime societies reliant on the sea, he observed, 'all the great historic cultures . . . have thriven through the movement of men and institutions and inventions and goods along the natural highway of a great river'. His exemplary rivers were the Yellow River, Tigris, Nile, Euphrates, Rhine, Danube and Thames.[3]

## Mercantile and Musical Mersey

When Botero wrote his book about the greatness of cities, Liverpool was a fishing village of about a thousand inhabitants of no larger consequence than hundreds of other small communities across Britain. Not much had changed since the settlement was granted a royal charter to establish a borough in 1207; and little would change over the next few centuries.[4] But Mumford's neglect of the Mersey was surprising. When *Technics and Civilization* appeared in 1934, Liverpool was one of the world's greatest ports, a rank it had attained by combining the advantages of riverine and maritime cities; in fact, the Mersey struck more than one observer as being more like an arm of the sea than a river – not least because the quantity of water flowing in from the sea was vastly in excess of the volume flowing down into the tidal estuary 'from the country'. (Liverpool Town Hall [1754], whose ground floor functioned as the cotton exchange, features a sculpture with Neptune as god and protector of the Mersey.)[5]

Many of the world's greatest cities are estuarine, connected by a river to the outside world and their hinterland. Due to their volatile deltas, neither Danube nor Po host great port cities at their mouths: at the Danube's exit perches Sulina, whose population peaked somewhat short of 8,000 just before the First World War and which remains accessible only by boat. The Mersey, by contrast, has no delta to compromise its navigability or suitability for large-scale human settlement. Of my six rivers, in fact, it is the only one whose lower reaches support a great port city. San Pedro, the port of Los Angeles, sits near the mouth of the Los Angeles River, but would exist with or without its presence.

Alexandria would not have become great without the Nile. And Liverpool would not have become a world city without the Mersey. Baines acknowledged, though, that in physical terms, the Mersey was an 'insignificant stream'. And an earlier commentator noted that it was 'not distinguished for its beauty'.[6] Looking beyond mere size and aesthetics, local pride, since Baines in the 1850s, has accorded the Mersey a place in the 'premier league' of world rivers, comfortable in the company of the Nile, Amazon and Ganges.[7] Michael Heseltine, the UK government's Minister for Merseyside in 1981, hailed 'this huge majestic river flowing through this great British city . . . the river that had given life to that part of England', adding that 'Without it there would be no Liverpool'.[8] Nearly two centuries earlier, James Wallace had paid a similar tribute, hailing the river as 'the key of its commerce and the source of its wealth'.[9]

At 48 miles (70 from the origin of its main source stream), the Mersey is short, even by modest British standards. Baines, who euphorically announced the city's imminent global supremacy, noted that 'great numbers' of the tributaries of the Paraná and Uruguay, which became the river

Plate, were larger than the Mersey.[10] Yet among England's rivers, only the Thames, Severn, Trent, Humber and Great Ouse have larger watersheds.[11] Moreover, like the Po, it drains one of Europe's most densely populated and heavily industrialized regions: over five million people currently live within its 2,900 square mile catchment. For three centuries, this liquid 'highway of commercial expansion' provided the outlet for the products of the world's first industrial revolution, manufactured in wool, cotton and paper mills on tributaries such as the Bollin, Tame and Goyt.[12] In particular, the Mersey and its main tributary, the Irwell, which flows through the centre of Manchester, linked Britain's biggest manufacturing centre with its major port.

The establishment of technological mastery over the Mersey also bears comparison with the establishment of human dominion over other world-class rivers. Many great cities rely for their greatness on great rivers, yet great rivers do not automatically make great cities. The relationship between rivers, people and human affairs is dynamic and reciprocal. 'Rivers', explains Ron Freethy, 'are far too valuable in human affairs to be left alone'.[13] The river that once formed the frontier between the Anglo-Saxon kingdoms of Northumbria and Mercia (*Merse/Maere* means 'boundary') has been spanned over the centuries. Bridges, tunnels, overhead viaducts carrying canals and railways, and an underwater aqueduct that delivers drinking water from an impounded valley in North Wales pro-gressively eliminated the natural barrier the river once represented.

In the 1300s, the Normans erected the first bridge at the Roman settlement of Warrington. Nearby Runcorn remains the lowest bridging point. The absence of a bridge between Liverpool and its opposite shore at Birkenhead (which an American visitor characterized as the 'Brooklyn of Liverpool'[14]) is a distinctive feature of the upper river. What Merseyside has instead is three tunnels (two road and one rail) punched through the bedrock at the river's narrow mouth. Speaking on 18 July 1934 at the opening of the Queensway Tunnel that links Liverpool and Birkenhead – at the time the world's longest and largest underwater road tunnel – an enraptured George V inquired:

> Who can reflect without awe that the will and power of man which in our own time have created the noble bridges of the Thames, the Forth, the Hudson . . . can drive also tunnels such as this, wherein many streams of wheeled traffic may run in light and safety below the depth and turbulence of a tidal water bearing the ships of the world![15]

Yet human authority over the Mersey, or any river for that matter, remains incomplete.

The Mersey's immense importance as a *Wasserstrasse* is almost matched by its cultural significance. Well into the twentieth century, Vienna enjoyed a largely unchallenged reputation as the music capital of the world, gathering musical influences from the east (Slavic and Magyar), the North (Germanic) and the South (Latin).[16] Early twentieth-century pilgrimages to the sites where the 'Blue Danube' waltz was written and first performed have been superseded by treks to Liverpool's Cavern Club, where The Beatles performed, the boyhood homes of Lennon and McCartney, and the locations that feature in songs such as 'Penny Lane'.[17]

A bronze statue of Billy Fury has graced Liverpool's riverscape since 2003. Before getting his break as a rock'n'roll singer (and becoming Britain's first rock'n'roll star), Ronald William Wycherley (as he was then called) worked as a deck hand (1956–8) on the *Formby*, a Mersey tug. Between tides, he and fellow crew members played skiffle, an American genre derived from jazz and blues that was enjoying a British rediscovery. While the *Formby* was tied up, they sang and played to passengers on the decks of nearby liners.[18] 'The Beat Goes On: From the Beatles to the

View from the Mersey ferry of Liverpool Pier Head with the Three Graces and the Mersey ferry landing.

Zutons', an exhibition at Liverpool's World Museum (2008–9) that chronicled the soundscape of Merseyside, highlighted the river's enshrinement in names: the Merseysippi Jazz Band (Britain's oldest surviving jazz ensemble, founded in 1949, and the first band to play the Cavern, in 1957); and the River City People (a late 1980s folk-rock band). Not least, though commentators identified a 'Liverpool Sound' in the early 1960s, it was the river rather than the city that gave its name to the fortnightly music paper: *Mersey Beat* (July 1961 to November 1964).[19] And it was also the river that lent its name to the parallel efflorescence of poetic talent dubbed the *Mersey Sound*.[20]

The Merseysippi Jazz Band performed songs entitled 'A Dip in the Mersey' and 'Mersey Tunnel Jazz'. And the city of Liverpool's signature tune is 'Ferry Cross the Mersey', by Gerry and the Pacemakers (a UK top ten chart success in 1964 and performed aboard the *Woodside* ferry in the 1965 film of the same name).[21] Otherwise, though, the river did not loom large in lyrics. Nor, with Fury's exception, did the river directly shape the lives of Liverpool musicians. In a statement that undermined the very notion of a Mersey Sound (or Merseybeat) phenomenon, a predictably iconoclastic John Lennon reflected in 1964 that it was 'just something journalists cooked up, a name. It just so happened we came from Liverpool, and they looked for the nearest river and named it.'[22] Nonetheless, Lennon did not give the river the credit it deserved for its contribution to Liverpool's peerless position within popular music by acting as a conduit for outside influences. In musical terms, the Mersey is a tributary of the Mississippi. Through mercantile connections with the Americas (that date back to the 1660s), jazz, rhythm and blues, calypso, gospel, folk, doo-wop and country flowed up the river during the 1940s and '50s.[23]

Liverpool shipping lines connected the city to ports around the Americas. The Mississippi and Dominion Steamship Company sailed to New Orleans, Boston and Quebec. The Brazil and River Plate Line, the Booth and Singlehurst Lines and the Liverpool Pacific Line plied routes to Montevideo, Buenos Aires, Rio de Janeiro and the Amazonian ports of Belém and Manaus.[24] However, the company that dominated Liverpool's North American routes after its first sailing to Boston in 1840 (weekly mail and passenger service to New York City began in 1852 and 1868, respectively) was Cunard. In 1874, Cunard's fleet for the Boston and New York runs consisted of 22 vessels.[25] As late as the mid-1950s (shortly before the advent of jet airliner service), Cunard still had twelve ships criss-crossing the Atlantic. The 'Cunard Yanks' – British merchant seamen on the company's

Adolphe Augustus Boucher, 'New Liverpool – From the Mersey', photomontage view of the signature waterfront and buildings at George's Pier Head, 1912.

transatlantic liners – were instrumental in introducing local musicians to dance band, country and jazz recordings not yet released in Britain.[26]

Commercially and culturally famous, the river is ecologically infamous. Heseltine noted the bitter irony that, despite Merseyside's enormous debt to the Mersey, it had been 'treated with total and utter contempt'.[27] The Mersey is a glaring (then shining) example of a river that has taken an enormous battering from industrialization before experiencing an uplifting recent rejuvenation. The instructions to the mid-Victorian commissioners appointed to a pioneering investigation of the polluted condition of British rivers in 1868 recommended a case study of the Mersey Valley (including feeder streams such as the Irwell). For here was a prime example of a river basin 'most extensively polluted by all forms of manufacturing refuse'.[28] By the early 1900s, according to one wit, Mersey salmon were 'to be compared with the snakes of Ireland – there are none there!'[29]

Today, the Mersey again supports trout, lamprey and dace as well as (a few) salmon, which, in turn, has encouraged the return of estuarine predators, including grey seals, octopus and harbour porpoises (the latter sometimes visible from the Liverpool-Birkenhead ferries). In 2009, speakers at the conference marking the end of the 25-year Mersey Basin Cam-paign announced that the river was in better shape than at any time since the onset of the Industrial Revolution.[30] A process that goes hand-in-hand with the ecological revival of rivers is the reinstatement of positive human connections. In this respect, Merseyside and its major city also typify a wider European and North American phenomenon. Liverpool's Anglican cathedral occupies a commanding position overlooking the river, and in the early 1980s, its bishop, David Sheppard, dropped an enormous iron ring into the estuary to seal the marriage between city and river.[31]

## Source and Course

The identification between Merseyside and the Mersey is so strong it usually overshadows the rest of the river. Just as few Berliners know where the Spree rises, few Liverpudlians can pinpoint their river's source. Unlike the Spree and the Po, but like the Danube, the Mersey is formed by the convergence of other rivers. There are three main contenders for the title of Merseyhead: the sources of the Etherow, Goyt and Tame. The Etherow rises in the tri-county border region of Yorkshire, Derbyshire and Cheshire – though, for Daniel King, writing in the mid-seventeenth century, there was no Etherow, just the Mersey.[32] Dammed in the nineteenth century to supply drinking water to Manchester, the Etherow is the tributary that begins farthest to the east and is most faithful to the Mersey's general direction. For many Victorian authorities, however, the Mersey proper began at 'Water Meeting', near the mill town of Compstall, where the Etherow joins the Goyt – a point of origin that received the *Encyclopaedia Britannica*'s official blessing.[33] Other authorities placed the river's beginning at the 'union' of Goyt and Tame in downtown Stockport.[34] Since then, these debates have lost whatever relevance they may once have possessed.

The start of the Mersey, where the Tame and Goyt meet, in Stockport. Freight from the port of Liverpool is carried against the flow on the adjacent dry artery of commerce.

By general consensus, the Mersey originates four miles below 'Water Meet-ing'. Just as the Danube begins where the Breg flows into the Brigach, the Mersey starts in Stockport.[35] As the wrought-iron lettering reads: 'Here rivers Goyt and Tame become Mersey flowing clear from Stockport to the sea.'

Despite the attractive sculpture that includes this inscription, the spot is inauspicious. The larger Goyt roils in from the south, emerging from a culvert that carries it under an ASDA supermarket. The 20-mile Tame joins from the north. Rising on Saddleworth Moor on the border between Lancashire and Yorkshire, it flows through a string of factory towns before running out from under the M60 motorway. The infant Mersey is encased between a brick wall on the south bank and a high concrete wall on the north side, above which the motorway (the Manchester Orbital) runs parallel. Vehicles hurtle past, their occupants oblivious to the river's presence. The pedestrian underpass is graffiti-smeared and the pathway littered with broken glass. There is no bench or promenade, just the sculp-tured railing above the sharp-angled meeting point of two concrete retain-ing walls. 'This is not how a mighty waterway should begin', reflected the Manchester-based *Guardian* correspondent David Ward after locating the spot behind Sainsbury's in the Merseyway Shopping Centre (built over the river in 1965).[36] The place that he and other recent pilgrims favour is the source of the Goyt.[37] Few now dispute that the Mersey rises in the Peak District, near the Cat and Fiddle Inn, on the main road between Maccles-field and Buxton. The world-changing river's cradle, at 1,600 feet on Axe Edge, is a peat bog blanketed with sphagnum, heather and bilberry.[38]

The Mersey's first major tributary is the Irwell. Though shorter by over 20 miles, the Irwell contributes a larger flow. The Irwell, rather than the Mersey itself, was also the locus of manufacturing, with more industrial establishments crammed along its banks mid-nineteenth century than on any other British river.[39] But just as the Spree relinquishes its identity to the Havel on Berlin's western edge, the Irwell gives up its name to the Mersey on Manchester's south-western fringes. So far, the Mersey possesses no particu-larly distinctive morphological qualities. It has passed through the first three zones of Kathleen Carpenter's four-zone (fish focused) classification for British rivers (1928): headstream (highland) brook; minnow reach and lowland reach.[40] The fourth and final zone, the estuarine, is when the Mersey emerges as exceptional.

As well as occupying nearly a third of the Mersey's entire length (un-usual for such a short river), this 'great arm of the sea' is a very peculiar

Landsat Thematic Mapper (TM) image of Liverpool showing the Mersey's mouth and estuary.

shape.[41] Unlike the adjacent Dee, whose estuary is V-shaped, the Mersey has an entrance that constricts to a mile between Liverpool and Seacombe (the 'Narrows'). It also has a broad lower estuary resembling a lake (or, as one commentator put it in 1913, 'a curious similarity in shape to a side view of the skins of the water carriers which are yet familiar objects in some parts of the East'[42]). The basin is widest – three miles – between Speke and Ellesmere Port, then contracts again to less than half a mile between Runcorn and Widnes, where the first bridges could be raised.

This shape conspires with the Mersey's tides to present a particular challenge to human activity. According to the distinguished nineteenth-century water engineer, Thomas Hawksley, the estuary was a 'raging beast of a river'.[43] 'By which Mr Hawksley, who was not given to paying unmerited compliments either to men or to things', explained fellow engineer W. Henry Hunter, 'meant that he regarded the Mersey as a difficult river to deal with'.[44] At the bottleneck where the port of Liverpool was founded, the tide flows at the remarkably high speed of between 4.5 and 5.5 miles an hour. This produces the third fastest tidal rip in Europe, running and ebbing at up to 6 knots.[45] Moreover, depending on the season, the tidal variation is enormous. At high spring tides, the difference between low and high water is 31 feet – after the Severn, the highest UK range – while the autumn (neap) tidal range is still a respectable 10 feet. The tidal capacity of the inner estuary between low and high water, at 'springs', is about 710 million cubic yards, and at 'neaps' about 280 million cubic yards.[46] Howley Weir, four miles above Warrington, is the upper limit of the 'springs', and where the Upper Estuary begins. At the confluence with the navigable Weaver at Runcorn, the river widens to form the Inner Estuary.

Low tide is especially low in summer, when, in the Middle Ages and early modern period, seasonal fords operated opposite Sankey Brook and at Hale Head, where cattle, sheep and horses were driven across.[47] In the summer of 2006, as a charity stunt, Graham Boanas (6 feet 9 inches tall) walked across a broader, one-and-a-half mile stretch between Ince Banks, near Ellesmere Port, and Oglet Shore, by Liverpool John Lennon Airport, in just over an hour. At low tide, the channel between the mudflats and sandbanks is just 5–6 feet deep.[48] Botero emphasized that, to be navigable, a river needs width as well as length. Yet he also recognized that width without depth compromises utility, making it 'unfit for navigation'. This was the drawback of the Plate, 'which through overmuch widenesse, is for the most part lowe and of uneven bottome, and full of rocks and little islands'[49] (a disadvantage that did not prevent its selection for Bernini's fountain). The Mersey was potentially afflicted by the Plate's problem, but tidal extremes were the saving grace of a category of river that the nineteenth-century Chinese dubbed 'sons of the ocean'.[50]

No river channel is immutable. But the Mersey provides an arch-example of mutability. Fretting – the process whereby the main channel at low water swings over from the Lancashire side to the Cheshire side, under-cutting the concave banks of bends – was a regular activity of the Mersey. In 1922, the main low water channel migrated one and a half miles southward. By any standards, however, the 'Great Fret' of 1873 was abnormal: the nibbling away of the southern bank continued for over a year, until, halted by a rocky reef, the current swung across and began eating away at the embayment immediately to the north at Ellesmere Port (the terminus of the Shropshire Union Canal). Whereas previous fretting on the southern shore had been harmless, this event destroyed the port at Ellesmere by undermining the foundations of the river walls, which toppled backwards. Thereafter, according to Hunter, 'apparently satisfied with the results of its excursion to the Cheshire side of the estuary, [the channel] reverted to the Lancashire shore, and remained there more or less for several years'.[51]

Ever changing channels as the river enters the Outer Estuary in Liverpool Bay compounded the disadvantages of perilous inter-tidal mudflats and sandbanks and a powerful and capricious tide. On the other hand, the river also offered 'superb advantages'.[52] At the estuary's upper end, the natural scouring action of the tides (Baines called it the 'grand operation of nature') served the needs of shipping. Concentrated by the 'Narrows', where, even at low tide, the water is up to 100 feet deep, the vigorous two-way flow maintained the navigability of the river's entrance.[53] By contrast, the wide-mouthed Dee, separated from the Mersey by the blunt-ended Wirral peninsula, was 'powerless to clear its channels'.[54]

## Mastered Mersey

As a Liverpool-based geographer explained, converting a 'masterful adversary' into a 'useful servant' was the challenge.[55] Despite its drawbacks (silting was already a headache for the port at Chester in Roman times), the neighbouring Dee had for centuries been the preferred point of embarkation to Ireland. After Chester silted up, the fishing village of Parkgate, 12 miles upriver, took over as the main port for Anglo-Irish traffic.[56] By the late 1600s, however, Parkgate was clogged up too and the Irish link moved over to the Mersey, where Liverpool's shipping interests were determined to avoid Chester's and Parkgate's fates.[57] By the late nineteenth century, observes James Winter, the river was so extensively dredged and channelized that 'on the scale of artificiality, the Mersey [and the Irwell] would have found places near the top'.[58]

The river was initially trained for the sake of millers. In medieval Stockport (founded at a fording point between Lancashire and Cheshire), bankside waterwheels ground corn into flour (there was no equivalent to the Po's floating mills). Repeated destruction of the wheels during spate, however, prompted the lord of the manor to divert the flow into tunnels, which also suited the early cotton and silk industries.[59] In 1626, Charles I granted Liverpool a charter to levy tolls on the river and organize navigation. But the first improvements to the upper Mersey were not executed until the late seventeenth century.[60] The Mersey Conservancy Act of 1842 vested regulatory powers in three crown-appointed commissioners, who appointed an Acting Conservator. The Conservancy's mandate was to tackle 'impediments, encroachments, nuisances and annoyances' that inhibited the movement of commercial traffic.[61] The Mersey's mouth provided an enviable anchorage and its tidal vigour and estuarine configuration represented further assets.

The river's natural values, however, did not extend to upstream navigability. Ocean-going ships, assisted by the surging tidal flow, could press upriver as far as Warrington, but not beyond.[62] And even the larger tributaries were inadequate for the brisk two-way flow of goods between Liverpool and its hinterland's coalfields, salt fields and textile towns. Baines believed that Liverpool laboured under 'a worse river communication' with its hinterland 'than any other English port' (casting an envious glance across the Atlantic at New York City's location at the mouth of the Hudson, which thrust directly into the interior of the 'Empire State'). The deepening and straightening of channels and the cutting of canals ('dead water' transportation) supplied the initial remedy.[63] James Brindley, creator of the Bridgewater Canal (1761), one of the Mersey basin's earliest commercial canals, was once asked his opinion of the purpose of rivers. 'To feed canals, of course', he reputedly replied.[64] The 35-mile extension (1776) of the Bridgewater Canal, to connect Manchester with the Mersey at Runcorn (where a flight of ten locks linked it to the river, 90 feet below), more than halved the cost of carriage between Manchester and the Port of Liverpool.[65]

The watershed's two leading cities were mutually dependent. Land-locked Manchester received the bulk of its cotton through Liverpool and its textile products contributed a large chunk of Liverpool's outbound cargo. At the same time, Manchester's reliance on Liverpool's port bred resentment. When Manchester began to explore options for circumventing its rival in the early nineteenth century, one proposal involved by-passing the Mersey completely by cutting a canal across to the Dee at Dawpool.[66] Though persisting problems with silting, among other difficulties, rendered this a non-starter, an equally radical proposal to reduce Manchester's dependence eventually gained traction. The desire of Mancunian industrialists and politicians for a direct connection to the Irish Sea deep and wide enough for sea-going vessels took the form of a proposed ship canal. Those preoccupied with the commercial consequences for Liverpool also cited the potentially negative impact on tidal flows and vital estuarine scouring. For the original plan proposed to run the canal straight down the middle of the estuary beyond Runcorn, by means of a training wall and dredged channel.[67] Witnesses in parliamentary committee hearings (1882) pointed out that Chester harbour silted up because an eighteenth-century navigation company had ignored the natural channel and made a 'trained cut' through the Dee estuary.[68] Once the promoters came up with a revised plan to place the canal along the estuary's southern rim, which persuaded politicians in London (if not local opponents) that the Mersey's mouth would not silt up, Parliament authorized the scheme (1885).

Construction of the world's eighth longest canal took six years. The filling of the 36-mile seaway – as deep as Suez and more than 50 feet wider – was complete by late November 1893. 'Manchester-sur-Mer' (as *Punch* dubbed the city) had finally wrested control of its transportation from Liverpool and the Mersey when the canal opened for business on 1 January

'Manchester-sur-Mer. A Sea-Ductive Prospect', *Punch*, 7 October 1882.

At the Mersey Weir, where the Mersey joins the Manchester Ship Canal, 2009. They share a bed for four miles.

1894. Like the completion of the Danube modernization works at Vienna twenty years earlier, the formal opening ceremony was a royal occasion. Boarding the royal paddle steamer *Enchantress* at Trafford Wharf in the Port of Manchester on 21 May 1894, Queen Victoria steamed up the canal to Mode Wheel Docks (where, reputedly, as well as pushing the button to open the gates, she commented on the 'smell' of which the authorities were all too well aware).[69]

The Ship Canal consolidated the Mersey's high position on the scale of river artificiality. For it did not just replace the river in a commercial sense. It also entailed a drastic physical modification by creating a surrogate river. Over some sections, the 'Big Ditch'[70] parallels the Mersey, from which, at times, it is separated by mere inches. Indeed, for nearly eighteen miles, between Irlam Weir and where the Bollin enters, river and canal share the same bed. And whilst the canal's waters are partly saline, it draws most of its volume from the Irwell, Irk and Medlock. The Ship Canal has effectively converted these rivers from Mersey tributaries into canal feeders (fulfilling the pre-ordained purpose of rivers, as defined by Brindley). Rather than demonstrating an imperious desire to conquer rivers, however, the upper canal's layout simply indicates that it made sense to follow existing watercourses. To locate and cut an alternative route through this thickly settled and intensively used area would have constituted an enormous challenge (and expense).

## Manufacturing Mersey

Dredged and channelized, the Mersey and its tributaries enabled the fuller exploitation of their watershed's rich endowment of natural resources. The Mersey became the outlet not just for Lancashire and Cheshire, but – thanks to navigational improvements and canal construction – also for Staffordshire's Potteries, the 'Black Country' around Birmingham and the West Riding of Yorkshire. As well as Cheshire's salt, the river Weaver brought earthenware, iron and coal up from Staffordshire.[72] The shipment to London of Cheshire cheese (brought down the Weaver by barge) also flourished at pre-modern Liverpool, where the London cheesemongers' ships docked in the shallow, sheltered creek entrance known as the pool.[73] As the Mersey replaced the Dee as the major regional river, port facilities along the largely unmodified riverside in Liverpool proved inadequate. The 'state of nature' that still prevailed along the river's banks in the early 1700s was broken by construction of Britain's first modern (wet) dock.[74] Maintaining a constant level of water regardless of the stage of the tide and able to accommodate a hundred ships, the facility was fully operational by 1719 (comparison between the dockland complex that eventually spread along five miles of riverside and the pyramids of Egypt were rife in the high Victorian age[75]).

In a robust endorsement of the popular early twentieth-century ethos of environmental determinism, Dixon Scott (a Tynesider) argued for the river's 'dominion over the City'. The opening chapter of his book about Liverpool, published at a time when the city was at its zenith, was given over entirely to the River (invariably capitalized) of which the city was the 'historical result'. Remove the city's 'river-born attributes' and 'you leave her utterly dismantled'. Rivers in other cities were not the central feature: 'In London, there are a score of Londons, in Glasgow a dozen Glasgows; but here there is only one Liverpool – Liverpool-on-the-Mersey.' Even if Scott's evocation of a river dependency distinguished by its totality was overblown, his emphasis on Liverpool as a 'pure product of the nineteenth century', an instant city, was spot on.[76] In the 1790s, Liverpool outstripped Bristol in tonnage to become Britain's second port.[77] By the 1850s, Liver -

pool had captured almost half of Britain's export trade (pushing London into second place).[78] Moreover, the Mersey basin was now the world's leading manufacturing region, containing two million inhabitants by 1861 (nearly half a million in Liverpool itself).

The Mersey bestrode a global network of commerce. Commodities shipped from the Mersey, boasted a reviewer of Baines's *History of the Commerce and Town of Liverpool* (1852) could be found in every corner of the world. Crockery from Stoke-on-Trent, cotton shirts from Manchester, firearms from Birmingham and cutlery from Sheffield – these items were to be found in households across Europe, from the 'mouth of the Tagus to the river of the Don Cossacks which divides Europe from Asia'. These goods were also all around Africa, from Alexandria to the Cape of Good Hope and points north up to the Red Sea; and across Asia from Smyrna to Shanghai. On the other side of the Atlantic, products shipped out of the Mersey were distributed down the east coast of the Americas from the St Lawrence to the river Plate. Cheshire salt (exported in enormous quadrangular blocks) preserved 'the flesh of the millions of animals fatted in the forests or the corn-fields of America'. On the Pacific side, cotton, silk and linen textiles loaded up at Liverpool were spread from San Francisco to Valparaíso.

At the same time, the Mersey was the gateway for the bulk of Britain's raw cotton and grain imports.[79] Britons, Baines explained, were 'clothed with the cotton grown on the banks of the Mississippi, the Amazons, the Indus, and the Nile'.[80] They ate bread baked from wheat grown in the fields of Romania and Bulgaria and despatched to the lower Danubian ports of Galatz and Brăila; in Wellington Dock, Scott pointed out, a ship owned by Glynn and Son (the *Bulgarian*, for instance) 'will always be unloading grain from the Danube'.[81] The Canetti family personified the grain and cotton trades that connected Mersey and Danube. When the future novelist was a young boy, his father, a grain merchant, moved the family from Bulgaria to Manchester to join his brother-in-law's business: the export of cotton goods to the Balkans. Canetti recalled Sunday walks with his father down by the Mersey, along the riverside path that meandered through the meadows.[82] However, his first encounter with the river that flowed not far from his family's first Manchester home in the Sephardic Jewish community of West Didsbury was something of a disappointment. It was 'called a river, but what a narrow stream (*Rinnsal*) it was'.[83] The six-year-old boy's point of reference for this invidious comparison was obviously the mighty Danube on whose banks he had grown up. Nonetheless, the three years

Near where the novelist Elias Canetti walked with his father as a boy, a colourful embankment mural of a bucolic River Mersey (with salmon) brightens up a grey wintry dawn at Didsbury, Manchester, 2011.

In case the pastoral mural lulls riverside visitors into a false sense of security, a sign warns that this is still a river of peril at Didsbury, 2011.

Canetti spent in Manchester shortly before the First World War may have shaped how he recalled the Danubian mercantile hub of Ruse (Ruschuk) in his autobiographical writings.

Liverpool's global reach and the world-wide reverberations of the industrialism born within its river's basin prompted Ian Wray to subtitle his book 'the river that changed the world'. 'Is it absurd', he inquired, 'to compare the Mersey with the Nile?'[84] Baines and many other proud and confident Victorian Britons would not have considered the analogy far-fetched. Nineteenth-century commentators conceded that it could not compete with the Severn or Thames in terms of a picturesque ancient history. And they wasted no time on the Mersey's upper, rural reaches. Nonetheless, its 'rapid development' and 'present glory' made it just as worthy of attention. Unlike the Severn and Thames, the Mersey was making history.[85] By the 1860s, Liverpool was the world's leading port, outstripping London, New York and New Orleans in imports and exports combined.

## Mucky Mersey

The rivers that equipped the region for a vanguard role in the industrialization process also bore its brunt. Since the late eighteenth century, the Mersey has only flowed clear from Stockport to the sea in the sense that the river underwent no further changes in name: its waters were not clear and they were certainly not clean. A New Yorker visiting Merseyside in springtime in the early 1850s was eager to enjoy some English countryside. He found what he was looking for twelve miles from the centre of Liverpool near the picturesque village of Hale, located at a former fording point. From the village tavern, he strolled down to the river along a hedge-lined lane profuse with blossom. The river he reached presented a pastoral tableau: 'the river gleamed in the sun; and upon it were small sailing vessels going slowly up into the English country, or coming down from it to the city.' This echoed the sentiments of a Scottish visitor to Merseyside less than a decade earlier. Hale 'answers at last to our full idea of a sweet English village'; he, too, had been enchanted by the view of the 'rich and winding shores' of the Mersey. The Scot also reflected that Hale lived up to its name, enjoying a reputation for 'salubrity'. Since the summer of 1847, though, the industrial era had firmly arrived in Hale's backyard. Awakening from his reverie, the New Yorker noted that industry was not far away – too close, in fact, for his liking: 'Beyond the river . . . the tall chimneys of some manufactories sent out lines of wriggling smoke over the lower sky, which looked like great flying serpents.'[86]

Though the visiting American provided no details, the factories of nearby Widnes probably emitted the wriggling smoke that stained the lower sky. This most recently emerged cluster of industrial establishments in the Mersey basin was dominated by the Gossage soap works on Spike Island (a landscape feature created by the cutting of the St Helens Canal). Long before what was then the world's biggest soap factory began operation, serpent-like smoke was a familiar feature of the basin's skyscape, belched out by a host of bleaching, dyeing, and finishing works associated with the textile industry's spinning and weaving mills.

Industrialization blighted water as well as the air. Thirteen miles from Hale, at Warrington, was the centre of northern England's tanning industry. Between eight and ten thousand hides were processed weekly, mostly for shoe soles: British soldiers marched and policemen walked the beat on leather tanned with copious quantities of Mersey water.[87] Producing soles generated three forms of effluent that returned to the river as wastewater.[88] Further upstream, Stockport's silk, cotton and felt hat industries poured in their share of toxic waste.

The textile finishing industries of Stockport and the soap- and glass-making operations of Widnes depended on alkali (caustic soda). Alkali was traditionally made from natural substances such as the ash of kelp and bracken. However, the chimneys of the manufactories that adopted the chemical (Leblanc) production method in the early 1800s (based on coal, salt and limestone) emitted hydrogen chloride gas (muriatic acid) into the lower sky, which fell as acid rain.[89] Meanwhile, solid toxic waste (galligoo) oozed into the river or mingled with rainwater to generate hydrogen sulphide (recognizable by its rotten egg smell). 'It is permissible to imagine', ruminated a 'well-known' but anonymous 'expert' on the river in 1888, 'that the ashes of Sodom and Gomorrah immediately after the destruction of those wicked cities emitted no more pestiferous vapours, or were more devoid over all their wide area of one single green leaf or sign of vegetation, than those twin-sister towns of the Mersey – Widnes and Runcorn'.[90] Hedges like those in Hale that the American visitor admired were blasted to year-round leaflessness. Widnes had previously been renowned for its eel pies.[91] Within twenty years of the Gossage works' arrival in 1855, the fame of eel pies had been replaced by the fame of soap and the infamy of noxious vapours. In the 1880s, Élisée Reclus introduced Widnes as 'a town of evil odour', horticultural expert and gardening writer William Robinson dismissed it as a 'negatively healthy town', and the *Daily News* candidly described it as 'the dirtiest, ugliest and most depressing town in England'.[92]

The load of hydrogen sulphide from the chlor-alkali industry was so high on the Mersey and its tributaries that – like the Spree and the Cuyahoga – its surface occasionally combusted spontaneously.[93] Initial concern over pollution, though, had more to do with the flow of commerce than biology. Nobody fretted over the impact on fish or human health. Focusing on solid rather than chemical ('liquid') waste, a report of 1860 calculated that disposal of refuse such as slag cinders raised the Irwell's bed a couple of inches a year. To combat this widespread unfettered discharge, the Mersey and Irwell Navigation Company secured the Mersey and Irwell Protection Act of 1862.[94] But malpractice persisted. The Longworthy Brothers, operators of the Greengate cotton mills on the Irwell's Salford bank, freely admitted to the unfiltered release of vast quantities of the 'liquid refuse' of washing, bleaching, printing and dyeing. Yet the company complained to the Rivers Pollution Commission (1868) that the incorri-gible dumping of ash, cinder and other rubbish had raised the river-bed 3–4 feet in their vicinity over the previous twelve years.[95] When barred from direct disposal, factories less scrupulous than the Longworthys' (who ostensibly carted away their solid refuse) simply left trash on the banks for flood waters to wash away.[96] In 1899, to preserve navigability, Admiral Sir George Ware, Conservator of the Mersey Docks and Harbour Board, demanded action, singling out, on this occasion, the discharge of sewage.[97]

The river's health, though a subordinate concern, began to receive some attention in connection with efforts to improve public health. Again, it was human waste and other solid substances that initially exercised sanitation officers. In the early 1800s, the Irwell and its tributary, the Medlock, were already 'open sewers that bore to the sea the refuse of many towns on a stream so slow that the sparrows could find footing on the filth that encrusted its surface'.[98] The condition of the Irk, another Irwell tributary, deeply shocked Friedrich Engels during his sojourn in Manchester in the 1840s. Instead of flowing, the river 'disgorges a narrow coal-black, foul-smelling stream full of debris and refuse'. In dry conditions, 'a long string of the most disgusting, blackish-green slime pools are left standing . . . from the depths of which bubbles of miasmic gas constantly arise and give forth a stench unendurable even on the bridge forty or fifty feet above the surface'.[99] Twenty years later, the Longworthy Brothers recorded that sewers transported the 'excrements of workpeople' into the Irwell.[100]

Appointed Borough Engineer for Liverpool in 1847 (the first post of its kind in Britain), the specific mandate of James Newlands was to provide a sewer system to combat the city's regular cholera and typhoid fever epidemics. Yet he quickly realized that this solution simply trans- ferred the sewage problem from land to water. In 1848, Newlands informed Liverpool City Council that relieving the Mersey of its burden of pollutants was a 'consideration of vital importance'.[101] To highlight the Irwell's plight, the Report of the Rivers Pollution Commission (1870) contains the fac-simile of a letter written with fluid from the Irwell instead of ink.[102] (References to the Irwell as the 'Sewage Canal' proliferated after Suez opened in 1869.[103]) So much human waste sloshed around in it that Salford was regularly awash in sewage (the currents were stronger on the Manchester side).[104] A sanitary official noted that the Irwell held the dubious honour of being 'the hardest worked and foulest stream in the world'.[105]

An obstacle to these concerns being taken seriously was the wide- spread belief in a river's capacity for self-help. Many Victorians, who did not exempt rivers from this powerful ethos, were confident that the Mersey estuary in particular, with its large volume of water and strong tides, had the ability to degrade, dilute, digest and disperse without lasting ill-effect any quantity of untreated household and industrial waste. Even sanitary reformers insisted that a river operated its own self-cleansing process; so chucking filth into a river was the 'natural' disposal method. (A non- commercial objection to the proposed Manchester Ship Canal was that it would carry the same dirt yet lack a river's built-in purification system.[106]) Even when the existence of a pollution problem in the Mersey or Irwell was acknowledged, few officials adopted Newlands' stance. More heavily contaminated rivers seemed a reasonable price to pay for the health bene- fits of cleaner cities with falling death rates.[107]

An eminent Victorian who did share Newlands's holistic approach was Charles Kingsley. Inspired by the mucky Mersey, the prominent Christian Socialist, literary figure and fisherman became a campaigner for clean water. Kingsley grew up on rural Devon's Dart and angled for trout in the pellucid chalk streams of the home counties. During an appointment as canon of Chester cathedral (1870–73), Kingsley became acquainted with another two rivers: the Dee on his doorstep and its very different neigh- bour, the Mersey. He preferred the Dee. Protected from the blight of industrial progress by its incorrigible silt, it still hosted salmon. The Dee, in other words was a fit subject for his poetry ('The Sands of Dee'). The

*Mersey*

Mersey, by contrast, was the river that featured in his social commentary. A vigorous critic of industrialism's unsavoury side effects, Kingsley knew that pollution defiled people and water in equal measure. 'The Tide River', one of the songs in *The Water Babies* (1863), his novelistic paean to pure and cleansing river water, closely fitted the Mersey.[108] In a passage that recent Mersey regenerators like to quote, Kingsley compared the river's 'undefiled' higher reaches, where it ran 'cool and clear', with the 'sin-defiled' persona of its lower industrial stretch.[109]

> Dank and foul, dank and foul,
> By the smoky town with its murky cowl;
> Foul and dank, foul and dank,
> By wharf and sewer and slimy bank;
> Darker and darker the farther I go,
> Baser and baser the richer I grow

Finally, the ocean purifies the degraded river:

> Strong and free, strong and free,
> The floodgates are open, away to the sea.
> Free and strong, free and strong,
> Cleansing my streams as I hurry along
> To the golden sands and the leaping bar,
> And the taintless tide that awaits me afar.[110]

Kingsley was a sought-after speaker on the imperative for sanitary reform. In June 1870, he preached in Liverpool on behalf of Kirkdale Ragged School. He warned his audience of prominent Liverpudlians that, as well as fouling the air, soil and water, the rampant pursuit of profit produced 'human soot'. 'Capital', he explained, 'is accumulated more rapidly by wasting a certain amount of human life, human health, human intellect, human morals, by producing and throwing away a regular percentage of human soot' (symbolized, in *Water Babies*, by Tom, the young sweep).[111] Capital, he might have added, is also amassed more swiftly by squandering a large portion of a river's health. Yet for many Victorian industrialists, a dirty river was a natural by-product of wealth creation – a symbol of economic well-being. The most visible casualties of the soiled river were fish. In 1656, King noted that the Mersey held 'great store' of salmon, conger eel, plaice, flounder, smelt (sparling) and

*181*

shrimp.[112] Probably the last recorded salmon catch in the Mersey basin was a fish taken with a fly by Lord de Tabley at the mill on Peover Brook, Cheshire, in 1847. For any lingering salmon, the Manchester Ship Canal was the final straw; an 'unfortunate' specimen was trapped in a lock in 1894.[113]

After 1945, sewage that deprived fish of oxygen and created anoxic bottom conditions that eliminated their invertebrate food supply was supplemented by a new order of noxious chemicals and petrochemicals. Pesticides such as DDT (Manchester's Trafford Park area, within the Mersey catchment, was a pioneering production site[114]) and persistent organic contaminants like polychlorinated biphenyls (PCBs) and pentachlorophenol (PCP) were much more insidious than the simple inorganic compounds of previous industrial waste. Twentieth-century chemicals, in lethal combination with heavy metals (mercury, lead, cadmium and zinc) and deteriorating, sewage-leaking Victorian era pipes and drains, spelled biotic disaster.

The Mersey and Weaver River Authority instigated monthly water quality surveys in the early 1960s. By the 1970s, anecdotal evidence suggested that the river was largely devoid of fish; a Department of the Environment survey of 1970 confirmed that, though the percentage of grossly polluted rivers had fallen by a quarter since a previous survey in 1958, more industrial effluent was discharged into the Mersey catchment than any other British river's.[115] As fish disappeared, herons and kingfishers also vanished. Precisely when the brook-fed tidal inlet at Otterspool in south Liverpool – a valuable salmon fishery for medieval monks at Woolton grange – became a name without substance is not recorded. However, sightings and trappings across the estuarine zone were increasingly rare by the 1860s and the tidal area as a whole was ruled otter-less by the early 1900s.[116]

## Mercy on the Mersey

On the eve of the petrochemical industry's arrival on Merseyside, William Palmer delivered a poignant lament for a defiled and pitiful river. A well-known author of guides to Britain's wilder places, Palmer was much more at home by the rivers of his native Lake District, which featured in *Lake County Rambles* (1901) and *The English Lakes* (1905). During the First World War and the 1920s, however, he lived in Liverpool, from where he initially struck out for Wales. But the river on his doorstep also attracted him, perhaps as a counterpoint to unsullied Welsh and Lakeland streams. Palmer excoriated the degraded state of this 'much-abused stream' and its equally shackled and debased tributaries. One headwater, the Kin, is allowed a 'brief period of rejoicing' before being 'trapped' in a reservoir. Likewise, the Sett quickly becomes 'the slave of humanity, the driver of mill-wheels, the washer of fabrics, the scourer of refuse'. Then, from Stockport, the Mersey 'flows sadly' with no more enlivening tributaries, every inch of this 'tired' 'working stream' intensively used, regulated and disciplined – pooled, pumped and piped out and back in, interrupted by weir and sluice.[117]

Palmer's Mersey narrative was one of loss and terminal decline. It held out no realistic expectation of a reversal in fortunes. In 1971, the Depart - ment of the Environment classified the condition of the river's non-tidal section as 'bad'. And in the early 1980s, the Mersey estuary and river system bore the dubious distinction of being Britain's most polluted (according to some sources, it was also peerless within western Europe).[118] But no river can ever be written off. There is no such thing as a river of no return (even after two centuries' worth of hard days and nights). Even Palmer expressed the hope in 1944, however vague, that 'one day in the age of universal electricity and clean manufacture it may win again its clarity and charm'.[119] The demise of dirty, heavy industry, here as elsewhere, and a steady decline in Liverpool's population since the 1930s (by 2008, the number of residents had shrunk by almost half), created the opportunity for the river's return from the brink.

For the Mersey to benefit directly, however, it took a riot and the strong personal commitment of a prominent politician. Michael Heseltine, Secretary of State for the Environment in the newly elected Conservative government of Margaret Thatcher, was appointed Minister with special responsibility for Merseyside following the riots in the inner city's Toxteth area in July 1981. This twelve-month appointment involved spending a day a week in Liverpool. In the spirit of Kingsley, Heseltine tackled the city's ills on a wide front. For him, the river's poor condition was symp matic of the city's overall state.

Heseltine's leonine mane (and flamboyant brandishing of the ceremo- nial mace during an outburst in Parliament in 1976) earned him the nick - name 'Tarzan' from the opposition benches. *Tarzan's Secret Treasure* (1941) and *Tarzan's New York Adventure* (1942), starring former American Olym- pic swimmer Johnny Weissmuller, were filmed at Wakulla Springs, Florida, at the head of the 9-mile Wakulla River. The Mersey – of which one of the biggest beasts in the British political jungle enjoyed a splendid panorama from his room in the recently built Atlantic Tower Hotel – could not have been any more different from the piercingly limpid, spring-fed, alligator-rich Wakulla, whose temperature is a consistent, year-round 21.1°C. 'Alone, every night, when the meetings were over and the pressure was off', Heseltine recalled in his autobiography, 'I would stand with a glass of wine, looking out at the magnificent view over the river and ask myself what had gone wrong for this great English city. The Mersey, its lifeblood, flowed as majestically as ever down from the hills.'[120]

Heseltine did not mention the river in the 21-page memorandum to cabinet colleagues ('It Took a Riot') based on his initial two-and-a-half week sojourn on Merseyside. But its clean-up could be construed as a prime example of a 'worthwhile scheme' creating jobs to which he recommended the commitment of public resources.[121] In November 1982, Heseltine's Department of the Environment issued a consultation paper on regenerating the river. In his covering letter, the Secretary remarked that:

> The haunting grandeur of the Mersey creates its own unforgettable impressions. To earlier generations the Mersey and its tributaries were the essence, the life-spring of Liverpool and of a whole host of towns in the textile and industrial belt of the North West . . . But today the river is an affront to the standards a civilised society should demand of its environment.

Heseltine further claimed that the river's polluted mess was 'perhaps the single most deplorable feature of this critical part of England'. His Merseyside initiative duly included a campaign (launched on 22 November 1982) to save an ailing river 'bearing the foul legacy of the Industrial Revolution'.[122]

Though Heseltine left to become Defence Secretary in early 1983, sufficient momentum had built up to carry his successors at the Department of the Environment. His vision informed the establishment of the Mersey Basin Campaign (1985), a partnership of public, private and voluntary sector agencies and organizations. Backed by central government, European Community funds and a 25-year mandate, the Campaign spearheaded the conversion of the river and its associated watercourses from liabilities to assets, ecologically, economically and recreationally.[123] A core partner in this catchment-wide campaign was the local water authority. When the North West Water Authority (privatized in 1989 and superseded by United Utilities in 1995) launched its own water improvement initiative in 1981, the most pressing problem was the low levels of dissolved oxygen stemming from ever higher levels of raw (untreated) domestic sewage – that offset gains from de-industrialization.[124]

Success has exceeded expectations. The Campaign's prime objective was to raise the quality of all watercourses within the catchment to at least Class 2 ('fair') by 2010. When the Campaign released its mid-term report (1997), the official satisfaction expressed over being well on course to meet targets was justified.[125] International recognition of the Mersey's rapid resuscitation followed in September 1999. At the Second International River Management Symposium in Brisbane, Australia, the Campaign won Riverfestival's inaugural Thiess International Riverprize for best clean-up, in competition with 37 other entries, including the Rhine, Mississippi and Thames.[126]

Assisted by Liverpool's economic decline and dwindling population (the 1970s was the decade that registered the most drastic loss since 1930) as well as the improved pollution controls, the load of organic pollution that the watershed's rivers carried fell by 80 per cent between 1975 and 2000. Meanwhile, mercury discharge declined by 90 per cent between 1980 and 2000 – an improvement reflected in the lower mercury content of the fatty tissues of long-living species like eels. Even at the river's ecological nadir, in the early 1970s, the estuary was far from lifeless. The Department of the Environment noted in 1983 that the upper estuary's intertidal marshes and mudflats, with their rich invertebrate fauna and salt marsh flora, designated a Site of Special Scientific Interest in 1951, provided nationally and internationally important habitat for large numbers of overwintering wildfowl and waders, as well as valuable spring and autumn staging posts for migrating birds.[127] Nonetheless, a cleaner and more oxygenated river supported a greater number and range of invertebrates such as shellfish and worms. The population of ducks (shelduck, teal and pintail) and waders (dunlin, redshank, curlew and turnstone) increased by 80 per cent between 1990 and 2000.[128]

In Japan, the litmus test of a river's status as a river, its *river-ness* or *river-hood*, is the presence of fish. The question Japanese river restorers pose is: 'what's a river without fish?'[129] UK water quality criteria operate with the same yardstick, the indicator species for Class 2 (fair) being coarse fish. Though the target date for the return of a significant number of species (and in significant numbers) was 2010, the species count rose spectacularly to fifty by the mid-1990s, of which ten are comfortably re-established. These include bass, cod, squid, lesser octopus, lumpfish, mullet, anchovy, brown trout and sea trout – species proudly paraded on signage aboard Mersey ferries. The presence of trout was particularly encouraging. In Britain, as elsewhere in the northern hemisphere, the best indicator species for Class 1 water ('good' or 'very good' quality) are fussy salmonids such as trout.[130]

Further ecological success stories followed. One of them featured the cormorant's return. The cormorant is the original 'liver bird', which – clutching a spring of laver seaweed in its beak – has been a fixture on Liverpool's coat-of-arms since 1797 (it also sits atop the Liver Building and is the logo of Liverpool Football Club). About the size of a heron, with long slender neck and thick bill, the cormorant is particularly fond of the returning flounder. By 2007, cormorants were fishing in the river by Princes Dock in central Liverpool.[131] The most newsworthy story, how-ever, involved fish. In 1999 and 2000, Environment Agency staff recorded video footage of large salmonids trying to surmount a weir at Heatley on the River Bollin, which joins the Manchester Ship Canal 4 miles above the upper tidal limit. In November 2001, a fish trap at Woolston Weir, Warrington, caught three salmon (perhaps strays from the Ribble or Dee). Then, in 2005, three young salmon (parr) were detected in the Goyt, prompting speculation that the species may be spawning in the Mersey headwaters.[132] At Northenden Weir, a salmon ladder has been installed to assist upstream migration to spawning grounds on the Goyt. Parr have also been logged (appropriately) at Parrs Wood (near Didsbury, Greater Manchester), named for the parr that flourished hereabouts before 1800. At nearby Heaton Mersey, Mersey Vale Nature Park occupies the site of a former riverside cotton bleaching works (Mellon and Coward), demol-ished in 1992.[133] Gracing a spot overlooking the weir is Simon O'Rawke's rustic (and now mossy) wooden salmon sculpture, installed in September 2006 (when the park opened), to celebrate the fish's return.[134]

The Mersey may be on its way to becoming an octopus's garden, but the Mersey Basin Campaign's contribution to World Environment Day in 2007 pivoted on the salmon's return. A baton in the form of a carved wooden salmon named Sammy was carried in relay from Stockport to Liverpool's Pier Head, with the mayors of the two cities present, respec-tively, at the start and finish of the high-media-profile event.[135] Salmon have re-connected the river with its headwaters by incorporating the Ship Canal – which shares the river's bed for a stretch – into their migratory route. A sign aboard the *Snowdrop*, the Mersey Ferries vessel that operates recreational cruises along the Ship Canal between May and October, explains that dolphins are sometimes found in the canal. They interpret this as a vote of confidence in the canal water's unprecedented cleanliness – even if, as they freely concede, the canal is hardly a suitable place for a dolphin. No wonder those involved in the Mersey's robust recovery were indignant when American scientists working for the UN Environment Programme inadvertently proposed to include the Mersey estuary on its expanded list (*Global Environment Outlook Year Book*, 2007 edition) of around 200 marine 'dead zones': areas, monitored globally since the 1970s, where oxygen levels are so heavily depleted that marine life is unsustainable.[136]

## From Merseyside to Mersey

The author of a late-nineteenth-century essay about the Mersey as a river of industry was only interested in the river 'at the proud consummation of its career, when the wealth of nations is entrusted to its keeping, and the mercantile navies of half the world float upon its broad bosom'.[137] Liverpool and the Mersey have been more or less synonymous for over a century, whether at the port's early twentieth-century global zenith, or during the city's music and poetry boom of the 1960s. One of the main galleries at the former Museum of Liverpool Life (which closed in 2006) was the 'River Room', which showed how the Mersey shaped the lives of Merseysiders. This feature has not been re-created within its replacement, the new Museum of Liverpool, which opened in July 2011. Though the new museum concentrates more on the city and port than their host river, one of the highlighted exhibits in the 'Global City' gallery is the 'River Mersey dress' – a brownish-green outfit adorned with crab, starfish and fish motifs as well as shells, worn by Astrid Caroe, daughter of the Danish consul, for a fancy dress party at the Town Hall in 1912.[138] And for David Fleming, director of National Museums Liverpool, the city is all about the river: 'For me, the nature and character of this city is completely dependent on its river.' He regards the city's creative genius as a product of the immense wealth generated by those who 'used the river'.[139]

Yet there is more to the Mersey than Merseyside. The Mersey Basin Campaign (which concluded in 2010) was precipitated by the state of the river in Liverpool. But its vision and activities embraced the entire watershed. An exhibition of photographs that toured the catchment in 2007 and 2008, 'Mersey: The River that Changed the World', also evolved to encompass the entire river. The exhibition – and companion book – which feature the work of Liverpool photographer Colin McPherson, were supported by the Campaign, one of whose main objectives was to raise awareness of the river among its residents, many of whom had 'turn[ed] their backs' to a river dismissed as beyond repair and redemption.[140] Scott's eulogy to Liverpool, published a century earlier, had contended that the river provided a strong, if fluid adhesive that stuck together the diverse and otherwise unconnected peoples that had gathered on its banks: 'they are all unmistakeably of the Mersey'. In similar fashion, Wray's ode to the city contains a feature on 'Mersey People' – a series of portraits ranging from ferryboat deckhand to police diver, of individuals glued together by a common fluvial bond, a quality that Scott identified as a 'subtle solidarity'.[141] Most of the Mersey People, though, are from the Liverpool Mersey.

Moving upstream from Liverpool, the exhibition culminated at Stockport Art Gallery, not far from the river's official beginning.[142] Bringing the exhibition to Stockport, a city with little meaningful current connection to the river, was part of an effort to re-establish the link. When the landlord of the Jackson's Boat public house in nearby Sale, where Farmer Jackson ferried people across before an iron footbridge was built, informs his customers that the body of water is the Mersey rather than a canal, they reply: 'it can't be, that's in Liverpool'.[143] Likewise, artist Helen Clapcott, despite spending her teenage years in Stockport, followed by art college in Liverpool in the early 1970s, 'never related the Mersey in Liverpool to the Mersey in Stockport', not least because the latter was inaccessible, walled off by mills.[144]

Those who learned of the river's local presence in the Stockport gallery and then sought it out will have found no shortage of local echoes. The route from the gallery follows the Merseyway (built over the river in the 1930s), passes the Mersey Café and then cuts through Merseyway Shopping Centre, which also sponsored the exhibit. But there is no sign for the river or named riverside walk. The path that runs past the confluence is the Fred Perry Way (Stockport's famous, tennis-playing son clearly enjoys greater local renown and official recognition). 'I bet very few people can find [the confluence] . . . or know about it', wagered a visitor in the feedback relayed to McPherson via a comments card at the exhibition.

At the same time, visitors to the Stockport exhibit who were already aware of the river's local presence were irked by its 'Liverpool focus'. The companion book would not be purchased, another visitor's feedback indicated, because there was insufficient input 'for the Mersey near here'. 'People tend to think', the visitor complained, 'that the Mersey *starts* and ends at Liverpool. More info of its roots near here should be illustrated'. Another visitor expressed disappointment that these local roots merited just one photograph, while conceding that the confluence was thoroughly un-photogenic, and recommending that it was shifted to make a more emphatic and atmospheric focal point for where it all began.[145]

If the Po is *il Mississippi italiano*, then the Mersey that begins so miserably in Stockport supplies another kind of bridge to the new world. The leaving of Liverpool from the mouth of the Mersey is a fine point of departure for the rivers of America. Through the musical influences that flowed up it, the Mersey spans the Atlantic. Yet the river's commercial sway extended beyond the mouths of the Hudson and Mississippi. The 'Yankee clipper ship' from the renowned folksong 'The Leaving of Liverpool', was headed for California during the gold rush of the late 1840s. Between 1897 and 1900, gold seekers from across Europe who were bound for another gold rush also embarked from Liverpool. In response to a high volume of

Postcard of RMS *Campania*, *c.* 1890–1900. One of the two flagships of the Cunard passenger fleet, the *Campania* entered service in 1893 as the largest and fastest passenger liner of her day, covering the distance between Liverpool and New York in under six days. Some Klondikers began their journey to the Yukon basin on this liner. She retired from service in 1914.

inquiries in the winter of 1897, the Allan Line published a map of the
upper Yukon that showed the various routes to the Klondike goldfields
from Vancouver, and began quoting through rates for travel in the spring
of 1898.[146] And Cunard regularly advertised its Klondike service in the
*Liverpool Mercury*. The Klondyke and Columbian Passenger Agency
offered an all-in service so the 'intending gold-seeker can leave Liverpool
with no more luggage than a Gladstone bag'. The Company promised a
trip of no more than 28 days between Liverpool and Dawson City, the
settlement near the goldfields, along the 'shortest and best', all-year route
to the Klondike: via New York, Vancouver, Victoria, British Columbia and
the Alaskan port of Dyea, with the final stretch by boat down the Yukon.[147]
Iredale and Porter even offered a direct service from Liverpool to the
mouth of the Yukon on the *Garonne*.[148]

Newspapers across Britain were stuffed with Klondike news. But
coverage in the weekly *Liverpool Mercury* was particularly thick. Not
surprisingly, some local crewmen jumped ship to join the ranks of their
gold-seeking passengers on arrival in New York, Vancouver or (having
taken the 'all-water route') St Michael at the Yukon's mouth. The scale of
desertion was serious enough for local shipping firms to provoke debate
at a meeting of the Prenton Literary and Debating Club, based on the
Birkenhead side of the river.[149] Yet the liquid highway from the Mersey
to the Yukon that presented an unforeseen problem for the ship owners
who resided in Birkenhead (perhaps in a villa overlooking the park that
inspired the designer of Manhattan's Central Park) offered Jack London
a literary opportunity. In the Klondike short story, 'Siwash', an 'English
sailor', 'Tommy', up to his neck in Yukon frontier life, caught himself
'wondering if the folks in Liverpool could only see me now'. And in a late
story, 'Like Argus of Ancient Times' (1916), the name London chose for
another strapping, energetic sailor from the other side of the Atlantic is
also revealing. The name of the man who becomes 'boss' of a boat party
bound for Dawson from the lakes of the upper Yukon in the summer of
1897 – perhaps a fictional persona for himself – was 'Liverpool'.[150]

FIVE

# *Yukon*

In the spring of 1999, the seasoned white-water kayaker Steve Chapple, veteran of rivers like the Yellowstone and Zambezi, was ready for a fresh challenge. The next river for this resident of rural Montana and well-known writer on the outdoors was deliberately ironic. He decided to tackle the Los Angeles River because, unlike the Yellowstone and Zambezi, it was a 'symbol not of wilderness, but of its absence, of its extirpation, of all that had gone wrong with Western civilization'. His three-day voyage down to the Pacific was not without incident. At one point, shortly before entering The Slot (the central groove in the river's concrete bed that he compares to Deep Throat at the end of the Zambezi's Batoka Gorge), his party, spotted by a helicopter patrol, was obliged to wait midstream in the 'non-river river' for five police officers to show up.[1]

The Los Angeles River is even shorter than the Mersey. But none of my selected rivers, bar one, is particularly long by global standards. That exception is the 3,185-kilometre Yukon. The Yukon is also the kind of river more usually associated with adventurous paddling of the sort that Chapple normally pursued. A few minutes searching the Internet reveals the scale of the Yukon's current appeal to those in search of waterborne challenge: guidebooks and rafting companies constitute a mini-industry. But the untouched quality of the river that exerts such a powerful attraction as an antidote to the world symbolized by the LA River is deceptive. The Yukon may be largely devoid of the trappings of industrialism and modernity. But today's unpeopled stretches were much busier in the late nineteenth century and early twentieth century. At that time, canoes, rafts and other barques bearing an assortment of native peoples, explorers, scientists and gold-seekers were thick on the water. If a river's suspended load consists of history as well as silt, then the Yukon carries an enormous burden of both.

The first survey of the entire river was undertaken by members of the Scientific Corps attached to the Western Union Telegraph Company's expedition of 1865–7 to investigate the feasibility of an overland connection

191

between the western and eastern hemispheres via British Columbia, the Yukon Valley in Russian America, the Bering Strait and Siberia (numerous attempts to lay an Atlantic cable having proved fruitless to date). The chief of the Scientific Corps, William H. Dall, whose task was to collect specimens for the Smithsonian Institution, described his first sight of the river on 26 October 1866 in rhapsodic prose. Mushing overland from St Michael via Unalakleet on Norton Sound, he stopped his dog team half a mile below Kaltag. Spread out before him was a 40-mile stretch of snow-clad river, 'with broken fragments of ice-cakes glowing in the ruddy light of the setting sun'. 'This', he proclaimed, 'was the river I had read and dreamed of, which had seemed as if shrouded in mystery, in spite of the tales of those who had seen it'.[2]

Dall's travelling companion, the British artist Frederick Whymper, was equally impressed (though his point of reference was the Thames): 'I had been prepared to see a large stream, but had formed no conception of the reality. Neither pen nor pencil can give any idea of the dreary grandeur, the vast monotony, or the unlimited expanse we saw before us.'[3] On arrival at Fort Yukon, the river's most northerly point, in 1867 Dall felt 'a pardonable pride in being the first American' to reach, from the sea, what was also the (British-owned) Hudson's Bay Company's most westerly post.[4] By 1890, however, following a flurry of voyages, the 'most copious of all American rivers flowing to the Pacific' was 'well-known' from source to mouth.[5]

All who live with or encounter the Yukon are struck by its size and length. For the Gwitch'in Indian peoples of its inner watershed – just as the Po was *il grande fiume* for Italians – it was simply 'the river' (or 'the great river'): *Yu-kun-ah* (*Yukonah*).[6] For the Yupik, a people who dwell further downstream and in the delta region, it was *Kwiguk* ('large stream'). Russian explorers adopted a close version of the Yupik name: *Kwikhpak* (or *Kvichpak*).[7] However, English-speaking incomers eventually adopted an adaptation of the Gwitch'in name. In 1846, John Bell of the Hudson's Bay Company, who reached it by descending the Porcupine, first attached the name *Youcon* to the river downstream from Fort Yukon.[8] Continuing aboriginal practice, us army explorer Lieutenant Frederick Schwatka routinely referred to it as the 'great river' in the account of his expedition in 1883 (the first comprehensive survey of the entire river).[9]

Following the United States' acquisition of Alaska in 1867, the Missouri's and Mississippi's pre-eminent positions among American rivers were no longer undisputed. Ivan Petroff, the us Treasury agent responsible for the federal census of 1880 in the territory of Alaska, travelled upriver at least as far as where the Nowitna enters as part of his data-gathering exercise. A few years later, he reflected on how Americans would receive the new information about the Yukon and its magnitude, wagering that they 'will not be quick to take to the idea that the volume of water in an Alaskan river is greater than that discharged by the mighty Mississippi; but it is entirely within the bounds of honest statement to say that the Yukon river . . . discharges every hour one-third more water than the "Father of Waters".[10]

Whether or not the Yukon is greater than the Mississippi (or the second, third or fourth river of the United States), it is unrivalled by European standards. (So, of course, are any number of American rivers; a Kentuckian aboard Frances Skene's steamer in 1845 dismissed the Danube as 'nothing in comparison of the Ohio'[11]). By modest British standards, it is colossal. John Burns may have beaten his breast about the Thames's global role (size, in this instance, did not matter). However, French geographer Élisée Reclus used Britain's modest dimensions to drive home the Yukon's scale: its watershed could easily accommodate the British Isles three times over. The Canadian government surveyor William Ogilvie, lecturing on the Yukon Basin at the Royal Geographical Society in London (1898), employed a similar analogy: 'it is a very long river, so long that you might wrap it round this little island, and then tie a knot with the ends'.[12] The Briton, Whymper, was also suitably awed by the Yukon (whose side streams 'would be large rivers in Europe').[13] Nonetheless, this was precisely the sort of puffery closely associated with new world sources that goaded the likes of Burns and Mitton, who sprang to the defence of a small but momentous river.

This distinction between a river that was significant as a natural object but insignificant as a piece of history lay behind the objections of Burns and Mitton. Martin Heidegger did not care to draw such a distinction. He had a low opinion of the United States and all things American (*Amerikan-ismus*). As he associated in his better line and Hölderlin'. The later American culture was not only devoid of history (*geschichtslos*) but positively unhistorical (*ungeschichtlich*).[14] Though Heidegger never expressed an opinion of American rivers, there is no reason to believe that it would have been any higher than his evaluation of other American attributes. Yet what Heidegger regarded as a fatal flaw in things American, others have regarded as a monumental asset. Disregarding, for the moment, the centuries of aboriginal pre-history on the Yukon before the first Euro-Americans showed up 250 years ago, it is precisely this ahistorical or non-historical quality that has so deeply charmed more recent observers – many of whom are, in fact, Heidegger's fellow nationals. Such is the German penchant for 'floating' the river that an American who voyaged downriver in the mid-1980s felt as if the Yukon was a tributary of the Rhine.[15] Compared to other North American rivers, the Yukon has a shallow Euro-American history: it was the final river on the North American frontier that they explored, tentatively settled, and converted to their uses. 'Of all America's rivers', noted Richard Mathews, 'it has the longest prehistory and shortest recorded history'.[16]

As Constance Lindsay Skinner explained in the manifesto for her 'Rivers of America' series that ran until 1974 and totalled 65 volumes, she wanted to create a grand, fluvio-centric 'Folk Saga' of American history: 'We began to be Americans on the rivers . . . By the rivers the explorers and fur traders entered America.'[17] Since Frederick Jackson Turner solemnly announced the closing of the frontier in 1893, the Yukon is where Americans have sought to keep the frontier and its role as the crucible of Americanization alive, whether by continuing the time-honoured practice of exploiting untapped natural resources or working for a permanently frozen frontier by preserving the environmental status quo.

For many 'Rivers of America' authors – Skinner sought contributions from well-known novelists, poets and other writers ('artists') with a strong attachment to a particular river instead of historians ('scholastics') – the quality of the wild and the autonomous was their chosen river's leitmotif. The Colorado is 'an outlaw' that 'belongs only to the ancient, eternal earth. As no other, it is savage and unpredictable of mood, peculiarly American in character'. The book on the Allegheny, according to the rear dust jacket, was written in the style of 'masculine, unfettered writers who recorded the life of the wild American frontier'.[18] Oddly enough, the book on the Yukon, the wildest of American rivers – though planned, apparently, since 1944 – was one of the last to appear, in 1968. Mathews (who had a degree in modern European history) was moved to write the book about the Yukon after reading Leslie Roberts' contribution of 1949 on Canada's longest river, the Mackenzie, which reminded him that the series' reach did not yet extend to Alaska.

Mathews then spent his honeymoon (and publisher's advance) in the spring and early summer of 1966 on an extended field trip. After driving from New York City to Whitehorse, Yukon Territory, in a vw camper van, he and his wife embarked on a voyage down the river in a 'small, underpowered' boat. The newlyweds quit the river at the Yupik village of Marshall in the delta region. As he had written the book just before the discovery of Arctic oil that triggered a 'black gold' rush, Mathews could conclude that little had changed since the Russians first entered the river; it was still largely wild and 'primitive'. As the dust jacket's back flap informed readers: 'Today, the Yukon is an abandoned waterway, a beautiful wilderness river with deserted ghost towns and stern-wheelers rotting along the banks.'[19]

More than 40 years later, the Yukon remains one of the wildest of North America's long rivers. Just four road bridges span it. The newest, the E. L. Patton Bridge on the Dalton Highway, was constructed in 1974–5 as part of the Trans-Alaska Pipeline project and remains the Alaskan Yukon's only one. Before 1957, the river was entirely unfettered, with salmon enjoying a full, unimpeded run, scaling the White Horse Falls to spawn in the upper tributaries. That year, the river was dammed just above Whitehorse to provide the town with power, flooding White Horse Canyon to create Lake Schwatka. Yet this remains the only dam and impoundment. No other river in this study is so spectacularly unmodified. And, despite the effluents of mining, past and present, that affect some stretches, no other is so clean.

Despite its comparatively undeveloped condition, the Yukon has decisively shaped the history of its enormous catchment, which is larger than France. Nearly two-thirds of this third of a million square-mile watershed is located in Alaska. But Canadians feel just as entitled to sing the praises of a truly North American river. 'Of all Canada's great rivers', reflects the Canadian Council for Geographic Education, the Yukon is 'the one that has most retained its natural glory, while still being visibly marked by great human events'.[20] Within Alaska, the river serves as a far northern, apolitical version of the Mason-Dixon Line, more or less dividing the state into equal halves. As a result, until transportation links were forged between points south and north (kicking off with the Alaska Railroad that connected the coast at Seward to Fairbanks in the 1920s and culminating with the first Alaskan bridge over the river [1975]), the Yukon served as Alaska's principal highway. The far northwest's equivalent to the Mississippi has organized the flow of Alaskan history on an east-west rather than a north-south axis.

## Source, Course and Exploration

Though the only river in this study whose origins are glacial or lacustrine rather than spring, the Yukon is not exempt from the customary dispute over the precise location of a source. The contest is not just between advocates of a 'remote' source and those of the 'proper' (actual) source. It also reflects the piecemeal nature of the river's early exploration and mapping in self-contained portions, none of which commanded an overview. Wholesale confusion reigned as a rapid succession of explorers gave different names to the same features and offered estimates of length that varied by as much as 800 kilometres.[21]

Various glaciers in the coastal mountains of northern British Columbia are candidates for the 'remote' source. One of them sits above Lake Lindeman. Also in the running is the Choda Glacier at the southern end of Lake Atlin, that connects with Lake Taglish, which, in turn, flows into Lake Marsh. And according to Petroff, eastern and western Kussoa lakes (Lake Arkell), at the foot of the Chilkat Trail, were the 'real heads'.[22] If the origin of the tributary furthest from the mouth is the supreme criterion applied, then, strictly speaking, the source is the headwaters of the Nisutlin River in the Pelly Mountains, Yukon Territory. Others proposed that the northern end of Marsh Lake, just south of Whitehorse, is the source in practice. No matter that the freshly emerged river then quickly widens out into 50-kilometre-long Lake Laberge.

The complications raised by this chain of finger lakes that occupy the sites of ancient fjords doubtless influenced the judgment of Captain Charles W. Raymond of the US Corps of Topographical Engineers, who voyaged 1,673 kilometres upriver to Fort Yukon in 1869.[23] At the 'James - town of the Yukon' (as fellow American explorer Hudson Stuck dubbed it), Raymond's duty was to inform the Hudson's Bay Company that it was trespassing on American territory and to raise the American flag over the fort.[24] For Raymond, whose secondary purpose was to gather information about the new acquisition's natural resources and natives, the Yukon proper did not begin until the confluence with the Porcupine just downriver from Fort Yukon. He designated the river between Lake Laberge and Fort Yukon as the Lewes.[25] This was standard nomenclature at the time, whether in the United States or Canada. Adopting a stance between the extremes, others indicated that the 'true' Yukon began at the junction of the Lewes and Pelly, 483 kilometres below Whitehorse, where the river is already as broad as the Mississippi at St Louis.[26]

On the eve of the Western Union expedition (1865), it was not even clear whether the river the Russians called the *Kwikhpak* and the river the British called the Yukon were one and the same. The majority view (based on the account of the Hudson's Bay Company explorer, Alexander Murray) held that the Yukon was a separate entity, connecting with the Colville, and debouching to the north in the Arctic Ocean.[27] In the summer of 1866, Frank Ketchum and Michael Labarge, Canadian members of the Western Union expedition's Scientific Corps, were the first North Americans to travel from the mouth to Fort Yukon, establishing beyond doubt that the Yukon and the *Kwikhpak* were the same river.[28]

For half a century, the names for the upper and lower halves of the same river, Yukon and Lewes, more or less co-existed, separate but equal. Sorting out the bewildering tangle became a matter of increasing urgency, however, at the time of the Klondike stampede. National pride was also involved. Whether to continue the search for the upper reaches of the Yukon via the Lewes or Pelly was a decision that faced the Alaska Military Reconnaissance of 1883, under Schwatka's command, whose purpose was to pinpoint the Yukon's headwaters. Schwatka calculated, after measuring water flow, width and depth, that the Lewes was 'superior' to the Pelly. Riding roughshod over local custom, he unilaterally changed its name: 'I abandoned the name [Lewes], and it appears on the map as the Yukon to Crater Lake at its head'. (By extension, he identified Lake Lindeman as the source.) The subtitle of Schwatka's subsequent book said it all: *An Adventurous Expedition down the Great Yukon River, From its Source in the British North-West Territory, to its Mouth in the Territory of Alaska* (1890).[29]

Schwatka's conclusion that the 'old Lewis river' was 'undoubtedly the Yukon proper' was not well received in Canada.[30] Across the border, the desire to retain the autonomy of the Lewes (which Robert Campbell, a Hudson's Bay Company explorer, named in honour of John Lee Lewes, the Company's chief factor, in 1842) remained strong.[31] In its first annual report, in 1898, the Geographical Board of Canada nomenclature committee ruled against Schwatka's re-designation (and adjusted the spelling from Lewis to Lewes).[32] The recommendation of the Canadian government explorer, George M. Dawson, who followed shortly after Schwatka (1887), perhaps influenced the Board. For Dawson, a geologist who compiled the first report on the Yukon region's mineral resources, it was also a question of establishing the source of the Lewes or the Pelly as the Yukon's ultimate source. But he had no intention of meddling with established nomenclature, denouncing Schwatka's decision as 'arbitrary and unjustifi-able'.[33] The (renamed in 1948) Canadian Board on Geographic Names finally capitulated in May 1949 and eliminated the Lewes from all future maps.[34] When it issued its *Principles and Procedures for Geographical Naming* (1990), Natural Resources Canada's Canadian Permanent Committee on Geographical Names cited the Yukon's replacement of the Lewes as an example of adherence to Principle Four ('Naming an Entire Feature and Identifying its Extent').[35]

Accepting the 'remote' source in Lake Lindeman or Atlin as the source proper – now the conventional wisdom – gives the Yukon a highly unusual course. Rising within view of the Pacific, the divide between the Yukon's watershed and waters flowing south to the Pacific is astonishingly close. Tidal waters, at the head of Dyea Inlet, are just 24 kilometres from Yukon headwaters.[36] The river initially follows an upward curving trajectory north-westward into Alaska and then drops south-westward toward the same ocean, into which it finally emits at a point 1,600 kilometres north of its source.

From Dawson City, epicentre of the Klondike stampede, the Alaskan border is 145 kilometres. Two hundred and nine kilometres beyond the border is Circle City, at the head of the Yukon Flats and at the centre of the so-called 'Great Arctic Bend'.

For 370 kilometres, the river disperses into the maze-like Flats, a labyrinthine area of multiple channels, islands and sloughs that reminded one Briton of a hugely magnified Norfolk Broads and gave numerous visitors the feeling that they had entered the delta proper prematurely.[37] This Spreewald of sorts (a big difference, though, is that the current's strength does not dissipate) was characterized by us army explorer and cartographer William Yanert as a 'jungle' of thick scrub, relieved only by 'niggerhead swamp'.[38]

Below the Flats, the river enters Rampart Canyon, where castellated sandstone bluffs rise 330 metres as the channel narrows to under a kilo-metre. 'Going down to salt water' (the Middle Yukon Indian term for travelling to the mouth[39]) over its final 480 kilometres, the river crosses lowland tundra, finally debouching into the Bering Sea at Norton Sound, after passing through a marshy delta region considerably larger than the Danube's and Po's (the head of the delta is 161 kilometres short of the ocean). The sea leaves its imprint along the Mersey for a considerable distance, if the sea's stamp is defined as its highest tidal reach. The Yukon's estuarine portion is greater than the Danube's and the Po's,

198

Aerial photograph of the intricately braided river that flows through the Yukon Flats in central Alaska.

H. W. Elliott, 'Looking Back at the End of the Ramparts', illustration from W. H. Dall, *Travels on the Yukon and in the Yukon Territory* (1898).

if proportionately less than the Mersey's. Dall reported seals at Nulato – not to mention a white (beluga) whale – 966 kilometres from traces of salt water.[40]

The Yukon's liquid content is also exceptional among my six rivers. For much of its length, it is clouded with silt. Dawson characterized the upper river (Lewes) as 'slightly opalescent', akin to the Rhône that emerges from Lake Geneva.[41] Lavrentii A. Zagoskin, a Russian naval lieutenant who led the first Russian scientific exploration of the Yukon in 1842, described the water at Nulato as greyish-yellow and mentioned that a three-pail keg, after standing for three days, had an accumulation of sediment equivalent to a sixth of its volume (though the water itself, 'like that of our blessed Mother Volga', was entirely potable).[42] Tributaries contribute their own thick and granular loads. The White River is aptly named; chalky ash from a prehistoric eruption bestows the milky quality of 'pulverized pumice-stone'.[43] Schwatka described its flow as 'almost liquid mud' – the distinction between the flow and mud bars hard to discern. A gold-seeker compared it to soup.[44] The White mingles instantly, converting the Yukon into milky coffee. Stuck, the Episcopal Archdeacon of the Yukon between 1904 and 1920, took great exception to how the White 'completely befouled' the Yukon, ruining its fair appearance for good. The London-born frontier missionary also objected to the impact of another glacier-draining tributary, the Tanana, whose potability, consistency and colour were so deplorable that 'the drainage of London' could not make them any worse.[45] The load of suspended silt is so heavy (but suspended nonetheless because of the swift current) that boat paddles hiss as if being rubbed with sandpaper and moving boats make a scraping sound.

The massive burden of suspended silt and other debris (including whole trees) that discharged into the sea, especially after spring break-up, built up sand and mud banks at the mouth that extended 112 kilometres out to sea at the time the United States began to explore its latest territorial acquisition. Not only did this discolour the eastern Bering Sea for as far as the eye could see; it was difficult for a large steamer to travel safely across the delta region, let alone enter the river.[46] An Argonaut from California, who voyaged from San Francisco to the river's mouth in June 1898 and remarked on the 'power' of the river in 'shallowing' the sea, noted that the Bering Sea was only ten feet deep 40 miles from the shore.[47] St Michael, the trading station that the Russian American Fur Company founded north of the delta in 1833, on the northeast-facing promontory of a small island that marshes connected to the mainland, was at the point closest to the mouth that oceangoing vessels could reach – and, even here, they had to anchor offshore and transfer cargo to barges for transhipment.[48]

## Yielding Yukon

The Yukon valley, a migration route for the first settlers of the Americas who trekked across the Bering Land Bridge from Eurasia, has an ancient history as an artery of commerce. Harry de Windt, a British adventurer headed in the opposite direction in 1896 (his original purpose was to travel overland from New York to Paris via the Bering Strait), hailed the Yukon as the 'great highway of this vast northern land, where there was not a single road'.[49] Upstream Indians voyaged downstream in spring after the ice left the river (break-up) and spent the summer hunting muskrat, beaver, duck and geese, and fishing for salmon. At winter's approach, they retreated into the interior to hunt large mammals. When newcomers penetrated the region in search of furs for the Chinese market, the river supported a linear trading empire in which 'first nation' peoples exchanged furs for flour, textiles, tea and liquor and vied for the upper hand with Russians, Britons and Americans.[50]

The lower river's characteristic watercraft was the *baidarra*, a sealskin boat that could accommodate a party of twenty to 30. After overwintering at Nulato, the first non-native settlement on the river (1838) at the mouth of the Tanana, and the Russian American Company's easternmost trading post, Dall and Whymper made the 966-kilometre journey to Fort Yukon in a 'baidarre'.[51] The smaller *baidark*, made of the same material, had a maximum capacity of three. These boats required considerable mainten-ance. After a few days in the water, sealskin became soggy; periodic layovers (preferably every ten days) were needed for drying out and re-oiling.[52] Zagoskin left Nulato for the upper river on 4 June 1843. But heavy rain rotted his skin boat. He learnt too late what Dall knew from the start: these boats required regular waterproofing with marine mammal grease.[53] On the upper (Canadian) river and the middle river (US border to the Tanana), some boats were made of moose hide. The typical native boat, however, was the 12-foot, sharp-ended birch bark canoe, whose frame was sewed with roots of white spruce (this thickly wooded region's dominant tree) and calked with spruce gum. The birch canoe was so light it could be carried in one hand. Yet lightness had its drawbacks. These boats were extremely frail and easily damaged.

The Yukon's mercantile value to outside traders was partly grounded in its favourable physiology. Given the overall absence of rapids, even larger vessels could negotiate most of its length (if only in summer). Ogilvie, who ascended in 1895–6 on behalf of the Canadian Topographical Survey, was

Eric A. Hegg, shooting the White Horse Rapids during the Klondike Era, photograph, 1898.

struck that 'a river so long, and flowing as it does for more than two-thirds of its length through a veritable sea of mountains', challenged boats just once: at the 'grand canyon' of the Yukon, upstream from the future site of Whitehorse. This confirmed the Yukon's status as 'a strange river in a strange land'.[54]

The Yukon's busiest human moment was 1898, when the river and its major tributaries hummed with activity relating to prospecting for and extracting gold. The first (smallish) strikes were in Alaska at Forty Mile Creek (1886) and Birch Creek (1891), which gave birth to Circle City (by July 1896, with almost a thousand inhabitants, the 'Paris of Alaska' was the world's largest log cabin city).[55] However, the river's international renown is based on a discovery across the border. On 17 August 1896, gold was struck in the gravels of Rabbit Creek, which fed into the Klondike, a 200-mile tributary of the Yukon. The native name indicates its former source of wealth. For centuries, the most precious commodity in the Klondike and its related streams was dark red and mobile: *Tronduick* (or *Thron-Duik*) translates as Hammer-water, a reference to the stakes driven into the gravel river-bed across its mouth to divert salmon into traps. When he passed on 1 September 1887, Ogilvie noted that the entire mouth was staked, with a fish camp consisting of six families on a nearby island.[56] George Carmack's renaming of Rabbit Creek as Bonanza Creek was entirely apt: the precious metal deposits were literally found within the rivers.[57] These were truly rivers of riches. Centuries of freezing, thawing and erosion had loosened the ore from the surrounding strata. Heavier than adjacent substances, these particles sank into stream bed gravels until checked by a denser mineral. To wrest the ore from the auriferous gravel, miners ripped creeks apart, wrecking them for other human pursuits such as fishing and eliminating their capacity to sustain biotic life. Rivers were entirely remade, stripped of their basic biological capacities, boiled down to a repository of gold.

When the first steamer from St Michael docked in San Francisco on 14 July 1897, laden with over half a million dollars' worth of gold, 'Klondicitis' reached epidemic proportions worldwide. Perhaps as many as 1,000,000 fortune-seekers set out to make their 'pile'. Getting there was no mean feat; only about 50,000 arrived. There were two ways to reach the Klondike: downstream from the Yukon's headwaters ('inside passage') or upstream from its mouth ('outside passage'). Those who chose the first route landed in the south-east Alaska 'panhandle', crossed the daunting barrier of the coastal range, and then headed downriver. The alternative, much longer route, was to enter at the mouth and travel upstream from St Michael

('Fort Get-There').[58] This route had the advantages of comfort (roughing it was not part of the deal; three meals a day were) and avoided the hard work of traversing the coastal passes.[59] The drawbacks, however, were the extra cost and distance; as explained by Liverpudlian Frank Richards, a captain in the Liverpool Battalion of the Boy's Brigade who had travelled extensively on the Yukon, the trip from St Michael to Dawson, the settlement closest to the goldfields, took as long as the voyage from Liverpool to New York.[60] The first route, being cheaper and shorter, as well as, in theory, open all year, was by far the most popular, and the one recommended for gold seekers leaving from Liverpool.

Three-quarters of gold-seekers took a boat from San Francisco, Portland, Seattle, Tacoma, Vancouver or Victoria up the Inside Passage and disembarked at Skagway or Dyea. There were two routes over the mountains: White Pass and Chilkoot Pass. Chilkoot Trail was the main Indian route to the interior. White Pass was an easier but lesser-known route. Both crossings had to be made on foot. And supplies had to be shouldered for the last few thousand feet of Chilkoot Pass, which was too sheer for pack animals.[61] Once across, prospectors entered Canada and dropped down to Lake Bennett, where they assembled makeshift boats or crude rafts from timber whipsawed into lumber and paddled through a chain of lakes to Lake Marsh. Dawson City lay 885 kilometres upstream. Miners crossed into the Yukon watershed in spring, prospected over the summer and then floated down to St Michael before winter closed in.

Steamboats had appeared on the Danube, Spree and Mersey by the early 1830s. They penetrated the upper Yukon in the spring and summer of 1898; by the start of the following year's springtime upriver travel season, they had entirely displaced miners' rudimentary boats. The journey to Dawson was completed in two legs: one steamer shuttled between the upper lakes and Miles Canyon, while the other ran between Whitehorse and Dawson. Whereas the Danube confronted river craft with three major obstacles – the Wirbel, the Strudel and the Iron Gate – the only serious impediment the Yukon raised in the path of the herd of gold-seekers that stampeded down the river in the wake of the explorers of the 1880s was the 'Grand Cañon'. Though the 'only dangerous spot on the river' (Ogilvie), it was still a formidable proposition.[62]

The most renowned of the explorers who passed through the canyon before the gold rush was 33-year-old Schwatka and his military party of six, which built a raft at Lake Lindeman after crossing Chilkoot. The preface to his best-selling book about the expedition (*Along Alaska's*

'The Raft at the End of its Journey', engraving from a photograph by Mr Homan, 1883.

'Prying the Raft off a Bar', engraving from a sketch by Sergeant Gloster, 1883.

Eric A. Hegg, photograph of rafts and rough-hewn scows negotiating Squaw Rapids, between Miles Canyon and White Horse Rapids, *c.* 1898.

'Miles Canyon', with a raft in the middle of the river, some time between 1896 and 1913.

*Great River*, published in 1885, the same year as *Huckleberry Finn*) billed it as 'the longest raft journey ever made, in the interest of geographical science'. They built the raft from the largest available spruce and pine logs. Initially measuring 30 feet by 15, after locating better timber, they enlarged it before setting off. The final dimensions were 42 feet by 16. A canvas sail fashioned from a wall tent topped off the *Resolute*. Schwatka expected to have to replace the 'primitive' craft a couple of times en route, but the *Resolute* lived up to its name by proving astonishingly resilient.[63]

Entering Miles Canyon (as Schwatka renamed it), the river narrowed from 300 to 30 metres. The 8-kilometre canyon, within which the river drops 12 metres, included a kilometre-long section walled with perpendicular, six- and seven-sided columns of basalt rising up 20–25 metres – a monumental curiosity of nature that Schwatka compared to the legendary Fingal's Cave off the Scottish island of Mull. 'Through this narrow chute', he recorded, 'rushes the water of the great river, a perfect mass of milk-like foam, that can be heard reverberating for a long distance'. Hot on the heels of the walled section came a whirlpool and, lower down, another slender chute formed 'a perfect funnel of boiling cascades, not much wider than the raft and higher than the mast at its outlet'.[64] This stretch, which the first prospectors named White Horse Rapids because the water resembled a flowing mane, was the final rapid before calmer waters returned.[65] Nearly a kilometre long, it required a portage of goods and passengers – and sometimes the boats themselves.[66]

Local Indians 'confidently' expected Schwatka's raft to be smashed to smithereens. In fact, his party survived Miles Canyon unscathed. Yet Dawson also warned against attempting to run these rapids.[67] In the summer of 1897, bound for the Klondike goldfields, an assortment of 7,000 improvised wooden watercraft known as scows (rough hewn, flat bottomed and raft-like) confronted Miles Canyon. Many 'greenhorns' erred on the side of caution. They hired pilots, both Indian and white, to take their vessels through with just enough weight to keep them stable, while they portaged the bulk of their gear (including the most valuable items) around the canyon on the west bank (or, when it became available, took the tramway). One British fortune-seeker, Robert Kirk, provided an extended account of his party's passage through Miles Canyon in the autumn of 1897. After portaging 600 pounds of equipment and supplies around the canyon, the trio shot the rapids in three and a half minutes by steering a steady course straight down the middle. Though Kirk's party found White Horse Rapids much more intimidating, it also came through

Larss & Duclos, horse-pulled tram cart loaded with two canoes, equipment and dog for the portage around White Horse Rapids and Canyon Tramway, Klondike era.

unruffled the following day (admittedly with an experienced borrowed helmsman). Jack London, already a seasoned sailor at the age of twenty, also breezed through, unfazed (according to his second wife) by an audience of a thousand.[68]

Needless to say, an impatient minority tried to run through without unloading cargo (the portage could consume up to two days), causing the wreckage of hundreds of boats crammed with precious supplies, as well as the loss of several lives. During its successful passage down Miles Canyon, Kirk's party witnessed several smash-ups. And White Horse Rapids had claimed at least one victim the previous day. By the spring of 1898, seasoned boatmen had set themselves up guiding novices for a fee of between $5 and $20.[69] Nonetheless, in the early summer, the banks around Miles Canyon were festooned with soggy groceries and provisions spread out to dry on canvas sheets and blankets. All around, upturned boats were being repaired.[70] That same summer, a tramway system that ran the full 8 kilometres from the head of Miles Canyon to the bottom of White Horse Rapids was constructed. Horse-drawn flat car-style wagons ran along its 8-inch diameter wooden rails. Soon, the North-West Mounted Police arrived and established rules for portaging and piloting. A swift and safe portage around the reefs was now available for all who wished to avail themselves of this service.[71] The upriver portage of Mary Hitchcock and Edith Van Buren ('born and reared in luxury and refinement') in the autumn of 1898 was thoroughly uneventful – a 4.5 mile ride atop the last wagon in a seven-car procession along a 'fine road with the most gorgeous scenery'.[72]

The only other stretch of white water that regularly attracted attention – initially as a hazard and later as a tourist attraction – was Five Finger Rapids. Here, below the trading post of Carmacks, five 30-metre, tree-topped basalt pillars split the river into four channels, just one of which – on the far right – was navigable. The passageway was reputedly so slender that boats grazed the jagged rocks on each side. Hell's Gates, immediately below Five Finger, was another hairy stretch, the 'treacherous chute' so narrow that, allegedly, a passenger on a boat could shake hands with someone standing on the rocky bank. Nevertheless, an ascending steamer could pull through with a warping winch and line attached to the shore.[73]

The route between Dawson (the metropolis of the Yukon, with a peak population of 35,000 in the early 1900s) and the mouth was plied by Mississippi-style (if smaller) steamers and increasingly staffed by Mississippi-trained captains and crews (the first pilots were local Yupik).[74] Steamers arrived on the lower river 30 years before they began to operate on the upper river during the gold rush. The brig *Commodore*, on which Raymond travelled to St Michael in 1869, carried a 50-foot stern-wheel steamer, the *Yukon*, which, bearing him and his survey party, was the first steamboat to enter the river on 4 July 1869.[75] Hereafter, upriver passengers

Looking down Miles Canyon.

and goods transferred at St Michael to the smaller, stern-wheeled river steamers with shallower draughts that were required to negotiate the shallow delta channels.[76] The closest point of entry to the multiple-mouthed river – though the sandbank hazard meant that most steamers could only enter at high tide – was 75 miles south of St Michael (Kwikhpak channel).[77]

As the stories of traffic flow on the Po, Mersey and Danube indicate, white water is not the only impediment to navigation. Low water, multiple channels and bars also cause headaches. Running aground on bars of sand, mud and gravel was a constant hazard for prospectors rafting down the upper river; sometimes it was necessary to unload, refloat and then reload at the first convenient stopping point downstream.[78] In the summer of 1898, low water following snow and ice melt detained two female travellers at St Michael, who, having arrived from San Francisco, wished to transfer to a Dawson-bound river steamer.[79]

To negotiate the innumerable braided channels, shoals and dead-end sloughs of the Yukon Flats, native pilot hire was mandatory. Moreover, since the main channel's position shifted during break-up, native navigators plotted a fresh steamboat channel each spring.[80] Even a shallow draft steamer had to pick its way through gingerly. Low water during the brief sub-arctic summer season, with its aridity and unexpectedly fierce heat

Travellers en route to the Klondike Gold Fields, standing above Five Finger Rapids, postcard, 1896–1913.

The steamboat *White Horse* passing upriver through Five Finger Rapids, Yukon
Territory, 1904.

('the sun came through with a blistering effect that made one feel as
though they were floating on the Nile or Niger — anywhere, except under
the shadow of the Arctic circle'[81]), was an associated problem, especially
in the Flats. It might take ten days for even an expert pilot to re-float a
grounded steamer with the assistance of cordwood and soapy skids, or the
heavy spar and tackle stored on the forward deck.[82] In August 1897, only
22 inches of water remained in the main shipping channel through the
Flats. Just above Fort Yukon, reported Lieutenant W. P. Richardson on
13 September 1897, the water was only 2 feet deep; yet his boat drew 3.5

Walter W. Hodge, 'Midnight Sun on Yukon River', *c.* 1930–32.

to 4 feet of water. Steamers carrying food, hardware, tobacco and liquor up to Dawson were marooned here until October (as tributaries froze, they compounded the low water problem).[83] By mid-August, panic gripped Dawson. The Mounted Police and the two resident trading companies urged those without enough food to see out the winter to get out before freeze up. Hundreds abandoned Dawson for Fort Yukon or headed upriver.[84]

## Unyielding Yukon

Whether voyaging upstream or downstream, explorers and travellers faced the problem of a short (four-month) ice-free season. The first batch of gold-seekers who crossed the coastal passes in the autumn of 1897 were at the mercy of the imminent ice; if caught in the upper lakes, this meant eight months of enforced inactivity, consuming limited supplies. Twenty-year-old Jack London and his party spent three demoralizing days trying to made headway down Lake Laberge on the homemade *Yukon Belle* in the face of a gale. 'Today we've got to make it', he declared, 'or we camp here all winter'.[85] Of nearly 2,000 gold seekers who survived the first hurdle and tried to descend to Dawson by steamboat, only 43 arrived; the others, their vessels trapped in the ice, over-wintered where they could.[86] The river was usually closed until the first of June.[87] Nor did break-up proceed at the

H. W. Elliott, 'The Frozen Yukon, from Dawson City', *c.* 1867.

same pace along the entire river. The upper reaches broke first, but on the still waters of the lakes the ice took longer to go out; miners crossed the passes from the coast in April and built boats while awaiting break-up. At the mouth, the ice also went out later, sometimes as late as the Fourth of July.[88]

Break-up, when it arrived, was a spectacular phenomenon that no first-time visitor failed to describe with as much eloquence as could be mustered. 'After the first crack, mountains of ice reared up on the sand bars', recorded Zagoskin at Nulato on 5 May 1843. 'After a minute every-thing broke loose: the ice heaped up again, and again broke apart – death again was magnificently vanquished by life.'[89] No matter how sublime, break-up is not an overnight process. The Russians had learnt to be patient, to wait until the entire river was completely clear – a period that might last two weeks – before ascending from Nulato to Fort Yukon.[90]

The melting and movement of ice up to four feet thick held many perils for late-going and other early river users and bankside dwellers. As on the Danube, meltwater backed up behind ice dams caused regular and heavy springtime flooding (particularly at bends). The impact is particu-larly severe along the Yukon because the lowest reaches remain frozen for up for a month after the rest of the river is free of ice and sending ice careering headlong downstream. Dall recorded that an ice barrier 15 feet high formed near Nulato in late May 1868, shortly after break-up, where it stuck around for several days. When the blockage eventually shifted, his craft narrowly avoided being crushed between slabs of ice and the bluffs. He also reported an incident in which a birch canoe sank after being 'nipped between the ice-cakes'.[91] And unless they were firmly beached, descending ice would sweep away or crush steamers overwintering on the river.[92]

The danger of collision with driftwood created further concern. Swollen with snowmelt (Whymper recorded that the river at Nulato ran 14 feet above its winter level at the height of break-up), the river dislodged huge logs berthed on sandbars and floated them off. Even when canoes managed to avoid these marauding logs, the merest brush could slice through the sealskin or birch bark.[93] Live trees that tumbled into the river created more disorder. The melting ice was a powerful agent of erosion, undermining the banks on the concave bend where the current is strongest. Eventually, the bank's overhanging roof collapsed into the river. This not only altered river morphology but generated tremendous quantities of hazardous driftwood. Before finally toppling over, bankside trees hung precariously, attached only by their roots. Schwatka found his reference point in the *chevaux de frise*, an anti-cavalry device consisting of interlocking wooden spikes that remained in use as late as the American Civil War.[94] By the early 1860s, erosion from melting ice had encroached literally to the doorstep of the trading post established at Fort Yukon in 1847 – a substantial fortress designed to withstand assault by local Indians or the formal owners of the territory (though, in practice, it was well beyond the Russian sphere of influence).[95] In 1864, the Hudson's Bay Company relocated the fort a mile downriver. When Dall and Whymper visited in 1867, the new fort was not yet finished and some of the original structure's foundation timbers now stuck out well into the river.[96]

Travel did not cease during the eight frozen months. Frozen rivers in arctic and sub-arctic regions tend not to be smooth surfaced like their counterparts in temperate regions. The texture is rough and jagged and not suitable for travel until snow has filled the crazy paving of gaps and crevasses. Even then, the ride is rocky, with relatively few patches of smooth ice and much meandering to and fro between 'a mass of tilted ice blocks'.[97] Moreover, for two months, the river was effectively unusable. In late spring, when the ice was melting, all movement came to a complete standstill. (During early spring, refreezing at night extended the winter travel season by a week or two.[98]) For half the year, though, people moved goods on sleds pulled by dogs fuelled with dried salmon.[99] Zagoskin, for

The steamboat *General Jefferson C. Davis* breaking through ice on the Yukon, Alaska, postcard, *c.* 1920s.

Party negotiating a passage through ice floes in an open boat, near Ruby, Yukon Flats, Alaska, *c.* 1920s.

Frederick Blount Drane, photograph of crossing the Yukon with the mail at the Tanana Mission during the early stages of freeze-up (24 October), 1913–39.

Break-up at Circle City, Alaska, 21 May 1897, photograph by E. A. Sather.

'Falling banks of the Yukon just below Nuklakayet'. This engraving from a sketch by Sergeant Gloster (1883) illustrates the *chevaux de frise* effect.

example, left St Michael on 4 December 1842 with five sleds, 27 dogs, and 1,600 pounds of supplies, adding another 800 pounds en route. They reached Nulato, 600 miles upriver, on 15 January 1843.[100]

Some gold-seekers who did not want to wait until the next spring in the event that they crossed the coastal passes too late in the year brought along or procured a bicycle.[101] A group of New Yorkers devised a 'Klon-dike Bicycle' specially adapted for the Chilkoot Trail.[102] Weighing 50 pounds, it possessed a strong steel tubing frame (wound with rawhide so it could be handled in low temperatures), and 1.5 inch diameter tyres of solid rubber (which froze hard). The Klondike bike was reputedly capable of carrying half the requisite 1,000 pounds of kit without which the Mounties would prohibit passage over the coastal range.[103]

The river's value as a winter cycling route was particularly evident in 1899–1900, when thousands of Klondikers headed west for the latest dis -coveries on the beaches of Nome, 1,200 miles to the northwest on the northern shore of Norton Sound, across from the delta. The majority mushed to Nome. A few skated. Others cycled. Edward R. Jesson owned a dog team but was deterred by the state of many of the first wave of Nome-bound stampeders who passed his trading post 120 miles down-river from Dawson at Star City in the winter of 1899. They were already in poor condition, their dog teams overloaded and exhausted. It apparently took Jesson eight days to learn to ride the 'wheel' he acquired (the trick was to keep the front wheel firmly placed in the groove of a dog sled track).[104]

He pedalled out of Dawson on 22 February 1900 and the journey, in temperatures as low as minus 48 degrees Fahrenheit, took five weeks. His daily average rate was 30 miles; on good days, he covered 100 miles. (Since many Indians and old timers had never seen a bicycle before, his passage caused quite a commotion.) This was impressive going, given that, as Jesson wrote in his diary on the first day out: 'the oil in the bearings was frozen and I could scarcely ride it and my nose was freezing and I had to hold the handlebars with both hands not being able to ride yet with one hand and rub my nose with the other'. He arrived at Nome covered in bruises but without breaking a single spoke or suffering a puncture. One big advantage over dogs was that his trusty metal steed 'didn't eat anything and I didn't have to cook dogfeed for it'[105] (though, unlike a dog, a bicycle was inedible if it broke down).

Since the Yukon gold rushes attracted such a motley crew, whose motives were so varied and multi-layered, it makes little sense to try to distinguish between those who participated for strictly pecuniary reasons and those who desired adventure first and foremost. Nonetheless, even during the peak years of 1897–8, persons who regarded the Yukon primarily as a river of recreation can be identified. These travellers regarded the voluntarily assumed rigours of travel as part of the undertaking's appeal and any scrapes – provided they were fairly effortlessly survived – spiced up their take-home experience.

## Ever Youthful Yukon

Henry David Thoreau, who preferred his unassuming local brooks to storied rivers in distant places, was left cold by the Rhine. He had never visited Europe, but based his opinion on a panorama in a gallery. The heavy hand of the past weighed down the Rhine. The river's legends, the Roman bridges, the vine-clad hillsides and ruined castles – these features impoverished rather than enriched the Rhine. Snapping out of 'the spell of enchantment' that the artwork had cast on him, Thoreau shifted his attention to the Mississippi, which, at the time of writing (1850s), he had not seen either, except as another gallery panorama.[106] Yet the river that bisected North America's inland empire served his purpose by supplying the Rhine's polar opposite. He awoke from the 'dream of the Middle Ages' into which the old world's river had transported him to find himself firmly in the present, among the 'rising cities' and the steamboats 'wooding up'.

Voyaging along a river not yet spanned by bridges and along which cities were just being founded, he felt that '*this was the heroic age itself*'. The importance of rivers like the Rhine, Ganges and Nile and their associated basins was historical, for they had 'yielded their crop'. All eyes were now on rivers of the Americas such as the Amazon, Plate, Orinoco, St Lawrence and Mississippi: 'it remains to be seen what [they] will produce'.[107] A river such as the Mississippi was not living off or dwelling in the past; like the Mersey, it was busy making history.

Thoreau did not include the Yukon on his list of robust new world rivers. Yet travellers did compare the Yukon to the Amazon.[108] And in the final years of the nineteenth century, the heroic age in the making and yet to be harvested potential could be located on the banks of the Yukon. Visiting in 1903, the American travel writer William Seymour Edwards shared Thoreau's grand vision of fluvial futures. Between Whitehorse and Dawson (the stretch he surveyed from the *White Horse* steamboat in September 1903) the river reminded the West Virginian of the Ohio Valley on the eve of colonization: 'an immense and unknown land, not yet taken possession of by man!' Ignoring the permafrost, he insisted that the soil was fertile and would yield prodigious crops when ploughed.[109] But after the gold rush, the region quickly returned to relative obscurity.

The saving grace was scenic grandeur. What farmers found sorely wanting (Edwards' 'distant day' when towns and villages will dot the banks remains very distant), tourists found abundantly present. A place inhospitable for cultivation and defined by a boom-bust economic cycle associated with mineral extraction by outside interests (here today, gone somewhere else tomorrow) turned out to be entirely hospitable for those in search of a non-extractable natural resource: the experience of wildness and scenery in the raw. The spell of enchantment that the Yukon's scenery and mystique cast was not instant or intrinsic. The first generation of explorers was largely immune to the charms later detected and to the experiential, non-monetary commodity value invested in the river as land - scape rather than land.

In June 1847, Alexander Murray voyaged down the Porcupine to its junction with the Yukon, under instructions to found a Canadian trading post on Russian territory. Seeing the Yukon for the first time was not the overwhelmingly positive experience it would be for Dall and Whymper twenty years later. ('Stolid indeed must he be, who surveys the broad expanse of the Missouri of the North for the first time without emotion', reflected Dall.[110]) In fact, Murray's reaction was overwhelmingly negative:

> As I sat smoking my pipe and my face besmeared with tobacco
> juice to keep at bay the d—d mosquitoes still hovering in clouds
> around me . . . my first impressions of the Youcon were anything
> but favourable . . . I never saw an uglier river, every where low
> banks, apparently lately overflowed, with lakes and swamps
> behind, the trees too small for building, the water abominably
> dirty and the current furious.[111]

The entire river did not benefit, however, from Dall's and Whymper's
aesthetic and emotional appreciation. Some stretches were more valued
than others. Schwatka explained that another hazard of the Yukon Flats,
besides the bugs and the navigational obstacles, was boredom: 'the
everlasting flat country through which we had been drifting for days
produced a peculiar depression hard to describe and harder to bear'.[112]
And though he was more kindly disposed toward the more conventionally scenic stretches of the river, where it was squeezed within defiles
(like the Rhine gorge or the Iron Gate on the Danube), Schwatka found
it hard to envisage or promote the Yukon Valley as 'a paradise to future
tourists'.[113]

Nevertheless, two women from the east coast who ascended to Dawson
in July 1898 were thoroughly charmed by the scenery, which they routinely
described as magnificent, grand, glorious and marvellous. Hitchcock
(widow of a naval commander) and Van Buren (grand-niece of former
president Martin Van Buren) were unflappable travellers as well as blue-
blooded and 'fearless Anglo-Saxon' women. A 21-day trip upriver on the
*Flora* to the 'very skirmish line of civilization' in the 'terrible Wonderland
of the North' was unadulterated adventure.[114] As they steamed upriver
(with what a fellow-voyager referred to as 'the strangest agglomeration
of cargo that ever women's wits devised'[115]), the scenery just kept getting
better: 'If the scenery yesterday was grand, what can be said of that through
which we have been passing to-day [Rampart Canyon]? Mountains and
relays of mountains, narrow gorges, rapids, all that is most wild and
picturesque!'[116] A fellow passenger also lauded the 'primeval beauty'
that begged the landscape painter's attention.[117]

A few years earlier, a Londoner heaped more grudging praise: the
scenery in the vicinity of Rampart Canyon was 'not at all unpleasing', with
the 'picturesque' views from his party's camp reminiscent of a 'familiar
"burn" in far-away Scotland'.[118] Stuck also merrily mixed the aesthetic
categories of the picturesque and the sublime established by the eighteenth-

century canon of taste in landscape. Mushing along the river on one of his many ministrations to the spiritual and practical needs of the basin's far-flung and sparsely distributed native peoples, he hailed the Rampart region as 'one of the most picturesque portions of this great river' yet also 'very bold and wild'.[119] Stuck's composite account of his summer travels (1917), which complemented his earlier amalgam, *Ten Thousand Miles With a Dogsled* (1914), was more consciously addressed to an emerging tourist constituency. The upper river, as a riverscape, had few rivals, and the Rampart gorges were the epitome of the picturesque, with their 'gloomy depth and lofty height'.[120]

The place of the human element within the Yukon's wild tableaux was unclear in the early 1900s. For Whymper, one of the great enticements of Yukon travel was the opportunity to encounter the '"red-skin"' (who, within a few generations, would be extinct) in a state of 'greater perfection' than anywhere else in North America.[121] But for Americans less captivated than Europeans by the notion of noble savagery, the aboriginal population was decidedly unromantic and non-picturesque. The Yukon River's appeal resided partly in its unpeopled quality – its property as a blank canvas. However, this *tabula rasa* was not an end in itself. It was waiting for a particular type of person to inscribe its meaning. The key human ingredient in the powerful spell that the Yukon cast at the turn of the twentieth century was manifestly Anglo-Saxon.[122]

That Edwards's account went through three editions between 1904 and 1909 suggests the enormity of the 'old stock' American appetite for tales of the Yukon within the environment of a rapidly industrializing and urbanizing nation that many members of this group found uncomfortable at best and distressing at worst.[123] *In to the Yukon* delivered a soothing antidote to *fin de siècle* anxiety arising from the evaporation of unsettled country and the formal end of the long frontier phase that formed the core of the American experience. Edwards told his readers what they badly wanted to hear: that the spirit of the frontier had not vanished. It had simply moved north, where, 'in the keen faces of the men and women of the Yukon', he detected unmistakeable evidence of 'the living spirit of the great West, of the West half a century ago; of Virginia and New England two hundred years ago' – the spirit 'which gives the future of the earth to the yet virile Anglo-Saxon race'. Jack London, whose nine months on the Yukon provided a rich and almost inexhaustible seam to mine for literary material, dutifully recorded the ubiquity along the river of the 'adventurous Anglo Saxon, always at home in any environment'.[124]

Though at home in any habitat, the accomplished and enterprising Anglo-Saxon was especially comfortable on the Yukon, which was no place for the faint-hearted or defeatist. On being advised to turn back and return to their homes by a dejected boatload of men coming down to St Michael from Dawson, Jeremiah Lynch from California, about to embark upriver, exclaimed: 'It reminded me, in its dreariness, of the cry of Stanley's crew going down the Congo: 'Sennenneh! Sennenneh! Sennenneh!' – the river of the Equator and the river of the North Pole tingling with like sounds, in men's voices, of doubt and despondency'.[125] The frontier was not dead; it had just moved north: 'The Great Yukon River flows on amidst the stupendous wilderness', Edwards reflected in the preface to his book's third edition, 'man's presence is here a mere passing incident . . . The Lure of the Wild still broods over the great valley and the great river'.

That 'passing incident' of human presence was surely a reference to the gold rush. George Francis Berton, father of Canadian author and Klondike historian Pierre Berton, was one of the 20,000 who descended the river from Lake Bennett to Dawson in the summer of 1898. The recently graduated civil engineer from Saint John, New Brunswick, did not strike it rich on the creeks. Nonetheless, he stayed and made a life in Dawson for 40 years, working at a variety of jobs and professions. Berton the younger was born in Whitehorse in 1920, spent his first twelve years in what was left of Dawson, and toiled in a Klondike mining camp to pay his college fees. In 1972, the author of *The Klondike Fever* (1958) retraced his father's watery footsteps. His party spent eleven days on motorized inflatable rafts, covering the 600-mile distance from Lake Bennett to his hometown. Berton, now in his early fifties, had not been down the river since the age of nineteen.[126]

Berton found the Canadian stretch more or less unchanged apart from Lake Schwatka reservoir (which has domesticated the turbulent canyon that his father negotiated without mishap on 7 July 1898, as related in a postcard to his mother).[127] Yet the ghosts and relics of the gold rushes that Berton logged (not least the decaying steamboats) are not the only traces of the Euro-American past along the Yukon. Though the river and its valley reverted to wildness after the price of fur plummeted and gold-dredging operations ceased during the depression of the 1930s, the eastern Alaskan stretch of river attracted another group of seekers to replace the trappers and miners (people the u.s. National Park Service refers to as 'rugged individualists').[128] In the early 1970s, a new breed of pioneers emerged from the countercultural impulse and back-to-nature ethos of the 1960s.

Steeped in the woodcraft and sourdough lore of an earlier frontier generation, they emulated trappers, homesteaders and prospectors by heading
out to live off the fat of the land and water. Some of these 'river people'
(also known as 'White Indians', not least because some of them insisted
they were keeping the flame of indigenous subsistence culture alight)
acquired nationwide exposure when John McPhee portrayed them and
their backcountry lifestyles in a series of *New Yorker* articles and his
subsequent bestseller, *Coming into the Country* (1977).[129]

McPhee's 'river people', though relatively few in number, constituted
the area's only noteworthy influx of settlers since the 1930s. Sixteen years
spent chugging up and down the Yukon and its tributaries at the wheel of
his 32-foot launch, the *Pelican*, and snow-shoeing along its frozen surface
for thousands of miles, had afforded Stuck plenty of time to ponder the
region's future. He could not imagine a scenario in which the native residents (the 'helpless Indian flock' that, according to a British obituary, he
endeavoured to protect from exploitation and corruption by 'white adventurers') would be displaced by incomers. For mining was an ephemeral
pursuit and there was no pasture or cropland to attract decent farming folk
(as distinct from disreputable adventurers).[130] This view was widely shared
and nothing happened over the next half-century to encourage a more san-
guine outlook.

Reviewing Mathews's 'Rivers of America' book in 1969, an historian
of Alaska commended him for being 'rightly pessimistic about the Yukon
basin's economic future'.[131] This pessimism was deep-rooted. In the report
of his reconnaissance of 1869, Raymond had conceded that, despite the
river's almost unbelievable quantities of salmon, the agricultural potential
of adjacent lands was very limited.[132] This early sobriety regarding the last
frontier's agricultural potential persisted, despite the strong desire to see
Alaska as a place to continue the venerable American tradition of clearing
the land to husband the soil. The Yukon basin was not what Stuck called
a 'good white man's country' in a traditional agrarian sense.[133] Despite
the enormous, record-breaking cabbages and root vegetables raised
under the sub-arctic midnight sun during the fleeting but intense growing season, agriculture has remained what Raymond predicted: a merely
incidental pursuit.

In the light of a river-based boom in recreation since the early 1980s,
however, this downbeat assessment of the Yukon's economic future
requires modest adjustment. Some idea of how lively with traffic the river
was during the gold rush era can be gained from the terse entries in the

diary that the scurvy-ridden London kept of his journey from Dawson to St Michael in a 'frail open boat' in June 1898. Despite the earliness of the season, during the first ten days of the 23-day voyage, he logged twelve steamers (including one 'high and dry' on a sandbar with 170 stranded passengers).[134] Now, during the boating season between late May and early September, the river bustles again, for it has turned out to be very good country for a fresh batch of recreational adventurers that Stuck could not have envisaged.

The most popular section of the Alaskan Yukon for canoeists, kayakers and rafters is the 158-mile stretch from Eagle down to Circle, a trip that typically takes five days.[135] Most of this journey lies within the Yukon-Charley Rivers National Preserve (established in 1980), whose 2,527 acres include 128 miles of river between Eagle and Circle. Stuck reckoned that this stretch of river was world-class on the scale of the 'exceedingly pictur-esque'. The 108-mile Charley was even more distinguished in his view. Charting 75 miles of this fast flowing river in the 1910s, the roving archdeacon was 'struck by its ever-varying beauty and romantic charm', qualities that were peerless among the Alaskan rivers he knew (and his knowledge of Alaskan rivers was unrivalled).[136] Unlike many local tribu-taries of the Yukon, the Charley runs clear because it rises (at 4,000 feet) in glacier-free mountains. The Charley, a designated wild and scenic river under the Wild and Scenic Rivers Act of 1968, is also atypical in being comparatively undisturbed by human activity. Stuck noted 'a little desul-tory mining' on a few side creeks, but its own bed is devoid of gold ore. Today's float down the Charley (inflatable rafts only) averages six days and the upper two-thirds offer a challenging white-water experience.[137]

Just as Berton had followed in his father's paddle strokes, Alaskan author Dan O'Neill retraced McPhee's 30 years after the publication of *Coming Into the Country*. O'Neill wanted to find out what had become of the river people that featured in McPhee's account.[138] He discovered that they were gone, a string of decomposing cabins the only sign of their presence along a 'ghost river'.[139] On the other hand, the National Park Service is protective of events, sites and objects associated with the gold rush (roadhouses, mail trails, trappers' cabins, bucket dredges and other mining paraphernalia) on the National Park System's 'largest natural, free-flowing river'.[140] Just over a century ago, the Yukon was producing history. Today, it is cashing in on that auspicious past. Without necessarily seeking a vicarious frontier experience, Americans who float the Yukon are, in part, acting on Skinner's belief that 'our rivers typify for us our living link with the pioneers'.[141] Those who make the trip between Eagle and Circle can camp on gravel bars or 'take' themselves 'back in time' by overnighting in one of seven 'public use' cabins, some of which, though rebuilt or restored in the past two decades, stem from the 1930s.[142]

Winter travel also provides the opportunity to indulge in commemorative activity. Inspired by the exploits of Jesson and Max Hirschberg, another prospector (but seasoned cyclist, unlike Jesson) who peddled to Nome in the spring of 1900, two Canadians and an American recreated their journeys in the spring of 2003.[143] Among the items in the saddlebags of the 'Bikes on Ice' expedition that left Dawson on 3 March were Jesson's and Hirschberg's accounts. Averaging between 48 and 80 daily kilometres, the trio reached Nome after 49 days in the saddle, though warming temperatures and thaw (evidence of climate change) were a problem over the home stretch. Most of the people they met en route, mainly Native Alaskans, were familiar with the original journeys, their grandparents having handed down the stories. What really struck the cyclists, though, was that the river was more isolated and empty than the inhabited wilderness that Jesson and Hirschberg had described.[144]

The status of the Yukon basin – and other parts of Alaska and Yukon Territory – as inhabited wilderness gives the river a distinctive quality absent from debates over wilderness preservation in the 'lower 48' (as Alaskans refer to the contiguous United States), where designated wilderness is visited rather than lived in.[145] The biggest single threat since the gold rushes to the Yukon wilderness still populated mostly by Natives (as Stuck predicted) was posed in the early 1960s. The u.s. Army Corps of Engineers wanted to replace the Yukon Flats with a reservoir bigger than Lake Erie (so vast it would take twenty years to fill) by damming the river at the head of Rampart Canyon.[146] Campaigning for the presidency in Anchorage, John F. Kennedy foresaw 'the greatest dam in the free world . . . producing twice the power of TVA to light homes and mills and cities and farms all over Alaska'. To counter criticism of the mega-project on economic and environmental grounds, Yukon Power for America, the most enthusiastic local booster outfit, echoing a string of explorers and prospectors, zoomed in on the Flats' dearth of scenic value.[147] Since 1945, however, conventional notions of landscape value based on visual beauty had been under revision to accommodate ecological value, and, on these grounds, lowlands – especially wetlands – were deemed as valuable as uplands (if not more so, in terms of biodiversity content). This newly assigned value was reinforced by a growing awareness among federal decision-makers of the importance of the Flats' furbearers, waterfowl and fish to the livelihoods of its Native residents (seven Indian villages, including Fort Yukon, would be drowned).[148]

Since the boondoggle was shelved in 1967, the power of the Yukon for America and the rest of the over-developed world has become understood in a more potent, if less tangible form than the number of kilowatts generated for customers thousands of miles away. Rampart 'pumpers', who recruited the poet Robert Service ('Bard of the Yukon') and the beckoning promise of the Yukon during the Klondike era, argued that the bold project embodied the precious and peerless American frontier spirit.[149] More electrifying, though, was the Yukon's power to remind Americans of European descent of the wilderness that once covered the entire continent, the priceless but dwindling raw material of the frontier from which white Americans carved the most powerful nation in history. Not that the Yukon's appeal is restricted to those for whom the wilderness, as both physical condition and cultural construct, is a central facet of their national heritage. The call of the El Dorado of the Yukon wilderness is also heard loud and clear by growing numbers of western Europeans (witness the German paddlers enamoured of a primitive river) whose appetite cannot be satisfied by the modified and humanized landscapes, however beautiful, of their home nations.

The homes, mills, cities and farms that Kennedy conjured up in 1960 have not materialized. The trees felled to feed the furnaces of steamboats have grown back.[150] Mine tailings remain visible on side creeks and a dam has quietened Miles Canyon. And yet, compared to the extensive hydraulic works that have reconfigured and embanked the Danube, Spree, Po and Mersey, the Yukon has experienced the lightest of engineering touches. This minimal impact is thrown into particularly acute relief in the company of the heavily reconstructed Los Angeles River. An Alaskan supporter of the Rampart scheme lambasted small-minded critics for failing to appreciate the Yukon's potential as *Lebensraum* for an increasingly over-crowded nation and for refusing to 'admit the necessity of industrial progress here to relieve the situations like L.A.' Another frustrated proponent had a dream that one day, 'a housewife in Phoenix or L.A. will fry her eggs at breakfast with electricity generated on the far-off Yukon'.[151] The belief that densely populated areas of the country such as burgeoning Los Angeles had run out of the supposedly bottomless cornucopia of natural resources that was the leitmotif of frontier regions on the eve of Euro-American colonization becomes much more plausible when situated within the context of the anything but illustrious river of Los Angeles. By the 1960s, it had been straightened, encased and wrung dry to support factories, cities, farms and wall-to-wall homes in the El Dorado of perpetual sunshine.

# SIX

# *Los Angeles River*

In his contribution to 'Rivers of America', Henry Seidel Canby was almost apologetic about his choice of a 60-mile river, distinguished by its absence of traits rather than its assets. The Brandywine river of Pennsylvania and Delaware lacked an association with a great city: it was no Thames or Hudson. It did not form a border: it was no Rio Grande. It was not a highway of commerce like the Mississippi. It did not open up a vast inland empire like the St Lawrence. It did not even boast any grand scenery: it was no Colorado. The little Brandywine was 'so small a stream, even when judged by European standards, that its historian's first task is to prove that it is a river at all!'[1] At 51 miles, the Los Angeles River is my little river – much shorter than the Spree and even shorter than the very short Mersey. Its drainage basin, at 825 square miles, is also by far the smallest.

Unsurprisingly, there was no room among the 'Rivers of America' for the Los Angeles. California had three representatives (four, if the Colorado is included): the Sacramento (1939), the Salinas (1945) and – the series' final volume – the American (1974). None of these is particularly long either. But the first and third were obvious choices. Their subtitles speak volumes: *River of Gold* and *River of Eldorado*. The subtitle of the book on the Salinas was more cryptic: *Upside-down River*. In somewhat Yukon-esque fashion, though rising within 25 miles of the sea, the Salinas, forced by the Santa Lucia coastal range, flows north-westward for 150 miles parallel to the coast before debouching into the Pacific. More important than the vagaries of morphology, though, was the role of the Salinas in watering one of the world's richest agricultural bottomlands – dignified by the soubriquet American 'Valley of the Nile'.[2] Moreover, in terms of literary riverscapes, if the Yukon was the river of Jack London, then the Salinas was the river of fellow Californian John Steinbeck.

The Los Angeles River cannot compete on any of these terms. It may be unique among this book's selection in having a precise moment of recorded discovery (at least by Europeans). But for most of its written history, it has consistently maintained the lowest profile among my

company. During the Depression, when Los Angeles was the last resort for
many Americans seeking a place to start over, Harry Carr displayed a rare
historical consciousness: 'When I was a schoolboy in Los Angeles, I never
heard of . . . Portolá or . . . Anza. Now I never cross the river over the North
Broadway bridge that I do not look down into the arroyo half expecting to
see the herders in their leather armor, guarding the war horses of Portolá.'
Two-thirds of a century later, Kevin Starr, noted historian of California,
optimistically placed Los Angeles in the august company of river cities
such as London, Rome, Paris, Budapest and New York – though even he
conceded that, unlike, the Thames, Tiber, Seine, Danube and Hudson,
the river that gives Los Angeles its name and on whose banks the city
was founded 'does not sweep majestically past its city in unchallenged
supremacy'.[3] Yet, until recently, even within the City of Los Angeles
(which encompasses 32 of the river's 51 miles), the acute awareness of
the river displayed by local boosters like Carr and Starr – and particularly
their pride in the river – was exceptional.

More representative were the sentiments of an elderly African
American in the opening scene of the pilot episode of *Boomtown*, a short-
lived NBC crime drama about Los Angeles that aired in September 2002.
Standing on a bridge, gazing down at the river, he ruminates: 'London's got
the Thames. Paris got the Seine. Vienna's got the Blue Danube. LA's got a
. . . concrete drainage ditch'. Whether a source of pride or shame for some
Los Angelenos, numerous others – just as many in Stockport are oblivious
to the Mersey's local presence – remain unaware that their city has a river.

Moreover, given the watercourse's current condition, many who do
know of its existence doubt its qualifications as a bona fide river. 'Used
to flood like a son of a bitch back when I was a boy', the old man on the
bridge reminisces. But then 'they paved it all up'. For almost two-thirds
of its length, the river flows in a concrete bed whose artificiality is emphasized by a central groove (low flow channel), up to twenty feet wide and
three feet deep, that is designed to funnel low flow even more effectively
(kayaker Steve Chapple's The Slot). 'Not quite the Ganges, is it? Not really
a river anymore', reflects the elderly man in *Boomtown*. A reporter who
tried to kayak down to the sea in 2003 summed it up as a 'glorified trench'.[4]
As if this was not enough, 'every indignity has been visited upon it' (except
for painting its walls Danubian blue).[5]

The ignoble river narrative raised its ugly head in Roman Polanski's
*Chinatown* (1974), a neo-noir murder-mystery located in a thirsty city
locked in drought, which, though set in 1937, derives its historical ambience

Akili-Casundria Ramsess, photograph of the LA River trickling through downtown within its expansive concrete bed, 1989.

from the shadowy machinations of early twentieth-century water 'theft'.[6] On a visit to the county morgue, private detective J. J. 'Jake' Gittes (investigating the alleged marital infidelities of the city's water czar) recognizes the corpse of a notorious local drunk who allegedly drowned in an intoxicated stupor on the river bed. Gittes is sceptical of this diagnosis, dismissive of the 'bone dry' river's capacity to drown anyone, even an incorrigible drunk. When the assistant coroner protests that the river is not entirely dry, Gittes retorts: 'he ain't gonna drown in a damp river-bed either. I don't care how soused he was. That's like drowning in a teaspoon.'[7] Robert Towne, who wrote the award-winning screenplay, reflects that 'in movies, the river is the symbol of the ass end of Los Angeles.'[8]

Whether or not repeated use as a Hollywood film set qualifies as an insult, this habit has at least performed the useful service of keeping memories of the river alive. The downtown river's shortage of water and its concrete jacket's similarity to a roadway attracted the attention of a string of post-war movie makers. In the sci-fi classic *Them!* (1954), giant mutant ants bred by atomic fallout emerge from their nests in the storm drains to mass for an invasion in the river-bed (the first person to spot them is a drunk who hangs out in the concrete channel's demi-monde). The drag race scene in *Grease* (1978), when the T-Birds face off against the Scorpions and Sandra Dee (Olivia Newton John) blossoms into Sandy, was filmed in the spillway under one of the city's most famous bridges:

the steel-truss-arched, late Art Deco Sixth Street Bridge and Viaduct – in its day (1932) the world's longest concrete bridge (3,500 feet). This city centre stretch between First and Seventh streets – the section of river the old man surveys in 'Boomtown' – featured again in *Terminator 2: Judgment Day* (1991). The Harley Davidson-riding Arnold Schwarzenegger is hotly pursued by the T-1000 (an alien made of liquid metal) driving a tractor-trailer.[9] More prosaically, the Metropolitan Transportation Authority trained bus drivers and Toyota test-drove new cars down there.

Not that the LA River's appeal is restricted to film buffs. It provides a particularly instructive example of the close relationship between water and power (the Los Angeles Department of Water and Power [1925] is a name that says it all). The river merits attention as an outstanding instance of our capacity to change a river in a fundamental sense. 'There may not be another river anywhere that has been as thoroughly transformed by humans as the Los Angeles River', reflects Blake Gumprecht, who concludes that 'the river as it now exists has almost nothing in common with the stream the Gabrieleño [Gabrielino] hunted beside or that Father Juan Crespi so eloquently described'.[10] As a river ostensibly altered to within an inch of its life, the LA River occupies the opposite end of the spectrum to the Yukon. And while we can at least distinguish between the rural and

Looking upriver (north) from above the Sixth Street Bridge.

An arrow indicates the body of a man (probably a murder victim) located in the river-bed, 1949.

urban stretches of the Spree and Mersey, the Los Angeles River is almost wholly urban. There is no internal counterpoint or foil. Yet if the American River was the focal point of nineteenth-century California, then the Los Angeles River is the essential river of twentieth-century California.

Philip Fradkin, who has travelled its length, claims that 'Los Angeles *is* the river and the river is Los Angeles.'[11] But to appreciate this umbilical connection requires a major leap of the imagination. For many locals, the river is little more than a joke (at least the 'burning' Cuyahoga was a *national* joke), a notorious dumping ground for just about everything, including murder victims and dead horses.[12] The following wisecrack was once popular in the yearbooks of high school seniors: 'Yours till the L.A. River wets its bed.'[13] Joke or no joke, any river that offers better opportunities for skateboarding than for aquatic forms of recreation is undeniably a weird river. Looking down from the Beaux Arts-style César Chávez Avenue Bridge (1926; formerly Macy Street Bridge), with its Spanish colonial revival design, where I first saw the river, I could scarcely believe my eyes: trucks trundled along the bed. In 1989, in an op-ed piece in the *Los Angeles Times*, state assemblyman Richard Katz actually recommended

Looking upriver (northeast) from above the César Chávez Avenue Bridge.

Highway officials evaluate the river-bed's potential as a freeway, 1947.

its conversion into a 'bargain' freeway with car-pool and truck lanes to relieve pressure on adjacent highways (and received a state grant for a feasibility study).[14]

Others feel that the river should not be judged by standard criteria. After all, Los Angeles is not a normal city. So why expect it to have a normal river?[15] (A harsher verdict is that, 'back East', there are real people and real rivers.[16]) There can be few better springboards for consideration of what makes a river a river than the dispute over the LA River's fluvial credentials. Can a river whose morphology, ecology and role have been as drastically redesigned as Gumprecht insists, and which has suffered such extraordinary abuse at human hands, reduced to a culvert, still lay claim to be a river? 'A River Runs Through It?' is the rhetorical question posed on the back cover of *Down by the Los Angeles River*, a guide prepared by Friends of the Los Angeles River (FOLAR).[17] 'Let us turn back the clock and have a real river again', was the challenge state senator Art Torres issued twenty years ago.[18] When the U.S. Army Corps of Engineers and the LA County Public Works department 'rechristened the river the flood control channel' in the 1930s, observes the Los Angeles-based nature writer Jennifer Price, they transformed it from a biological entity into a component of infrastructure: 'They decreed it was no longer a river – and to the public, the concrete channel no longer looked wild enough to count as nature. And this is how LA lost its river – not lost as in no longer had one, since LA actually did, but lost as in could no longer see or find it'.[19]

If the Yukon remains a largely pre-modern river, then the LA River may be an example of a post-modern river. 'That's all we got. It'll have to do', shrugs the old man in the *Boomtown* pilot. But others are not so resigned. As if to compensate for its long-standing neglect by locals and lack of recognition (never mind renown) beyond the confines of its watershed, the river is now the beneficiary of one of the world's most imaginative and robust river restoration campaigns, spearheaded by FOLAR since the mid-1980s. The river that became largely invisible in local consciousness as it was deprived of much of its flow and river-ness has received an astonishing amount of publicity over the past twenty years. Over the past quarter century, the river has been found with a vengeance. Indifference toward a river that is no more has been converted into enthusiasm for a river that once was and could be again ('under the concrete, the Los Angeles River is laughing'[20]). Measured in terms of recent media coverage, books, artwork and photography exhibits, as well as internet presence, the LA River enjoys its highest ever profile among the world's rivers.

## Source and Course

The LA River's flow is highly irregular – even more so than the Po's often mercurial regime. This partly reflects its location (alone among my rivers) within a semi-arid, Mediterranean climatic zone, where rainfall is concentrated in the winter months.[21] Moreover, the river's course is abrupt, descending nearly 800 feet. (A raindrop that falls in the 10,000 foot San Gabriel Mountains can reputedly reach the Pacific in under an hour.[22]) The character and soil structure of the river basin – an alluvial plain hemmed in by the steep mountains of the Santa Monica, San Gabriel and Santa Susana ranges – thus aggravate the impact of seasonal variations in volume based on rainfall patterns. In the absence of a regular, year-round flow, the unmodified river was unable to cut a firmly entrenched or durable channel. This shallow bed was ill-equipped to cope during the rainy season, when large volumes of water transporting tremendous amounts of debris flowed swiftly off the hills.

Over half the river's watershed is floodplain and channel changes were once as frequent as the Po's. Until 1825, the river turned right near

John Humble, 'Headwaters, the Los Angeles River, Confluence of Arroyo Calabasas and Bell Creek, Canoga Park', 2001.

Akili-Casundria Ramsess, photograph of the mouth of the river with the *Queen Mary* on the horizon, 1989.

the original pueblo site and headed due west through the future sites of Hollywood and Beverly Hills to Santa Monica Bay. Following a bout of incessant rain that year, the channel shifted dramatically, plunging directly south to debouch into San Pedro Bay – a course it has maintained since.[23] Startling hydrological statistics associated with flood times abound. Once, in the 1930s, discharge at Long Beach was judged equal to the Mississippi's usual flow through St Louis, Missouri.[24] The volume has been known to increase three-thousand fold within 24 hours.[25]

Since modifications by the Los Angeles County Flood Control District in the 1930s, the river officially begins in the far western San Fernando Valley at the confluence of the Arroyo Calabasas and Bell Creek in present-day Canoga Park (above this point, all pursuable traces disappear, whether along the Calabasas or Bell).[26] Near the local high school's playing fields, circa 795 feet above sea level, the two creeks' high white retaining walls come together sharply like the prow of a ship. Prior to the Spanish era, the river's waters merged with the Tujunga and Verdugo Washes and various natural springs to blanket the San Fernando Valley with lush wetlands, ponds and lakes. During the dry season, what water did flow in the river derived from the subterranean reservoir (underflow), 175 square miles in extent, that collected beneath the Valley and was thrust to the surface where the floodplain met the northern foothills of the Santa Monica range. At other times, though, the river ran entirely underground. The watershed encompasses much of west and central Los Angeles. Sliding eastward past

236

Warner Brothers and Universal Studios, it makes a southward turn as it enters the Glendale Narrows and slices through downtown. Continuing past Maywood, Cudahy and Compton, it emits into the Pacific at Long Beach. Moored (in cement) at the entrance to the river is the decommissioned liner RMS *Queen Mary* (1937–67), a ship built by and belonging to Cunard, whose former headquarters lord it over at the Liverpool waterfront.

## Lush and Limpid LA River

Today, the site that Spanish settlers selected for a pueblo outpost at the confluence of the LA River and Arroyo Seco, one of the largest of its seven tributaries, is an unappetizing scene criss-crossed by a veritable 'spaghetti junction' of railroad tracks, graffiti-smeared freeway bridges and Riverside Drive bridge ('one of the [river's] ugliest, most devastated spots'[27]). Nearby is the stadium of the Los Angeles Dodgers baseball team. This spot is even more inauspicious than the beginning of the Mersey in Stockport. Two hundred and fifty years ago, this was a fertile mosaic of ponds and marshes that supported the largest concentration of Indians in California.[28] To treat a river as the lifeblood of a human community makes particular sense

Aerial view of the confluence with Arroyo Seco.

within the context of arid and semi-arid regions. Whether directly or indirectly, the river and its watershed supplied every need of the Tongva
branch of the Gabrieleño. They caught the steelhead trout that migrated
upstream to spawn and hunted the deer and antelope that came down to
the river to drink and graze. Extracts from the bark of riparian trees provided medicine. They harvested riparian willows for the frames of their
beehive-shaped huts (the Spaniards called them *jacales* and the American
word was 'wickeups') and sweat lodges, which they thatched with tule
reeds. They also wove reeds and the inner bark of willows and cotton-
woods into baskets, which, coated with local tar (*brea*), hauled water.[29]
Though the Secretary of the Historical Society of Southern California in
1901 characterized the area's pre-contact Indian as 'so ardent a lover of
nature that he never defaces her face by attempting to make improvements
– particularly if it requires exertion to make the changes', Gabrieleño
culture was actively flood adaptive. They tolerated periodic disruption
because of the benefits of proximity to the river and adjusted to its variable
flow by locating their dispersed dwelling places (*rancherias*) on the highest
available ground. On raised platforms they stored acorns and chia seeds.
When heavy winter rains converted much of the lower river into a wetland,
the indigenes navigated their water world in reed boats.[30]

Europeans entered this fluvial domain in 1769. Gaspar de Portolá's
expedition was en route from Vellicatá to Monterey, where it intended to
establish a garrison, and missions and forts (*presidios*) at points in between.
Having more or less traced the coast of Alta California up from San Diego,
they reached a point just north of present-day downtown Los Angeles. On
the evening of 2 August 1769, according to the diary of Father Juan Crespi,
they 'entered a very spacious valley, well grown with cottonwoods and
alders, among which ran a beautiful river' that came from the northwest
and headed due south. Crespi, the expedition's missionary and Franciscan
friar, recorded that it was a 'good sized, full flowing river . . . with very
good water, pure and fresh'. It was the explorers' good fortune to have
chanced on the only stretch of river (the Glendale 'narrows') that flowed
all year. About nineteen yards wide, the river here was fringed with
Western cottonwood, Western sycamore (*aliso*), Arroyo willow and live
oak of prodigious size. Crespi also noted the profusion of wild roses,
grapes and sage, as well as the fertility of the black, loamy soil. Antelope
on which the Spaniards would feed descended to the riverbank.

Though not as big as the San Gabriel and Santa Ana rivers they had
recently forded, the padre considered this one to be the best. The expedi-

tion camped at a 'delightful place' immediately to the north of its confluence with a dry watercourse that local Indians called the *Hahamungna*
('flowing water, fertile valley') and the Spaniards dubbed the Arroyo Seco.
In view of the site's attractions, the area's principal native community, the
village of Yangna, was located nearby. And soon after the expedition had
pitched camp, a detachment of eight 'heathen' approached, bearing shell
necklaces and grass baskets filled with dried maize and chia seeds.[31]
On the expedition's return journey (17 January 1770), Crespi remarked
on the river's volatility. A large volume of floodwater a few days earlier
had directed the river into a new bed and pools and fallen trees littered
the area.[32]

A sign at the Los Angeles River Center and Gardens (established
2000), a verdant oasis in the grounds of a former restaurant and spice
packing plant, near the historic confluence with the Arroyo Seco, tells the
story of the next European visitors. A group of soldiers and their families
under the leadership of Juan Bautista de Anza, en route from Sonora to
establish a *presidio* in San Francisco, and accompanied by horses and cattle,
crossed the river hereabouts on 21 February 1776. The expedition's priest,
Father Pedro Font, was just as impressed by the river and its environs
as Crespi had been, noting that it contained 'a great deal of water' and
coursed through lands that were 'very green and flower-strewn'.[33] These
early Spanish accounts refer to the river as the Porciúncula. The full name
was quite a mouthful: *El Rio y Valle de Nuestra Señora la Reina de Los
Angeles de la Porciúncula* (The River and Valley of Our Lady the Queen of
the Angels on the River Porciúncula).[34] In 1781, not far from the discovery
site, a pueblo outpost was founded, near present-day Olvera Street in
downtown Los Angeles; eleven families (46 colonists in total) were brought
up from Mexico to form the nucleus of *El Pueblo de Nuestra Señora La
Reina de Los Angeles de la Porciúncula*.[35] The *Californios* dug irrigation
canals with hoes and spades so that *El Pueblo de La Reina de Los Angeles*
(as it became known) could supply food (especially wheat) to the Californian missions of San Fernando and San Gabriel, and, eventually, turnon
Mexico itself. Inhabitants of the largest civilian community in Spanish
California also grazed cattle (for meat and tallow) and grew watermelons
as well as grapes for wine and brandy (California's first vineyards, irrigated
by the river, occupied its banks). When California became Mexican in
1822, *El Pueblo* housed circa 800 residents. Yangna (near present-day
Union Station) clung on with a few hundred Indians until relocated
in 1836.[36]

When California became American (1850), the pueblo transmuted into Los Angeles (City Hall occupies the former site of Yangna) and the river, which assumed the settlement's name, was put to work even harder. The pueblo's community-owned lands were broken up and sold off. The great exception to privatization was the river itself, though, in 1868, the Los Angeles City Water Company received a 30-year franchise to supply water to the fledgling city's 5,000 inhabitants. The main flow was also harnessed to drive woollen and flour mills, as well as the town's earliest printing presses. The network of irrigation ditches (*zanja*) inherited from the *Californios* was extended to irrigate ever larger quantities of crops. Indeed, the most powerful public official in the river-reliant city between 1854 (when the first one was appointed) and 1904 (when the post was abolished) was the *zanjero*, the water commissioner responsible for the *zanja* system. One of the main components of the network (*Zanja Madre*) tapped water from the river at a point opposite present-day Griffith Park and carried it to a reservoir in today's Elysian Park.

In 1878, one of the ditch tenders on the *Zanja Madre* was William Mulholland. The young Irishman's job was to keep the ditches clear of sludge, weeds, brush and other debris. He quickly worked his way up to superintendent within the privately owned Los Angeles City Water Company. Not long afterwards, he rose to the position of chief engineer and general manager of the new municipal body, the Los Angeles Bureau of Water Works and Supply, that bought out the City Water Company in 1898.[37] In a statement FOLAR frequently quotes, Mulholland later recalled the charm that the river exerted when he first arrived on horseback from San Francisco in 1877: 'The country had the same attraction for me that it had for the Indians who originally chose this spot as their place to live. The Los Angeles River was a beautiful, limpid little stream with willows on its banks. It was so attractive to me that it at once became something about which my whole scheme of life was woven. I loved it so much'.[38]

Until the early twentieth century, the highly productive local agricultural economy, distinguished visually by vineyards and citrus groves, was supported entirely by water extracted from the river. In the volume of his mammoth geography of the world devoted to the United States, Élisée Reclus, without mentioning the river by name, remarked that the banks of the streams of Los Angeles resembled 'a vast garden'.[39] Growing competition over an increasingly scarce resource, however, intensified reliance on water tapped from the underflow and stored in reservoirs, which, in turn, ratcheted up direct confrontation between the interests of the city of Los

Angeles and those of the San Fernando Valley's ranchers. The struggle pivoted on which party could make the strongest legal case for ownership of the river's water, both surface and subsurface.[40]

Seeking a more permanent solution, City of Los Angeles water department officials targeted the distant Owens River, fed by snowmelt from the eastern slopes of the Sierra Nevada mountains.[41] In 1913, the first water diverted from the Owens River down a 233-mile aqueduct – Mulholland's grandest hydraulic engineering achievement – arrived to liberate both the city and the Valley from dependence on their expended local river.[42] With - out this fresh supply to fill swimming pools, wash cars and refresh lawns, Los Angeles would not have grown from a city of nearly 500,000 in 1913 into a metropolis of 3.7 million by the twentieth century's end.

## Leashed LA River

Though the Owens River had superseded the LA River as a supplier of the city's water, the local river remained a powerful presence in the lives of Angelenos. For Spanish and American settlers, its munificence had always been mixed with malevolence. But few now could see beyond its troublesome nature. The threat its floodwaters continued to pose after it had outlived its usefulness to the city it had nurtured, comments Starr, was 'as if – or so it seemed', the river 'were angry at the insult of its displacement'; however 'humiliated' it felt at being cast aside, it refused 'to be ignored'.[43] In the same anthropomorphic vein, Greg Ercolano (of the spoof organization Friends of Vast Industrial Concrete Kafkaesque Structures) presented the river as a wayward, unpredictable and predatory beast. 'Before flood control', he commented in 2000, 'the deceptively quiescent river transformed into a wild torrent during seasonal floods, and like a renegade river, would jump its banks, carving out new random meandering riverbeds throughout Los Angeles, killing people, destroying highways, businesses, residences and livestock'.[44]

Yet no river is inherently destructive; it all depends on what we place in its path and on how we manage risk. An indigenous society that had learnt to live with inundation and uncertainty gave way to a Spanish-Mexican transitional era, during which floods were an occasional disruptive element. High water in 1815 shifted the river's course within the pueblo's precincts, washing out fields or burying them in sand. When the waters subsided, a fresh area was opened for cultivation. And the new church erected in 1814 (the city's first) was relocated to higher ground (the site it still occupies) a few years afterwards.[45] The culture that came next, however, was less flexible and highly risk averse. The American city of Los Angeles received its first real taste of how devastating the river could be in spate when it tried to improve on the customary method of water delivery by cart and cask. A powerful flood in the late 1850s ripped out the wheel installed on the bank to raise water to the level of a new network of wooden pipes.[46]

'The application of water produces marvellous results', remarked a travel writer from the east coast who was smitten by the 'almost continuous fruit garden' of the Los Angeles basin.[47] However, with the large-scale influx of easterners after the first transcontinental railroad arrived in 1876 (a second national rail link followed in 1888) and a massive recruitment drive that played up the climatic and environmental charms of 'Our Italy', the dominant use of riverside land switched from agricultural to residential. Human action aggravates a river's tendency to flood. But inactivity in the face of this challenge was not an economic or political option in Los Angeles.[48] Among the periodic floods, those of 1914, 1934 and 1938 were particularly severe. Three days of heavy rain in February 1914 that followed several wet months effectively cut the city off from the outside world. The city not only rebuilt the levees, but installed retention basins and deepened channels along certain sections. And still, the pace of urban growth outran the implementation of flood protection schemes. Soon after midnight on 2 January 1934, after three days of uninterrupted rain, a huge flood ripped down the San Gabriel Mountains, laying waste to the foothill communities of La Cañada, Montrose, and Glendale. In 'The New Year's Flood' (1934), folksinger Woody Guthrie commemorated the 'cloud burst' and flood that 'came a-rumblin' down' and 'swept away our homes . . . [and] our loved ones', 'blockaded' highways and 'wrecked and scattered' houses.[49]

Ever tighter training seemed like the only way forward. Yet an alternative vision was articulated in the early twentieth century by a Congregationalist minister who was a pioneering proponent of the City Beautiful Movement. Dana Webster Bartlett's work to improve the lives of the city's many immigrants incorporated the river, which, he believed, could be transformed into a 'line of beauty'. Undismayed by the factories, warehouses, yards and other industrial establishments that clogged its disciplined banks, he felt that the river retained 'all its ancient possibilities of beauty and adornment'. The settlement house operator recommended the establishment of a special commission to reclaim the river from 'base uses' and dignify both sides with an esplanade stretching as a 'natural boulevard', perhaps as far as the sea.

Bartlett's most imaginative suggestion was to clean the river-bed of rubbish and undergrowth between First Street and Elysian Park. This would provide a 'riverbed playground' for the children of the densely populated adjoining districts during the dry season that occupied three-quarters of the year.[50] Fellow City Beautiful crusader, Charles Mulford Robinson, was a firm believer in a river's capacity to ennoble a city. Particularly impressed by the grouping of riverside buildings on Museum Island in downtown Berlin and the 'monumental' Schloss Brücke across the 'unimportant' Spree, he made the larger point that the many notable cities of Europe located on rivers usually derive 'a large part of their splendour' from tasteful deployment of their waterfronts (Berlin, Budapest, Dresden, London, Paris, Prague and Rome).[51]

Despite this admiration for river-front embankment and enhancement with stately buildings, Robinson retained his fondness for the 'charm of nature's gentler lines and fringing vegetation'. He hoped that modern cities could find a way to incorporate some stretches of linear parkland between their rivers and the adjacent buildings, to preserve, 'in semblance at least, nature's softer treatment' within the urban environment. Predictably, Robinson, like Bartlett, advocated an aesthetic upgrade for the LA River in his 'suggestions' to the Los Angeles Municipal Art Commission in 1907. The river constituted a 'very serious problem' and one that was hard to resolve to complete 'aesthetic satisfaction', given that it was dry for much of the time and that railroads ran along both banks. The amount of sand in the river-bed (tapped by the construction industry) also bothered him and he recommended its removal along with the accumulated garbage (the river-bed provided prime habitat for transients). Like Bartlett, he urged the planting of willows and sycamores to create 'a varied and beautiful screen of verdure'.[52]

The visions of Bartlett and Robinson lived on in a report of 1930 for the Los Angeles Chamber of Commerce that resurrected some of the ideas of the City Beautiful movement and the proposals that the Los Angeles Park Department had advanced in 1910 and 1911 for riverside greenways, parks and drives (the only outcome of which was the Arroyo Seco Parkway). Based on a three-year investigation, the landscape architects Frederick Law Olmsted, Junior (son of the designer of Central Park) and Harlan Bartholomew offered a series of recommendations for the provision of places for outdoor recreation in the Los Angeles area. These included proposals for public purchase of riverside lands to provide parkland, 'pleasure' parkways and flood protection zones, by keeping private housing and other forms of land development out of areas with the highest risk of inundation, a practice we would now refer to as hazard zoning.[53] The specific suggestion for re-planting the banks with cotton-woods, sycamores, willows and wild grapes evoked Crespi's description of the river (1769), and Olmsted and Bartholomew also flagged up the retention of surviving riverside vegetation to avoid creating even more 'ugly vacant channel'.[54]

Despite (or because of) these bold suggestions, the report had no impact. Dramatically out of tune with the pro-private development ethos of the city's ruling class (the timing of publication – five months after the stock market crash of 1929 – was also unfortunate), it was promptly shelved.[55] The conversion into a drainage channel of those parts of the river that were still more or less unmodified proceeded unchecked. Having failed to finance flood protection by raising bonds, the Los Angeles County Flood Control District sought the federal funding and expertise of the U.S. Army Corps of Engineers, a body freshly empowered by the Flood Control Act of 1936. Two years into the Corps of Engineers' comprehensive project to straitjacket the river in cement, the most catastrophic flood in the history of Los Angeles County was unleashed after a week of precipitation dumped nearly two feet of rain in the mountains and over a foot on the flatlands. The rains that began on 27 February 1938 and continued unbroken until 3 March brushed aside many of the Corps' newly installed works and the swaying river washed out twenty bridges. The floodwaters claimed 87 lives (some victims were transfixed spectators watching the surging river from bridges that collapsed; and objects in the river also included escapees from the alligator farm near Lincoln Park[56]). The catastrophe destroyed 1,500 houses and the show did not go on: the Academy Awards ceremony was postponed by a week as numerous actors, actresses and movie industry folk were marooned in Malibu.[57]

Nonetheless, embankments of reinforced concrete tended to withstand flood waters. And though much of the San Fernando Valley became a shallow lake, Los Angeles itself was relatively unaffected. The Corps, far from being rebuffed, redoubled its resolve to finish its grand scheme of straightening, deepening and encasing the unruly river (a programme of works that Mike Davis dubs the 'killing' of the river).[58] With the exception of three short stretches, the bed and sides were lined with concrete and

Excavations to enlarge the channel were part of flood protection works in the Resenda area, 1956.

fenced in to eliminate public access. The length of the river was even extended at its upper end with a 7-mile training channel, which provided an entirely new official starting point in the western San Fernando Valley.[59] This flood protection programme, which continued through the 1950s, achieved a measure of success. Debris basins the size of sports arenas on feeder streams in the mountains intercept most of the dislodged earth, vegetation and boulders before they enter the concrete channel.[60] So there has been no flood comparable to that of 1938 since the river's wholesale re-engineering into a new kind of *Wasserstrasse* or 'water freeway'.

Whether on the LA River or the Po, however, measures intended to calm the flow and carry winter storm water or snowmelt off to the sea with a minimum of fuss can sharpen destructive capacity. The current's force and speed (clocked on the LA, during spate, at 45 miles per hour[61]) is greater in a straightened river because the banks are steeper and there are no bends to impede the flow. Here and elsewhere, the amount of damage from cyclical floods also increases in step with the quantity of permanent structures assembled on a floodplain, the number of people who live within its bounds and the extent to which hard, impermeable surfaces replace porous surfaces. Urbanization removes the vegetation that checks the movement of floodwater and helps the ground absorb rainfall. Sixty per cent of the LA River's watershed is now paved over. Asphalt and concrete (as well as roofs) exacerbate run off into the storm drains that feed directly into the river and starve aquifers of replenishment. Arroyo Seco in particular remains a dangerous place after heavy rain – a place all too well known to the Los Angeles Fire Department's Swiftwater Rescue Unit (established 1983).

In the light of a 25 per cent growth in the city's population between the early 1970s and the mid-1990s, the Corps of Engineers reviewed the local flood defence system, concluding that the associated expansion in the acreage of non-absorbent surfaces had further reduced the river basin's ability to soak up floodwater before it reached the river. To tackle the potential return of the inundation threat, the Corps embarked on an upgrade/retrofit of the flood defences (including higher and stronger levees). The El Niño-driven storms of the early 1990s visited widespread flooding on the river's lower reaches, in the communities of Torrance, Carson and Long Beach. In the autumn of 1997, the Federal Emergency Management Agency (FEMA) designated a 75-square-mile zone as a 'special flood hazard area'.[62] As on the Po, total security is a fond technocratic delusion.[63]

## Lamentable, Ludicrous, Lost, Lauded and Liberated LA River

The return of the river as a flood hazard was accompanied by the return of a sense of the river as something more than a drainage channel. Between October 1985 and January 1986, Dick Roraback, a *Los Angeles Times* staff writer, made a tongue-in-cheek journey from mouth to source. This trip triggered a spate of excursions that almost compares to the volume of trips up and down the Yukon in the wake of Dall and Whymper. The Los Angeles River explorer faced a whole set of challenges as well. No rapids, freeze-up or break-up complicated their journeys. But they, too, grappled with shallow water and the requirement to portage around obstacles, with resort to walking and cycling when necessary. Moreover, unlike the Yukon voyagers, they confronted widespread inaccessibility and inhospitable conditions in the shape of freeways, railroads, insurmountable

Canoeing down the river, 1996.

fences, barbed wire, padlocked gates, 15-feet high retaining walls and
vast swathes of impenetrable railroad yards as well as industrial and
commercial premises.

Roraback's trip took three months to complete (in sections) on foot
and bicycle. Along the way, he sent dispatches to the *Times*, which
appeared as an eleven-part series between 20 October and 30 January.[64]
Roraback knew his rivers. He had grown up on the Hudson, lived on
the Yukon, 'paddled on the Po', 'dabbled in the Danube', 'chugged up the
Congo' and meandered along the Mersey (he fondly recalled the rock in
the river bearing the slogan 'The Quality of Mersey is Not Strained'[65]).
This knowledge and experience made him particularly ashamed of his
ignorance of the river in the city where he had lived for a decade. At least
he was not alone in his innocence of the source of the river he characterized as emasculated.[66] And one person he encountered, whose backyard
abuts against the river, exclaimed: 'I don't know where it starts or ends,
and I don't care. It's an eyesore.'[67] Though he was not an advocate of
river restoration, Roraback's series raised public awareness of the river's
condition.[68]

The year Roraback completed his LA River odyssey, the campaign
group, American Rivers (set up in 1973), began to issue an annual list of
the top ten most endangered U.S. rivers. In 1995, it ranked the LA River

Bill Watson, photograph of two boys cycling along the river-bed while raw sewage pours in, 1955.

as the most endangered urban river (and second overall). The river re-appeared as the eighth most threatened in 1994 and featured again in 1996 among the twenty most threatened. The immediate danger facing the river in 1996 was a flood control proposal to string 21 miles of 8-feet high concrete walls along the lower section, which largely passes through low-income communities. According to American Rivers, just 13 miles of river remained in a 'mostly natural state' and it was the single most serious source of pollution along the southern California coast, spilling into the ocean a melange of toxic runoff from streets and parking lots, the residue of fertilizer and pesticides from nearby farms and gardens, sewage from outdated storm water systems, and chemicals from riverside factories.[69]

De-industrializing cities across North America and Europe are redis-covering the positive aspects of once degraded rivers. In the United States, the grassroots movement to revivify urban waterways emerged in the late 1980s and early 1990s with groups such as the Coalition to Restore Urban Waters and Friends of Trashed Rivers.[70] FOLAR rode in the vanguard of this impulse that stood the traditional notion of river improvement on its head. The group's origins are usually traced back to two events in September 1985. One morning, local poet Lewis MacAdams visited a particularly unsavoury stretch of downtown river with some friends. Having accessed the river by cutting a large hole in a chain-link fence, they clambered down the concrete walls into the bed, where 'we felt like we were exploring the moon'. Extending their act of civil disobedience, they hiked up to the con-fluence with Arroyo Seco, where the scenario was 'latter-day urban hell'. Because of the infernal din, MacAdams recalled, 'when we asked the river if we could speak for it in the human realm we didn't hear it say no; and that was how Friends of the Los Angeles River began'. The second seminal moment transpired that evening. For an eccentric performance piece at the Los Angeles Museum of Contemporary Art, entitled 'Friends of the LA River', MacAdams painted his face a watery colour, dressed up in a white suit and delivered a grandiloquent monologue in the style of William Mul-holland. He wrapped up with a series of impressions of river-associated animals (owl, hawk, rattlesnake and frog).[71]

The Los Angeles River's best-known tributary simultaneously attracted artist-activist attention. *Arroyo Seco Release*, by veteran 'earthwork' artists Helen Mayer Harrison and Newton Harrison, was exhibited (1985) in Pasadena at the California Institute of Technology's Baxter Art Gallery. The exhibit consisted of a multi-media installation including collages, maps, photographs and short, hand-written poems that represented what the Harrisons identified as a 'wound in the land' – a reference to the concrete spillway, enclosed by fences ten feet high and crowned with barbed wire, that housed the river. The Harrisons' remedy was to stitch this 'incision' in a two-stage process. Firstly, to cap the conduit with concrete, thereby preserving its flood control function. Secondly, to create a new linear park stretching from Devil's Gate Dam to the confluence with the LA River by covering the buried conduit with soil and vegetation and re-establishing the stream.[72] As curator Jay Belloli commented in the

exhibit catalogue: 'The technology remains, but it is placed underground
. . . the river becomes continuous, the banks are continuous, the Arroyo is
again made whole.' The local reporter who covered the exhibit challenged
Los Angeles to follow the lead of cities like Denver, Phoenix and San
Antonio in 'rediscovering' its river's potential.[73]

The fundamental activity that unites river improvement groups from
Los Angeles to Liverpool is the clean-up. During the 25-year life of the
Mersey Basin Campaign (established the same year that MacAdams was
gearing up for FOLAR), children representing 200 out of the 4,000 schools
within the Mersey catchment participated in the Campaign's annual
(October) Mersey Basin Weekend clean-ups.[74] Similarly, FOLAR's best
known activity has become the annual Great LA River Cleanup, held each
spring, when tons of rubbish, ranging from portable toilets, cars, phone
booths and mysterious bones to more mainstream items like plastic bags,
supermarket trolleys and hub caps, are retrieved from the water and banks.
First held in 1989, when it attracted 30 volunteers, *La Gran Limpieza*
has since grown into a large-scale, trans-generational, multi-racial event
involving over 3,000 people (including, in 2011, FOLAR's 25th anniversary,
Mayor Antonio Villaraigosa) and backed by a range of commercial, non-
governmental and governmental sponsors, from Coca-Cola and Toyota
to Keep California Beautiful and the Port of Long Beach.

Fishing out bicycle wheels, umbrellas, underwear and CDs as part of
the nation's biggest urban river clean-up event is not a means to the end
of returning the river to a primordial condition. Undoing some of the
re-engineering works of the past 75 years is plain common sense. As
Price has observed, in the mid-1980s, 'proposals to paint the concrete
blue and to use the channel as a dry-season freeway for trucks met with
far more serious consideration' than FOLAR's recommendations.[75] Twenty
years later, though, the preposterous could be contemplated. In 2002, LA
City Council set up an Ad Hoc Committee on the Los Angeles River.[76]
Thanks to MacAdams's efforts, commented a committee member whose
constituency includes some stretches of river in May 2003, the river is
'now on your standard politician's check off list, along with affordable
housing, more cops and fire fighters, and doing something about smog
and earthquakes'.[77]

Stripping some of the concrete out of the river is no longer regarded
as an eccentric activity at best and a reckless pro-flood measure at worst.
City officials and local politicians increasingly understand that a colossal
amount of water that could replenish the basin's aquifers and provide for

the city's needs is currently squandered by being routed straight out to sea. They are also responding to citizen pressure for greater access to the river that goes hand in hand with efforts to improve the river's health and capacity to supply clean water: in a city with the lowest per capita ratio of public parkland and open space of any major American urban centre,[78] the river represents the wanton waste of a prime recreational space for congested communities.

In 2004, the Los Angeles Department of Water and Power stumped up $3 million to develop a comprehensive plan covering 30 miles of river between Canoga Park and Boyle Heights.[79] Four years later, the City of Los Angeles issued a comprehensive Los Angeles River Revitalization Master Plan for the development and management of the 32-mile portion of river within the city boundaries. The blueprint's objectives for the next 25 to 50 years are: to establish guidelines for land use that, building on the Taylor Park initiative, balance the needs of environmental protection and urban living requirements;[80] to restore the river to ecological health and diversity; to improve public access and boost provision of riverside recreational space; to tighten up flood controls; and to enhance community awareness of the river in their midst and promote inter-community connection by reinstating a 'green ribbon'. As Ed P. Reyes, chairman of the Ad Hoc Committee, points out in his introduction, the master plan is the outcome of 'tireless efforts' by those who 'never stopped believing that the River, a trench entombed in concrete, could be renewed, brought back to life'.[81]

The Master Plan has already delivered a string of riverfront mini-parks that will help convert the urban river way into an 'emerald necklace'.[82] One mini-park, Los Angeles River Steelhead Park, commemorates the migratory steelhead trout that was a casualty of the canalization that eliminated resting and spawning areas as well as shade (the last recorded catch was near Glendale in 1940).[83] The Master Plan envisages restoration of steelhead trout habitat through provision of fish passages, fish ladders, riffles, pools and gravel. A sign (in English, Spanish and Chinese) in the pleasant Glendale Narrows, maintained by the Los Angeles River Greenway, invites the passer-by to: 'Imagine the LA River as a clean and protected environment that is a source of community pride. Parks, bicycle trails, places to walk under a green canopy of trees, clean air, water, and wildlife habitat are all a part of what the future holds for the river.'

The ultimate objective is nothing less than the river's restoration to its ancient role as the city's heart and soul.[84] Mayor Villaraigosa believes it is time for the city to repay its debt: the river gave the city life; now the city needs to give life back to the river.[85] In this spirit, FOLAR has campaigned for a mini-park at the insalubrious confluence with Arroyo Seco that will communicate a sense of the attractions that commended the site to the Portolá expedition. This park, in Price's words, will help 'commit' to 'civic memory' the 'founding of LA, and the centrality of the LA River to LA and its history'.[86] However, we should not misconstrue the impulse behind the liberal use of phrases such as 'paradise reclaimed' and river 'resurrection' and 'redemption', MacAdams's dream of being able to see a steelhead heading upriver again, and the general call for 'a city the river can be proud of'.[87] These do not express a yearning to return the river to an original (pre-human) condition or to how it looked and operated on the day that Crespi wrote so effusively in his diary.

## LA River as River

Within this fresh context of appreciation, care and concern, what the main body of water that flowed (more or less) through the city was actually called became more than a question of semantics. The city's engineers and flood control officials maintained that it was inaccurate to refer to the Los Angeles River as a river, because they had re-created it to serve two specific purposes: to carry off flood waters and to receive treated sewage. But every time the deputy chief director of the Los Angeles County public works agency (Jim Noyes) referred to it as a 'flood control channel' at a meeting in 1997, MacAdams interrupted with 'you mean "river"'.[88] To concede that the river was no longer a river, no matter how tenuous its current identity as a river, was to capitulate to the terms of debate imposed by advocates of the non-river status quo. (Among those who simply went ahead and treated it like a 'real river', bemoaned an activist on behalf of the homeless, were undocumented immigrants, who 'insist[ed]' on washing, drinking and swimming in the river in the 1990s.[89])

Many river lovers had given up on the river and abandoned it to a permanent fate as a glorified trench entirely of the engineers' making. In his 'Rivers of America' study of the Santee, published just before the age of widespread public environmental awareness dawned, Henry Savage contended that when a river becomes overloaded with effluent it becomes a river in name only and is more accurately characterized as an open sewer.[90] Though he did not pursue this line of thought, the notion of nominal river-ness raises the possibility of a fluid identity, with a water-

course passing in and out of river-hood according to the condition of
its liquid content. It also begs the question: what is a river? This, in turn,
raises a further question: what is a dead river?

For Henry Van Dyke, a river was a combination of three elements:
contents (water), container (bed) and banks (shore). 'Fluid' content that
flowed through a channelized bed and banks was a river no more. To
support this point, he quoted Charles Lamb's early nineteenth-century
verdict on the Thames in London: a 'mockery of a river – liquid artifice –
wretched conduit!', no better than a canal or aqueduct. By the same token,
the most beautiful and natural container without contents was nothing
more than an 'ugly road with none to travel it; a long, ghastly scar on the
bosom of the earth'. A river's 'life', like a person's, consisted of the 'union of
soul and body, the water and the banks. They belong together'. Acting on
and reacting to one another, Van Dyke explained, the stream shapes the
shore ('hollowing out a bay here, and building a long point there') and
the shore modulates the stream ('now bending it in a hundred sinuous
curves, and now speeding it straight as a wild-bee in its homeward
flight').[91] Van Dyke would doubtless have described the LA as a wretched
conduit – and one far worse than the Thames, in that it was not even
dignified by a reliable fluid content.

Playing with the metaphors of life and death, Gumprecht refers to the
LA River's concrete bed and sides as a 'coffin' for a river already drained of
its vital juices.[92] Others, though, believe that a 'trench entombed in concrete' can be resuscitated.[93] What strikes them most forcibly is the river's
irrepressibility, its refusal to lie down and die.[94] In a technical sense, a river
is the law of gravity applied to water, a downward flow of liquid particles
carrying dissolved mineral and suspended organic substances, returning
to the sea the moisture that it gave to the land through the mechanism of
clouds. So, strictly speaking, whether a river's liquid content is polluted or
pure or somewhere in between is beside the point. The California poet and
nature writer Gary Snyder gave the LA River the benefit of the doubt in the
early 1990s. That much of the open flow was currently confined and dirty
did not demoralize him. Nor was he dismayed by the amount of river that
had been consigned beneath asphalt and concrete: 'in the larger picture the
Los Angeles River is alive and well under the city streets, running in giant cul -
verts'. Nor was the river itself disheartened or despairing. In fact, 'It is possibly
amused by such diversions'.[95]

For all the zealotry of the water engineers, for all the lamentations of
historians and ecologists, and despite all the jokes, the Los Angeles River's

fluvial identity was never completely wiped out. The final two-mile tidal stretch at Long Beach, below Willow Street, where it flows shallow, wide and brackish, bears the hallmarks of an estuarine river. Midway to the river's official start, for a total of some 8 miles within the Glendale Narrows, Griffith Park and Elysian Fields sectors, the river retains a soft bottom, prompting visitors to exclaim in shock: 'Wow! It really is a river.'[96] Though the course has been straightened and the sides armoured here as elsewhere, the bottom is cobbled instead of concrete-lined. This was not an act of grace, mercy or restraint. Lining was simply not feasible because the bedrock hereabouts forces the water table close to the surface – sometimes as little as 40 feet beneath ground – as indicated by the springs that bubble up into the riverbed and would rupture concrete. Unsurprisingly, this is the most hospitable section of river for flora and fauna. Vegetation provides dramatic visual evidence of precisely where a stretch of unpaved bottom begins and ends. Willows and cottonwoods colonize sandbars built up by winter runoff. Bulrushes and reeds grow along the littoral, which is also occupied by sycamore and oak (whose branches are often decorated with disintegrating plastic bags and clothes). Snowy egret and great blue heron patrol for crawfish. Ducks, sandpipers, lizards and turtles are often spotted. Along these soft-bottomed sections – where the retaining walls

Lush vegetation marks the soft-bottomed stretch of river in the Glendale Narrows, 2009.

also switch from vertical to sloping (that is, from 90 to 45 degrees), damp-ening the current's velocity – Gumprecht concedes that it 'acts and even looks like a river'.[97]

Ecologist Ellen Wohl has given considered thought to how a river should act and look. In her study of the mountainous upper South Platte basin in Colorado, she identifies – as Van Dyke did more casually – the two essential characteristics of a river: the physical form (container) and the physical and biological functions (contents). The tendency of human activity over the centuries has been to simplify diversity of fluvial form and function.[98] By these standards of river 'impoverishment', the Los Angeles River has been reduced to a fairly abject state of poverty. And yet, in a biological sense, the river is not, never has been and probably never will be dead (even if many of those forms of life it currently supports are invasive non-native species).

Richard Pike Bissell adopted a more personal set of criteria than Wohl to define a river. For the native of the Mississippi river town of Dubuque, Iowa, who worked as a pilot on the upper Mississippi, Ohio and Mononga-hela rivers before becoming a novelist and playwright, 'the important thing about a river is that it is made of water, has fish in it, and steamboats, row-boats, or floating logs on its surface'. The Yukon passes that test with flying colours. But many rivers in the semi-arid and arid American Southwest fall far short of the exacting, Mississippi-basin specific standards of a man whose rollicking novels set on the Mississippi (*A Stretch on the River* [1950], *High Water* [1954] and *River in my Blood* [1955]) earned him a reputation as a latter-day Mark Twain. Edwin Corle quoted Bissell's eccentric state-ment in his 'Rivers of America' book on the Gila, a 600-mile tributary of the Colorado in New Mexico and Arizona. The Gila, he explained, had 'never known a steamboat, very few rowboats, some floating logs, and only a fair assortment of fish'.[99]

Like the Gila, the Los Angeles is a river 'of unpredictable liquid con-tent'.[100] Still, it fares better than most of its regional compatriots in this department. The flow of water has increased substantially since 1984, when a wastewater treatment plant opened in the Sepulveda Basin on the upper river. Most of the water in the river outside the winter rainy season is now treated discharge from this and a couple of neighbouring plants, which guarantees a consistent year-round flow unprecedented in the river's history. In the summer of 2003, for example, the average flow was 80 million gallons per day.[101] Treated effluent may sound unappetizing, but is actually much cleaner than storm water entering through drains. The presence of fish (and fishermen) are the proof of the pudding. Though none of the native species that survive in the watershed (Santa Ana sucker, Santa Ana speckled dace and arroyo chub) were among the specimens collected, FOLAR's fish study in the Glendale Narrows during the late summer and autumn of 2007 uncovered eight species (the most abundant being tilapia and mosquitofish).[102]

So the still-a-river river has water and fish. And official recognition: in 2004, the city erected Danubian blue 'Los Angeles River' signs bearing the county's heron logo on every bridge across the river.[103] Besides, during spate, it carries plenty of debris, if not so many logs as in the past, thanks to interception by debris basins. Returning to Bissell's criteria, there is just one recorded entry by a steamboat (carrying eminent geologist and all-round scientist W. H. Brewer in December 1860), and that was a small craft which only penetrated six miles upriver from San Pedro.[104] And rowboats (as distinct from Gabrieleño canoes and rafts) are and were a rarity. On the other hand, the navigability that was such a critical consideration for Bissell has been formally recognized as an attribute of the Los Angeles River. In *Rapanos v. United States* (2006) – a challenge to federal regulatory power under the Clean Water Act of 1972 by a Michigan developer fined for filling in 58 acres of wetland without a permit in the 1980s – the Supreme Court applied a broad definition of navigable waterway. Rapanos contended that the law on unlawful discharges into navigable waters did not apply to his actions because the wetland in question was not only non-navigable but 20 miles from any navigable body of water defined by historic use for commercial purposes. The court majority ruled, however, that the reach of the Clean Water Act was not restricted to waters that could float a boat and applied wherever there was a 'significant nexus' between the affected wetlands or tributary and the 'navigable-in-fact' waterway.[105] In other words, a navigable river was inseparable from other streams and water bodies within its watershed.

The ruling in 2006 may have settled this particular controversy in Michigan. But it did nothing to resolve a host of other disputes over the federal regulatory right as applied to individual waterways. Did the Los Angeles River qualify as navigable? Was its essential character that of an entity that qualified as one of the 'waters of the United States'? Or is that designation restricted to more or less permanent, standing and continuously flowing bodies of water (like those Bissell knew)? If the Los Angeles River was first and foremost a concrete flood control channel, then did it lie beyond the scope of federal environmental protection? At stake was the

A spoof photo printed in the *Los Angeles Herald-Examiner* on April Fool's Day 1950 shows a liner steaming downriver.

Clean Water Act's applicability not just to the LA River but to its entire watershed. From a strictly legal standpoint, waterways that have carried – or have the potential to bear – interstate or foreign commerce through boating of any sort (including recreational kayaking, whether solo or group) are 'navigable-in-fact' and thus subject to the Act's jurisdiction. In July 2010, FOLAR won a major victory when the U.S. Environmental Protection Agency (EPA) agreed that, despite its intermittent flow and mostly concrete bed, the main stem of the river nonetheless counted as 'a traditional navigable water' (TNW) and was therefore entitled to various protections under the Clean Water Act that did not previously apply. Having considered its current capacity to support watercraft, evidence of historic navigation by watercraft (the Gabrieleño fashioned rafts and canoes from tules and rushes), and the extent of current commercial and recreational uses (not least the so-called Los Angeles River Expedition of July 2008) and future potential (not least boat tours of famous filming locations), EPA concluded that the LA River was of no lesser ecological, economic, recreational or community importance than a river with a more regular flow[106] – or, they might have added, a river with a more illustrious and dignified history.

Yet not everyone who values the river wants to return it to a more natural condition. The role of local creative practitioners in particular is not restricted to publicizing the river's plight and to offering an alternative future. Some like it just the way it is. A connoisseur of the river's ambiguity, contradictions and strange beauty is photographer Anthony Hernández, for whom the river supplied a boyhood stomping ground when growing up in the nearby Latino district of Boyle Heights. In a show entitled 'Everything (The Los Angeles River Basin)', based on what he found during a series of walks between January 2003 and May 2004, the all-embracing, non-discriminating Hernández recorded (and in the process aestheticized) 'lost' objects that had washed down into the river-bed through storm channels or been discarded by the homeless, who, for decades, have sought refuge in this fluvial skid row. His images – among them a mouldy jar of olives, crumpled female underwear, a sodden cardboard box and a stalk of gladioli – qualify as still lives rather than landscapes. The river never features as a river, but in the form of individual components: a headless doll in the algae; Barbie's legs in the mud. But this is where the river resides for Hernández: 'You can't see it unless you're physically down there, unless you walk its concrete corridor.' And as M. G. Lord points out, much of the impact of these photographs relies on our notion of familiar objects uncomfortably out of place: in Freudian terms, a doll languishing in the mud has been translated from the sphere of the comfortingly familiar to that of the disquietingly uncanny: *das Heimliche* rendered *das Unheimliche*.[107]

Taking a different approach, the photographer John Humble has fully incorporated the river and its attendant structures into the modernist canon of the industrial sublime. His album *The Los Angeles River: 51 Miles of Concrete* (2001) enshrines the river's infrastructural features and revels in how its flow dissects the city's 'sociological archaeology'.[108] 'L.A. River Reborn' (2006), an exhibition that included 26 large format photographs by the likes of Humble and Hernàndez – as well as the '*River Madness*' video mash-up of clips from movies filmed in the sterile riverbed – was designed not just to illustrate the natural world's resilience. It was also intended to capture the river's unexpected beauty.[109] The juxtaposition, often cheek by jowl, of unscheduled beauty and expected ugliness, of the 'natural' and the 'artificial', the dichotomy between alternating stretches of soft (real) and hard-bottomed (unreal) river – these elements lie at the heart of a thoroughly post-modern river's identity and appeal. Much of the Los Angeles River's current attractiveness and noteworthiness resides in its interim

John Humble, 'The Los Angeles River at the Sixth Street Bridge', 2001, depicts a full
river at night. The preservationist campaign to save the bridge, which is suffering from
incurable concrete decay, was lost in November 2011. A design competition for a new
bridge was launched in April 2012.

condition as a river in recovery and a river with multiple lives that are
overlapping and intersecting rather than sequential. If and when the river
people of Los Angeles have shaped a city that the river can be proud of,
the river and its city will be more river-like and more liveable, but also,
perhaps, somewhat duller and less intriguing: enriched in nature but
impoverished as a site for cultural exploration.

The curators of the exhibit 'L.A.: light/ motion/ dreams' (2004–5), at
the Natural History Museum of Los Angeles County, openly embraced
these multiple fluvial meanings in a bid to shake off the dichotomy of
'environment as myth' (nature as dream or volatile environmental adventure) that
has straitjacketed regional historiography. The Los Angeles River featured
in the Rivers gallery, one of four galleries dedicated to the city's major
environmental ingredients (the others were foothills, coast and plains).
In fact, the Rivers galley was set up to mimic the river itself. Visitors
moved along between straight banks, beginning with native vegetation that
eventually gave way to concrete, which then also melted away. In step with
this journey through time and space, the display cases that flanked the

walkway initially contained specimens of native species: such as the grizzly bear, red-legged frog, steelhead trout and the extinct Los Angeles River shrimp.[110] Artefacts from the various phases of human use and occupation of the watershed succeeded these creatures; most evocative, perhaps, was a strip of wooden pipe from the city's pre-twentieth-century water distribution network. Further down the display was a vial of water collected on the red letter day that Owens River water first wetted the city in 1913.[111] Moving closer to the present, the display features the stillborn Olmsted-Bartholomew plan of 1930, and winds up with its belated fulfilment in today's vision of restoration for a peerless liquid artifice.

## The View from Under the Bridge

If the downtown river is a paragon of sterile (and sometimes arid) artifice, enlivened only by gangland graffito, the bridges that span it are astonishingly and unexpectedly beautiful examples of artifice. The ethos of the City Beautiful movement that failed to improve the river itself found abundant expression in the fourteen elegant and often ornate bridges flung across the river within the City of Los Angeles between 1909 and 1938. Built in the Beaux Arts, Streamline Moderne and Gothic Revival styles – and of the same reinforced concrete that lines the river – their gorgeousness casts into even sharper relief the bankrupt concrete sheath beneath (the City Council awarded Historic-Cultural Monument status to eleven bridges in 2008). '72 Los Angeles River Bridges', the subtitle of 'Poured in Place', photographer Douglas Hill's solo show of 2007, suggests that the display of fifteen selected bridges was more about the bridges than about the river.[112] Yet the most striking feature of these and Hill's other bridge shots for the fluviocentric historian is their comparability to Andreas Müller-Pohle's photographic perspective on the Danube and its associated human infrastructure. In contrast to the Danube's surging vitality and brim-fullness in Müller-Pohle's images, there is far less water in evidence (though there is usually water, and some of it has a noticeable flow). But Hill's view is not often down from the bridge. He, too, frequently took his photos looking up from the riverbed or riverbank at the underside of bridges. And sometimes, like his German counterpart, he also stepped into the water (though, in the shallow reaches of the Los Angeles River, this is nothing to write home about).

Hill is no artistic-activist like MacAdams. Yet his bridges, contrary to expectation, lord it over the river no more than Müller-Pohle's bridges.

Moreover, whereas expanses of sprawling concrete sometimes dominate
Hill's LA riverscapes, he usually includes some sign of a world beyond that
is not of our making. A tumbleweed keeps a shopping cart sprawled on its
side company in the river-bed. In another photo, a thick raft of uprooted
reeds as well as a sofa bed are wrapped around a jutting retaining wall. Just
as Hill wants to communicate the dialogue and dialectic between river and
bridge, this book's series of river portraits that meander in and out of each
other captures the dynamic between rivers and people that pumps through
the main artery of liquid history.

On the other side of the continent, in his *Please the Waters* installation
at Wave Hill's Hudson Quadricentennial exhibit (2009), Hock E Aye Vi
Edgar Heap of Birds presented the river as bearing witness to the often
painful past through a series of paired signs: for example, 'Muhheakantuck
Knows Salt Tides, Winds, Sea' (circa 4000 BC) and 'Muhheakantuck Knows
LGA Airbus A-320 USAIR 1549' (2009).[113] But his signs also work to bring

Douglas Hill, photograph of a shopping cart and a tumbleweed in the damp river-bed, 2007.

the river that forms a scenic backdrop to the gardens onto terra firma as a vital persona. At the end of the day, though, the river's most animated presence at Wave Hill was to be found indoors in one of the rooms of Wave Hill House, a mansion built in the style of an English country residence in 1843. *Currents*, a three-minute digital video projected into an elaborate picture frame, began with the tidal ebb and flow of the Muhheakantuck. In the centre of the frame, above the fireplace, a modern clock marked time. Words such as 'Conflict' streamed across the screen, evoking the confrontation between European colonists and the local Lenape triggered by the appearance on the lower river of Hudson's carrack, the *Half Moon*. But the flow of a river is not just downhill. Fluvial fortunes wax and wane like those of river people. No civilization lasts forever. No river remains clean – or dirty – forever. Before the video returns to the beginning and starts to replay the eternal cycle of the tides – the horizontally split screen showing the river's two-directional movement – a sentence flashes up: 'a river is like history, it has its own ebb and flow as does any historical narrative'. A moment later, the words disappear, carried off by the swift current of time.

# References

## Introduction

1 Rudolf Wittkower, *Gian Lorenzo Bernini: The Sculptor of the Roman Baroque* (London, 1966), p. 30.

2 Claude Lévi-Strauss, *Totemism*, trans. Rodney Needham (London, 1964 [1962]), p. 89. Widespread use has adapted the phrase to read 'good to think with'.

3 Marcus Aurelius, *The Meditations of the Emperor Marcus Aurelius Antoninus* (Glasgow, 1749), p. 164.

4 Ibid., p. 165.

5 According to Raymond P. Holden, a river's course, followed upstream, leads from present to past because upstream conditions are the least changed and the lower reaches the most altered: *The Merrimack* (New York, 1958), p. 21.

6 Aurelius, *Meditations*, p. 165.

7 Pancrazio Capelli, *Roma, Antica, e Moderna* (Roma, 1750), vol. II, pp. 20–21; Stanislao Fraschetti, *Il Bernini: La sua vita, la sua opera, il suo tempo* (Milan, 1900), pp. 180–81; Max von Boehn, *Lorenzo Bernini: Seine Zeit, sein Leben, sein Werk* (Bielefeld, 1912), pp. 81–2.

8 Volume of flow and scale of watershed are additional criteria to consider when measuring a river's size. Among North America's rivers, the St Lawrence ranks higher by volume than length and the Missouri rates higher by length than volume.

9 Torgil Magnuson, *Rome in the Age of Bernini*, vol. II: *From the Election of Innocent X to the Death of Innocent XI* (Stockholm, 1986), p. 83.

10 *Handbook of Rome and its Environs* (London, 1864), pp. 60, 93.

11 Frank Fehrenbach, '"Dissimilia concors", Gianlorenzo Berninis "Fontana dei Quatro Fiumi" (1648–51) als päpstliches Friedensmonument', in *Der Westfälische Friede: Diplomatie – Politische Zäsur – Kulturelles Umfeld – Rezeptionsgeschichte*, ed. Heinz Duchhardt (Munich, 1998), pp. 718, 725, 730; Magnuson, *Rome in the Age of Bernini*, p. 85.

12 Arne Karsten, 'Rom in Preußen', in *kunsttexte.de: Sektion Politische Ikonographie*, 1 (2001), p. 3.

13 Mary Christian, 'Bernini's "Danube" and Pamphili Politics', *Burlington Magazine*,

CXXVIII/998 (May 1986), pp. 354–5; Ann Sutherland Harris, *Seventeenth-century Art and Architecture* (London, 2005), pp. 111–12.

14  Wittkower, *Bernini*, p. 30.

15  H.F.M. Prescott, *Once to Sinai: The Further Pilgrimage of Father Felix Fabri* (New York, 1958), p. 170.

16  Simon Schama, *Landscape and Memory* (New York, 1995), p. 293.

17  Carl Ritter, *Comparative Geography*, trans. William L. Gage (Edinburgh, 1865), p. 175.

18  Frank Eyre and Charles Hadfield, *English Rivers and Canals* (London, 1945), p. 26.

19  Henry David Thoreau, *The Journal of Henry David Thoreau* (Boston, 1906), vol. II, pp. 96–7. Entry for 16 November 1850.

20  Henry Van Dyke, *Little Rivers: A Book of Essays in Profitable Idleness* (New York, 1895), pp. 18–19. From Van Dyke's North American perspective, the Thames and Arno, however famous, remained 'little' rivers.

21  Ibid., p. 33.

22  J.J.A. Hayman, *A Brief History of Holford* (Holford, Somerset, 1973), pp. 10–12.

23  Samuel Taylor Coleridge, *Biographia Literaria* (London, 1906 [1817]), pp. 100–01; Coleridge, *The Notebooks of Samuel Taylor Coleridge*, vol. I: *1794–1804*, ed. Kathleen Coburn (New York, 1957), p. 211; *The Complete Poetical Works of Samuel Taylor Coleridge*, ed. Ernest Hartley Coleridge (Oxford, 1912), vol. II, pp. 988–92; Frederic Stewart Colwell, *Rivermen: A Romantic Iconography of the River and the Source* (Montreal, 1989), pp. 89–90.

24  Richard White, *The Organic Machine: The Remaking of the Columbia River* (New York, 1995); Jeff Ingram, *Hijacking a River: A Political History of the Colorado River in the Grand Canyon* (Flagstaff, AZ, 2003); Philip L. Fradkin, *A River No More: The Colorado River and the West* (Berkeley, 1996); Marquis William Childs, *Mighty Mississippi: Biography of a River* (New Haven, CT, 1982); Mark Cioc, *The Rhine: An Eco-Biography, 1815–2000* (Seattle, 2002); Roland Recht, *The Rhine* (London, 2001); Gavin Weightman, *London's Thames: The River that Shaped a City and its History* (London, 2005); Patrick Wright, *The River: The Thames in our Time* (London, 1999); Jonathan Schneer, *The Thames: England's River* (New Haven, CT, 2005); Peter Ackroyd, *Thames: Sacred River* (London, 2007).

25  *The Prose of Philip Freneau*, ed. Philip M. Marsh (New Brunswick, NJ, 1955), p. 228.

26  W. G. East, 'The Danube Route-Way in History', *Economia*, 37 (August 1932), p. 321.

27  Tricia Cusack, *Riverscapes and National Identities* (Syracuse, NY, 2009), pp. 1–4, 10–15; Cusack, 'Riverscapes and the Formation of National Identity', *National Identities*, IX/2 (June 2007), pp. 101–04.

28  G. E. Mitton, *The Thames* (London, 1910), p. 6.

29  Henricus Glareanus, *De geographica liber unus* (Paris, 1572), pp. 50, 53.

30  C. A. Macartney, *Problems of the Danube Basin* (Cambridge, 1942), pp. 1, 8.

31  Christof Mauch and Thomas Zeller, 'Rivers in History and Historiography: An Introduction', in *Rivers in History: Perspectives on Waterways in Europe and North America*, ed. Mauch and Zeller (Pittsburgh, PA, 2008), p. 1.

32  Ellen Churchill Semple, 'Ancient Mediterranean Agriculture: Part 1', *Agricultural History*, II/2 (April 1928), p. 61.

33  Henry Skrine, *A General Account of All Rivers of Note in Great Britain* (London, 1801), p. 319.

34  Blair Niles, *The James: From Iron Gate to the Sea* (New York, 1939), p. 11; Ian Wray, ed. (photographs by Colin McPherson), *Mersey: The River that Changed the World* (Liverpool, 2007); William Maitland, *The History of London: From its Foundation by the Romans to the Present Time* (London, 1739), vol. I, p. 56.

35  Paul Du Noyer, *Liverpool: Wondrous Place. Music from Cavern to Cream* (London, 2002), p. 9.

36  The 'Three Graces' are the Mersey Docks and Harbour Board (1907) (now the Port of Liverpool Building), Royal Liver Building (1911) and Cunard Building (1916).

37  Anon., 'The Mersey', *Industrial Rivers of the United Kingdom, by Various Well-known Experts* (London, 1888), p. 20.

38  Élisée Reclus, *The Earth and its Inhabitants. Europe*, vol. IV: *The British Isles* (New York, 1881), p. 267.

39  Wordsworth, 'The River Duddon', in *The Poetical Works of Wordsworth*, ed. Thomas Hutchinson (London, 1959), p. 297.

40  International Riverfoundation, *River Journeys II* (Brisbane, 2010), pp. 1, 5, 12–15, 44–7. The Mersey Basin Campaign and the International Commission for the Protection of the Danube River won this prize in 1999 and 2007, at the first and third attempts respectively.

41  Frederick Schwatka, *Along Alaska's Great River* (New York, 1885), p. 143.

42  C. M. Wong et al., *World's Top 10 Rivers at Risk* (Gland, Switzerland, March 2007), p. 7.

43  Bill Thomas, 'The Yukon: A True Wilderness River', in *Great Rivers of the World* (Washington, DC, 1984), p. 401.

44  Élisée Reclus, *The Earth: A Descriptive History of the Phenomena of the Life of the Globe* (New York, 1879), p. 381.

45  Reclus, *The Earth: Descriptive History*, p. 382.

46  Robert T. Cooper, *Our Empire of Rivers* (London, 1886), p. 7; Henry Savage, *River of the Carolinas: The Santee* (New York, 1956), p. 395.

47  Robert Shackleton, *Unvisited Places of Old Europe* (Philadelphia, 1914), p. 289.

48  Élisée Reclus, *The Earth and its Inhabitants*, vol. IV: *Europe* (New York, 1883), pp. 206–8; Salvatore Ciriacono, *Building on Water: Venice, Holland, and the*

*Construction of European Landscape in Early Modern Times*, trans. Jeremy Scott (London, 2006), pp. 107–8, 117; Fynes Moryson, *An Itinerary Written by Fynes Moryson, Containing his Ten Yeeres Travell* (Glasgow, 1907 [1617]), vol. I, pp. 158–9.

49 Reclus, *Europe*, pp. 208–9; Thomas Bullfinch, *The Golden Age of Myth and Legend* (Ware, Hertfordshire, 1993 [1915]), p. 163.

50 Domenico Guglielmini, *Della natura de' fiumi trattato fisico-matematico* (Bologna, 1697); Cesare S. Maffioli, *Out of Galileo: The Science of Waters, 1628–1718* (Rotterdam, 1994), p. 266.

51 Jennifer McGregor, 'The Muhheakantuck in Focus', Wave Hill Glyndor Gallery, 1 August–29 November 2009, pp. 3, 6–7.

52 Written by Arthur Hamilton in 1953, this smash hit was first sung in 1955 by his former high-school classmate Julie London, who performed it again in the film *The Girl Can't Help It* (1956).

53 William Wordsworth, *The River Duddon, A Series of Sonnets; Vaudracour and Julia; and Other Poems* (London, 1820), 'Postscript', pp. 38–9.

54 Magnuson, *Rome in the Age of Bernini*, p. 88; *Handbook of Rome and its Environs*, p. 92; *New Guide of Rome, Naples and their Environs: From the Italian of Vasi and Nibby* (Rome, 1844), p. 109; *Handbook or New Guide of Rome and the Environs According to Vasi and Nibby* (Rome, 1845), pp. 294–5; Shakspere Wood, *The New Curiosum Urbis: A Guide to Ancient and Modern Rome* (London, 1875), pp. 6–7.

55 Van Dyke, *Little Rivers*, pp. 9, 12.

56 Skinner, 'Rivers and American Folk', postscript to Carl Carmer, *Hudson River* (New York, 1939), n.p.

57 J. E. Allison, *The Mersey Estuary* (Liverpool, 1949), p. 60.

58 Richard C. Bocking, *Mighty River: A Portrait of the Fraser* (Vancouver, BC, 1998), p. 11.

59 *The Life and Letters of Lord Macaulay,* ed. Otto George Trevelyan (London, 1881), vol. I, p. 350. On the Rhône, see Sara B. Pritchard, *Confluence: The Nature of Technology and the Remaking of the Rhône* (Cambridge, MA, 2011).

60 Ackroyd, *Thames*, p. 11.

61 Simon Winchester, *The River at the Center of the World: A Journey Up the Yangtze, and Back in Chinese Time* (New York, 1996), pp. 4, 13, 404.

62 Mao Zedong, *The Poems of Mao Zedong*, trans. and ed. Willis Barnstone (New York, 1972), p. 85; 'Chairman Mao Swims in the Yangtze', *China Reconstructs*, XV/9 (September 1966), pp. 4, 6.

63 *Up the Yangtze* (Eyesteelfilm/National Film Board of Canada) is based on one of the 'farewell cruises' operated by the New York City-based Victoria Cruises company. For 'high modernism', see James C. Scott, *Seeing Like a State: How Certain Schemes to Improve the Human Condition Have Failed* (New Haven, CT, 1998), p. 5.

64  John Graves, *Goodbye to a River: A Narrative* (New York, 1960), p. 8. Graves undertook the 175-mile canoe trip the book is based on in autumn 1957.

65  Philip L. Fradkin, *A River No More: The Colorado River and the West* (Berkeley, 1996); Katie Lee, *All My Rivers Are Gone: A Journey of Discovery Through Glen Canyon* (Boulder, CO, 1998), p. xi; Blaine Harden, *A River Lost: The Life and Death of the Columbia* (New York, 1997), p. 13.

66  Donald Worster, *The Wealth of Nature: Environmental History and the Ecological Imagination* (New York, 1993), pp. 214–19.

67  Robert Boyle, *The Hudson: A Natural and Unnatural History* (New York, 1969); Libby Hill, *The Chicago River: A Natural and Unnatural History* (Chicago, 2000).

68  Ellen E. Wohl, *Virtual Rivers: Lessons from the Mountain Rivers of the Colorado Front Range* (New Haven, CT, 2001), pp. ix–x, 34–7.

69  'Cologne', in *The Poems of Coleridge* (New York, 1906), p. 419.

70  Samuel Taylor Coleridge, *Anima Poetae: From the Unpublished Notebooks of Samuel Taylor Coleridge*, ed. Ernest Hartley Coleridge (London, 1895), p. 228.

71  Patrick McCully, *Silenced Rivers: The Ecology and Politics of Large Dams* (London, 2001).

72  Clay McShane and Joel A. Tarr, *The Horse in the City: Living Machines in the Nineteenth Century* (Baltimore, MD, 2007); White, *Organic Machine*, pp. ix, 59–60. See also Christopher Armstrong, Matthew Evenden and H.V. Nelles, *The River Returns: An Environmental History of the Bow* (Montreal, 2009), pp. 10–20.

73  Marcus Tullius Cicero, *De natura deorum,* ed. Arthur Stanley Pease (Cambridge, MA, 1955), vol. II, p. 1028; Clarence J. Glacken, *Traces on the Rhodian Shore: Nature and Culture in Western Thought from Ancient Times to the End of the Eighteenth Century* (Berkeley, 1967), p. xxviii.

74  Wong, *World's Top 10 Rivers at Risk*, p. 4.

75  These achievements included an increase in the amount of the river defined as having good water quality from 53 per cent in 1990 to 80 per cent in 2008: Alastair Driver, 'River Thames', presentation, 13th International Riversymposium, Perth, Australia, p. 4; 'River Thames Wins International Restoration Prize', 12 October 2010, at www.bbc.co.uk (accessed 16 March 2012).

76  Carl N. Tyson, *The Red River in Southwestern History* (Norman, OK, 1981), pp. 9, 181, 184; Henry Clune, *Genesee* (New York, 1963), p. 28; Thomas L. Stokes, *The Savannah* (New York, 1951), p. 12.

77  C.R.L. Fletcher and Rudyard Kipling, *A History of England* (New York, 1911), p. 4.

78  *Life and Letters of Macaulay*, pp. 350–51.

79  Van Dyke, *Little Rivers*, p. 15.

80  I owe this phrase to Allison, *Mersey Estuary*, p. 12.

81  Carmer, *Hudson*, preface; Henry Seidel Canby, *The Brandywine* (New York, 1941), p. 3.

82  A sequel to *London: The Biography* (2000), the American edition of *Thames: Sacred River* carried a more explicit subtitle: *The Biography* (2009).

83  Norman Maclean, *A River Runs Through It (and Other Stories)* (London, 1976), pp. 1–104.

84  E.P. Thompson, 'Socialist Humanism: An Epistle to the Philistines', *New Reasoner*, 1 (1957), p. 122.

85  Ted Steinberg, 'Down to Earth: Nature, Agency, and Power in History', *American Historical Review*, CVII/3 (2002), pp. 768–820; Richard C. Foltz, 'Does Nature have Historical Agency? World History, Environmental History, and How Historians Can Help Save the Planet', *History Teacher*, CCCVII/1 (November 2003), pp. 9–28.

86  William H. Sewell, 'Nature, Agency, and Anthropocentrism', post-dated 7 September 2002, at www.historycooperative.org (accessed 16 March 2012).

87  Francis Gooding, 'Of Dodos and Dutchmen: Reflections on the Nature of History', *Critical Quarterly*, XLVII/4 (2005), p. 33; Jonathan Burt, *Animals in Film* (London, 2002), pp. 30–31; Chris Philo and Chris Wilbert, 'Animal Spaces, Beastly Places: An Introduction', in *Animal Spaces, Beastly Places: New Geographies of Human-animal Relations*, ed. Philo and Wilbert (London, 2000), p. 16.

88  Emil Lengyel, *The Danube* (London, 1940), p. 23.

89  Wordsworth, *River Duddon*, p. 297.

90  Cioc, *Rhine*, pp. 5–6.

91  Jason Hribal, 'Animals, Agency, and Class: Writing the History of Animals from Below', *Human Ecology Review*, XIV/1 (2007), pp. 102, 106.

92  Bruno Latour, *Reassembling the Social: An Introduction to Actor-Network-Theory* (New York, 2005), pp. 71–92; *We Have Never Been Modern*, trans. Catherine Porter (Cambridge. MA, 1991), pp. 1–3.

93  Linda Nash, 'The Agency of Nature or the Nature of Agency?', *Environmental History*, X/1 (January 2005), pp. 67–8.

94  Tim Ingold, *The Perception of the Environment: Essays in Livelihood, Dwelling and Skill* (New York, 2000), pp. 3–4, 19, 396; Latour, *Reassembling the Social*, pp. 2, 22, 109, 111, 114–5.

95  Wray, *Mersey: The River that Changed the World.*

96  The phrase was adapted from Aldo Leopold, 'Thinking Like a Mountain', in *A Sand County Almanac* (New York, 1949), p. 132. MacLennan's use of the term dates from correspondence (1974) relating to the re-issue of his book *Seven Rivers of Canada* (1961): Neil S. Forkey, '"Thinking like a River": The Making of Hugh MacLennan's Environmental Consciousness', *Journal of Canadian Studies/Revue d'études canadiennes*, XLI/2 (Spring 2007), p. 50. Worster first used this phrase in 1984: Worster, 'Thinking Like a River', in Worster, *The Wealth of Nature*, pp. 125, 131. The Brower quotation is from an interview with Ken Verdoia, director of the PBS

documentary *Glen Canyon: A Dam, Water and the West*: transcript at ww.kued.org (accessed 16 March 2012).

97  See the anthology of poetry edited by Angela King and Susan Clifford: *The River's Voice* (Totnes, Devon, 2000).

98  Canby, *Brandywine*, p. 3.

99  A sixteenth-century French humanist regarded rivers as instruments of God's wrath: 'it pleaseth God that they should ouerflow to chastice men, by deluges and flouds': Pierre de la Primaudaye, *The Third Volume of the French Academie*, trans. R. Dolman (London, 1601), p. 265.

100 Mauch and Zeller, 'Rivers in History and Historiography', p. 1.

101 Mitton, *Thames*, p. 5.

102 As quoted (undated and non-contextualized) in Kim Wilkie Environmental Design/Thames Landscape Steering Group, 'Thames Landscape Strategy: Hampton to Kew' (Richmond, June 1994), p. 22; Philip Howard, 'Britain's Unsung Treasures', *The Times*, 27 June 1981.

103 Burns's biographer merely confirmed that the comparison involved 'new world' rivers: William Kent, *John Burns: Labour's Lost Leader: A Biography* (London, 1950), pp. 341–2, 283. According to some sources, the phrase is attributed to Burns by Liberal Party politician Frederick Whyte: John L. Gardiner, ed., *River Projects and Conservation: A Manual for Holistic Appraisal* (Chichester, Sussex, 1991), p. 165.

104 Arthur Bryant, *Liquid History: To Commemorate Fifty Years of the Port of London Authority, 1909–1959* (London, 1960); Stephen Croad, *Liquid History: The Thames through Time* (London, 2003). Croad's frontispiece features Burns's statement without further explanation, likewise Ackroyd (*Thames: Sacred River* (2007), p. 6) and Schneer (*Thames*, p. 4). For other examples of use – sometimes with reference to an American visitor/s, but without other contextual detail – see *The Times*, 14 June 1911; 'London's River: Neglected Pageantry', 4 August 1919; 'The Infant Thames', 13 February 1924; 12 October 1926; 'Mission Ship at Greenwich', 27 July 1932; 'Australia Looks at London', 22 August 1935; B. R. Leftwich, 'Liquid History' (letter to the editor), 13 November 1937; 'Secret History in the Thames', 2 August 1938; 'Mr John Burns: Obituary', 25 January 1943; 'London's River', 21 March 1951; 'The Gay River', 14 September 1971.

105 Ernest Wild (Conservative MP for Upton, 1918–22), quoted in 'Round Table Knights', *The Times*, 27 June 1921.

106 In November 2008, as part of the third annual European Month of Photography, the exhibition was displayed at Berlin's Uferhallen gallery.

107 Tom Fort, *Downstream: Across England in a Punt* (London, 2008), pp. 1–2, 4.

108 Roman Schmidt, 'Blue Danube: Andreas Müller-Pohle's '"Danube River Project"', *Eikon: International Magazine for Photography and Media Art*, 54 (June 2006), p. 34.

109  Ivaylo Ditchev, 'The Danube Frontier', in Andreas Müller-Pohle, *The Danube River Project* (Berlin, 2007), p. 13. The Danube Project consisted of 80 photos selected from over 4,000 taken at 21 locations during four field trips between July and November 2005; a ten-minute video projection of the river's surface at Dunaújváros, Hungary; and a twelve-minute soundtrack of an underwater recording at Kilometre Zero (Sulina, Romania), extracted from five hours of recording with a device wedged into the silt: Ulf Erdmann Ziegler, 'A Specific View: The Danube River Project by Andreas Müller-Pohle', at www.riverproject.net (accessed 16 March 2012); 'And the Danube Flows On', *Vagabond: Bulgaria's English Monthly*, 25 (October 2008), pp. 84–90.

110  David Blackbourn, *The Conquest of Nature: Water, Landscape, and the Making of Modern Germany* (New York, 2006), pp. 15–16, 19.


# 1 Danube

1  Melville Chater, 'The Danube, Highway of Races: From the Black Forest to the Black Sea, Europe's Most Important River Has Borne the Traffic of Centuries', *National Geographic*, LVI/6 (December 1929), pp. 643–97; Mike Edwards, 'The Danube: River of Many Nations, Many Names', *National Geographic*, CLII/4 (October 1977), pp. 455–85.

2  R. T. Claridge, *A Guide Down the Danube* (London, 1837), pp. 86–7. The Danube Steamship Company (1829) sent its first steamer from Vienna to Pest in 1830.

3  Walter Jerrold, *The Danube* (London, 1911), p. vi.

4  Claridge, *Guide*, p. 87.

5  Cliff Tarpy, 'The Danube: Europe's River of Harmony and Discord', *National Geographic*, 200 (March 2002), at http://ngm.nationalgeographic.com (accessed 16 March 2012).

6  C. A. Macartney, *Problems of the Danube Basin* (Cambridge, 1942), pp. 1, 8.

7  Richard Bernstein, 'The Danube Transformed: From River of Blood to River of Hope', *New York Times*, 1 August 2003.

8  Emil Lengyel, *The Danube* (London, 1940), pp. 11–12, 21, 173, 239; Ross S. Bennett, 'The Danube: The March of Empires', in *Great Rivers of the World*, ed. Margaret Sedeen (Washington, DC, 1984), pp. 95–130.

9  Andrew Charlesworth, 'The Topography of Genocide', in *The Historiography of the Holocaust*, ed. Dan Stone (London, 2004), p. 221.

10  Aleksandar Tišma, *The Book of Blam* (New York, 1988 [1972]), pp. 124, 150, 162.

11  Joshua Hirsch, *After Image: Film, Trauma, and the Holocaust* (Philadelphia, 2004), pp. x, 119, 134. The shoes featured on the cover of *QJM: An International Journal of Medicine*, CI/9 (September 2008).

12 The International Danube Commission (IDC) is not be confused with the European Danube Commission (EDC, also set up in 1856). EDC enjoyed absolute authority over the Maritime Danube, levying its own taxes and hiring its own police and pilots to ensure free navigation between Brăila and Sulina. IDC (whose status was not formalized until 1920) controlled navigation along the rest of the river. In 1948, a commission in charge of the entire river whose membership consisted exclusively of riparian states superseded both commissions, which represented various non-Danubian states (notably Britain, France and the United States): Nicholas Spulber, 'The Danube-Black Sea Canal and the Russian Control over the Danube', *Economic Geography*, XXX/3 (July 1954), p. 238.

13 Otto Popper, 'The International Regime of the Danube', *Geographical Journal*, 102 (November–December 1943), p. 252.

14 Barbara Miller, 'This Europe: Blue Danube Sputters Back to Life as Wars and Disputes Recede', *The Independent*, 28 May 2002; Neal Asherson in *Danube: River of Life*, ed. Neal Asherson and Sarah Hobson (Athens, 2002), p. 2.

15 Hinnerk Dreppenstedt, 'Die Donau', in Uwe Oster et al., *Flüsse in Deutschland* (Darmstadt, 2007), p. 147. The last *Schachtel* succumbed to railway competition in 1897. In 1907, Eduard Hahn, a professor of economic geography in Berlin, rowed a specially commissioned replica from Ulm to Vienna: Wolf-Henning Petershagen, *Kleine Geschichte der Ulmer Schachteln* (Ulm, 2009), pp. 8–13, 44–7.

16 Hartmann Schedel, *Die Schedel'sche Weltkronik* (Dortmund, 1978 [1493]), CXCI, XCVIII.

17 Henry Cord Meyer, 'German Economic Relations with Southeastern Europe, 1870–1914', *American Historical Review*, LVII/1 (October 1951), p. 86.

18 Elias Canetti, *Die Gerettete Zunge: Geschichte einer Jugend* (Frankfurt am Main, 1977), pp. 19, 10–14, 16. Published in English as *The Tongue Set Free* (1979).

19 'Quite Neglected is the Blue Danube: It Far Outshines the Castled Rhine in all that Makes that River Famous' (review of Jerrold's book), *New York Times*, 3 December 1911.

20 Jerrold, *Danube*, pp. 27–8, vi.

21 Loredana Polezzi, 'Journeys along the River: Claudio Magris's "Danubio" and its Translation', *Modern Language Review*, XCIII/3 (July 1998), p. 682; Magris, *Danube: A Sentimental Journey from the Source to the Black Sea*, trans. Patrick Creagh (London, 1986).

22 Magris, *Danube*, pp. 59, 64. The chapter section Magris dedicates to Neweklowsky's three-volume opus, *Die Schiffahrt und Flösserei im Raume der oberen Donau* (1952–3) – which translates as 'Navigation and Rafting on the Upper Danube' – is entitled 'Two thousand one hundred and sixty-four pages and five kilos nine hundred grammes of Upper Danube'.

23 Lengyel, *Danube*, p. 361.

24 Johann Georg Kohl, *Austria, Vienna, Prague, Hungary, Bohemia, and the Danube* (London, 1843), p. 255.

25 Jennifer Speake, ed., *Literature of Travel and Exploration: An Encyclopedia*, vol. I: A–F (New York, 2003), p. 372.

26 B. Granville Baker, *The Danube with Pen and Pencil* (London, 1911), pp. xv, xvi, 1, 2, 3, 9, 26, 30, 15.

27 George Meredith, *Ballads and Poems of Tragic Life* (London, 1887), pp. 99–100; Raimund Hinkel, *Wien an der Donau* (Vienna, 1995), p. 15; Theodore Murdoch Andersson, *A Preface to the Niebelungenlied* (Palo Alto, CA, 1987), pp. 82, 41, 101, 119.

28 George Macaulay Trevelyan, *The Poetry and Philosophy of George Meredith* (London, 1906), p. 54.

29 The Savannah starts at the confluence of the Seneca and Tugaloo. From here to the Atlantic it separates South Carolina and Georgia. Determining whether the Tugaloo-Chattooga or the Seneca-Keowee was the Savannah's parent stream was a weighty business for the two states. If the decision went in its favour, Georgia would own a large slice of what became South Carolina. The Tugaloo-Chattooga was designated the border in 1787, benefiting South Carolina: Thomas L. Stokes, *The Savannah* (New York, 1951), p. 17.

30 *Schriften des Verein für Geschichte und Naturgeschichte der Baar und der angrenzenden Landesteile in Donaueschingen. 1. Jahrgang. 1870* (Karlsruhe, 1871), pp. 27, 29, 62; *Oberrheinkarte* von Martin Waldseemüller, in 'Donauquelle in Donaueschingen', at www.fg.vs.bw.schule.de (accessed 15 May 2012). Donaueschingen's most famous son, painter Anselm Kiefer, published a mixed media book entitled *Die Donauquelle* (*The Source of the Danube*) (Cologne, 1978).

31 Jerrold, *Danube*, p. 5; Bernard Everke, 'Die Geschichte der Donauquelle: Die Donauquelle in Donaueschingen', December 1995, p. 1, at www.donaueschingen.de; http://webuser.hs-furtwangen.de; Günther Reichelt, *Die Baar: Wo Donau und Neckar Entspringen* (Donaueschingen, 1990), all at www.fg.vs.bw.schule.de (accessed 16 March 2012).

32 Magris, *Danube*, p. 41. Julius Caesar named the river Danuvius (Danubius) in *De Bello Gallico, Liber Sextus*, ed. J. T. Phillipson (London, 1900), pp. 44–45, iii.

33 Andrew Eames, *Blue River, Black Sea: A Journey Along the Danube into the Heart of the New Europe* (London, 2009), p. 10.

34 Poultney Bigelow, *Paddles and Politics down the Danube* (London, 1892), pp. 18–19.

35 *Tacitus' Germania*, ed. H. Schweizer-Sidler (Halle, 1902), p. 21; Max Rieple, *Land um die Junge Donau: Ein Besinnlicher Heimatführer* (Konstanz, 1951), p. 6.

36 Philippi Clüveri, *Germania antiqua libri tres* (Leiden, 1616), p. 746; Ernst

Zimmermann, 'Die historische Donauquelle' (Donaueschingen, n.d. [but post-1996]), p. 3, at www.donaueschingen.de (accessed 16 March 2012).

37  Hartmann Schedel, *Die Schedel'sche Weltkronik* (Dortmund, 1978 [1493]), Blat XCVIII, CXCI, CC, CCCXXXII. Author's translation.

38  Sebastian Münster, *Cosmographia* (Basel, 1628 [1544]).

39  *Tacitus' Germania*, ed. H. Schweizer-Sidler (Halle, 1902), pp. 4–5, 11; Clüveri, *Germania antiqua libri tres*, p. 746.

40  Clüveri (Clüver) also questioned Donaueschingen's claim: *Germania antiqua libri tres*, pp. 518, 745–6.

41  An early eighteenth-century Italian soldier-scientist who decided for the Breg over the Donauquelle supported his case with detailed maps: Luigi Ferdinando Marsili, 'De fontibus Danubii', *Danubius Pannonico-Mysicus, Observationibus Geographicis, Astronomicis, Hydrographicis, Physicis Perlustratus et in sex Tomos digestus*, vol. VI (The Hague, 1726), pp. 3–6.

42  Jerrold, *Danube*, p. 4; Jerrold, *The Silvery Thames* (Leeds, 1906), p. 8. See also *Hansard*, House of Commons, 320 (25 February 1937), 2185–6.

43  Tarpy, 'Danube'.

44  Gesellschaft von Gelehrten und Vaterlandsfreunden, *Universal-lexikon vom Grossherzogthum Baden* (Karlsruhe, 1844), pp. 174, 191.

45  *Universal-lexikon*, p. 278; Höhengasthof Kolmenhof, 'Vom Ursprung der Donau' [undated], p. 1. Perhaps the most famous visitor to the *Martinskapelle* spring was French oceanographer and conservationist Jacques-Yves Cousteau, who spent a week in the vicinity in 1990 filming with his crew for the first of a four-part documentary about the Danube ('*The Danube Rediscovered – Charlemagne's Dream*').

46  Conflict flared up again in 1981, after the mayor of Donaueschingen, Bernhard Everke, complained to Baden-Württemberg's ministry for interior affairs about a state-published touring map that showed the Breg spring as the source, without reference to Donaueschingen's connection with the river's origins. In response, the ministry ordered the removal of references to the Breg spring as the Danube source from all official materials. The city fathers of Furtwangen regarded this as the politically motivated liquidation of their leading tourist attraction: 'Alte Eselsbrücke', *Der Spiegel*, 14 September 1981, pp. 88–90.

47  Francis Davis Millet, *The Danube from the Black Forest to the Black Sea* (New York, 1892), p. 16. Millet's party included Poultney Bigelow and the British landscape painter and illustrator Alfred William Parsons, who illustrated Millet's book.

48  'Bed of the Danube Leaks', *New York Times*, 3 December 1911.

49  This phenomenon was established in 1877 using salt, shale oil and fluorescent tracer dye: Adolf Knop, 'Über die hydrographischen Beziehungen zwischen der Donau und der Aachquelle im badischen Oberlande', *Neues Jahrbuch für*

*Mineralogie, Geologie und Paläontologie*, 16 (1878), pp. 350–63. Since 1992, Rhine and Danube (and, by extension, North Sea and Black Sea) have been connected via the 171-kilometre Main–Danube Canal, which starts at Bamberg and joins the Danube at Kelheim.

50  Eduard Suess, 'The Danube', *Geographical Journal*, XXXVII/6 (June 1911), p. 643.

51  Johann Jacob Scheuchzer, *Hydrographia Helvetica: Beschreibung der Seen, Flüssen, Brünnen…des Schweitzerlandes* in *Der Natur-historie des Schweitzerlandes*, vol. 2 (Zürich, 1716–18) p. 31.

52  *Langenscheidlsche Bibliotek sämtlicher griechischen und römischen Klassiker, 53. Band: Strabo II (Erdbeschreibung, Buch 6–10)* (Berlin, 1855), p. 77; *The Geography of Strabo*, trans. Horace Leonard Jones (London, 1917), vol. I, pp. 21, 169, 185, 211, 493; vol. VIII, p. 309; *The Geography of Strabo*, trans. H. C. Hamilton (London, 1854), vol. II, p. 302. According to Greek mythology, the Istros rose in the region of Istria in the north-east Adriatic.

53  Claudius Ptolemy, *The Geography*, trans. and ed. Edward Luther Stevenson (New York, 1991), pp. 81–2 (Book III/chapter 8). For Ernst Neweklowsky, the *Obere Donau* began at Ulm, the head of navigation, and ended at Vienna: *Die Schiffahrt und Flösserei im Raume der oberen Donau* (Linz, 1952–3), vol. I, pp. 11–12.

54  Thomas Wilson, *Lowlands of the Danube* (London, 1855), p. 63; Thomas Forester, *The Danube and the Black Sea: Memoir* (London, 1857), p. 15.

55  Edward Daniel Clarke, *Travels in Russia, Tartary and Turkey* (Edinburgh, 1839), p. 121.

56  Herbert Hager and Helmut Schume, 'The Floodplain Forests along the Austrian Danube', in *The Floodplain Forests in Europe: Current Situation and Perspectives*, ed. Emil Klimo and Herbert Hager (Leiden, 2001), p. 85.

57  David Shukman, 'Danube Reveals its Metal Graveyard', *BBC News*, 19 September 2003, at http://news.bbc.co.uk/1/hi/sci/tech/3122128.stm (accessed 16 March 2012).

58  Peter Payer, 'Eiszeit in Wien', *1000 and 1 Buch* 1 (2009), pp. 12–13.

59  Kohl, *Austria*, pp. 249–50.

60  *Statistisches Jahrbuch der Haupt and Residentzstadt Budapest 30 (1942)* (Budapest, 1942), p. 1.

61  Julia Pardoe, *The City of the Magyar, or, Hungary and her Institutions in 1839–40* (London, 1840), vol. II, pp. 2–9; Pardoe's account is based on a contemporary record by a local physician: Augustus Schoepff, 'The Inundation of Pesth, With an Account of its Moral and Physical Effects' (pp. 1–2).

62  Meredith, *Ballads and Poems*, pp. 99–100.

63  Pardoe, *City of the Magyar*, p. 35; Meyer (*Begleiter der Donau*), quoted in William Beattie, *The Danube: Its History, Scenery and Topography* (London, 1844), p. 189.

64  Kohl, *Austria*, p. 250.

65  Christopher H. Gibbs, '"Just Two Words: Enormous Success": Liszt's 1838 Vienna Concerts', in Christopher Howard Gibbs and Dana Andrew Gooley, eds, *Franz Liszt and his World* (Princeton, NJ, 2006), pp. 180 82; *Essays und Reisebriefe eines Baccalaureus der Tonkunst*, in *Franz Liszt's Gesammelte Schriften*, ed. Lina Ramann (Leipzig, 1881), vol. II, pp. 223–4.

66  Pardoe, *City of the Magyar*, p. 35; Alan Walker, *Franz Liszt: The Virtuoso Years, 1811–1847* (New York, 1983), pp. 253–4.

67  *Liszt's Gesammelte Schriften*, vol. II, pp. 223–4.

68  Franz Heiderich, 'Die Donau als Verkehrsstrasse', *Zeitschrift der Gesellschaft für Erdkunde zu Berlin*, 5 (1916), p. 303.

69  Patrick Leigh Fermor, *A Time of Gifts: On Foot to Constantinople: From the Hook of Holland to the Middle Danube* (New York, 2005 [1977]), p. 146.

70  For the unimproved Danube's challenges to navigation, see W. G. East, 'The Danube Route-Way in History', *Economia*, 37 (August 1932), pp. 322–45.

71  Neweklowsky, *Schiffahrt*, p. 86.

72  Kohl, *Austria*, p. 108; Kohl, *Pesth und die mittlere Donau* (Dresden, 1842), p. 128.

73  Review of James Robinson Planché, *Descent of the Danube, from Ratisbon to Vienna, during the Autumn of 1827* (London, 1828), *London Literary Gazette*, 5 July 1828, p. 421.

74  Beattie, *Danube*, p. 100.

75  Ibid., p. 108.

76  Planché, *Descent of the Danube*, p. 201; Jerrold, *Danube*, p. 118. Locals claimed that the collected monies contributed to towpath maintenance and the burial of washed-up bodies.

77  An early pioneer who travelled from Ratisbon (Regensburg) to Vienna in 1716 on a type of rowing boat ('wooden house'), commented on the 'charmingly diversified' nature of the scenery, which ranged from elegant cities to 'the most romantick solitudes': *Letters of the R.H. Lady Mary Wortley Montague: Written during her Travels in Europe, Asia, and Africa* (Paris, 1800), pp. 17–18.

78  Beattie, *Danube*, p. 99.

79  Review of Planché, *Descent of the Danube*, p. 421.

80  Planché, *Descent of the Danube*, p. 189. In classical mythology, Scylla and Charybdis were two monsters that terrorized the sides of the Strait of Messina that separates Sicily from the Italian mainland. The mariner's dilemma was how to avoid one without falling prey to the other.

81  Bigelow, *Paddles*, pp. 100–01.

82  Petershagen, *Kleine Geschichte der Ulmer Schachteln*, p. 40; Beattie, *Danube*, p. 103; For the chief engineer's account, see J. Walcher, *Nachrichten von den bis auf das Jahr 1791 an dem Donau-Strudel zur Sicherheit der Schiffahrt fortgesetzten Arbeiten:*

*nebst einem Anhange von der physikalischen Beschaffenheit des Donau-Wirbels* (Vienna, 1791).

83 Beattie, *Danube*, p. 105.

84 Bigelow, *Paddles*, p. 172.

85 Beattie, *Danube*, p. 217.

86 Claridge, *Guide*, p. 160.

87 Beattie, *Danube*, p. 218.

88 Michael Joseph Quin, *A Steam Voyage down the Danube: With Sketches of Hungary, Wallachia, Servia, and Turkey* (London, 1835), vol. I, p. 144.

89 Bigelow, *Paddles*, p. 191.

90 Claridge, *Guide*, p. 160. Edmund Spencer, who claims to have been aboard the first steamboat to negotiate the Iron Gate (1836), reports traces of a former canal hewed out (most likely by the Romans) to circumvent the Iron Gate: *Travels in Circassia, Krim-Tartary & including a Voyage down the Danube, from Vienna to Constantinople, and Round the Black Sea, in 1836* (London, 1837), vol. I, p. 69.

91 Popper, 'International Regime', p. 248.

92 Stephen Széchenyi, essays in *Társalkodó* (13 October and 9 December 1834) in *Über die Donauschiffahrt* (Buda, 1836), trans. Michael v. Paziazi; as reproduced in Henry Hajnal, *The Danube: Its Historical, Political and Economic Importance* (The Hague, 1920), pp. 130, 132–3.

93 Popper, 'International Regime', p. 248; East, 'Danube Route-Way', p. 341.

94 Anton Holzer, 'Through the Cataracts', in *Blue: Inventing the River Danube*, trans. Steven Grynwasser and Akos Doma (Salzburg, 2005), pp. 97–8. This is the exhibition catalogue for 'Blue: Inventing the River Danube', Technisches Museum Wien, 15 June – 27 November 2005.

95 Jerrold, *Danube*, pp. 276–7.

96 East, 'Danube Route-Way', p. 341; Heiderich, 'Donau als Verkehrsstrasse', p. 283.

97 George Kiss, 'TVA on the Danube?', *Geographical Review*, XXXVII/2 (April 1947), pp. 277, 302.

98 Bigelow, *Paddles*, pp. 188–9, 184.

99 Kohl, *Austria*, p. 220.

100 Radu Băncilă and Edward Petzek, 'The History of the Romanian Danube Bridges', *Proceedings of the Third International Congress on Construction History*, Cottbus, Germany, May 2009, pp. 99–100; Marsili, *Danubius Pannonico-Mysicus*, vol. II, pp. 25–32.

101 Claridge, *Guide*, pp. 166–7; John Hungerford Pollen, *A Description of The Trajan Column* (London, 1874), p. 86; John Paget, *Hungary and Transylvania; With Remarks on their Condition, Social, Political and Economical* (Philadelphia, 1850), vol. II, p. 45.

102  Paget, *Hungary and Transylvania* (London, 1839), vol. I, p. 219.

103  Some piers rotted; others were removed as navigation hazards: Pollen, *Trajan Column*, p. 81; Băncilă and Petzek, 'History of Danube Bridges', p. 100.

104  Dejan Vučković, Dragan Mihajlović and Gordana Karović, 'Trajan's Bridge on the Danube: The Current Results of Underwater Archaeological Research', *Istros*, 14 (2007), pp. 119–30; Marko Serban, 'Trajan's Bridge over the Danube', *International Journal of Nautical Archaeology*, XXXVIII/2 (2009), pp. 331–42.

105  Some holes remained visible just above the waterline in the late 1930s: Korbinian Lechner, *Sommer in Rumänien* (Berlin, 1940), p. 8.

106  The most striking feature of the 30-metre column (completed in 113), is the spiral bas relief wrapped around huge marble drums. The upper and lower halves of the 190-metre frieze depict Trajan's victorious Dacian campaigns.

107  Pollen, *Trajan Column*, pp. 69, 71; Paget, *Hungary and Transylvania*, vol. II, p. 37.

108  Millet, *Danube*, p. 201.

109  Băncilă and Petzek, 'History of Danube Bridges', p. 101. The tablet was designated a Monument of Culture of Exceptional Importance in 1979.

110  Meyer, 'German Economic Relations', p. 86.

111  East, 'Danube Route-Way', p. 342.

112  David Urquhart, *The Mystery of the Danube, Showing how through Secret Diplomacy, that River has been Closed, Exportation from Turkey Arrested, and the Re-opening of the Isthmus of Suez Prevented* (London, 1851), pp. 107–8. Plans for a short cut gained little traction. Contruction did not start until 1949 (with Nâvodari the chosen port). Suspended in 1953, work resumed in 1976. The southern arm (64 kilometres) and northern arm (32 kilometres) of the Danube-Black Sea Canal were finished in 1984 and 1987.

113  Heiderich, 'Donau als Verkehrsstrasse', pp. 274–5.

114  Suess, *Erinnerungen*, p. 280; John Stokes, 'Notes on the Lower Danube', *Journal of the Royal Geographical Society of London,* 30 (1860), p. 164. Stokes was the EDC's first British representative.

115  Charles Hartley, 'On the Changes That Have Taken Place Along the Sea Coast of the Delta of the Danube', *Minutes of Proceedings of the Institution of Civil Engineers*, 36 (1873), pp. 239–40.

116  The quantity of cereals exported from Sulina between 1901 and 1905 was five times the average annual figure between 1861 and 1867: Henry Trotter, 'Danube', *Encyclopaedia Britannica*, 11th edn, vol. VII (Cambridge, 1910), pp. 822–3. Trotter represented Britain on the EDC.

117  Spencer, *Travels in Circassia*, p. 92. For a plant ecologist's appreciation of the delta's distinctive floating fens (*Plav*), see Laura Cameron and David Matless, 'Benign

Ecology: Marietta Pallis and the Floating Fen of the Delta of the Danube, 1912–1916', *Cultural Geographies*, 10 (2003), pp. 253–77.

118 Jerrold, *Danube*, pp. 173, 175; Millet, *Danube*, p. 102.

119 Jerrold, *Danube*, viii; Millet, *Danube*, p. 134; Kohl, *Pesth und die mittlere Donau*, pp. 170, 211.

120 Jerrold, *Danube*, pp. 204–5.

121 Albert Speer, *Inside the Third Reich: Memoirs*, trans. Richard and Clara Winston (London, 1966), p. 99.

122 Kohl, *Die Donau von ihrem Ursprunge bis Pesth* (Triest, 1854), quoted in Anton Holzer and Elisabeth Limbeck-Lilienau, 'Inventing the River Danube', in *Blue*, pp. 13–14.

123 Kohl, *Austria*, p. 109.

124 A. Chovanec et al., 'Constructed Inshore Areas as River Corridors through Urban Areas – The Danube in Vienna: Preliminary Results', *Regulated Rivers: Research and Management,* 16 (2000), p. 177.

125 Neweklowsky, *Schiffahrt*, vol. I, pp. 12, 42, 437–530, 539–620.

126 Elisabeth Strönmer, 'Das Allerheiligenhochwasser', in *Umwelt Stadt: Geschichte des Natur- und Lebensraumes*, ed. Karl Brunnar and Petra Schneider (Vienna, 2005), p. 310; Franz Michlmayr, 'Gegen den Strom: Die Regulierung der Donau', in *Umwelt Stadt*, p. 312; Helmut Zisser, 'Die Hochwässer der Donau', Diplomarbeit, Institut für Hydraulik, Gewässerkunde und Wasserwirtschaft der Technischen Universität Wien, February 1989, p. 3.

127 Martin Andreas Schmid, 'Rivers' Role in Urban Metabolism: Vienna and the Danube *c.* 1500', unpublished conference paper, American Society for Environmental History, Tallahassee, Florida, 28 February 2009.

128 On risk aversion and accommodation, see Greg Bankoff, 'Cultures of Disaster, Cultures of Coping: Hazard as a Frequent Life Experience in the Philippines, 1600–2000', in *Natural Disasters, Cultural Responses: Case Studies Toward a Global Environmental History*, ed. Christof Mauch and Christian Pfister (Lanham, MD, 2009), pp. 265–84.

129 'Inaugurirung der Donau-Regulirungs-Arbeiten', *Neue Freie Presse* (Vienna) 2051 (15 May 1870); Suess, *Erinnerungen*, pp. 214–15. Over its five-year construction period, the 24.6-million florint project engaged a workforce of nearly a thousand Italians, Poles, Czechs and Slovakians. Anton Holzer, 'A New River, A New City: The Regulation of the Danube in Vienna', in *Blue*, pp. 67–8.

130 'Die Durchstechung des Rollerdammes', *Neue Freie Presse*, 3821 (16 April 1875); 'Vom neuen Donaubette', 3824 (19 April 1875); 'Die Schiffahrt-Eröffnung im neuen Donaubett', 3865 (31 May 1875); Suess, *Erinnerungen*, pp. 263–6.

131 Millet, *Danube*, p. 193.

132 'Schiffahrt-Eröffnung im neuen Donaubett'.

## References

133 Gustav Wex, Supplement II, 'Reply to the Pamphlet of Sir Lorenz, Minsterial Counsellor', in Wex, *A Lecture on the Progress of the Works of Completion of the New Improved Bed of the Danube at Vienna, and the Lessons Taught Thereby; Together with a Description of the Catastrophe Produced by the Ice Gorge of 1880* [from *Journal of the Society of Austrian Engineers and Architects* 3 (1880)], trans. Godfrey Weitzel (Washington, DC, 1881), pp. 29–30; Raimund Hinkel, *Wien an der Donau* (Vienna, 1995), p. 68; Jan Mokre, 'The Environs Map: Vienna and its Surroundings, *c.* 1600–*c.* 1850', *Imago Mundi*, 49 (1997), pp. 92–3.

134 Wex, *Lecture on Progress of Works*, p. 14. Wex was the Danube Regulation Commission's Chief Director of the Improvement of the Danube at Vienna.

135 Suess, *Erinnerungen*, pp. 266–7; Wex, in *Lecture on Progress of Works*, pp. 8–10.

136 Wex, 'Supplement I: Description of the Catastrophe Caused by the Ice Gorge in the Danube, at Vienna, in 1880', in *Lecture on Progress of Works of Completion*, pp. 19–21; Anton Holzer, 'Ice Drifts: A Catastrophe and Spectacle', in *Blue*, pp. 75–6; Bertrand Michael Buchmann, 'Historische Entwicklung des Donaukanals', in Buchmann, Harald Sterk and Rupert Schickl, *Der Donaukanal: Geschichte – Planung – Ausführung* (Vienna, 1984), pp. 3–73.

137 Franz Michlmayr, 'Gegen den Strom', in *Umwelt Stadt*, p. 313.

138 In the 1970s, to counter the negative connotations of 'canal', to recognize its historic role in the city's physical and commercial landscape and to signal its recreational potential, the new name of *Kleine Donau* was proposed: Marin Knoglinger, 'Donaukanal', Diplomarbeit, Institut für Landschaftsplanung und Gartenkunst der Technischen Universität Wien, April 1995, pp. 10, 14.

139 Neweklowsky, *Schiffahrt*, vol. I, p. 75.

140 Only men were admitted: Viktor Mekarski von Menk, *Notizen über Gymnastik . . . mit bes. Rücksicht auf d. öffentl. Donau-Bade-Anstalten* (Vienna, 1831), pp. 97–100. A nearby *Damenschwimmschule* was set up in 1831.

141 Gerhard Hofer, *100 Jahre Gänsehäufel* (Vienna, 2007), pp. 60–61.

142 Baker, *Danube*, pp. 117–18.

143 Ernst Gerhard Eder, 'Freizeit am Wasser: Baden, Schwimmen, Bootfahren, Segeln in der Donaulandschaft bis 1870', in *Umwelt Stadt*, p. 525.

144 Menk, *Notizen über Gymnastik*, p. 104; Hinkel, *Wien*, p. 44. The Schwedenbrücke site has become the location of a contemporary, Spree-style Badeschiff.

145 Hofer, *100 Jahre Gänsehäufel*, p. 88.

146 Helmut Gruber, 'Sexuality in "Red Vienna": Socialist Party Conceptions and Programs and Working-Class Life, 1920–34', *International Labor and Working-Class History*, 31 (Spring 1987), pp. 50, 54, 38.

147 Eve Blau, *The Architecture of Red Vienna, 1919–1934* (Cambridge, MA, 1999), pp. 75, 470.

148  Gerhard Kletter and Leopoldine Lendaric, *Das Gänsehäufel* (Vienna, 2007), p. 55.

149  Hofer, *100 Jahre Gänsehäufel*, p. 86.

150  Kletter and Lendaric, *Gänsehäufel*, p. 56. The island reopened on 21 June 1950.

151  'Das Gänsehäufel feiert seinen 100. Geburtstag', Press release, 2007, Bundesdenkmalamt, Vienna, at www.bda.at (accessed 16 March 2012). To improve water quality, half the Alte Donau was drained in December 1993 and replaced with water from the New Danube: Martin T. Dokulil and Katrin Teubner, 'Eutrophication and Restoration of Shallow Lakes – the Concept of Stable Equilibria Revisited', *Hydrobiologia*, XXIX/35 (2003), pp. 30–31.

152  Eva Kausel, 'Arkadien an der Donau: Freizeit in der Grossstadt am Beispiel der Wiener Donauinsel', Doktorarbeit, Geisteswissenschaftlichen Fakultät der Universität Wien, 1991, pp. 30–31, 41–3, 48.

153  Michlmayr, 'Gegen den Strom', in *Umwelt Stadt*, p. 316.

154  Kausel, 'Arkadien an der Donau,' p. 35.

155  Chovanec, 'Constructed Inshore Areas as River Corridors', p. 178.

156  International Commission for the Protection of the Danube River, *Convention on Cooperation and Sustainable Use of the Danube River*, Sofia, Bulgaria, 29 June 1994, pp. 3–4, 12–13, 18.

157  Marsili, *Danubius Pannonico-Mysicus*, vol. IV, pp. 31–7.

158  Ernst Gerhard Eder, 'Heimisch in der Wiener Donaulandschaft: Fische, Amphibien und Schildkröten', in *Umwelt Stadt*, p. 378.

159  Fermor, *Time of Gifts*, p. 149.

160  'Appendix: Thoughts at a Café Table Between the Kazan and the Iron Gates', in Patrick Leigh Fermor, *Between the Woods and the Water: On Foot to Constantinople from the Hook of Holland: The Middle Danube to the Iron Gates* (New York, 2005 [1986]), p. 257.

161  Rhoda Margesson, 'Reducing Conflict over the Danube Waters: Equitable Utilization and Sustainable Development', *Natural Resources Forum*, XXI/1 (1997), pp. 26–8.

162  Krista Harper, '"Wild Capitalism" and "Ecocolonialism": A Tale of Two Rivers', *American Anthropologist*, CVII/2 (2005), pp. 224, 228.

163  Judit Vásárhélyi, quoted in Harper, '"Wild Capitalism"', p. 228.

164  Harper, '"Wild Capitalism"', p. 227.

165  János Varga, quoted in Mark Schapiro, 'The New Danube', *Mother Jones*, XV/3 (April 1990), p. 72; Ronnie D. Lipschutz, 'Damming Troubled Waters: Conflict over the Danube, 1950–2000', *Intermarium*, I/2 (1997), p. 7.

166  Schapiro, 'New Danube', p. 50.

167  Krisztian Szabados, quoted in Richard Bernstein, 'East on the Danube: Hungary's Tragic Century', *New York Times*, 9 August 2003; Walter Schwarz, 'Green Issues Rise in the East', *The Guardian*, 26 November 1988.

168  Ursula Schmedtje, ed., *The Danube Basin District, Part A (Basin-Wide Overview [WFD Roof Report 2004]* Doc. IC/084 (Vienna, 18 March 2005), pp. 75, 109. In 1997, following a lawsuit filed by NGOs including Greenpeace and the World Wildlife Fund, the International Court of Justice ruled that the river's diversion into wholly Slovakian territory was illegal.

169  Nicholas Wood, 'Floods Persuade Some to Give Danube Room', *International Herald Tribune*, 27 April 2006.

170  Schmedtje, *Roof Report*, p. 77.

171  Karen F. Schmidt, 'A True-Blue Vision for the Danube', *Science*, CCXCIV/5546 (16 November 2001), pp. 1444–5, 1447.

172  Schmedtje, *Roof Report*, p. 109; Nicolae Panin, 'Living Force', in *Danube: River of Life*, p. 30.

173  Catherine M. Pringle, 'U.S. – Romanian Environmental Reconnaissance of the Danube Delta', *Conservation Biology*, V/4 (December 1991), p. 443.

174  Wood, 'Floods Persuade Some to Give Danube Room'.

175  UNESCO, Romania/Ukraine, *Danube Delta: MAB Biosphere Reserve Directory* (Vilkovo, Ukraine: Administration of the Danube Delta Biosphere Reserve, 2005).

176  Erika Schneider, Marian Tudor and Mircea Staraş, eds, *Ecological Restoration in the Danube Delta Biosphere Reserve: Evolution of Babina Polder after Restoration Works*, trans. Danièle Reuland (Frankfurt, 2008), pp. 14–15, 63–4, 69, 71, 13; Schmidt, 'True-Blue Vision', p. 1445.

177  Kiss, 'TVA on the Danube?', pp. 279–80.

178  Neal Asherson, 'Introduction: Danube – Europe's Messenger', in *Danube: River of Life*, pp. 1–2.

179  Opening Keynote Speech, 17 October 1999, in *Danube: River of Life*, p. 13.

180  Bartolomew to Prodi, 25 October 1999, in *Danube: River of Life*, pp. 178–9. The Danube was declared open again in November 2001, with navigation channels completely unblocked by June 2003.

181  WFD's objective is a political, legal and economic framework to prevent further deterioration of water bodies and to protect and improve aquatic ecosystems.

182  Schmedtje, *Roof Report*, pp. 95, 146, 132, 147, 169, 110, 113; Asherson, *Danube: River of Life*, p. 4.

183  Quoted in Elisabeth Rosenthal, 'The Danube Blues: Decades of Misuse: A New Study Has Alarming Findings', *International Herald Tribune*, 6 October 2005.

184  Schmedtje, *Roof Report*, pp. 77, 94, 96, 98, 142.

185  Catherine Lovatt, 'An der Schönen, Braunen Donau', *Central Europe Review*, I/12 (13 September 1999) at http://www.ce-review.org (accessed 16 March 2012).

186  Schmedtje, *Roof Report*, p. 109.

187  Ibid., p. 105; Asherson, *Danube: River of Life*, p. 5.

188 Emma Batha, 'Death of a River', BBC News, 15 February 2000, at http://news.bbc.co.uk (accessed 16 March 2012).

189 Robert Koenig, 'Wildlife Deaths are a Grim Wake-up Call in Eastern Europe', *Science*, CCLXXXVII/5459 (10 March 2000), pp. 1737–8.

190 Baia Mare Task Force, *Report of the International Task Force for Assessing the Baia Mare Accident* (Brussels, 15 December 2000), pp. 2, 12, 14–16, 19, 30.

191 Emma Batha, 'Death of a River'; Gyula Lakatos, Ernő Fleit and Ilona Mészáros, 'Ecotoxicological Studies and Risk Assessment on the Cyanide Contamination in Tisza River', *Toxicology Letters*, CXL/141 (2003), p. 334.

192 Schmedtje, *Roof Report*, p. 105; Asherson, *Danube: River of Life*, p. 168; www.danubeday.org (accessed 16 March 2012).

193 Quoted in Ida Miro Kiss, 'The Blond is Dead: The Tisza River Disaster', *Central Europe Review*, II/7 (February 2000), at www.ce-review.org (accessed 16 March 2012).

194 Ronnie D. Lipschutz, *Global Civil Society and Global Environmental Governance: The Politics of Nature from Place to Planet* (Albany, NY, 1996), p. 167.

195 Magris, *Danube*, p. 29.

196 Lewis Spence, *Hero Tales and Legends of the Rhine* (New York, 1915), pp. 2–3. The Quadalquivir is Spain's second longest and only navigable major river. *Die Wacht am Rhein*, adopted as unofficial national anthem during the Franco-Prussian War (1870–71), originated as a poem (1840) by Max von Schneckenburger.

197 Lipschutz, *Global Civil Society*, p. 159; Harper, '"Wild Capitalism"', p. 226; Kiss, 'Blond is Dead'.

198 Kiss, 'Blond is Dead'.

199 Lengyel, *Danube*, p. 45. For the concept of symbolic ecology (though not applied to Europe or rivers), see Philippe Descola, 'Constructing Natures: Symbolic Ecology and Social Practice', in *Nature and Society: Anthropological Perspectives*, ed. Philippe Descola and Gísli Pálsson (London, 1996), pp. 87–9.

200 'Johann Strauss: The Waltz King', *Musical Times*, L/798 (1 August 1909), p. 513; H. E. Jacob, *Johann Strauss: Father and Son, A Century of Light Music* (New York, 1939), pp. 208–9. The original German text reads: 'An der schönen blauen Donau/Liegt mein Dörfchen, still und fein/Reich an weltberühmten Wein'. For Leigh H. Bailey's translation, sanctioned by the Wiener Institut für Strauss-Forschung, see www.johann-strauss.at (accessed 16 March 2012).

201 Helen Hirsch, 'A Collection of Rare Straussiana', *Music Educators Journal*, XLVII/3 (January 1961), p. 68; 68–70. Defeat precipitated fears of a Prussian invasion of Vienna and was accompanied by dire economic straits.

202 Jacob, *Strauss*, pp. 209–10.

203 'Strauss: Waltz King', p. 513.

204 Of all the Danubian nations' national anthems, only Bulgaria's mentions the river. Written in 1885 by Tsvetan Radoslavov, on the eve of his departure for the Serbo-Bulgarian War, and adopted in 1964, '*Mila Rodino*' (Dear Motherland) opens with the lines: 'Proudly rise the Balkan peaks, At their feet Blue Danube flows'.

205 Kletter and Lendaric, *Gänsehäufel*, p. 25; Ludwig Bemelmans, *The Blue Danube* (London, 1946), p. 91.

206 Millet, *Danube*, frontispiece, p. 97; Jerrold, *Danube*, p. 27.

207 'Schiffahrt- Eröffnung im neuen Donaubett'.

208 Gabriele Zuna-Kratky, 'Preface', and Holzer and Limbeck-Lilienau, 'Inventing the River Danube', in *Blue*, pp. 9, 15–16; *Bockkeller*, XII/1 (January 2006), p. 3.

209 'The Current Cinema', *The New Yorker*, 17 December 1949, p. 116.

210 Fermor, *Between Woods and Water*, p. 254.

211 Eunice Buckley's novel *Blue Danube* (London, 1943) does not mention the river. Part one focuses on Viennese social life and part two is about London (dignified, by contrast, as 'City on the Thames').

212 Friedrich Hölderlin, 'The Main', in *Poems and Fragments*, trans. Michael Hamburger (London, 2004), pp. 138–9.

213 Hölderlin, 'The Neckar', in *Poems and Fragments*, pp. 191–3.

214 Martin Heidegger, *Hölderlin's Hymn 'The Ister'*, trans. William McNeill and Julia Davis (Bloomington, IN, 1996), pp. 14, 10.

215 Hölderlin, 'The Ister', in *Poems and Fragments*, p. 581.

216 Friedrich Hölderlin, 'The Ister', p. 58; Heidegger, *Hölderlin's Hymn*, p. 14. Given that some of the Danube's flow ducks underground, resurfaces at the *Aachtopf* and ends up in the Rhine, Hölderlin's symbolic reversal of flow is not entirely fanciful.

217 Heidegger, *Hölderlin's Hymn*, pp. 6, 12, 18–20.

218 Ibid., pp. 146, 42, 48, 21.

219 Ibid., pp. 153, 164.

220 Ibid., p. 20.

221 Hölderlin, *Hyperion and Selected Poems*, ed. Eric L. Santner (New York, 1990), p. 271.

222 Heidegger, *Introduction to Metaphysics*, trans. Gregory Fried and Richard Polt (New Haven, CT, 2000 [1935]), p. 40.

223 Heidegger, Bremer und Freiburger Vorträge Vorträge (Frankfurt am Main, 1994), p. 27; Heidegger, *Basic Writings*, ed. David Farrell Krell (London, 1993), pp. 308–9, 320.

224 Heidegger, *Bremer und Freiburger Vorträge*, p. 29. This lecture was re-worked as 'The Question Concerning Technology' (1953).

225 The large dam era on the Upper Rhine, between Lake Constance and Basel, where the river falls sharply between rocky walls, began in 1898. Heidegger may have had the most recent (Reckingen, Switzerland, 1946) in mind.

226 Heidegger, *Basic Writings*, p. 321; David I. Waddington, 'A Field Guide to Heidegger: Understanding "The Question Concerning Technology"', *Educational Philosophy and Theory*, XXXVII/4 (2005), p. 573.

227 Heidegger, *Basic Writings*, p. 321.

228 *The Ister* consists of five chapters within two parts; three in part one and two in the second. Chapter 1 voyages as far upstream as Vukovar (struck by Serbian forces in 1991), where the river separates Croatia from Serbia (with Stiegler ruminating on technology). Chapter 2 meanders through Hungary (with Nancy examining democracy, tyranny, and Heidegger's political ideology). Moving up from Vienna in chapter 3, the film-makers visit Mauthausen, where Lacoue-Labarthe confronts Heidegger's analogy between industrialized farming and Nazi death camps.

229 James Lewis Hoberman employs the term *Wasserstrasse* film to group '*The Ister*' with Werner Herzog's *Aguirre: Wrath of God* (1972) and Francis Ford Coppola's *Apocalypse Now* (1979). In all three films, he argues, the river leads into the heart of darkness, which, in this instance, is Heidegger's Black Forest cabin: Hoberman, 'Mystic River: Heideggerian Cine-Essay Treks up the Danube', *Village Voice*, LI/6 (14 February 2006), p. 48.

230 Hölderlin, 'The Ister', p. 585.

231 Heidegger never expressed a view on the river's most historic bridge. Presumably, though, given how he felt about wooden bridges on the Rhine, he would not have regarded Trajan's bridge as a fundamental violation of its spirit.

232 Daniel Birnbaum, 'A River Runs Through It', *Artforum*, XLIII/10 (Summer/22 June 2005), p. 87.

## 2 Spree

1 F.M.F. Skene, *Wayfaring Sketches among the Greeks and Turks and On the Shores of the Danube* (London, 1847), pp. 259–60, 284.

2 Heinz Götze, *398 Kilometer Spree: Von den Quellen in der Oberlausitz bis zur Mündung in Spandau* (Berlin, 1993), pp. 185, 188; Ed Gennerich, *Die Flüsse Deutschlands* (Dresden, 1908), p. 96.

3 Gerd Conradt und Jörg Welke, 'An der Spree', at www.spree2011.de (accessed 16 March 2012).

4 'Letter to his Father: On a Turning-Point in Life (1837)', in *Marx on Religion*, ed. John C. Raines (Philadelphia, 2002), p. 26; 'Peace', in *The Poems of Heine*, ed. Edgar Alfred Bowring (London, 1859), p. 239.

5 Erdmann Wirker, *Märckische Neun Musen, Welche sich Unter den Allergrossmächtigsten Schutz Sr. Königl. Majestät in Preussen . . . Bey glücklichen*

*Anfang Ihres Jubel-Jahres Auff dem Franckfurtischen Helicon Frohlockend auffgestellet* (Berlin, 1706), p. 59; Lothar Müller, 'The Beauty of the Metropolis: Toward an Aesthetic Urbanism in Turn-of-the-century Berlin', in *Berlin: Culture and Metropolis*, ed. Charles Werner Haxthausen and Heidrun Suhr (Minneapolis, MN, 1990), p. 40.

6 Walter Rathenau, 'Die schönste Stadt der Welt [1899]', in *Impressionen* (Leipzig, 1902), pp. 139–40, 148–9, 158. Henry Vizetelly, Berlin correspondent for the *Illustrated London News*, drew the same invidious comparisons with the riverscapes of London and Paris: *Berlin under the New Empire* (London, 1879), vol. I, p. 77.

7 Siegbert Stehmann, ed., *Am grünen Strand der Spree: Die Reichshauptstadt als Heimat* (Berlin-Steglitz, 1940); Erich Hobusch, *Am grünen Strand der Spree; Zur Geschichte des Erholungswesens an Spree und Dahme bis 1945* (Berlin, 1986), p. 5.

8 Werner Bergengruen, *Am Himmel wie auf Erden* (Berlin, 1940), pp. 7–18; Lida Kirchenberger, 'Bergengruen's Novel of the Berlin Panic', *Monatshefte*, XLVI/4 (April 1954), pp. 10, 199–200, 204.

9 Engelhardt Kühn, *Der Spreewald und seine Bewohner* (Cottbus, 1889), p. 9; Siegfried Passarge, *Vergleichende Landschaftskunde*, vol. I: *Aufgaben und Methoden* (Berlin, 1921), pp. iv–v, 1–3; J. F. Unstead, 'The Regional Geography of Siegfried Passarge: Review', *Geographical Journal*, LXXVIII/2 (August 1931), p. 165.

10 Lilian L. Stroebe, 'The Real Knowledge of a Foreign Country', *Modern Language Journal*, IV/7 (April 1920), p. 355; Emma Gertrude Kunze, 'Summer Study Abroad', *Modern Language Journal*, XIII/5 (February 1929), p. 357.

11 Johann Benedict Carpzov, *Neueröffneter Ehren-Tempel Merckwürdiger Antiquitäten des Marggraffthums Ober-Lausitz* (Leipzig, 1719), pp. 213–25.

12 Kühn, *Der Spreewald und seine Bewohner*, p. 3; www.neugersdorf.com (accessed 16 March 2012); Götze, *398 Kilometer Spree*, pp. 17–18; Andreas Luber, 'Quellen von Flussen/Die Spreequellen', in Ludwig Ellenberg and Nadia Hörrmann, 'Die Spree: Ergebnisse eines Oberseminars', Heft 114, Geographisches Institut, Humboldt-Universität zu Berlin, 2005, pp. 48–9; Horst Vollrath und Bernd Lammel, *Wiedersehen am Strand der Spree: Ein Fluss und seine Geschichte* (Berlin, 1990), p. 25.

13 *Oberlausitzer Wanderparadies* (Dresden, 2010), pp. 9, 17; Wolfgang Richter, 'Der Spreequellenstreit zum 100. Geburtstag des Spreeborns', *Ebersbacher Mitteilungsblatt*, 82 (1996), p. 20.

14 Gennerich, *Flüsse Deutschlands*, p. 98.

15 Der Senator für Bau- und Wohnungswesen, *Berlin: Die Stadt am Wasser* (Berlin, 1963), p. 1; Hans-Joachim Melzer, *Berlin: Die Stadt am Wasser* (Berlin, 1989).

16 Élisée Reclus, *The Earth and its Inhabitants. Europe*: vol. III *(Austria-Hungary, Germany, Belgium, and the Netherlands* (New York, 1883), p. 326; Kurt Groggert,

*Personenschiffahrt auf Spree und Havel* (Berlin, 1988), pp. 11, 14.

17  Heinz Trost, *Zwischen Havel, Spree und Dahme: Aus der Geschichte der Berliner Fahrgastschiffahrt* (Wesselburen, 1979), p. 9; Uwe Oster, 'Havel und Spree: Flüssepaar im märkischen Sand', in *Flüsse in Deutschland*, ed. Uwe Oster (Darmstadt, 2007), pp. 56–7.

18  Groggert, *Personenschiffahrt*, pp. 15–17.

19  Hansjürgen Vahldiek, *Cölln an der Spree: Ursprung und Wandel der Berliner Spreeinsel* (Berlin, 2004), p. 45. Mill use ceased in the 1920s; they were demolished in the 1930s.

20  'Germany', *The Economist*, 2333 (12 May 1888), p. 599; Walter Winkler, *Die Ufer der Spree in der Berliner Innenstadt* (Berlin, 1936), pp. 9–13.

21  Wolfram Bäumer, 'Neue Ausstellung "Lebenswelt Schiff" im Deutschen Technikmuseum Berlin', *Die Museums-Eisenbahn*, 1 (2004), p. 16. Carl-Peter Steinmann, *Im Fluss der Zeit: Geheimnisse Links und Rechts der Spree* (Berlin, 2008), p. 54. In September 2003, the water-borne commerce of Danube and Spree were united symbolically when a small flotilla of *Ulmer Schachteln* boats moored at the Regierungsviertel to represent Ulm's chamber of commerce. The boats were placed in the Elbe at Bad Schandau and then crossed to the Havel through the Elbe-Havel Canal: Wolf-Henning Petershagen, *Kleine Geschichte der Ulmer Schachteln* (Ulm, 2009), p. 70.

22  Luc Gersal, *Spree-Athen* (Leipzig, 1893), pp. 20–21.

23  Heinrich Eduard Jacob, trans. Richard and Clara Winston, *Felix Mendelssohn and his Times* (Englewood Cliffs, NJ, 1963), p. 7.

24  Vizetelly, *Berlin*, vol. II, p. 361.

25  Hans J. Reichardt and Gerd Müller, *Zwischen Oberspree und Unterhavel: Von Sport und Freizeit auf Berlin's Gewässern* (Berlin, 1985), pp. 43–4; Götze, *398 Kilometer Spree*, p. 121.

26  Steinmann, *Im Fluss der Zeit*, p. 83; Erich Hobusch, *Am grünen Strand der Spree; Zur Geschichte des Erholungswesens an Spree und Dahme bis 1945* (Berlin, 1986), p. 34.

27  Hans Halter, 'Als die Berliner schwimmen lernten', *Der Tagesspiegel*, 24 July 2005; Emil Pusch, *Friedrich Friesen: Ein Lebensbild* (Berlin, 1938), p. 26.

28  Ulrike Zoister, 'Von den Anfängen der Schwimmkunst in Berlin', *Berliner Ärzteblatt*, 112 (1999), pp. 366–7. An earlier swimming station (1802) soon closed.

29  Isabel da Silva Matos, et al./Verein zur Förderung des H2O Museum e.V., *Stadt-Bad-Fluss: Berliner Bade- und Wasserkultur im Wandel* (Berlin, 2010), p. 6; Winkler, *Ufer der Spree*, pp. 55, 120–21; Jörg Welke and Ralf Steeg, 'Geschichte der Spreebäder'; Welke, 'Flussbäder Berlin', at www.spree2011.de (accessed 16 March 2012).

30  Reichardt and Müller, *Zwischen Oberspree und Unterhavel*, p. 44.

31 Pusch, *Friedrich Friesen*, p. 26; Bernard von Gersdorff, *Ernst von Pfuel* (Berlin, 1981), p. 55; Karl Wippermann, 'Ernst Von Pfuel', *Allgemeine Deutsche Biographie*, (Leipzig, 1887), vol. xxv, p. 707; Bärbel Holtz, 'Ernst Von Pfuel', *Neue Deutsche Biographie*, vol. 20 (Berlin, 2001), pp. 362–3; Otto Julius Bernhard von Corvin-Wiersbitzki, *Die Schwimmkunst: zum Selbstunterricht und zum Gebrauch fur Schwimmschulen bearbeitet nach den Grundsätzen des Generallieutenants Herrn von Pfuel* (Saarlouis, 1835), p. 13.

32 Zoister, 'Von den Anfängen der Schwimmkunst', p. 367.

33 Ernst von Pfuel, *Über Das Schwimmen* (Berlin, 1827 [1817]), pp. 31, 55–6; Alexander Meyer, 'Bei Pfuel', in *Aus guter alter Zeit: Berliner Bilder und Erinnerungen von Alexander Meyer* (Leipzig, 1909), pp. 151–8.

34 Zoister, 'Von den Anfängen der Schwimmkunst', p. 368.

35 Meyer, 'Bei Pfuel', p. 154. Appreciative pupils also issued a commemorative coin.

36 'Ascension' in *The Poems of Heine*, ed. Edgar Alfred Bowring (London, 1859), p. 528; Jost Hansen and Horst Mauter, *Berlin am Wasser: Fotografien, 1857–1934* (Berlin, 1993), p. 33.

37 Robert Blachford Mansfield, *The Water Lily on the Danube: Being a Brief Account of the Perils of a Pair-Oar during a Voyage from Lambeth to Pesth* (London, 1853), p. 34.

38 Wilhelm Oehlert, *Moabiter Badeanstalten ehedem und jetzt* (Berlin, 1893); Winkler, *Die Ufer der Spree*, p. 78; Cornelia Carstens et al., *Frauen an der Spree: ein Spaziergang durch die Geschichte* (Berlin, 1999), p. 113.

39 Letter dated 9 July 1834, in *'Die Musik will gar nicht rutschen ohne Dich': Briefwechsel 1821 bis 1846*, ed. Eva Weissweiler (Berlin, 1997), p. 171.

40 Helmut Gruber, *Red Vienna: Experiment in Working-Class Culture, 1919–1934* (New York, 1991), pp. 121–2.

41 Agathe Nalli-Rutenberg, *Das Alte Berlin: Erinnerungen* (Berlin, 1913), p. 35; StadtSportBund Halle, *Salzspuren in Halle: Beiträge zur Halleschen Sportgeschichte* (Halle, 2006), pp. 10–11.

42 Continental Europe's first steam-powered boat (1816) plied the Spree from Schloss Bellevue to Charlottenburg and Potsdam. However, its commercial life was short-lived. Hansen and Mauter, *Berlin am Wasser*, p. 30.

43 Hansen and Mauter, *Berlin am Wasser*, p. 31; Trost, *Zwischen Havel, Spree und Dahme*, p. 27; Kurt Groggert, *Spreefahrt tut not!: Berliner auf dem richtigen Dampfer* (Berlin, 1972), pp. 11, 40–41. In 1860, Louis Sachse, Maass's successor, introduced a second steamer.

44 Günther Bohm, 'An den Ufern der Spree – Die Städtische Flussbadeanstalten Alt-Berlins, 1850–1925', *Der Berliner Bär*, 11 (1962); Reichardt and Müller, *Zwischen Oberspree und Unterhavel*, p. 46.

45  Carstens, *Frauen an der Spree*, pp. 113–14; Reichardt and Müller, *Zwischen Oberspree und Unterhavel*, p. 48.

46  Friedrich Rückert, 'Ein Winter in Berlin', *Blätter für literarische Unterhaltung*, 48 (17 Februar 1844), p. 189; Rudolf Gottschalk, 'Friedrich Rückert: Ein literarisches Porträt', *Unsere Zeit: Deutsche Revue der Gegenwart*, 2/1 (1866), p. 331.

47  Carstens, *Frauen an der Spree*, p. 111.

48  Günther Bohm, *Die städtischen Flussbadeanstalten Alt-Berlins* (Berlin, 1961), p. 2; Heinrich Zille, *Rund ums Freibad* (Berlin, 1926), p. 7.

49  Peter Baumann and Carl Hatebur, *Berlin: Landschaften am Wasser* (Berlin, 1982), p. 43; Mark Twain, 'The German Chicago', in *The Complete Essays of Mark Twain*, ed. Charles Neider (Garden City, NY, 1963), p. 88. This essay originally appeared as 'The Chicago of Europe', *Chicago Daily Tribune*, 3 April 1892.

50  Rathenau, 'Die schönste Stadt der Welt', p. 144.

51  Reclus, *Europe*, vol. III, p. 327; Karl Baedeker, *Berlin and its Environs: Handbook for Travellers* (Leipzig, 1908), pp. 201, 45; Isidor Kastan, *Berlin wie es war* (Berlin, 1925), pp. 20–21.

52  David Stradling and Richard Stradling, 'Perceptions of the Burning River: Deindustrialization and Cleveland's Cuyahoga River', *Environmental History*, 13 (July 2008), pp. 515–35.

53  Zille, *Rund ums Freibad*, p. 6. The lakes that ring Berlin also provided fresh opportunities once the ban on swimming in them (1852) was lifted (1907).

54  Winkler, *Die Ufer der Spree*, pp. 5–6.

55  Dirk Westphal, 'Berlin, vom Wasser aus betrachtet', *Welt am Sonntag*, 30 March 2008; Brian Ladd, *The Ghosts of Berlin: Confronting German History in the Urban Landscape* (Chicago, 1997), p. 228.

56  Frederick Taylor, *The Berlin Wall: 13 August 1961–9 November 1989* (London, 2007), pp. 435–9; 'Berlin: Spree on the Spree', *Time*, LXXIX/24 (15 June 1962).

57  The exception was islands, all of which were granted to Georgia by fixing the boundary mid-way between island and the opposite shore: Thomas L. Stokes, *The Savannah* (New York, 1951), p. 17.

58  Quoted in David Rising, 'New Research Says 136 Died at Berlin Wall', *Associated Press*, 7 August 2008, p. 1; Hans-Hermann Hertle and Maria Nooke, *The Victims at the Berlin Wall, 1961–1989: A Biographical Handbook* (Berlin, 2011), pp. 244–5.

59  'World: The Escape Continues', *Time*, LXXX/17 (26 October 1962).

60  Ingrid Pitt, *Ingrid Pitt: Darkness Before Dawn* (Baltimore, MD, 2004), pp. 85–7; Obituary, *The Independent*, 25 November 2010.

61  Christine Brecht. 'Krüger, Ingo', 'Chronik der Mauer/Bau und Fall der Berliner Mauer/Opfer der Mauer/1961/', at www.chronik-der-mauer.de (accessed 16 March 2012); Hertle and Nooke, *Victims at the Wall*, pp. 65–6.

62  Hans-Hermann Hertle and Maria Nooke, 'Die Todesopfer an der Berliner Mauer, 1961–1989', Zentrum für Zeithistorische Forschung Potsdam, Potsdam/Berlin, May 2010, pp. 3–5.

63  Christine Brecht, 'Düllick, Udo', at www.chronik-der-mauer.de (accessed 16 March 2012).

64  Werner Filmer and Heribert Schwan, *Opfer der Mauer* (München, 1991), pp. 111–112; Hertle and Nooke, 'Die Todesopfer an der Berliner Mauer, 1961–1989', pp. 10–11; Christine Brecht, 'Räwel, Hans', at www.chronik-der-mauer.de (accessed 16 March 2012).

65  Filmer and Schwan, *Opfer der Mauer*, p. 115; Heiner Sauer and Hans-Otto Plumeyer, *Der Salzgitter Report: Die Zentrale Erfassungsstelle berichtet über Verbrechen im SED-Staat* (Munich, 1991), p. 295.

66  Christine Brecht, 'Probst, Werner', at www.chronik-der-mauer.de (accessed 16 March 2012); Christopher Hilton, *The Wall: The People's Story* (Stroud, Gloucestershire, 2002), p. 161.

67  Christine Brecht, 'Krüger, Ingo', at www.chronik-der-mauer.de (accessed 16 March 2012); Hilton, *Wall*, pp. 177–8. For details of others who tried to swim the river, see Sauer and Plumeyer, *Salzgitter Report*, p. 293.

68  Günter Matthes, 'Ein Grenzfall', *Der Tagesspiegel*, 15 September 1966; Hertle and Nooke, 'Die Todesopfer an der Berliner Mauer, 1961–1989', p. 7.

69  Udo Baron, 'Katranci, Cengaver', www.chronik-der-mauer.de (accessed 16 March 2012); *Die Welt*, 31 October 1972; *Berliner Morgenpost*, 31 October and 2 November 1972.

70  Hilton, *Wall*, p. 264.

71  GDR army divers eventually recovered his body just 5 metres from the western bank. Nonetheless, they took it to East Berlin and retained it for a few days, precipitating days of protest in Kreuzberg's Turkish community.

72  *Berliner Morgenpost*, 15 May 1975; 'A Matter of Status', *The Economist*, 6874 (24 May 1975), p. 47.

73  *Berliner Morgenpost*, 13 May 1975; 'Vereinbarungen des Berliner Senats und der DDR-Regierung über Rettungsmasnahmen bei Unfällen an der Berliner Sektorengrenze' [Rescue Measures for Accidents at the Zone Borders], correspondence between the GDR (Ministerium für Auswärtige Angelegenheiten, Joachim Mitdank) and West Berlin Senate (Senator für Inneres, Heinz Annussek), 29 October 1975, in: Bundesministerium für innerdeutsche Beziehungen (ed.), *Zehn Jahre Deutschlandpolitik* (Bonn, 1980), pp. 287, 454–60; Gerhard Kunze, *Grenzerfahrungen. Kontakte und Verhandlungen zwischen dem Land Berlin und der DDR, 1949–1989* (Berlin, 1999), pp. 404–5; 'Der nasse Tod', in *Der Monolog der Lautsprecher und andere Geschichten aus dem geteilten Berlin*, ed. Peter Pragal and

Eckart D. Stratenschulte (Munich, 1999), pp. 58–65. Life-saving equipment and emergency telephones were installed along the West Berlin bank in spring 1976.

74 Karl-Heinz Starick, *Gurkenfass und Himmelbett* (Lehde, 2002 [1997]), p. 3.

75 'Spree', in *Grosse vollständige Universal Lexicon aller Wissenschaften und Künste,* vol. XXXIX (Leipzig, 1744), p. 482.

76 Christel Lehmann, Wilfried Lehmann and Ute Henschel, *Museums-Führer, Spreewaldmuseum, Lehde* (Lübbenau, 1993), p. 10; Reclus, *Europe*, vol. III, p. 292.

77 Carsten Rasmus and Bettina Klaehne, *Biosphärenreservat Spreewald: Wanderungen, Radtouren und Spatziergänge* (Berlin, 1999), pp. 8, 23.

78 Kühn, *Spreewald*, p. 44; Rasmus and Klaehne, *Biosphärenreservat Spreewald*, p. 20. The *Kahn* at the open-air folk museum (*Freilandmuseum*) in Lehde (est. 1957) dates from 1816. Made from a 200-year oak trunk, it was initially hollowed out with fire and then hand-tooled.

79 Starick, *Gurkenfass und Himmelbett*, p. 16. A picture (1920) of a funeral processsion on skates hangs in the gherkin museum.

80 Kühn, *Spreewald*, p. 34; Wilibald von Schulenberg, *Wendisches Volkstum in Sage, Brauch und Sitte* (Leipzig, 1934), p. 218; Starick, *Gurkenfass und Himmelbett*, pp. 31–2. This ancient ritual had also been observed in Berlin (at midnight, under a full moon) since the founding of the twin towns, surviving well into the nineteenth century. See 'Der letzte Tag im Vaterlande', *Erheiterungen: Belletristiches Beiblatt zur Aschaffenburger Zeitung*, 134 (June 1866), pp. 534–5.

81 Matthew Kossick, Mato Kosyk and Matthäus Kossick, *Basni-Gedichte-Poems*, trans. Pĕtš Janaš, Roland Marti and Gerald Stone (Saarbrücken, 2003), pp. 15, 43, 55, 92; Gerald Stone, 'Review Article: Mato Kosyk: Poet of the Lower Sorbs', *Slavonic and Eastern European Review*, LXXXV/2 (April 2007), p. 325.

82 Baedeker, *Berlin*, p. 208.

83 Starick, *Gurkenfass und Himmelbett*, p. 34; Oster, 'Havel und Spree', p. 57.

84 Lawrence P. Ralston, 'The Lusatian Question at the Paris Peace Conference', *American Slavic and East European Review*, XIX/2 (April 1960), p. 249; Klaus J. Dippmann, 'The Legal Position of the Lusatian Sorbs since the Second World War', *Slavonic and East European Review*, LIII/130 (January 1975), p. 63; Bergengruen, *Am Himmel wie auf Erden*, pp. 10, 14, 199, 201, 235–6, 238, 579–607, 620.

85 'Spreewald', Biosphere Reserves Directory, Man and Biosphere Programme, UNESCO (2005).

86 Bernard O'Connor, *The Law of Geographical Indications* (London, 2004), p. 135.

87 Christel Lehmann-Enders, *Nicht rumgurken, sondern reinbeissen! Das echte Spreewälder Gurkenbuch* (Lübben, 1998), p. 8.

88 Ursula Heinzelmann, `Spreewälder Gurken: Pickled Cucumbers from the Spreewald', *Gastronomica: The Journal of Food and Culture*, IV/3 (Summer 2004),

p. 14; Joachim Seyppel, *Ein Yankee in der Mark: Wanderungen nach Fontane* ([East] Berlin, 1969), pp. 14, 25; Karl Friedrich von Rumohr, *Geist der Kochkunst* (Frankfurt am Main, 1966 [1822]), p. 157. Leading gastronomist Rumohr nonetheless preferred the Dutch product.

89  Starick, *Gurkenfass und Himmelbett*, p. 30.

90  Starick, *Gurkenfass und Himmelbett*, pp. 22–3; Heinzelmann, 'Spreewälder Gurken', p. 13; Lehmann-Enders, *Nicht rumgurken, sondern reinbeissen!*, p. 10.

91  Vizetelly, *Berlin*, vol. I, p. 129.

92  Groggert, *Personenschiffahrt auf Spree und Havel*, p. 30; Vizetelly, *Berlin*, vol. I, p. 76. Fontane's novel, *Der Stechlin* (1899), includes an account of an excursion by steamer to Treptow.

93  Fontane, *Von Zwanzig bis Dreissig, Sämtliche Werke, Band 15* (Munich, 1967), p. 111.

94  Frido Mětšk, 'Theodor Fontanes Begegnung 1859 im Spreewald', in *Theodore Fontanes Werk in unserer Zeit*, ed. Theodor-Fontane-Archiv (Potsdam, 1966), p. 67.

95  Theodor Fontane, *Wanderungen durch die Mark Brandenburg, Vierter Band: Spreewald* (Munich, 1963 [1881]), pp. 9, 13; Fontane, *Eine Fahrt in den Spreewald* (Leipzig, 1929), pp. 56, 61; Fontane, 'In den Spreewald', in Luise Berg-Ehlers und Gottfried Erler, eds, *'Ich bin nicht für halbe Portionen': Essen und Trinken mit Theodor Fontane* (Berlin, 1985), pp. 43–4.

96  *Märkisches Wanderruderbuch* (Berlin, 1925), p. 24.

97  Gersal, *Spree-Athen*, pp. 23–4; *Märkisches Wanderruderbuch* (Berlin, 1925), pp. 7–41; Paul Schneider, *Rund um Berlin: 1 Teil: Spreewanderungen* (Berlin, 1926), pp. 46–53.

98  Reclus, *Europe*, vol. III, p. 307; Mathilde Edith Holtz, 'Project: Re-discovering Germany for German Classes', *Monatshefte für deutschen Unterricht*, XX/6 (October 1928), p. 180.

99  Eva G. Fremont, 'The Green Canals of the Spreewald', *Los Angeles Times*, 2 April 2002; Eve Schaenen, 'A Quaint and Watery Refuge', *New York Times*, 18 July 1999.

100  Many visitors explore the reserve in traditional punts navigated by rustic gondoliers. The level terrain is also ideal for cycling. The local tourist authority has developed the 250-kilometre *Gurkenradweg* (Gherkin Cycle Path).

101  Gordon Craig, *Theodor Fontane: Literature and History in the Bismarck Reich* (New York, 1999), pp. 66–77.

102  Gerd Conradt, *An der Spree: Der Fluss, Die Menschen* (Berlin, 2007), p. 63.

103  Spremberg Dam and Reservoir (*Talsperre Spremberg* and *Spremberger Stausee*) (1958–65) interrupt the Spree to supply the nearby lignite processing plant (1955), Europe's biggest, with cooling water.

104  Gennerich, *Flüsse Deutschlands*, p. 98; Sebastian Leber, 'Spree? Na Klar!', *Berliner Tagesspiel*, 4 April 2010.

105 Natalia Sosin (trans. Olia Yatskewich), 'Media Spree on Berlin's River: Swim next to Offices', *CafeBabel.com* ('The European Magazine'), 24 June 2008, at www.cafebabel.co.uk; Matthias Oloew, 'An der Spree is alles im Fluss', *Berliner Tagesspiegel*, 30 September 2007, at www.tagesspiegel.de (accessed 16 March 2012).

106 Anschutz operates O$_2$ World (2008), Gemany's second largest multiple use indoor arena (capacity: 17,000), controversial not least because of perceived incongruity with the nearby East Side Gallery, the longest surviving stretch of Wall, designated a site for artists in 1990 and awarded historic monument status in 1993.

107 'Mediaspree Versenken', at www.ms-versenken.org; 'Flood Mediaspree Demo-parade', 10 July 2010, at www.demotix.com (accessed 16 March 2012).

108 Tamsin Walker, 'Sprucing up the Spree', *Deutsche Welle*, 10 August 2005, at www.dw-world.de (accessed 16 March 2012).

109 Courtney Davis, 'A Chilly Float Down the Aare River in Bern, Switzerland', *Dallas Morning News*, 28 August 2010. Bernese swimmers move around a horseshoe bend at a brisk 6.5 kilometres per hour. Handrails jut out at seven exit points so that swimmers can clamber up concrete steps.

110 Conradt, *An der Spree*, p. 126.

111 Leber, 'Spree? Na Klar!'

112 Claudia Fuchs, 'Die Rettungsinsel', *Berliner Zeitung*, 1 August 2008; Leber, 'Spree? Na Klar!'

113 Quoted in Walker, 'Sprucing up the Spree'.

114 Clemens Niedenthal, 'Die Spree war mal ein Badefluss', *Berliner Zeitung*, 31 May 2006.

115 Beween 1849 and the 1920s, *Lohmühleninsel* was the site of a swimming station taken over in 1859 by the *Sachse'sche Flussbadeanstalt*, whose special attraction was the *Wellenbad*, a pool with waves generated by steam engine: Groggert, *Spreefahrt tut not!*, pp. 40–41.

116 The facility extends 44 metres into the river and includes two wooden pontoons in addition to the pool, which, in summer, serve as sunbathing decks. In winter, the decks support two saunas, a relaxation area and a bar. Tube-like plastic membranes cover everything.

117 Conradt, *An der Spree*, p. 131.

118 Kyle James, 'A Pool with a View', *Deutsche Welle*, 22 July 2004, at www.dw-world.de (accessed 16 March 2012); Niedenthal, 'Die Spree war mal ein Badefluss'.

119 Conradt, *An der Spree*, p. 124.

120 Conradt and Welke, 'An der Spree'.

121 Jiri Kolaja and A. W. Foster, '"Berlin, The Symphony of a City" as a Theme of Visual Rhythm', *Journal of Aesthetics and Art Criticism*, XXIII/3 (Spring 1965), p. 357.

122 *Spreebabylon* ('Babylon-on-the-Spree') refers to 1920s nightlife: David Clay Large, *Berlin: A Modern History* (New York, 2001), pp. 96, 181, 224.

## References

123 *Deutsches Volkstum*, XII/1 (January 1930), p. 8, in Jochen Mayer, 'Aufstand der Landschaft gegen Berlin: Wilhelm Stapel und seine Zeitschrift *Deutsches Volkstum*', in *Berlin – Provinz: Literarische Kontroversen um 1930*, ed. Jochen Mayer (Marbach, 1985), p. 11; Wolfgang Natter, 'The City as Cinematic Space: Modernism and Place in *Berlin, Symphony of a City*', in *Place, Power, Situation, and Spectacle: A Geography of Film*, ed. Stuart C. Aitken and Leo Zonn (Lanham, MD, 1994), p. 215.

124 Benjamin, *The Return of the Flâneur* (1929), *Berliner Chronik* (1932) and *Berlin Childhood* (1932–8).

125 Gersal, *Spree-Athen*, p. 5; Vizetelly, *Berlin*, vol. I, p. 177.

126 Roth, 'Spatziergang', *Berliner Börsen-Courier*, 24 May 1921, in Joseph Roth, *Werke*, vol. IV, ed. Hermann Kesten (Cologne, 1956), pp. 793–6.

127 Roth, 'Das Haus der 100 Vernünftigen', *Frankfurter Zeitung*, 17 February 1923; 'Wahlkampf in Berlin', *Frankfurter Zeitung*, 29 April 1924; 'Das Museum', *Frankfurter Zeitung*, 14 March 1929; 'Typoskript von 1924 (?) [at Leo Baeck Institute, New York]', p. 833, in Roth, *Werke*, vol. IV, pp. 15, 31, 147.

128 *Am grünen Strand der Spree: Ein Gruss der Reichshauptstadt an unsere Kameraden im Felde* (Berlin, 1943), p. 5.

129 Quoted in Jens Mühling, 'Das Gedächtnis des Wassers: Spree-Porträt', *Tagesspiegel*, 27 August 2007. In this interview, Conradt ponders whether water has a memory. In his mytho-poetic version of the hydrological cycle, he sees atmospheric moisture as an element in search of its particular river, like a homing salmon.

130 Conradt and Welke, 'An der Spree'; Conradt, *An der Spree*, pp. 33–6, 58–64, 75–82, 95–101, 109–20, 121–8, 131–4. Spree and Havel provide 70 per cent of Berlin's drinking water.

131 Tamsin Walker, 'In Berlin, A River Remade', *DW-World*, 24 July 2004, at www.dw-world.de (accessed 16 March 2012).

132 Götze, *398 Kilometer Spree*, p. 7.

133 Roth, *Die Flucht ohne Ende*, in Roth, *Werke*, vol. I, pp. 389–90.

134 Karl Wilhelm Ramler, *Das Opfer der Nymphen und Flussgötter: Ein Vorspiel* (Berlin, 1775), p. 4.

135 'Beisessung des Sarkophags des verst. Prinzen Heinrich von Preussen', *Zeitung für die elegante Welt*, III/51 (18 April 1803), p. 103.

136 *Der Bär von Berlin: Jahrbuch des Vereins für die Geschichte Berlins, Bande 44–48* (Berlin, 1995), p. 55; *Die Kunst: Monatshefte für freie und angewandte Kunst* 17 (1908), p. 480; *Allgemeines Lexikon der Bildenden Künstler, Sechster Band*, ed. Ulrich Thieme (Leipzig, 1912), p. 538; Bernd Unger, *Der Berliner Bär: Ein Streifzug durch Geschichte und Gegenwart* (Münster, 2000), pp. 41–2; Winfried Löschburg, *Spreegöttin mit Berliner Bär: Historische Miniaturen* (Berlin, 1987), pp. 249–53.

137 Vollrath, *Wiedersehen am Strand der Spree*, p. 160.

138 Jenny Kähler, 'Marmor-Göttin soll umziehen', *Berliner Zeitung*, 25 January 1995; Lothar Münner, 'Kaufleute spenden för die Spreegöttin "Sprea"', 13 June 1995; Claudia Fuchs, '100 Jährige "Sprea" ist vom sauren Regen bedroht', 27 March 1999; Kathrin Kempe (letter to the editor), 20 April 1999; Marcel Gäding, 'Umzug einer Göttin: "'Sprea" kommt ins Märkische Museum', 14 August 2001. Sprea remains in her current location: emails from Gundula Ancke (Stiftung Stadtmuseum Berlin), 12 and 13 December 2011.

## 3 Po

1 *The Histories of Herodotus*, trans. Henry Cary (New York, 1904), pp. 195–6; Robert Brown, *Eridanus: River and Constellation* (London, 1883), p. 36.

2 P. L. Gibbard, 'The History of the Great Northwest European Rivers During the Past Three Million Years', *Philosophical Transactions of the Royal Society, B. 318* (1988), pp. 559–602; Eduard A. Koster, *The Physical Geography of Western Europe* (Oxford, 2005), p. 96; Brown, *Eridanus*, pp. 35–7, 41.

3 *The First and Second Books of Ovid's Metamorphoses*, ed. William T. Peck (Boston, 1907), p. 157; Christoph Gottlieb Groskurd, *Strabons Erdbeschreibung in siebenzehn Büchern, Vierter Theil* (Berlin, 1834), p. 341.

4 *Ovid's Metamorphoses*, trans. John Dryden et al. (London, 1826), p. 36; *Ovid's Metamorphoses in Fifteen Books* (London, 1736), p. 53.

5 Frank Fehrenbach, '"Discordia concors": Gianlorenzo Bernini's "Fontana dei Quatro Fiumi" (1648–51) als päpstliches Friedensmonument', in *Der Westfälische Friede: Diplomatie – Politische Zäsur – Kulturelles Umfeld - Rezeptionsgeschichte*, ed. Heinz Duchhardt (Munich, 1998), pp. 726–8.

6 *Ovid's Metamorphoses*, trans. Dryden, pp. 38, 40; *Ovid in Six Volumes*, III: *Metamorphoses*, trans. Frank Justus Miller (Cambridge, MA, 1916), p. 83.

7 Brown, *Eridanus*, p. 34.

8 *The Geography of Strabo*, trans. H. C. Hamilton (London, 1856), pp. 87–8; *Histories of Herodotus*, pp. 195–6; Brown, *Eridanus*, pp. 35, 38.

9 Apollonius Rhodius, *The Argonautica*, trans. R. C. Seaton (London, 1912), Book IV, p. 335.

10 Richard Hinckley Allen, *Star-names and their Meanings* (New York, 1899), p. 474.

11 *Eratosthemis Catasterismorum Reliquiae*, ed. Carolus Robert (Berlin, 1878), pp. 214, 217; Johann Konrad Schaubach, *Geschichte der griechischen Astronomie bis auf Eratosthenes* (Göttingen, 1802), pp. 316, 318, 343, 361.

12 *Nonnos Dionysiaca*, Book 3, trans. W.H.D. Rouse (Cambridge, MA, 1940), pp. 116–21, 123: Allen, *Star-Names*, p. 215.

## References

13 *The Etymologies of Isidore of Seville*, ed. and trans. Stephen A. Barney et al. (Cambridge, 2006), p. 282.

14 Ismail Sirry Bey, *Irrigation in the Valley of the River Po, Northern Italy: Being an Account of a Mission Undertaken in the Summer of 1899 for the Egyptian Government* (Cairo, 1902), p. 23.

15 H.J. Fleure, 'Cities of the Po Basin: An Introductory Study,' *Geographical Review* 14/3 (July 1924), pp. 345–61; Piero Bevilaqua, 'The Distinctive Character of Italian Environmental History', in *Nature and History in Modern Italy*, ed. Marco Armieri and Marcus Hall (Athens, OH, 2010), p. 18.

16 Jean Gottmann, *Megalopolis: The Urbanized Northeastern Seaboard of the United States* (Cambridge, MA, 1961), p. 27; Alla Ricerca del Grande Fiume, 'La salute del Po: Dal Monviso al Delta, problemi e criticità' (2007), p. 1, at www.allaricercadel-grandefiume.it (accessed 16 March 2012); Eugenio Turri, *La Megalopoli Padana* (Venice, 2000).

17 Carl T. Schmidt, 'Land Reclamation in Fascist Italy', *Political Science Quarterly*, 52/3 (September 1937), p. 340.

18 'Decreto che dichiara il fiume Po fiume nazionale', 12 April 1849, *Bibliografia degli scritti di Giuseppe Mazzini*, ed. Giulio Canestrelli (Rome, 1892), p. 23; Oscar Mammi, 'Dichiariamo il Po fiume nazionale: *La Repubblica*, 15 September 1996.

19 Mauro Calzolari, *Il Po in età romana: geografia, storia e imagine di un grande fiume europeo* (Reggio Emilia, 2004).

20 Giuseppe De Santis, 'Towards an Italian Landscape', in *Springtime in Italy: A Reader on Neo-realism*, ed. and trans. David Overbey (London, 1978), p. 128. This essay first appeared as 'Per un paesaggio italiano', *Cinema*, 116 (25 April 1941).

21 Michelangelo Antonioni, 'Concerning a Film about the River Po', in *Springtime in Italy*, p. 79. This essay first appeared as 'Per un film sul fiume Po', *Cinema*, 68 (25 April 1939).

22 Geoffrey Newell-Smith, 'Away from the Po Valley Blues', *Pix*, 1 (Winter 1993/94), pp. 24–30.

23 Fausto Guzzetti, Mauro Cardinali and Paola Reichenbach, 'The AVI Project: A Bibliographical and Archive Inventory of Landslides and Floods in Italy', *Environmental Management*, 18 (1994), pp. 623–4. Between 1980 and 2002, Italy accounted for 38 per cent of European flood fatalities: European Commission, Research Directorate-General, Directorate I – Environment, 'Floods: European Research for Better Predictions and Management Solutions, Dresden, 13 October 2003 (Background Information for Press Release)', p. 1, at http://ec.europa.eu (accessed 16 March 2012).

24 Erla Zwingle, 'Po: River of Pain and Plenty', *National Geographic*, CCI/5 (May 2002), p. 100.

25  Bolton King, 'Statistics of Italy', *Journal of the Royal Statistical Society*, LXVI/2 (June 1903), p. 245; Fleure, 'Cities of the Po Basin', p. 357; Goodrich Smith, 'History and Progress of Irrigation', in *Executive Documents, House of Representatives, 1860–61* (Washington, DC, 1861), pp. 186–7.

26  'Caratteristiche del bacino del fiume Po e primo esame dell'impatto ambientale delle attività umane sulle risorse idriche' (Parma, Aprile 2006), pp. 12–13.

27  Davide Zanchettin, Pietro Traverso and Mario Tomasino, 'Po River Discharges: A Preliminary Analysis of a 200-Year Time Series', *Climatic Change*, 89 (2008), p. 415.

28  Élisée Reclus, *The Earth and its Inhabitants: Europe*, vol. I (New York, 1883), p. 212.

29  W. E. Frye, *After Waterloo: Reminiscences of European Travel, 1815–1819* (London, 1908), pp. 352, 199.

30  R. Larry Todd, *Fanny Hensel: The Other Mendelssohn* (New York, 2009), p. 241.

31  A. C. Ramsay, 'The River Po', *Macmillan's Magazine*, XXVII/158 (December 1872), p. 125. This article was reproduced in Italian in *Les Inondations en Italie: Fiume Po* (Turin, 1873), pp. 6–12.

32  David L. Wheeler, 'Land Reclamation in the Po River Delta of Italy', *Land Economics*, XLI/4 (November 1965), p. 376.

33  Frye, *After Waterloo*, p. 197.

34  M. Tullii Ciceronis, *De Natura Deorum, Libri Tres*, vol. II, ed. and trans. Joseph B. Mayor (Cambridge, 1883), Book II, p. 279.

35  Machiavelli, *The Prince*, trans. and ed. Peter Bondanella (Oxford, 2005 [1532]), p. 84. For the failed project to make Florence a seaport and deprive Pisa of water (1503–6), see Roger D. Masters, *Fortune is a River: Leonardo da Vinci and Niccolò Machiavelli's Magnificent Dream to Change the Course of Florentine History* (New York, 1998), pp. 2–3, 16, 20.

36  *Virgil: The Ecologues Translated by Wrangham, The Georgics by Sotheby, and The Aeneid by Dryden* (London, 1830), vol. I, pp. 86–7. The Latin inscription reads: 'Proluit insano contorquens vertice silvas fluvorium rex eridanus. Composque per omnis cum stabulis armenta tulit'.

37  Riccardo Bacchelli, *The Mill on the Po*, trans. Frances Frenaye (London, 1952), p. 331. This English translation of *Il Mulino del Po* (1938) contains the trilogy's first two volumes.

38  Ermanno Cavazzoni, *The Voice of the Moon*, trans. Ed Emery (London, 1990), pp. 154–6.

39  Historical and geomorphological analysis of channel patterns revealed two broad changes: the sudden and dramatic transformation of the channel of the old Sesia river before 1500; and the more recent neotectonic movements that are raising the external margin of the Apennine chain, and causing the Po to migrate northward: G. Braga and S. Gervasoni, Evolution of the Po River: An Example of the

Application of Historic Maps', in *Historical Change of Large Alluvial Rivers: Western Europe*, ed. G. E. Petts, H. Möller and A. L. Roux (New York, 1989), pp. 113–26; Ramsay, 'River Po', p. 128.

40  Bey, *Irrigation*, p. 36.

41  George Davidson, *Irrigation and Reclamation of Land for Agricultural Purposes as Now Practiced in India, Egypt and Italy, etc.* (Washington, DC, 1875), p. 74.

42  Paolo Squatrini, *Water and Society in Early Medieval Italy, AD 400–1000* (Cambridge, 2002), pp. 69–74.

43  Cesare S. Maffioli, *Out of Galileo: The Science of Waters, 1628–1718* (Rotterdam, 1994), pp. 6, 12, 23. Venice emerged as the acknowledged world centre of hydraulic engineering expertise, academic and managerial: Karel Davids, 'River Control and the Evolution of Knowledge: A Comparison between Regions in China and Europe, *c.* 1400–1850', *Journal of Global History*, 1 (2006), pp. 69, 71, 77.

44  Maffioli, *Out of Galileo*, pp. 156–8; Gian Antonio Stella, 'Venezia "taglia" il Po e vince la sfida con il Papa', *Corriere della Sera*, 15 September 2004; Umberto Simeoni and Corinne Corbau, 'A Review of the Delta Po Evolution (Italy) Related to Climatic Changes and Human Impacts', *Geomorphology*, 107 (2009), p. 65.

45  James L. Wescoat, 'Wittfogel East and West: Changing Perspectives on Water Development in South Asia and the United States', in *Cultural Encounters with the Environment: Enduring and Evolving Geographic Themes*, ed. Alexander B. Murphy et al. (Lanham, MD, 2000), p. 118.

46  Elwood Mead, *Irrigation in Northern Italy, Part 1* (Washington, DC, 1904), pp. 5, 7, 12–13, 56, 58, 60, 66, 77, 95.

47  D. H. Grist, *Rice* (London, 1965), p. 6; 'Italian Rice', *The Economist*, 6292 (28 March 1964), p. 1230.

48  Thomas Jefferson to Edward Rutledge, 14 July 1787; to William Drayton, 30 July 1787, Thomas Jefferson Papers, Series 1, General Correspondence, 1651–1827, Library of Congress, Washington, DC.

49  Mead, *Irrigation*, p. 94.

50  Frank M. Snowden, 'Mosquitoes, Quinine and the Socialism of Italian Women, 1900–1914', *Past and Present*, 178 (February 2003), pp. 178–86.

51  Mario Borsa, *The Farm on the River Po*, trans. L. E. Marshall (London 1971 [*La cascina sul Po* (1920)]), p. 52; 'Torna la resistenza', *Patria Indipendente*, 29 September 2002, p. 40; Reclus, *Earth and its Inhabitants. Europe*, vol. 1, p. 215.

52  Over the past half-century, pasture and agro-industrial plantations of Canadian poplar producing cellulose for newspaper have steadily replaced rice cultivation.

53  Sebastiano Vassalli, 'Silvana Mangano, Addio Mondo Contadino', *Corriere della Sera*, 2 August 1998.

54 Carlo Lizzani, '*Riso amaro*': *Un film diretto da Giuseppe De Santis* (Roma, 1978), pp. 53–4.

55 Antonio C. Vitti, *Giuseppe De Santis and Postwar Italian Cinema* (Toronto, 1996), pp. 36–7; Antonio C. Vitti, 'Riso Amaro', in *The Cinema of Italy*, ed. Giorgio Bertellini (London, 2004), pp. 53–60; Gregory D. Black, *The Catholic Crusade against the Movies, 1940–1975* (New York, 1998), pp. 89–90; Maurizio Porro, '"Riso Amaro", Il cult che lanciò un sex symbol', *Corriere della Sera*, 18 August 2007: XXXI/10 (3 September 1951), p. 63.

56 David Ward, *Antifascisms: Cultural Politics in Italy, 1943–46* (Cranfield, NJ, 1996), pp. 105–6.

57 De Santis, 'Towards an Italian Landscape', pp. 125–6.

58 Christopher Wagstaff, *Italian Neorealist Cinema: An Aesthetic Approach* (Toronto, 2007), p. 286.

59 Roberto Roda and Gabriele Setti, *Le ruote del pane: Mulini natanti e cultura molitoria della Pianura padana: Storia, cultura e immaginario* (Mantua, 2004).

60 The trilogy's final volume (*Mondo vecchio sempre nuovo*) appeared in English as *Nothing New Under the Sun*, trans. Stuart Hood (London, 1955).

61 'The Literary Scene in Italy [2 - Bacchelli]', *New York Times*, 19 February 1938.

62 Bacchelli, *Mill on the Po*, p. 15.

63 Ibid., pp. 46–7.

64 Brent J. Piepergerdes, 'Re-envisioning the Nation: Film Neorealism and the Postwar Italian Condition', *ACME: An International E-Journal for Critical Geographies*, VI/2 (2007), pp. 240–42.

65 This incident was probably based on a conflation of the rural proletariat's strikes of the 1880s and the 'great agricultural strike' of 1920, which affected the entire Po valley: Francesco S. Nitti, 'Strikes in Italy', *Economic Journal*, III/12 (December 1893), pp. 731–2; L. Salvatorelli and G. Mira, *Storia d'Italia nel periodo fascista* (Turin, 1964), p. 168.

66 Bosley Crowther, *New York Times*, 23 October 1951.

67 Historian Fiorella Dall'Olio, quoted in Jenner Meletti, 'Ferrara, il Mulino del Po rinasce tra storia e romanzo', *La Repubblica*, 10 June 2005. In the 1870s, the Ferrara district alone supported 173 mills. By the 1930s, barely a dozen remained.

68 Bacchelli, *Mill on the Po*, pp. 7, 558. Despite the product's high quality, river mills depended on the current's speed. From the 1880s, steam mills that delivered a more regular grinding regime replaced them.

69 Among the collection of historic river boats at Boretto's Museum of the Po and its Internal Navigation (*Museo del Po e della Navigazione interna*) is a 1,500-year-old pirogue hollowed out of a log – a type of boat also found in the Spreewald and Mississippi delta.

70  Kees de Roest, *The Production of Parmigiano-Reggiano Cheese: The Force of an Artisanal System in an Industrialised World* (Assen, Netherlands, 2000), pp. 24, 101.

71  Frank Bruni, 'Italy's Hog Heaven,' *New York Times*, 5 November 2006; Bill Buford, 'The Pasta Station', *The New Yorker*, 6 September 2004, pp. 114–15.

72  DOP/PDO status is more stringent than PGI/IGP status. Whereas DOP products must be produced, processed *and* prepared in a specific region, PGI products can be *either* produced, processed *or* prepared in the specified geographical area.

73  Frye, *After Waterloo*, p. 353.

74  De Santis, 'Towards an Italian Landscape', p. 127.

75  Vittorio Emiliani, 'Litigando lungo il Po', *Ferrara: Voci di una città,* XXVIII/6 (2008), at http://rivista.fondazionecarife.it (accessed 16 March 2012).

76  'Discovering the Great River: Establishing a New Academic Model for Research into the Memory and Identity of a Region', University of Gastronomic Sciences (*Universita degli Studi di Scienze Gastronomiche*), Bra, September 2007: 'Slow Fish: A Slow Food Campaign. Understanding the Oceans', at www.slowfood.com (accessed 16 March 2012). Slow Food and the regional governments of Piedmont and Emilia Romagna founded the university in 2004.

77  Bruno Gambarotta and Touring Club Italiano, *Il Viaggio nella Valle del Po di Mario Soldati*, February 2009.

78  Antonioni, 'Concerning a Film about the River Po', pp. 79–80.

79  *The River* (which Antonioni may have seen at the Venice Film Festival in 1938, where it won first prize) actually offered more than a condemnatory, declensionist visual chronicle of careless abuse. Sponsored by the Farm Security Administration, a New Deal agency, the film closed with a celebration of technology's power to heal damaged nature. Lorentz's images and Whitmanesque script portrayed the Tennessee Valley Authority's integrated dam construction and flood control project as a grandiose undertaking commensurate with the river's own epic character: Finis Dunaway, 'New Deal Jeremiads', *Environmental History*, XII/2 (April 2007), pp. 308–12.

80  Antonioni, 'Concerning a Film about the River Po', pp. 81–2.

81  Peter Brunette, *The Films of Michelangelo Antonioni* (Cambridge, 1998), p. 16. *Gente del Po* was supposed to be longer, but half the footage (mainly of flooding in the delta) was lost during the German occupation and post-war turmoil. Mark Shiel, *Italian Neorealism: Rebuilding the Cinematic City* (London, 2006), p. 96; Noa Steimatsky, 'From the Air: A Genealogy of Antonioni's Modernism', in *Camera Obscura, Camera Lucida: Essays in Honor of Annette Michelson*, ed. Richard Allen and Malcolm Turvey (Amsterdam, 2003), pp. 183–8, 201–05.

82  Steimatsky, 'From the Air', p. 205.

83  Seymour Benjamin Chatman, *Antonioni, or, The Surface of the World* (Berkeley, 1985), p. 8.

84  Giuliana Minghelli, 'Haunted Frames: History and Landscape in Luchino Visconti's *Ossessione*', *Italica* (22 June 2008), at www.thefreelibrary.com (accessed 16 March 2012).

85  Antonio Batramelli, *Da Comacchio ad Argenta: La Lagune et le Bocche del Po* (Bergamo, 1905), p. 2.

86  'Film of the Week: *Paisan*', *Life*, xxv/3 (19 July 1948), p. 44; Wagstaff, *Italian Neorealist Cinema*, pp. 188, 285–6.

87  Italy's sugar beet growing and refining capacity were concentrated on the lower Po: C. J. Robertson, 'The Italian Sugar-beet Industry', *Economic Geography*, 14 (January 1938), p.1; Anthony Lane, 'Rambling Man', *The New Yorker*, 9 November 2009, p. 5.

88  Ann Guerin, 'A Many-hued Ado About Nothing', *Life*, lviii/9 (5 March 1965), p. 12; Richard Brody, 'Getting Wasted', *The New Yorker*, 14 June 2010, p. 22.

89  Flavio Niccolini, 'Diary', trans. Maggie Fritz-Morkin, *Words Without Borders*, March 2011, at http://wordswithoutborders.org (accessed 16 March 2012).

90  Ettore Mo, 'Il Placido Po di Don Camillo e Peppone', *Corriere della Sera*, 26 September 1996.

91  Giovanni Guareschi, *Mondo Piccolo: Don Camillo* (Milan, 1948), p. x. The first British translation was *The Little World of Don Camillo* (London, 1951).

92  Guareschi, *Little World of Don Camillo*, in Guareschi, *The World of Don Camillo* (London, 1980), pp. 75–8.

93  Guareschi, 'The Little World', *Little World of Don Camillo*, in *The World of Don Camillo*, p.21. The first part of this passage is also inscribed on the chapel at Zibello.

94  Guareschi, 'Little World', *Don Camillo and his Flock: The Enchanting Adventures of a Loveable Parish Priest* (Mattituck, NY, 1952), p. 8.

95  For the original Italian version ('E spesso vado a sedermi come allora sulla riva del grande fiume e mentre mastico un filo d'erba. Penso "Si sta meglio qui su questa riva"'), see Guareschi, 'Mondo Piccolo', *Don Camillo e il suo Gregge* (Milan, 1953), p. 8. This statement is displayed at the Museum of Don Camillo and Peponne (Museo Don Camillo e Peppone), under photographs of Brescello submerged by floodwaters in 1951. It also features among the inscriptions on the wall of the chapel at Zibello.

96  'Italian Film Invasion', *Life*, xxxiii/16 (20 October 1952), p. 108. Since the Museum of Don Camillo and Peppone opened in 1999, Brescello has become an even more popular destination for *Don Camillo* enthusiasts.

97  Winthrop Sargeant, 'Anti-Communist Funnyman', *Life*, xxxiii/19 (10 November 1952), pp. 122, 125.

98  Guareschi, 'Little World', *Little World of Don Camillo*, in *World of Don Camillo*, p. 21.

99  Loss of woodland cover on Alpine and Apennine slopes reduced the soil's capacity to retain and evaporate water during heavy rainfall, converting streams into torrents that washed earth and rocks into the valley.

# References

100  Guareschi, *Little World of Don Camillo*, in Guareschi, *World of Don Camillo* (London, 1980), pp. 68–71.

101  Guareschi, *Don Camillo and the Prodigal Son*, in Guareschi, *World of Don Camillo* (London, 1980), pp. 189–93, 217–19, 220–22, 223–5. The American edition was titled *Don Camillo and his Flock* (1953).

102  Guareschi, *Don Camillo and the Prodigal Son*, in Guareschi, *World of Don Camillo*, pp. 218–20.

103  Guareschi, *Don Camillo and the Prodigal Son*, pp. 220–25.

104  Guareschi, 'Introduction', in Guareschi, *World of Don Camillo*, pp. 17–18.

105  'Ethnoscape' signifies how landscape is imbued with 'poetic ethnic meaning through the historicization of nature'. Ethnoscapes cited are places associated with sacred sites (Israel), battlefields and (in the case of the Swiss) mountains and lakes: Anthony D. Smith, *Myths and Memories of the Nation* (Oxford, 1999), pp. 16, 149–57.

106  Benito Giordano, 'The Contrasting Geographies of "Padania": The Case of the Lega Nord in Northern Italy', *Area*, XXXIII/1 (March 2001), p. 28.

107  Paulo Tripodi, 'Separatism the Italian Way: The Northern League', *Contemporary Review*, 270 (1 February 1997), p. 1.

108  Margaret Rigillo, 'Bossi Carries Separatist Dream in a Green Box', *Glasgow Herald*, 14 September 1996.

109  Nick Parsons, 'Padania Stirs Fact and Fantasy', *Scotland on Sunday*, 15 September 1996; Margaret Rigillo, 'Italian National Unity Breaks Out Thanks to Bossi's Flop on the Po', *Glasgow Herald*, 23 September 1996.

110  Margaret Rigillo, 'Bossi Takes Braveheart Role in Drive for Northern Breakaway', *Glasgow Herald*, 9 September 1997.

111  Miroslav Hroch, 'National Self-determination from a Historical Perspective', in *Notions of Nationalism*, ed. Sukumar Periwal (Budapest, 1995), p. 70.

112  Richard Owen, 'Italians Turn their Backs on the Birth of Padania', *The Times*, 16 September 1996.

113  Richard Owen, 'Cracks Appear as Ringmaster Bossi Leads his Troupe on Independence Trail', *The Times*, 14 September 1996.

114  'Young Padanian Movement: Who We Are', at www.giovaniliguri.leganord.org (accessed 16 March 2012).

115  'Declaration of Independence and Sovereignty of Padania', http://digilander.libero.it (accessed 16 March 2012).

116  John Hooper, 'Secession Goes Against the Flow', *The Guardian*, 14 September 1996.

117  Anne Hanley, 'Padania Dream Fades after Bossi's Big Flop', *The Independent*, 15 September 1996.

118  Giorgio Savona, 'The Secluded Giant', *Emilia Romagna*, 5 (2002), p. 47; Luciano

Ghelfi and Umberto Bonafini, *Le Città di Destra e di Sinistra: Dove la Padania ha Cuore (e Testa)* (Milan, 1999).

119 Gianni Brera, 'Invectiva ad Patrem Padum', at www.brera.net (accessed 16 March 2012).

120 Nicola Surian and Massimo Rinaldi, 'Morphological Response to River Engineering and Management in Alluvial Channels in Italy', *Geomorphology*, 50 (2003), p. 312; Zwingle, 'Po: River of Pain and Plenty', p. 108.

121 E. Marchi, G. Roth and F. Siccardi, 'The Po: Centuries of River Training', *Physics and Chemistry of the Earth*, xx/5–6 (1995), pp. 475, 477.

122 Ramsay, 'River Po', p. 129.

123 M. Ferronato, et al., 'Modelling Possible Structural Instabilities of the Po River Embankment, Italy, due to Groundwater Pumping in the Ferrara Province', in *Proceedings of the International Congress on Modelling and Simulation MODSIM07*, ed. L. Oxley and D. Kulasiri (2007), p. 1224; Umberto Simeoni and Corinne Corbau, 'A Review of the Delta Po Evolution (Italy) Related to Climatic Changes and Human Impacts', *Geomorphology*, 107 (2009), p. 69.

124 Bey, *Irrigation*, p. 24; Fleure, 'Cities of the Po Basin', p. 350; Robertson, 'Italian Sugar-Beet Industry', p. 3.

125 Ramsay, 'River Po', p. 129; Reclus, *Europe*, vol. i, pp. 212–13.

126 Frye, *After Waterloo*, p. 352.

127 *The Orlando Furioso of Ludovico Ariosto*, trans. William Stewart Rose (London, 1829), Canto 40, Verse 31, p. 137.

128 Mario Borsa, *The Farm on the River Po*, trans. L. E. Marshall (London, 1931), p. 21. Borsa was London correspondent for the Milanese newspaper, *Il Secolo*, and was also Milanese correspondent for the *Times*.

129 Borsa, *Farm on the Po*, p. 50.

130 Ibid., pp. 74–94.

131 Reclus, *Europe*, vol. i, pp. 210–11; Borsa, *Farm on the Po*, pp. 80, 81, 83, 89.

132 Enrico Marchi, Giorgio Roth and Franco Siccardi, 'The November 1994 Flood Event on the Po River: Structural and Non-Structural Measures Against Inundations', us-Italy Research Workshop on the Hydrometeorology, Impacts, and Management of Extreme Floods, Perugia, November 1995, p. 8.

133 'Floods Bring Disaster Down the Po', *Life*, xxxi/23 (3 December 1951), pp. 39–43; Fausto Guzzetti et al., 'Information System on Historical Landslides and Floods in Italy', unpublished paper, Urban Hazards Forum, City University of New York, 22–24 January 2002, p. 2.

134 Roberto Cervo, *Polesine Amaro* (Bergamo, 1953); *Anthology of Italian and Italo-American Poetry*, trans. Rodolfo Purcelli (Boston, 1955), p. 108; Gian Antonio Cibotto, *Cronache dell'alluvione: Polesine 1951* (Venice, 2001); 'La Rotta del Po

semina la morte e la rovina nelle terre del Polisine invase dalle acqua', *Il Gazzettino*, 14 November 1951.

135  The region's flood-prone character (it was badly struck again in 1994 and 2000) has deterred economic investment. On the other hand, it has preserved an ambience that appealed to Sandro Bolchi, much of whose televised version of Bacchelli's novel (1963) was filmed in Crespino.

136  Maurizio Chierici, 'Gente del Po: La paura corre con l'acqua', *Corriere della Sera*, 8 November 1994.

137  Cesare Zavattini and Paul Strand, *Un Paese* (Turin, 1955), pp. 6–7, 14; Calvin Tomkins, *Paul Strand: Sixty Years of Photographs* (New York, 1976), pp. 31–2, 166, 170–71, 103, 138.

138  Letter to Walter Rosenbaum (9 April 1953), quoted in Tomkins, *Strand*, p. 166.

139  Cesare Zavattini and Paul Strand, *Un Paese: Portrait of an Italian Village* (New York, 1997), p. 5; E. Gualtieri, ed. *Paul Strand, Cesare Zavattini: lettere e immagini* (Bologna, 2005), pp. 245–55. Francesco Faeta, *Fotografi e fotographie: uno sguardo antropologico* (Milan, 2006), pp. 129–30; Emiliano-Romagnioli nel Mondo, 'Reggio Emilia: Luzzara: il mondo in un paese', at www.emilianoromagnolinelmondo.it (accessed 16 March 2012).

140  A complex administrative structure matches the complicated hydrological infra-structure. The *Magistrato*, a centralized civil authority with basin-wide power to undertake public improvement works (*genio civile*), set up in 1806, was replaced a century later with a national body, the *Ufficio di Ispezione Superiore del Genio Civile per il Po* (also based in Parma). The flood of 1951 fuelled the desire for an authority with greater powers. The *Magistrato per il Po* was established (1956) as an agency within the Ministry of Public Works, responsible for all activities pertaining to river regulation and protection of adjacent lowlands, which ranged from the reconstruction of flood-damaged levees to water extraction for agricultural and industrial uses, as well as all research and planning matters. In the early 1990s, another Parma-based body was created to coordinate water management tasks delegated to regional governments in the 1970s. *L'Autorità di bacino del fiume Po* coordinates the work of the six regions represented within the Po Valley, for which it has assumed responsibility for general planning and water management issues. In 2003, the *Magistrato* was superseded by the *Agenzia Interregionale per il fiume Po* (AIPO, also based in Parma), whose primary tasks are to provide flood protection and river regulation.

141  'Museo Gialdini' opened in 2000 and features military bridge-building equipment. Near the site, a pontoon bridge connected the provinces of Reggio Emilia and Mantova between 1886 and 1967 (when it was replaced by a concrete bridge). This wooden plank bridge that rested on a string of boats featured in the opening credits

of the second Don Camillo film. The museum houses Gialdini's one-in-ten scale replica (*plastico*) of the old bridge.

142 See also Zavattini, *Un Paese*, p. 8.

143 Sperangelo Bandera, 'Il Po, un fiume in agonia', *Corriere della Sera*, 31 July 1992; Bandera, 'Il Po, un fiume in agonia', *Corriere della Sera*, 14 May 1996; Martino Spadari, 'Po, un lungo fiume di rifiuti', *Corriere della Sera*, 9 May 2001; Zwingle, 'Po: River of Pain and Plenty', p. 105.

144 Alla Ricerca del Grande Fiume, 'La salute del Po: Dal Monviso al Delta, problemi e criticità' (2007), p. 1, at www.allaricercadelgrandefiume.it (accessed 16 March 2012).

145 Alla Ricerca del Grande Fiume, 'La salute del Po', p. 2; Autorità di bacino del fiume Po, *Caratteristiche del bacino del fiume Po e primo esame dell'impatto ambientale delle attività umane sulle risorse idriche* (Parma: Autorità di bacino del fiume Po, Aprile 2006), p. 47; 'Worrying Diagnosis for River Po's Health', *Italy Magazine*, 10 October 2007, at www.italymag.co.uk (accessed 16 March 2012).

146 Figures from *Autorità di bacino del fiume Po* (2007), cited in 'La salute del Po', p. 1; Zwingle, 'Po: River of Pain and Plenty', p. 100.

147 Sperangelo Bandera, 'Addio chiare e dolci acque, il Po rientra dalle ferie', *Corriere della Sera*, 8 September 1996.

148 Photograph iss013-e–78295m, September 6, 2006, iss Crew Earth Observations Experiment and the Image Science & Analysis Group, Johnson Space Center. A photograph from October 1997 shows the cloud of contamination fingering its way up tributary valleys: www.redorbit.com.

149 R. Marchetti, A. Provini and G. Crosa, 'Nutrient Load Carried by the River Po into the Adriatic Sea', *Marine Pollution Bulletin*, xx/4 (1989), p. 168; Davide Calamari et al., 'Strategic Survey of Therapeutic Drugs in the Rivers Po and Lambro in Northern Italy', *Environmental Science and Technology*, xxxvii/7 (2003), pp. 1242, 1244–5.

150 'Sun, Sea and Slime', *The Economist*, 22 July 1989, pp. 42–3.

151 Ettore Zuccato et al., 'Cocaine in Surface Waters: A New Evidence-based Tool to Monitor Community Drug Abuse', *Environmental Health: A Global Access Science Source*, iv/14 (August 2005), pp. 1, 7. These traces translated into a total daily cocaine consumption within the Po basin of four kilograms (or 40,000 daily doses among a population of five million) – much higher than crime statistics and surveys suggested.

152 Carlo Cencini, 'Physical Processes and Human Activities in the Evolution of the Po Delta, Italy', *Journal of Coastal Research*, 14/3 (1998), pp. 779–800.

153 Alla Ricerca del Grande Fiume, 'La salute del Po', p. 1; Umberto Simeoni and Corinne Corbau, 'A Review of the Delta Po Evolution (Italy) Related to Climatic

Changes and Human Impacts', *Geomorphology*, 107 (2009), p. 70. An intact delta marshland serves as a sponge-like speed bump by absorbing storm-driven seawater surges.

154 The surviving remnant of the Bosco di Mesola, where, protected by malarial swamps, Italy's last population of native red deer took refuge, is now part of the Po Delta Natural Park (1988).

155 Mark McGinley, 'Po Basin Mixed Forests', in *Encyclopedia of Earth*, ed. Cutler J. Cleveland (Washington, DC, 2008), at www.eoearth.org (accessed 16 March 2012).

156 Jean Pourtet, 'The Poplar: Its Place in the World', *Unasylva: An International Journal of Forestry and Forest Industries*, V/2 (April–July 1951), at www.peupliersdefrance.org (accessed 16 March 2012).

157 Interview with John Tusa, BBC Radio 3, August 2003, at www.bbc.co.uk (accessed 16 March 2012).

158 Peter Bondanella, *Italian Cinema: From Neorealism to the Present* (New York, 2001), p. 190; Bilge Ebri, 'Bernardo Bertolucci' (Directors Profile), *Senses of Cinema*, 33 (October–December 2004), at www.sensesofcinema.com (accessed 16 March 2012); Pauline Kael, 'Starburst by a Gifted 22-year-old', *Life*, LIX/7 (13 August 1965), p. 12; Neel Chaudhuri, 'Clouds Pursuing Clouds: Bernardo Bertolucci's *Prima della rivoluzione*', *Senses of Cinema*, 36 (July–September 2005), at www.sensesofcinema.com (accessed 16 March 2012); Newell-Smith, 'Away from the Po Valley Blues', p. 25.

159 Tullio Kezich, 'Olmi "Old Man River" Padano', *Corriere della Sera*, 11 July 1992. See also Joe Sheppard, 'Po Valley Polemics: *One Hundred Nails*', *The Lumière Reader*, at: http://lumiere.net.nz. Though Oscar Hammerstein's and Jerome Kern's 'Ol' Man River' was first sung by Jules Bledsoe in the stage production of *Show Boat* (1927), this homage to the stoic, carefree Mississippi (who/which just keeps rolling along) became renowned after Paul Robeson sang it in the 1936 movie version.

160 The Po as a place of retreat is a narrative that also informs Gianni Celati's short story 'The Story of a Carpenter and a Hermit', in which one of the two characters is a reclusive fisherman (a former racing driver) who lives in a (rather less picturesque) sheet-metal hut on the banks: Celati, *Voices from the Plains*, trans. Robert Lumley (London, 1989 [*Narratori delle Pianure*, 1985]), p. 91.

161 The historic range of *siluro* was north of the Alps between the Rhine and the Volga. Transplanted to the Po in 1957 to satisfy anglers, it enjoyed spectacular success. Quickly acclimatizing to the slow-flowing, turbid waters, the absence of predators and its omnivorous habits assisted naturalization and expansion.

162 Once widely distributed in the Po valley, the otter was gone by the early 1980s, a casualty of riparian woodland retreat as well as water pollution: Claudio Prigioni, Alessandro Balestrieri and Luigi Remonti, 'Decline and Recovery in Otter *Lutra*

Lutra Populations in Italy', *Mammal Review*, XXXVII/1 (2007), pp. 71, 73, 75.

163 Giuseppe Spatola, 'Un Po per tutti: Il grande fiume in festa', *Corriere della Sera*, 15 June 2002.

164 Legambiente, *Operazione Po: Campagna nazionale per la valutazione ambientale del fiume Po e la promozione della sostenibilità* (Rome: [15 July 2005]).

165 The launch took place at Slow Fish, a biennial event in Genoa to raise awareness of sustainable fish consumption, at www.slowfood.com (accessed 16 March 2012).

166 Henry Skrine, *A General Account of All Rivers of Note in Great Britain* (London, 1801), p. 412; S. C. and A. M. Hall, *The Book of the Thames* (London, 1859), pp. v, 1. On the deterioration of the Thames's health in the nineteenth century, see Tricia Cusack, *Riverscapes and National Identities* (Syracuse, NY, 2010), pp. 72–82, 92–4.

## 4 Mersey

1 Giovanni Botero, *A Treatise Concerning the Causes of the Magnificencie and Greatnes of Cities, Devided into Three Bookes by Sig. Giovanni Botero, in the Italian Tongue; Now Done into English*, Book 1, trans. Robert Peterson (London, 1606 [1588]), pp. 26, 20.

2 Thomas Baines, *History of the Commerce and Town of Liverpool, and of the Rise of Manufacturing Industry in the Adjoining Counties* (Liverpool, 1852), pp. 27–9.

3 Lewis Mumford, *Technics and Civilization* (London, 1934), pp. 60–61.

4 City of Liverpool/James A. Picton, *Selections from the Municipal Archives and Records, from the 13th to the 17th Century Inclusive* (Liverpool, 1883), vol. I, p. xi.

5 Baines, *History of Liverpool*, p. 661; James Wallace, *A General and Descriptive History of the Ancient and Present State of the Town of Liverpool* (Liverpool, 1795), pp. 23, 92. On the other hand, a 12-foot statue of the god of the Mersey (by William Birnie Rhind and E. O. Griffith) topped one of the two end towers of the Cotton Exchange (1906). In his left hand, he holds an anchor, tiller and strip of rope. His right hand pours water from an urn onto a dolphin. The statue now sits on the pavement outside the building on Old Hall Street: Terry Cavanagh, *Public Sculpture of Liverpool* (Liverpool, 1997), pp. 74, 123.

6 Baines, *History of Liverpool*, pp. 38–9; Henry Skrine, *A General Account of All Rivers of Note in Great Britain* (London, 1801), p. 167.

7 Peter Elson (*Liverpool Daily Post* journalist), quoted in Lew Baxter and Guy Woodland, *Liverpool: World Waterfront City* (Chester, 2008), p. 40.

8 Kate Fox, 'Mersey People: The Politician: Michael Heseltine', in *Mersey: The River that Changed the World*, ed. Ian Wray (Liverpool, 2007), p. 62.

9  Wallace, *General and Descriptive History*, p. 23.

10 Thomas Baines, *Observations on the Present State of the Affairs of the River Plate* (Liverpool, 1845), pp. 8–9.

11 A late nineteenth-century campaigner for cleaner rivers recognized the Mersey as one of Britain's 'first class' rivers: Robert T. Cooper, *Our Empire of Rivers* (London, 1886), p. 17.

12 Francis E. Hyde, *Liverpool and the Mersey: An Economic History of a Port, 1700–1970* (Newton Abbot, Devon, 1971), p. xv.

13 Ron Freethy, *The Natural History of Rivers* (Lavenham, 1986), p. 3.

14 T. Q., *A Wall-street Bear in Europe, With his Familiar Foreign Journal of a Tour Through Portions of England, Scotland, France and Italy* (New York, 1855), p. 223.

15 'Great Britain: Queensway', *Time*, 30 July 1934, at www.time.com (accessed 15 May 2012). To mark the tunnel's sixtieth anniversary, the Royal Liverpool Philharmonic Orchestra performed 200 feet under the river on 17 July 1994.

16 Emil Lengyel, *The Danube* (London, 1940), pp. 118–19.

17 Bernard Newman, *The Blue Danube: Black Forest to Black Sea* (London, 1935), p. 69.

18 Billy Fury interview, BBC Radio 1, 1973, at www.bbc.co.uk/archive (accessed 19 March 2012); Paul Du Noyer, *Liverpool: Wondrous Place: Music from Cavern to Cream* (London, 2002), p. 10.

19 Bill Harry, 'Introduction', *Mersey Beat: The Beginnings of The Beatles*, ed. Bill Harry (New York, 1977), p. 14. The regular round-up of news items was called 'Mersey Roundabout': *Mersey Beat*, 1/2 (20 July – 3 August 1961), p. 1. In October 1963, the BBC screened a 30-minute documentary entitled 'The Mersey Sound': *Mersey Beat*, 24 October – 7 November 1963, in *Mersey Beat*, p. 60.

20 Leigh, *Let's Go Down the Cavern* (London, 1984), p. 49. *The Mersey Sound* (1967), volume 10 in the Penguin Modern Poets series, testifies to the power of place to shape creative expression. The best-selling poetry anthology of all time, dedicated to a trio of Liverpool poets of the 1960s (Adrian Henri, Roger McGough and Brian Patten), it was the only volume in the series that carried a specific name.

21 'Model Collaboration', *Research Intelligence* (University of Liverpool), 19 (February 2004), p. 1.

22 The Beatles, *The Beatles Anthology* (London, 2000), p. 101.

23 *The Beat Goes On: From the Beatles to the Zutons* (Liverpool, 2008), pp. 4–5; Anthony Wilson, 'Westward Ho!', in *Mersey: River that Changed the World*, pp. 98, 100.

24 Anon., 'The Mersey', in *Industrial Rivers of the United Kingdom, by Various Well-known Experts* (London, 1888), pp. 42–3; William Hadfield, *Brazil and the River Plate, 1870–76* (London, 1877), pp. 18, 61, 63, 73, 138.

25 John Haskell Kemble, *History of the Cunard Steamship Company* (Liverpool, 1886),

pp. 14, 16; *Official Guide and Album of the Cunard Steamship Company* (London, 1877), p. 16; Francis E. Hyde, *Cunard and the North Atlantic, 1840–1973: A History of Shipping and Financial Management* (London, 1975), p. 35.

26 *The Beat Goes On: From the Beatles to the Zutons*, p. 4; Noyer, *Wondrous Place*, pp. 53–5. The claim that the Cunard Yanks were also the main conduit for early rock 'n' roll records (Harry, 'Introduction', *Mersey Beat*, p. 7) is harder to substantiate. According to Spencer Leigh, early rock 'n' roll records were available for purchase in Britain soon after American release: Leigh, *Let's Go Down the Cavern*, p. 30; Leigh, 'Growing up with the Beatles', in *The Beat Goes On: Liverpool, Popular Music and the Changing City*, ed. Marion Leonard and Rob Strachan (Liverpool, 2010), pp. 35–6; Noyer, *Wondrous Place*, pp. 56–58. An additional source of access to American music was the radio station 'Air Force Network' that served GIs at the nearby Burtonwood air base: Text board, 'Sailors, Servicemen and Touring Musicians', 'The Beat Goes On: From the Beatles to the Zutons', Exhibition, World Museum, Liverpool, 12 July 2008 to 1 November 2009; Marion Leonard, 'Historical Approaches to Merseybeat', in *The Beat Goes On: Liverpool, Popular Music and the Changing City*, pp. 18–19. George Harrison's father worked for a while as a Cunard steward: Joshua M. Greene, *Here Comes the Sun: The Spiritual and Musical Journey of George Harrison* (Hoboken, NJ, 2006), p. 6; Sara Cohen, *Decline, Renewal and the City in Popular Music Culture: Beyond the Beatles* (Aldershot, 2007), p. 82.

27 Heseltine, 'The Politician', in *Mersey: River that Changed the World*, p. 62.

28 H. Waddington, 'Instructions to Commissioners', 30 May 1865, in *First Report of the Commissioners Appointed in 1868 to Inquire into the Best Means of Preventing the Pollution of Rivers (Mersey and Ribble Basins)*, vol. 1, *Report and Plans* (London, 1870), p. v.

29 James Johnstone, 'The Fishes of Cheshire and Liverpool Bay', in *The Vertebrate Fauna of Cheshire and Liverpool Bay*, ed. T. A. Coward (London, 1910), vol. II, p. 148.

30 Alan Weston, *Liverpool Daily Post*, 23 September 2009.

31 Ron Freethy, *The River Mersey* (Lavenham, 1985), p. 167.

32 Daniel King, *The Vale-royall of England, or, the County Palatine of Chester* (London, 1656), p. 21.

33 Thomas Baines, *Lancashire and Cheshire, Past and Present: A History and a Description of the Palatine Counties of Lancaster and Chester* (London, 1868), vol. I, pp. 94–102; 'The Mersey', *Encyclopaedia Britannica*, vol. XVIII (Cambridge, 1911), p. 174.

34 John Aikin, *A Description of the Country from Thirty to Forty Miles Round Manchester* (London, 1795), p. 40; Anon., 'Mersey', p. 21; Charles Knight, *The English Cyclopaedia: A New Dictionary of Universal Knowledge*, vol. II: *Geography* (London, 1854), pp. 441, 721.

35  Matthew Sutcliffe, 'Who Saved the Mersey?', *Source NW*, 20 (September 2009), p. 13.

36  David Ward, 'Along the Banks', in *Mersey: River That Changed the World*, p. 139. In 2001, Stockport council floated a proposal to fit glass panels within the shopping centre's pavements: 'Mersey View Plan for Shoppers', *Manchester Evening* News, 7 December 2001.

37  Freethy, *Mersey*, pp. 5–6; Chris Baines, 'Wild Mersey', in *Mersey: River that Changed the World*, p. 113; William Robinson, *The Mersey and Irwell With Their Principal Tributaries* (Manchester, 1888), p. 5.

38  Anon., 'Mersey', p. 19; Robinson, *Mersey and Irwell*, p. 6.

39  Baines, *Lancashire and Cheshire*, vol. I, pp. 100–02.

40  Kathleen E. Carpenter, *Life in Inland Waters, With Especial Reference to Animals* (London, 1928), pp. 135–77.

41  Skrine, *General Account of All Rivers of Note*, p. 167.

42  W. Henry Hunter, *Rivers and Estuaries, or, Streams and Tides: An Elementary Study* (London, 1913), p. 54.

43  Quoted in H. C. Darby, 'Foreword' to J. E. Allison, *The Mersey Estuary* (Liverpool, 1949), vii.

44  Hunter, *Rivers and Estuaries*, p. 52.

45  William T. Palmer, *The River Mersey* (London, 1944), p. 231.

46  Hunter, *Rivers and Estuaries*, p. 52.

47  Bosdin Leech, *History of the Manchester Ship Canal*, vol. II (Manchester, 1907), p. 24.

48  'Charity Walker Crosses the Mersey', *BBC News*, 13 August 2006; Rory Smith, 'River Walk Alone', *Daily Mirror*, 14 August 2006.

49  Botero, *Treatise*, pp. 26, 28.

50  Carl Ritter, *Comparative Geography*, trans. William L. Gage (Edinburgh, 1865), p. 171.

51  H. R. Wilkinson, *Merseyside: Introduction to Local Geography* (Liverpool, 1948), p. 10; Hunter, *Rivers and Estuaries*, p. 56.

52  Darby, 'Foreword', in Allison, *Mersey Estuary*, p. vii.

53  Baines, *Lancashire and Cheshire*, vol. I, p. 19; Graham H. Hills, *Essay on the Hydrography of the Mersey Estuary* (Liverpool, 1858), pp. 7–8.

54  Allison, *Mersey Estuary*, p. 17.

55  Ibid., p. 59.

56  J. S. Howson, *The River Dee: Its Aspect and History* (London, 1889), pp. 4–5, 98, 121–2.

57  Wilkinson, *Merseyside*, p. 45.

58  James Winter, *Secure from Rash Assault: Sustaining the Victorian Environment* (Berkeley, 1999), p. 117.

59  *Pigot and Company's Pocket Atlas, Topography and Gazetteer of England: Cheshire* (London, 1838), p. 16; 'Interview: Mersey People: Coral Dranfield: Local Historian',

Mersey Basin Campaign Archive, 1985–2010 (MBCA), at www.merseybasin.org.uk (accessed 19 March 2012).

60  *Selections from Municipal Archives and Records*, vol. I, p. 241; ibid., vol. II (1886), p. 240. The stretch from Runcorn to Warrington was rendered navigable by the end of the seventeenth century, and the Mersey and Irwell Navigation Company (1721) initiated further improvement works. By 1734, barges could travel to Manchester via weirs and locks: Ramsay Muir, *A History of Liverpool* (London, 1907), pp. 178, 256.

61  Mr Schoolbred, address, Liverpool Polytechnic Society, 18 December 1876, in Benjamin Blower, *The Mersey: Ancient and Modern* (Liverpool, 1878), pp. 54–5. The 1842 Act addressed objections from the upper river, represented by the Mersey and Irwell Navigation Company, to the Corporation of Liverpool's stranglehold over navigation decisions: Vawser, *Mersey*, pp. 6–7.

62  Aikin, *Description of the Country*, p. 105.

63  Baines, *History of Liverpool*, pp. 38, 560; *Selections from Municipal Archives and Records*, vol. II, pp. 144–5.

64  H. Yule Oldham, 'The Manchester Ship Canal', *Geographical Journal*, III/6 (June 1894), p. 485. The Bridgewater Canal connected the Duke of Bridgewater's collieries at Worsley with Manchester, 7 miles away.

65  The river lost even more of its immediate value as a liquid highway after 1830, when a railway joined the two cities.

66  Wilkinson, *Merseyside*, p. 45; Ted Gray, *A Hundred Years of the Manchester Ship Canal* (Bolton, 1993), p. 21; Owen, *Manchester Ship Canal*, pp. 18–21.

67  Oldham, 'Manchester Ship Canal', p. 486.

68  Winter, *Secure from Rash Assault*, p. 121; Leveson Francis Vernon-Harcourt, *A Treatise on Rivers and Canals* (Oxford, 1882), vol. I, pp. 263–5.

69  'Manchester-sur-Mer. A Sea-ductive Prospect', *Punch*, 7 October 1882, p. 158; Gray, *One Hundred Years*, pp. 33–49; Leech, *History of Manchester Ship Canal*, vol. II, pp. 210–12; 'Manchester Ship Canal Opened: Two Million of Her Subjects Cheer Queen Victoria on Her Way', *New York Times*, 22 May 1894; *Journal and Proceedings, Institute of Sewage Purification*, Part 1 (1949), p. 258; Queen Victoria, *The Letters of Queen Victoria*, 3rd Series, vol. II: *1891–95*, ed. George Earle Buckle (London, 1931), p. 401.

70  Cyril J. Wood, *Manchester's Ship Canal: The Big Ditch* (Stroud, Gloucestershire, 2005).

71  Three openings permit the influx of water from the estuary at high tide, to save this remarkably thin barrier from collapse under high tidal pressure.

72  Braithwaite Poole, *The Commerce of Liverpool* (Liverpool, 1854), pp. 34–6, 46; Baines, *History of Liverpool*, p. 763.

73  *Selections from Municipal Archives and Records,* vol. I, p. 300.

74  R. Vawser, *The Mersey* (Warrington, 1876), p. 5.

75  Blower, *Mersey*, p. 44. Only the powerful cheesemongers complained, maintaining their right to 'stick their ships in the mud as their fathers had done', without payment of duties: Hyde, *Liverpool and Mersey*, p. 13; *Selections from Municipal Archives and Records*, vol. II, p. 48.

76  Dixon Scott, *Liverpool* (London, 1907), pp. ix, 3–4, 6, 14.

77  Aikin, *Description of the Country*, p. 344.

78  Baines, *History of Liverpool*, p. 743.

79  Review of Baines, *History of the Commerce and Town of Liverpool* (1852), *The Economist*, 466 (31 July 1852), pp. 852–3; Baines, *History of the Commerce and Town of Liverpool*, pp. 764, 840; Baines, *Lancashire and Cheshire*, vol. I, pp. 17, 25.

80  Baines, *History of Liverpool*, pp. 764, 841.

81  Scott, *Liverpool*, p. 31; Baines, *History of Liverpool*, p. 812; Thomas Forester, *The Danube and the Black Sea* (London, 1857), p. 151; George J. S. Broomhall and John H. Hubback, *Corn Trade Memories: Recent and Remote* (Liverpool, 1930), pp. 36, 71–2, 101; Morton Rothstein, 'Centralizing Firms and Spreading Markets: The World of International Grain Traders, 1846–1914', *Business and Economic History*, 2nd Series, 17 (1988), p. 105; Rothstein, 'Multinationals in the Grain Trade, 1850–1914', *Business and Economic History*, Second Series, 12 (1983), p. 87.

82  Elias Canetti, *Die Gerettete Zunge: Geschichte einer Jugend* (Frankfurt am Main, 1977), pp. 54–5, 64–5.

83  '*Flüsse und Berge*' (discarded manuscript), Papers of Elias Canetti, Box 222, Central Library, Zurich, as quoted in Sven Hanuschek, *Elias Canetti: Biographie* (Munich, 2005), pp. 45, 696.

84  Ian Wray, 'Time and the River', in *Mersey: River That Changed the World*, p. 10.

85  Blower, *Mersey*, p. 7.

86  T. Q., *Wall-Street Bear in Europe*, pp. 224–5; Rev. George Gilfillan, 'Reminiscences of a Tour of England – No. 1', *Hogg's Weekly Instructor*, XVI/131 (28 August 1847), pp. 3–4.

87  Anon., 'Mersey', p. 21.

88  P. D. Jones, 'Water Quality and Fisheries in the Mersey Estuary, England: A Historical Perspective', *Marine Pollution Bulletin*, 53 (2006), p. 147. The first stage of tanning produced soak water, then treatment with lime and sodium sulphide resulted in lime water, and the final process contributed spent tan liquors heavy with carbon and nitrogen.

89  'Liverpool Chemists' Association Excursion', *Pharmaceutical Journal and Transactions*, 2nd Series, V/2 (1863–4), pp. 55–6; A. E. Jarvis and P. N. Reed, 'Where There's Brass There's Muck: The Impact of Industry in the Mersey Basin, c. 1700–1900', in *Ecology and Landscape Development: A History of the Mersey*

*Basin: Proceedings of a Conference Held at Merseyside Maritime Museum, Liverpool, 5–6 July 1996*, ed. E. F. Greenwood (Liverpool, 1999), pp. 60–62.

90  Anon., 'Mersey', p. 19; J. Fenwick Allen, *Some Founders of the Chemical Industry: Men to be Remembered* (Manchester, 1907), pp. viii–ix.

91  R. L. Sherlock, *Man as a Geological Agent: An Account of his Action on Inanimate Nature* (London, 1922), p. 294; Palmer, *Mersey*, p. 139; Eunice M. Schofield, 'Working Class Food and Cooking in 1900', *Folk Life: Journal of Ethnological Studies*, 13 (1975), p. 16.

92  Élisée Reclus, *Earth and its Inhabitants*, vol. IV: *British Isles* (New York, 1881), p. 271; Robinson, *Mersey and Irwell*, p. 15; George E. Diggle, *A History of Widnes* (Widnes, 1961), p. 71.

93  Freethy, *Mersey*, p. 114. In April 1970, petrol spilled onto the Manchester Ship Canal caught fire.

94  Arthur Redford, *The History of Local Government in Manchester*, vol. II (London, 1940), p. 380; Vawser, *Mersey*, p. 7.

95  Rivers Pollution Commission, *Basins of the Rivers Mersey, Ribble, and Their Tributaries*: Queries Relating to Cities, Boroughs, Towns and Local Board Districts Situate in these Watersheds; Answers on Behalf of the Corporation of the City of Manchester: Evidence – Answers to Queries – Part II, Series, A,B,C,D, Trades and Manufactures – Mersey Basin (River Irwell) (Manchester, 1868), pp. 6–7, 141.

96  Winter, *Secure from Rash Assault*, p. 118.

97  John Hassan, *A History of Water in Modern England and Wales* (Manchester, 1998), pp. 32, 121.

98  T. W. Freeman, 'The Manchester Conurbation', in *Manchester and its Region: A Survey Prepared for the Meeting Held in Manchester 29 August – 5 September 1962* (Manchester, 1962), p. 54.

99  Frederick Engels, *The Condition of the Working Class in England in 1844* (Teddington, 2009 [1845]), p. 51.

100  Rivers Pollution Commission, *Basins of the Rivers Mersey, Ribble, and Their Tributaries*, p. 141.

101  Quoted in Peter D. Jones, 'The Mersey Estuary – "Back from the Dead?", Solving a 150-Year Old Problem', *Journal of the Chartered Institution of Water and Environmental Management*, 14 (April 2000), p. 124.

102  Sherlock, *Man as Geological Agent*, p. 295.

103  L. R. Burton, 'The Mersey Basin: An Historical Assessment of Water Quality from an Anecdotal Perspective', *The Science of the Total Environment*, 314–16 (1 October 2003), p. 60; Cyril Bracegirdle, *The Dark River* (Altrincham, 1973), p. 52.

104  Jarvis and Reed, 'Where There's Brass There's Muck', p. 59.

105  R. Kane (1880s), quoted in Leech, *History of Manchester Ship Canal*, vol. II, p. 21.

106  Testimony of Thomas Baraham Foster (Trafford Estate representative) and W. H.
     Watson before a House of Commons committee in 1883; reported in Leech,
     *Manchester Ship Canal*, vol. 1, p. 161. In fact, with the combination of narrow neck
     and wide, shallow tidal basin, polluted water entering at the tidal limit in
     Warrington can require up to a month to flush out into Liverpool Bay: *Mersey Basin
     Campaign: New Life for the North West* (Liverpool, September 1986), p. 3, MBCA.
     On the boomerang effect of tides in this respect, see John Kempster, *Our Rivers*
     (London, 1948), p. 55.

107  Anthony S. Wohl, *Endangered Lives: Public Health in Victorian Britain* (London,
     1983), pp. 238–40.

108  Burton, 'Mersey Basin', p. 54; Palmer, *Mersey*, p. 39; Freethy, *Mersey*, p. 1.

109  Robert Wood et al./Mersey Basin Campaign (MBC), 'Building a Healthier Economy
     Through a Cleaner Environment: Mid-term Report', Manchester, November 1997,
     p. 6, MBCA.

110  Charles Kingsley, *The Water-babies: A Fairy Tale for a Land-baby* (London, 1863),
     p. 23; Kingsley, *Poems* (London, 1889), p. 302.

111  *Charles Kingsley: His Letters and Memories of his Life*, ed. Frances E. Kingsley,
     (London, 1877), vol. II, pp. 322–3.

112  King, *Vale-Royall of England*, p. 22. On pre-industrial salmon abundance, see also
     *Selections from the Municipal Archives and Records*, vol. 1, pp. 48, 87; Robert
     Griffiths, *The History of the Royal and Ancient Park of Toxteth, Liverpool* (Liverpool,
     1907), pp. 115–17.

113  Johnstone, 'Fishes of Cheshire and Liverpool Bay', pp. 148–9; *Manchester Guardian*,
     23 June 1894.

114  Winston M. Fox et al., 'The Use of Sediment Cores from Stable and Developing Salt
     Marshes to Reconstruct Historical Contamination Profiles in the Mersey Estuary,
     UK', *Marine Environmental Research*, 47 (1999), p. 318; Kenneth Mellanby, *The DDT
     Story* (Farnham, 1992), pp. 19–20.

115  Department of the Environment, *Report of a River Pollution Survey of England and
     Wales, 1970* (London, 1971), vol. 1, p. 23; vol. II *(Discharges and Forecasts of
     Improvement)* (1972), pp. 66, 122. The bulk of the Mersey was placed in the lowest
     class (four), which denoted 'grossly polluted'.

116  J. W. Eaton et al., 'Biological Change in the Freshwaters of the Mersey Basin', in
     *Ecology and Landscape Development*, pp. 139, 157–8; T. A. Coward and C. Oldham,
     'The Mammals and Birds of Cheshire and Liverpool Bay', in *Vertebrate Fauna of
     Cheshire and Liverpool Bay*, vol. 1, pp. 30–31; Griffiths, *History of Toxteth*, pp. 115–
     17. Otterspool on the Goyt, shortly beyond its confluence with the Etherow, was
     also otter-less by the 1880s: Robinson, *Mersey and Irwell*, p. 8.

117  Palmer, *Mersey*, pp. 10, 16, 18, 37–8.

118  Jones, 'Mersey Estuary – "Back from the Dead?"', p. 150; Sutcliffe, 'Who Saved the
     Mersey?', p. 11; [Peter Walton, Department of the Environment, North West
     Regional Office, Manchester], 'Cleaning up the Mersey: Contribution to a Mersey
     Conference Convened by the Secretary of State for the Environment', Department
     of the Environment Letter and Consultation Paper/Ward, Ashcroft and Parkman,
     Liverpool, February 1983, p. 3, MBCA. This briefing paper was prepared for a
     conference on the Mersey chaired by Heseltine's successor, Tom King, on 18 March
     1983, at Daresbury, Cheshire, a few miles south of the river: Ian Gilfoyle (Deputy
     County Planner, Cheshire), 'Memories of the Mersey Basin Campaign', 31 July
     2000, p. 1, MBCA; Freethy, *Mersey*, p. 27.

119  Palmer, *Mersey*, p. 39.

120  Michael Heseltine, *Life in the Jungle: My Autobiography* (London, 2000), p. 217;
     'Foreword by Michael Heseltine' and 'Reflections on the Saving of a Mighty River',
     in Baxter and Woodland, *Liverpool: World Waterfront City*, pp. 17, 46–7.

121  The unpublished memorandum was leaked to Peter Hennessy and *The Times*:
     'Private information', Peter Hennessy, *Whitehall* (London, 1989), p. 699.

122  Michael Heseltine, Foreword to [Walton], 'Cleaning up the Mersey', p. 1; Paul
     Unger, 'The Flow of Events', in *Mersey: River that Changed the World*, p. 122; Jones,
     'The Mersey Estuary – "Back from the Dead?"', p. 127; Alan Dunn, 'Start Made on
     £2 Billion Plan to Clean Up the Mersey', *Guardian*, 23 November 1982. The
     replacement of antiquated sewage plants began in the early 1960s: 'Millions Spent
     in Fight for Cleaner Rivers', *Guardian*, 15 January 1962.

123  Patrick Jenkin (Secretary of State for the Environment), 'Mersey Clean-up Initiative
     Moves to Third Stage', Manchester, 16 March 1984 (Press release, Department of
     the Environment), quoted in Freethy, *Mersey*, pp. 26–8; A. Wright and B. Bendell,
     'Mersey Basin Campaign: A Partnership Approach to River Basin Management',
     IWA Watershed & River Basin Management Specialist Group Workshop,
     Marrakech, Morocco, September 2004, pp. 1–2, 4–7.

124  [Walton], 'Cleaning up the Mersey', p. 4. Walton acknowledged that sewerage
     improvement works over the previous decade had already markedly improved
     water quality in the river (p. 5). The new £300 million primary wastewater treat-
     ment works at the former Sandon Dock (operational since 1989), part of the
     Mersey Estuary Pollution Alleviation Scheme, replaced 28 individual outfalls of
     crude sewage with the 'third Mersey tunnel' (Merseyside Interceptor Sewer): Wood
     et al./MBC, 'Building a Healthier Economy Through a Cleaner Environment', p. 13.

125  Wood et al./MBC, 'Building a Healthier Economy Through a Cleaner Environment',
     pp. 3–5.

126  'Revitalising Rivers', Transcript, 'Earthbeat,' ABC Radio National (Australia),
     8 October 1999, at www.abc.net.au (accessed 6 December 2012); Walter Menzies

(chief executive, Mersey Basin Campaign), 'The River that Changed the World', in International Riverfoundation, *River Journeys II* (Brisbane, 2010), pp. 12–15.

127 Substantial improvements have brought fresh designations. In 1995, the estuary was designated a Special Protection Area (SPA) and a Ramsar site (a designation under the International [Ramsar, Iran] Convention on Wetlands of International Importance). Currently the ninth most important UK wetland site, no European estuary hosts more birds.

128 Jones, 'Mersey Estuary – "Back from the Dead?"', p. 129; Wood et al./MBC, 'Building a Healthier Economy Through a Cleaner Environment', pp. 18–19. By 2003, the minimum recorded dissolved oxygen concentration in estuarine waters was 66 per cent: Jones, 'Water Quality and Fisheries in the Mersey Estuary', p. 150.

129 Paul Waley, 'What's a River without Fish?: Symbol, Space and Ecosystem in the Waterways of Japan', in *Animal Spaces, Beastly Places*, ed. Chris Philo and Chris Wilbert (London, 2000), pp. 159–81.

130 Wood et al./MBC, 'Building a Healthier Economy Through a Cleaner Environment', pp. 15, 17; S. J. Hawkins et al., 'Liverpool Bay and the Estuaries: Human Impact, Recent Recovery and Restoration', in *Ecology and Landscape Development*, p. 158; Elson, 'Quality of the Mersey is Now Famed'.

131 Elson, 'Quality of the Mersey is Now Famed'; S. J. Hawkins et al., 'Liverpool Bay and the Estuaries: Human Impact, Recent Recovery and Restoration', p. 159; Sutcliffe, 'Who Saved the Mersey?', p. 19.

132 Jones, 'Water Quality and Fisheries in the Mersey Basin', p. 152; Nick Towle, 'Salmon have been spotted in the River Mersey for the first time in 200 years', *South Manchester Reporter*, 25 August 2005, at www.southmanchesterreporter.co.uk (accessed 19 March 2012).

133 Owen Ashmore, *The Industrial Archaeology of North-west England* (Manchester, 1982), p. 139; 'Interview: Mersey People Part 2: Irene Dooley: The Bleachworker', p. 1, MBCA.

134 Correspondence from Rachel Bennett, Countryside Ranger, Heaton Mersey, Cheadle and Gatley Area, 3 August 2010; 'Interview: Mersey People Part 2: Rachael Bennett: The Ranger', MBCA.

135 'Saving the Celebrity Salmon' June 2007, MBCA.

136 United Nations Environment Program, 'Further Rise in Number of Marine "Dead Zones"', 19 October 2006, at www.unep.org (accessed 19 March 2012).

137 Anon., 'Mersey', pp. 20–21.

138 'River Mersey dress', www.liverpoolmuseums.org.uk at Accession Number 1979.269A (accessed 19 March 2012 and visited 16 April 2012).

139 David Fleming, 'Reflections on the Exoticism of Liverpool', in Baxter and Woodland, *Liverpool: World Waterfront City*, pp. 214–15.

140 John Tavaré, 'Introduction by the Chairman of the Campaign Organisation', *Mersey Basin Campaign: New Life for the North West* (Liverpool, September 1986), p. 2, MBCA.

141 Scott, *Liverpool*, pp. 7, 15.

142 Sophie Armour, 'Stockport Shows us Some Mersey', *Manchester Evening News*, 4 September 2008. The exhibition ran between 6 September and 1 November 2008.

143 'The Publican: Dave Hall', in *Mersey: River that Changed the World*, p. 61.

144 'Interview: Mersey People: Helen Clapcott', MBCA.

145 Curators responded to criticisms with a creative photography course to encourage locals to contribute their own images. Participants' photographs, based on a river walk in Stockport, suggested an effort to re-insert the river firmly into the city's identity.

146 'Map of Route to Klondike', *Liverpool Mercury*, 22 December 1897; 'Nautical Jottings', 24 December 1897.

147 Advertisement, *London Standard*, 4 April 1989; *The Times*, 5 April 1898.

148 Advertisement, *Liverpool Mercury*, 26 November 1897.

149 At www.wirraltalks.co.uk (accessed 19 March 2012); correspondence from Arthur Maltby, 19 September 2011.

150 Jack London, *The God of His Fathers and Other Stories* (New York, 1901), p. 104; London, *The Red One* (New York, 1918]), pp. 89–141; Franklin Walker, *Jack London and the Klondike: The Genesis of an American Writer* (San Marino, 1966), p. 80.

## 5 Yukon

1 Steve Chapple, 'Taming the Wild Trickle: A Gray-Water Adventure on the Mighty L.A.', *LA Weekly*, 11 March 1999.

2 W. H. Dall, *The Narrative of W. H. Dall, Leader of the Expedition to Alaska in 1866–1868*, in *The Yukon Territory* (London, 1898), p. 41. This chapter includes measurement in miles, feet and inches as well as kilometres, metres and centimetres. The use of the former reflects the system employed in a particular source.

3 Frederick Whymper, *Travel and Adventure in the Territory of Alaska* (London, 1868), p. 164. Whymper's 'excuse' for not including more sketches of the river was that, to do it justice, an artist would have to 'make its width out of all proportion to its height' (pp. 164–5).

4 Dall, *Narrative*, p. 102. A Russian and two Canadians had already undertaken this journey.

5 Élisée Reclus, *The Earth and its Inhabitants: North America; British North America* (New York, 1890), vol. I, pp. 125, 115.

6   William Ogilvie, 'The Geography and Resources of the Yukon Basin,' *Geographical Journal,* xii/1 (July 1898), p. 31.

7   George M. Dawson, *The Narrative of an Exploration Made in 1887 in the Yukon District*, in *The Yukon Territory*, p. 251.

8   George M. Dawson, *Historical Notes on the Yukon District* (Toronto, 1898), p. 6; Dawson, *Narrative of an Exploration*, p. 251; Alexander Hunter Murray, *Journal of the Yukon, 1847–48*, ed. L. J. Burpee (Ottawa, 1910), p. 19.

9   Frederick Schwatka, *Along Alaska's Great River* (New York, 1885).

10  Ivan Petroff, *Report on the Population, Industries, and Resources of Alaska* (Washington, DC, 1884), p. 10. Petroff's claim is disputed by Dawson, *Narrative of an Exploration*, p. 253; Eric Ingersoll, *Golden Alaska: A Compete Account to Date of the Yukon Valley* (Chicago, 1897), p. 76.

11  F.M.F. Skene, *Wayfaring Sketches among the Greeks and Turks, and On the Shores of the Danube* (London, 1847), p. 287.

12  Reclus, *North America*, vol. i, p. 125; Ogilvie, 'Geography and Resources,' p. 21. The Topographical Survey of Canada tasked Ogilvie with establishing where the international boundary (141st meridian) crossed the Yukon.

13  Whymper, *Travel and Adventure*, p. 196. Three Yukon tributaries (Porcupine, Koyukuk and Tanana) are over 500 miles long. At their confluence, the Tanana is almost as large as the Yukon: Dall, *Narrative*, p. 93.

14  Martin Heidegger, *Hölderlins Hymne 'Der Ister'* (Frankfurt am Main, 1984), pp. 68, 86; *Hölderlin's Hymn "The Ister"*, trans. William McNeill and Julia Davis (Bloomington, IN, 1996), pp. 54–5, 66.

15  John Hildebrand, *Reading the River: A Voyage down the Yukon* (Boston, 1988), p. 32.

16  Richard K. Mathews, *The Yukon* (New York, 1968), p. 7.

17  Skinner, 'Rivers and American Folk', Appendix to Carl Lamson Carmer, *The Hudson* (New York, 1939), n.p.; Dorothy D. Adams, 'Biographical Sketch', in *Constance Lindsay Skinner: Author and Editor*, ed. Ann Heidbreder Eastman (New York, 1980), p. 25. John Y. Cole, 'Preface', in Carol Fitzgerald, *The Rivers of America: A Descriptive Bibliography* (Washington, DC, 2001), vol. i, p. ix; Ivan R. Dee (book review), *New York Times*, 8 September 1974, p. 33.

18  Frank Waters, *The Colorado* (New York, 1946), p. xi; Frederick Way, *The Allegheny* (New York, 1942).

19  Fitzgerald, 'The Yukon', in *Rivers of America: A Descriptive Bibliography*, vol. ii, pp. 808–15; Mathews, *Yukon*, rear dust jacket and p. 7.

20  'Yukon River', at www.ccge.org (accessed 14 March 2012).

21  Hudson Stuck, *Voyages on the Yukon and Its Tributaries: A Narrative of Summer Travel in the Interior of Alaska* (New York, 1917), p. 17; Schwatka, 'Exploration of the Yukon River in 1883', *Journal of the American Geographical Society of New York,*

16 (1884), p. 382. There are no established rules for measuring a river. A calculation based on drawing a line straight down the middle – the axis (Dall's and Schwatka's method) – will differ from one based on the 'travelled' distance, which, following the navigation channel, often swings from side to side (Raymond's method). Direction also affects travelled distance: Captain Charles W. Raymond, *Report of a Reconnaissance of the Yukon River, Alaska Territory, July to September 1869* (Washington, DC, 1871), p. 61. National Park Service publications cite the figure 1,979 miles.

22  Petroff, *Report*, p. 81.

23  In situ astronomical observations confirmed that Fort Yukon was in fact 129 kilometres beyond the Canadian frontier. The trading post was relocated east of the border.

24  Raymond, *Reconnaissance*, p. 98.

25  Ibid., p. 21; Charles W. Raymond, 'The Yukon River Region, Alaska', *Journal of the American Geographical Society*, 3 (1872), p. 21; Dawson, *Yukon Territory*, p. 252.

26  William Seymour Edwards, *In to the Yukon* (Cincinnati, 1909 [1904]), pp. 122, 128; Ingersoll, *Golden Alaska*, pp. 62, 75.

27  Dall, *Narrative*, p. 4; Stuck, *Voyages on Yukon*, p. 99.

28  Whymper, *Travel and Adventure*, pp. 179–80, 227–8; Stuck, *Voyages on Yukon*, p. 99; Raymond, *Reconnaissance*, p. 7.

29  Schwatka, *Exploring the Great Yukon* (New York, 1890), pp. 207–8, 212; Schwatka, 'Exploration of the Yukon River', p. 346.

30  Schwatka, *Exploring the Great Yukon*, p. 212.

31  Dawson, *Narrative of an Exploration*, pp. 251, 352.

32  'Old Landmarks Removed: Names Associated with the Yukon Materially Altered', *Klondike Nugget* (1899), at http://explorenorth.com (accessed 15 May 2012)

33  Dawson, *Narrative of an Exploration*, p. 252.

34  The Board's decision caught up with local usage within the affected area, where it was advantageous to be part of the Yukon (the name Lewes lacked resonance). The Lewes continued to appear on some unofficial maps in the 1950s: Darrell Hookey, 'The Lewes River', at http://explorenorth.com (accessed 14 March 2012). This article was first published as 'Naming the Yukon River (Lewes, Yukon River)', *The Yukoner Magazine*, 11 (1999).

35  'Principles and Procedures for Geographical Naming', Canadian Permanent Committee on Geographical Names (Natural Resources Canada, 1990), at www.nrcan.gc.ca (accessed 6 December 2012).

36  William Ogilvie, *Early Days on the Yukon and the Story of its Gold Finds* (London, 1913), p. 4.

37  M.H.E. Hayne and H. West Taylor, *The Pioneers of the Klondyke* (London, 1897),

p. 36; William B. Haskell, *Two Years in the Klondike and Alaskan Gold-fields* (Hartford, CT, 1898), p. 217.

38  Stuck, *Voyages on Yukon*, p. 124. Yanert used the term 'jungle' in conversation with Stuck, who often passed the riverside retirement cabin where Yanert lived for over 30 years. 'Niggerhead' was a common nineteenth-century term for an unstable tussock created by the freeze-thaw cycle. Progress across such ground was only possible by jumping from tussock to tussock.

39  Schwatka, 'The Middle Yukon – II', *Science*, III/71 (13 June 1884), p. 708.

40  Dall, *Narrative*, p. 119.

41  Dawson, *Narrative of an Exploration*, p. 360.

42  *Lieutenant Zagoskin's Travels in Russian America, 1842–1844: The First Ethnographic and Geographic Investigations in the Yukon and Kuskokwim Valleys of Alaska,* ed. Henry N. Michael (Toronto, 1967), p. 169.

43  Ogilvie, *Early Days*, p. 97; Edwards, *In to the Yukon*, p. 132.

44  Schwatka, 'Middle Yukon – II', p. 706; Jeremiah Lynch, *Three Years in the Klondike* (Chicago, 1904), p. 22.

45  Stuck, *Voyages on Yukon*, pp. 38–40. In winter, when discharge from volcanic soils and glaciers is staunched, the Yukon flows clear beneath the ice.

46  Dall, *Narrative*, p. 71; Whymper, *Travel and Adventure*, pp. 124–8.

47  Lynch, *Three Years*, pp. 4–5.

48  Stuck, *Voyages on Yukon*, p. 209.

49  Harry de Windt, 'Through the Goldfields of Alaska to Behring Straits', Royal Societies Club lecture, 23 September 1897, as reported in 'The Goldfields of Alaska', *The Times*, 24 September 1897; 'The Alaska Goldfields: Mr De Windt's Views', *Liverpool Mercury*, 18 September 1897. De Windt aborted his overland journey on reaching the coast of Siberia, where 'unfriendly natives' and the absence of any discernible travel route stymied further progress.

50  John R. Bockstoce, *Furs and Frontiers in the Far North: The Contest among Native and Foreign Nations for the Bering Strait Fur Trade* (New Haven, CT, 2009), pp. 178, 189, 198–9, 212–24, 301. The river also served as highway for the penetration of disease. Imported epidemics that first struck the coastal Chilkats in the Skagway also spread swiftly downriver with Native movement throughout the Yukon basin.

51  They departed on 26 May 1867 and reached their destination after 29 days, returning to St. Michael in just 15 days, thanks to the rapid current: Whymper, *Travel and Adventure*, pp. 195, 218, 233.

52  Dall, *Narrative*, pp. 82, 227; Whymper, *Travel and Adventure*, p. 195.

53  *Zagoskin's Travels*, pp. 162, 171, 173. According to Dall, Zagoskin's party was forced to turn back at the junction with the Nowitna. But Stuck reckons he made it up to

Rampart Canyon, which he thought was the head of navigation: *Voyages on Yukon*, pp. 136–7.

54 Ogilvie, *Early Days on the Yukon*, p. 6; Stuck, *Voyages on the Yukon*, p. 15.

55 Stuck, *Voyages on Yukon*, p. 87; Haskell, *Two Years*, p. 162.

56 Ogilvie, *Early Days*, p. 117. Others translated the name as 'plenty of fish': De Windt, 'Through the Goldfields of Alaska to Behring Straits'.

57 Haskell, *Two Years*, p. 243.

58 'The New Gold Diggings', *The Times*, 2 August 1897.

59 Robert C. Kirk, *Twelve Months in Klondike* (London, 1899), p. 4; Hayne and Taylor, *Pioneers of the Klondyke*, pp. xi–x, 10; Stuck, *Voyages on Yukon*, p. 213; A.C. Harris, *Alaska and the Klondike Gold Fields* (Chicago, 1897), pp. 129–31; 'The Yukon Goldfields', *The Times*, 29 July 1897.

60 'The Gold Discoveries: Particulars by a Liverpool Man', *Liverpool Mercury*, 21 July 1897.

61 *Report of Mr. W. T. Jennings, C.E., On Routes to the Yukon* (Ottawa, 1898), pp. 18–19. Chilkoot, which local Indians largely controlled, became obsolete in 1900, when the 161-kilometre, narrow gauge White Pass and Yukon Railroad was completed between Skagway and Whitehorse, the uppermost point on the river with a regular steamer service to the goldfields. When the centre of gravity of gold exploitation shifted west to Alaska after 1901, with strikes at Forty Mile, Fairbanks and along the Tanana, the railway route's advantages were largely forfeited.

62 Ogilvie, 'Geography and Resources', p. 23. The 'Rapids of the Yukon' in Rampart Canyon – where the river, falling twelve feet in half a mile and split into two channels by a granite island, runs at an accelerated seven miles per hour – presented few difficulties for those voyaging up to the Klondike. Russian traders and local Indians warned Dall's party that these falls might impede their journey. However, vessels larger than a canoe were unfazed: Dall, *Narrative*, p. 93; Whymper, *Travel and Adventure*, p. 213. Schwatka dubbed them 'the mildest rapids I had ever seen': Schwatka, 'Exploration of Yukon River', p. 374.

63 Schwatka, 'Exploration of Yukon River', p. 346; *Along Alaska's Great River*, pp. 95, 99, 149. At Nuklakayet, Schwatka's party abandoned the 'Resolute' and completed the trip to St. Michael on a 10-ton schooner (*barka*): 'Exploration of Yukon River', p. 375.

64 Schwatka, 'Exploration of Yukon River', pp. 355–6.

65 Ogilvie, 'Yukon Expedition, 1887', *Science*, 11 (272) (20 April 1888), p. 184.

66 Ogilvie, 'Yukon Expedition', p. 184; Haskell, *Two Years*, p. 125.

67 Schwatka, 'Exploration of Yukon River', pp. 355–6; Dawson, *Narrative of an Expedition*, p. 366. Ogilvie claims the rapids took the lives of thirteen greenhorns in 1895: Ogilvie, 'Geography and Resources', p. 23.

68  Kirk, *Twelve Months*, pp. 71–8; Charmian London, *The Book of Jack London* (New York, 1921), vol. I, pp. 232–3. London spent the winter of 1897–8 in a cabin on the upper of two islands in the Yukon near its confluence with the Stewart, 80 miles short of Dawson. Charmian gleaned details of his inward journey and sojourn at Upper Stewart Island from the letters and diaries of two of her late husband's compatriots.

69  Haskell, *Two Years*, p. 121.

70  Kirk, *Twelve Months*, pp. 74–5; Kathryn Morse, *The Nature of Gold: An Environmental History of the Klondike Gold Rush* (Seattle, 2003), p. 56. For an engrossing account of a capsize in 1896 (and loss of a full load worth $800), despite hiring two pilots, see Haskell, *Two Years*, pp. 121–5.

71  Stuck, *Voyages on Yukon*, p. 28.

72  Mary E. Hitchcock, *Two Women in the Klondike: The Story of a Journey to the Gold-fields of Alaska* (New York, 1899), p. 431. Edwards, passing through in September 1903, marvelled that any early miners 'ever got through': *In to the Yukon*, p. 116.

73  Hitchcock, *Two Women*, pp. 421–2; Edwards, *In to the Yukon*, pp. 127–8; Stuck, *Voyages on Yukon*, p. 33; Ogilvie, 'Geography and Resources', p. 26.

74  William R. Sidall, 'The Yukon Waterway in the Development of Interior Alaska', *Pacific Historical Review*, XXVIII/4 (November 1959), p. 368; Edwards, *In to the Yukon*, p. 136.

75  Raymond, *Reconnaissance*, pp. 13–14; Arthur Cherry Hinton, *The Yukon* (Toronto, 1954), p. 41; Stuck, *Voyages on Yukon*, p. 100.

76  Nonetheless, a Captain Edwards (a seasoned Liverpool-based navigator) planned to lead an expedition from Liverpool in January 1898 aboard a light draft steamer, the *Manauense*, which, specially fitted for Amazonian travel, intended to go all the way to Dawson without transhipment at St Michael: 'Day to Day in Liverpool', *Liverpool Mercury*, 6 October and 9 December 1897; advertisements, *Liverpool Mercury*, 29 November and 3 December 1897.

77  Smaller steam launches would have struggled against the swift summer current: William Ogilvie, *Extracts from the Report of an Exploration Made in 1896–1897*, in *The Yukon Territory*, p. 396. Typically 70 feet, a Yukon steamer averaged less than half the length of a Mississippi steamer; Melody Webb, *The Last Frontier: A History of the Yukon Basin of Canada and Alaska* (Albuquerque, NM, 1985), pp. 206–8, 211. The Alaska Railroad (1923) revolutionized goldfield access. Freight sent up from Seward was transferred to boats at Nenana for distribution along the Yukon and its tributaries. Service along the Yukon continued until the all-weather Klondike Highway connected Dawson City and Whitehorse in 1955.

78  Schwatka, 'Exploration of Yukon River', p. 353.

79  Hitchcock, *Two Women*, p. 32.

80 Lynch, *Three Years*, p. 23–4; Stuck, *Voyages on Yukon*, p. 92; London, diary entry (11 June 1898), reproduced in London, *Book of Jack London*, vol. I, p. 250.

81 Schwatka, 'Exploration of Yukon River', p. 352.

82 Morse, *Nature of Gold*, p. 83.

83 P. H. Ray and W. P. Richardson, *Relief of the Destitute in the Yukon Region, Alaska, 1898*, in *Compilation of Narratives of Explorations in Alaska* (Washington, DC, 1900), pp. 523, 529; Ogilvie, 'Geography and Resources', p. 28.

84 Ray, *Relief of the Destitute in the Goldfields of Alaska, 1897*, in *Compilation of Narratives of Explorations in Alaska*, pp. 497–503; and Ray and Richardson, *Relief of the Destitute in the Yukon Region, Alaska, 1898*, pp. 531–43; Haskell, *Two Years*, pp. 478–80; 'Famine at Dawson City', *Pall Mall Gazette*, 13 December 1897.

85 Charmian London, *Book of Jack London*, vol. I, p. 230.

86 Morse, *Nature of Gold*, pp. 79–80; Pierre Berton, *The Klondike Fever: The Life and Death of the Last Great Gold Rush* (New York, 1958), p. 205.

87 20 May is the break-up date Dall gives. He cites 16 May and 25 May as the earliest and latest dates respectively in known memory: Dall, 'Springtime on the Yukon', *American Naturalist*, IV/10 (December 1870), p. 597.

88 Dawson, *Narrative of an Exploration*, p. 371; Stuck, *Voyages on Yukon*, p. 25; Haskell, *Two Years*, p. 557.

89 *Zagoskin's Travels in Russian America*, p. 159.

90 Dall, *Narrative*, p. 73.

91 Ibid., pp. 205, 70.

92 Ibid., p. 90.

93 Whymper, *Travel and Adventure*, pp. 194, 198; Dall, *Narrative*, p. 83.

94 Raymond, *Reconnaissance*, p. 23; Raymond, 'Yukon River Region, Alaska', p. 172; Schwatka, 'Exploration of Yukon River', p. 351; Whymper, *Travel and Adventure*, p. 216. The term derives from the horseless Frisians, who deployed this method to protect themselves, not least against mounted Spaniards.

95 Bockstoce, *Furs and Frontiers*, pp. 214–15; Murray, *Journal*, pp. 21–5, 55.

96 Dall, *Narrative*, p. 102; Whymper, *Travel and Adventure*, p. 221.

97 Kirk, *Twelve Months*, p. 199; Dall, *Narrative*, p. 42; Haskell, *Two Years*, p. 508; Ogilvie, 'Geography and Resources', p. 40.

98 Morse, *Nature of Gold*, pp. 60–61.

99 Raymond, 'Yukon River Region', p. 166; Stuck, *Voyages on Yukon*, pp. vii, 110–11.

100 *Zagoskin's Travels in Russian America*, pp. 128, 130, 144.

101 Harris, *Alaska and the Klondike*, pp. 77, 168–9. Harris considered the bicycle a preposterous form of transit in the Yukon because of the absence of decent roads.

102 The most striking entry in the fancy dress cycle parade held at Ormskirk, near Liverpool, in September 1897, was 'On the Road to Klondike'. Two cyclists carried

dried fish, onions, lemons and 'other provision for the rigours of the road': 'Cyclists and Cycling', *Liverpool Mercury*, 30 September 1897.

103 Lynch, *Three Years*, p. 241; Berton, *Klondike Fever*, pp. 128–9. Since it was impossible to carry such a large load in panniers, the Klondike model was equipped with two 14-inch retractable 'outrigger' wheels in addition to the main wheels. The rider dismounted, loaded up as much as he could, and then dragged the contraption along on four wheels for ten miles. After a certain distance, the rider would fold back the side wheels and return to pick up the remaining load: 'Prospectus: Klondike Bicycle', in Harris, *Alaska and Klondike*, pp. 441–2. There is no evidence that this particular bicycle was ever built or used: Cole, 'Introduction', *Wheels on Ice: Bicycling in Alaska, 1898–1908*, ed. Terrence Cole (Anchorage, 1985), p. 6.

104 Edward R. Jesson, 'From Dawson to Nome on a Bicycle', in *Wheels on Ice*, ed. Cole, pp. 9–10; Andy Sterns, 'Dawson to Nome on Two Wheels', *Spoke'N'Word*, VI/3 (October 2001), p. 7.

105 Terrence Cole, 'Gold Rush Bicycling', *Fairbanks Daily News-Miner*, 1 May 1978; Jesson, 'From Dawson to Nome on a Bicycle', pp. 10, 20. Jesson's account was first published (ed. Ruth Leat) under the same title in the *Pacific Northwest Quarterly*, XLVII/3 (July 1956), pp. 65–77.

106 Thoreau, 'Walking' (1862), in *Sunshine and Smoke: American Writers and the American Environment*, ed. David D. Anderson (Philadelphia, 1971), pp. 135–6; Thoreau, *The First and Last Journeys of Thoreau*, ed. Franklin B. Sanborn (Boston, 1905), vol. II, pp. 25, 27–8; John T. Flanagan, 'Thoreau in Minnesota', *Minnesota History*, 16 (March 1935), pp. 36–7.

107 Thoreau, 'Walking', pp. 135–6, 140.

108 Harris, *Alaska and Klondike*, p. 194.

109 Edwards, *In to the Yukon*, pp. 122, 127.

110 Dall, *Narrative*, p. 41.

111 Murray, *Journal, 1847–48*, p. 43.

112 Schwatka, 'Exploration of Yukon River', p. 374.

113 Schwatka, *Along Alaska's Great River*, p. 125.

114 Hitchcock, *Two Women*, pp. 65, 72, 76, 77, 92, 99, 170, 175, 398, Elisha Dyer, Preface, p. viii.

115 They carried a tent with a capacity of 75 people, a collection of pigeons and other birds, various musical instruments, a bowling alley, and tremendous quantities of *pâté de foie gras*, truffles and *olives farcies* (stuffed olives): Lynch, *Three Years*, p. 16.

116 Hitchcock, *Two Women*, p. 76.

117 Lynch, *Three Years*, pp. 23,

118 Hayne and Taylor, *Pioneers of the Klondyke*, p. 120.

119 Hudson Stuck, *Ten Thousand Miles With a Dog Sled: A Narrative of Winter Travel in Interior Alaska* (New York, 1914), p. 219.

120 Stuck, *Voyages on Yukon*, pp. 22, 40, 73, 136.

121 Whymper, *Travel and Adventure*, Preface.

122 'The Spell of the Yukon' is a phrase popularized by Robert Service's poem of that name (1907). Born in Preston, Lancashire, the 'Bard of the Yukon' emigrated to Canada in 1895 at the age of 21. In 1904 and 1905, he worked as a bank clerk in Whitehorse and Dawson City. 'Spell of the Yukon' and 'Law of the Yukon' refer to Yukon territory rather than the river specifically: *The Spell of the Yukon and Other Verses* (New York, 1907).

123 Edwards, *In to the Yukon*, pp. 168–9.

124 Jack London, diary entry (11 June 1898), reproduced in Charmian London, *Book of Jack London*, vol. i, p. 251.

125 Lynch, *Three Years*, p. 18; Henry Morton Stanley, *Through the Dark Continent, or, the Sources of the Nile Around the Great Lakes of Equatorial Africa and Down the Livingstone River to the Atlantic Ocean* (London, 1899), pp. 155, 166, 185. Hayne's *Pioneers of the Klondyke* appeared in the same series (Low's Popular Library of Travel and Adventure) as Henry M. Stanley's *How I Found Livingstone*, H. H. Johnston's *The River Congo* and Joseph Thomson's *Through Masai Land*.

126 Pierre Berton, *Drifting Home: A Family's Voyage of Discovery Down the Wild Yukon River* (Vancouver, 1973), pp. 16–17; Berton, *Klondike Fever*, pp. 431–2, 439.

127 Berton, *Drifting Home*, pp. 38–9, 41, 174.

128 'History and Culture', Yukon-Charley Rivers National Preserve, National Park Service, at www.nps.gov (accessed 14 March 2012).

129 John McPhee, *Coming Into the Country* (New York, 1977), pp. 175–417; Hildebrand, *Reading the River*, pp. 28–31, 94–6, 98–101.

130 Stuck, *Voyages on Yukon*, p. 191; 'Archdeacon Hudson Stuck: Obituary', *The Times*, 30 October 1920.

131 William H. Wilson, 'The Yukon: By Richard Mathews', *Journal of American History*, 56/1 (June 1969), p. 158.

132 Raymond, *Reconnaissance*, p. 39.

133 Stuck, *Voyages on Yukon*, p. 191.

134 Charmian London reproduced the diary (8–30 June 1898) in *Book of Jack London*, vol. i, pp. 248–57.

135 'Yukon Charley Rivers National Preserve: Floating the Yukon River Eagle to Circle', National Park Service, Department of the Interior, at www.nps.gov (accessed 14 March 2012).

136 Stuck, *Voyages on Yukon*, pp. 77, 83.

137 'Yukon Charley Rivers National Preserve: Floating the Charley River'.

## References

138 Dan O'Neill, 'Coming Out of the Country', in *Under Northern Lights: Writers and Artists View the Alaskan Landscape*, ed. Frank Soos and Kesler Woodward (Seattle, 2000), pp. 177–209; O'Neill, *A Land Gone Lonesome: An Inland Voyage Along the Yukon River* (New York, 2006), pp. 59–236.

139 O'Neill, *Land Gone Lonesome*, p. 40.

140 Public Land Law 96–487-December 2, 1980, 94 STAT.2371 (96th Congress), at http://alaska.fws.gov (accessed 14 March 2012); Yukon-Charley Rivers National Preserve, *Annual Report for 2005; 2006; 2007; 2008* and *2009* (Fairbanks: National Park Service), p. 4.

141 Skinner, 'Rivers and American Folk', n.p.

142 'Public Use Cabins', at www.nps.gov (accessed 14 March 2012).

143 Max R. Hirschberg, 'A Broken Chain and a Busted Pedal', in *Wheels on Ice*, pp. 21–3. Hirschberg wrote his first-hand account for his grandchildren in the late 1950s. Granddaughter Penni Busse submitted it for publication ('My Bicycle Trip Down the Yukon', *Alaska Magazine*, February 1978). Nineteen-year-old Hirschberg (a roadhouse owner) took twice as long as Jesson (ten weeks).

144 Dan Davidson, 'Extreme Bikers Undertake Strange, Historic Journey Challenge: Three Men Hope to Duplicate 1900 Gold Rush Trek by Pedalling from Dawson to Nome', *Whitehorse (Yukon) Star*, 7 April 2003; Brian Handwerk, 'Ice Bikes Complete Expedition Down Frozen Yukon', *National Geographic News*, 9 May 2003, at http://news.nationalgeographic.com (accessed 14 March 2012).

145 For this concept, though without specific reference to the Yukon, see Ted Catton, *Inhabited Wilderness: Indians, Eskimos, and National Parks in Alaska* (Albuquerque, NM, 1997), p. xix.

146 George Sundborg, 'The "Biggest Dam" on the Mighty Yukon', *Rural Electrification*, 17 (July 1959), p. 15.

147 *Anchorage Daily Times*, 3 September 1960; Paul Brooks, 'The Plot to Drown Alaska', *Atlantic Monthly*, 215 (May 1965), pp. 53–70; Yukon Power for America, *Addresses Presented at Rampart Dam Conference*, Fairbanks, Alaska, 1963, pp. 39–41.

148 Department of the Interior, *Rampart Dam Project, Alaska: Market for Power and Effect of Project on Natural Resources*, vol. III (Washington, DC, 1956), pp. 935–78.

149 Ernest Gruening (Senator for Alaska), 'A imperative the nation' (rough draft of speech, undated), Gruening Papers, Archives, Alaska and Polar Regions Department, University of Alaska, Fairbanks, Alaska (UAF).

150 Steamboats needed regular refuelling. On its maiden voyage upriver in 1869, the *Yukon* halted two to three times a day to chop wood, though drift timber often sufficed: Raymond, *Reconnaissance*, p. 14. According to a Briton who spent two years in the service of the North-West Mounted Police, on the upriver journey from St Michael to Dawson (July 1895), during these halts, 'passengers and crew alike

went on shore armed with axes . . . and set to work chopping wood to take them a
few miles further up the river'. To make any appreciable headway against the
current, this steamer burnt between 1.5 and 2 cords (a stack of wood whose
dimensions are 4 by 4 by 8 feet) every hour: Hayne and Taylor, *Pioneers of the
Klondike*, pp. 26–7, 47–8.

151  Phil Holland to Ernest Gruening, 20 February 1864, Gruening Papers; Anthony
Netboy, 'Fish Versus Dams – A New Look at River Development', Yukon Power for
America, annual meeting, Fairbanks, 20 June 1964, p. 3, Fairbanks Chamber of
Commerce Collection, UAF.

## 6 Los Angeles River

1  Henry Seidel Canby, *The Brandywine* (New York, 1941), pp. 3–4.

2  Anne B. Fisher, *The Salinas: Upside-down River* (New York, 1945), pp. xv–xvi.

3  Carr, *Los Angeles: City of Dreams* (New York, 1935), p. 14; Kevin Starr, 'Foreword'
to Patt Morrison and Mark Lamonica, *Río L.A.: Tales from the Los Angeles River*
(Santa Monica, CA, 2001), p. 16.

4  Charlie LeDuff, 'Los Angeles by Kayak: Vistas of Concrete Banks', *New York Times*,
8 December 2003. The counterpoint to the LA River within Southern California is
the Sespe, a 55-mile river passing through the Sespe Wilderness just 50 miles
northwest of downtown Los Angeles. Southern California's last undammed river –
31.5 miles of which are an officially designated wild and scenic river (1992), like
Alaska's Charley – though hardly untouched by human activity, has 'escaped the
fate' of many other rivers in the American West: Bradley John Monsma, *The Sespe
Wild: Southern California's Last Free River* (Reno, NV, 2004), pp. 5–6, 81–91.

5  Morrison and Lamonica, *Río L.A.*, p. 19.

6  Steven P. Erie, *Beyond Chinatown: The Metropolitan Water District. Growth, and the
Environment in Southern California* (Stanford, CA, 2006), pp. 29–53.

7  William Hare, *L.A. Noir: Nine Dark Visions of the City of Angels* (Jefferson, NC,
2004), p. 185.

8  Tad Friend, 'River of Angels', *The New Yorker*, 26 January 2004, p. 44.

9  As part of a programme of events entitled 'Re-Envisioning the Los Angeles River'
(2000), organized by Friends of the Los Angeles River (FOLAR) in conjunction with
Occidental College's Urban & Environmental Policy Institute and funded by the
California Council for the Humanities, film-maker Dana Plays produced '*River
Madness*': an eighteen-minute montage of scenes, more or less well known, from
more than twenty movies filmed on river-bed location. A screening at CBS Studio
Center (6 April 2000) was followed by a panel discussion with director Wim

Wenders and screenwriter Robert Towne about the river's place in the city: *Re-envisioning the Los Angeles River: A Program of Community and Ecological Revitalization. A Report on the 40 Forums, Events, Activities, and Projects Held during 1999–2000* (Los Angeles, August 2001), pp. 2, 5–6, 22. Other films that contain river-bed footage include *Repo Man* (1984), *To Live and Die in L.A.* (1985), *Escape from L.A.* (1996) and *Transformers* (2007): Ted Elrick and the Friends of the Los Angeles River, *Los Angeles River* (San Francisco, 2007), pp. 83–92.

10  Blake Gumprecht, *The Los Angeles River: Its Life, Death, and Possible Re-birth* (Baltimore, MD, 1999), p. 244.

11  Philip L. Fradkin, *The Seven States of California: A Natural and Human History* (New York, 1995), p. 326.

12  Sam Shepard, 'Cruising Paradise', in *Cruising Paradise: Tales* (New York, 1996), p. 40.

13  Morrison and Lamonica, *Río L.A.*, p. 23.

14  Lewis MacAdams, 'Let the Los Angeles River Go Green to the Sea', *Los Angeles Times*, 27 November 1989; Mark Gladstone, 'No Shortage of Opinions When the Topic is What to Do With the L.A. River', *LA Times*, 1 April 1990.

15  Morrison and Lamonica, *Río L.A.*, p. 22.

16  Dick Roraback, 'Up a Lazy River, Seeking the Source Your Explorer Follows in the Footsteps of Gaspar de Portola', *LA Times*, 20 October 1985.

17  Joe Linton, *Down by the Los Angeles River: Friends of the Los Angeles River's Official Guide* (Berkeley, CA, 2005).

18  Gladstone, 'No Shortage of Opinions'.

19  Jennifer Price, 'Thirteen Ways of Seeing Nature in LA', in *Land of Sunshine: An Environmental History of Metropolitan Los Angeles*, ed. William Deverell and Greg Hise (Pittsburgh, PA, 2005), p. 229. For later versions, see Price, 'Thirteen Ways of Seeing Nature in L.A.: Part 1', *The Believer* (April 2006), at www.believermag.com; 'Thirteen Ways of Seeing Nature in L.A.: Part 2', *The Believer* (May 2006), at www.believermag.com (accessed 16 March 2012).

20  MacAdams, quoted in Steve Chapple, 'Taming the Wild Trickle: A Gray-water Adventure on the Mighty L.A.', *LA Weekly*, 11 March 1999.

21  When I visited the river in November 2010, the flow through the Glendale Narrows was calm and relatively clear. Overnight rains transformed it into roiling, chocolate-brown water.

22  Gumprecht, *LA River*, p. 224.

23  J. M. Guinn, *Historical and Biographical Record of Los Angeles and Vicinity (Containing a History of the City from its Earliest Settlement as a Spanish Pueblo to the Closing Year of the Nineteenth Century)* (Chicago, 1901), p. 126. Major, if less drastic changes in course followed the floods of 1889 and 1914.

24  Gumprecht, *LA River*, p. 5.

25  Mike Davis, *Ecology of Fear: Los Angeles and the Imagination of Disaster* (New York, 1998), p. 17.

26  Dick Roraback, 'From Basin Camp, the Final Assault', *LA Times*, 30 January 1986.

27  Jennifer Price, ' Confluence Park, Los Angeles: Case Study', *Forum* 5 (1 May 2010), at www.laforum.org (accessed 16 March 2012).

28  According to one authority, the area that now comprises Los Angeles County contained 40 settlements (lodges) of between 500 and 1,500 huts each: Hugo Reid, *The Indians of Los Angeles County* (Los Angeles, 1926), p. 3.

29  Bernice Eastman Johnston, *California's Gabrielino Indians* (Los Angeles, 1962), p. 124; A. L. Kroeber, *Handbook of the Indians of California* (Washington, DC, 1925), pp. 628, 630; Reid, *Indians of Los Angeles County*, pp. 25–7. Spanish settlers named the Gabrielino, one of the so-called Mission Indian tribes, after the San Gabriel Mission.

30  Guinn, *Historical and Biographical Record*, p. 33; William McCawley, *The First Angelinos: The Gabrielino Indians of Los Angeles* (Banning, CA, 1996), pp. 29–30; Johnston, *California's Gabrielino Indians*, p. 78.

31  Fray Juan Crespi, 'The Portolá Expedition: As Told in Crespi's Diary', *Fray Juan Crespi: Missionary Explorer on the Pacific Coast, 1769–1774*, ed. Herbert Eugene Bolton (Berkeley, 1927), pp. 147–8. Chia, a grey oblong seed from a thistle-like plant, was roasted and ground into meal.

32  Crespi, 'Portolá Expedition', pp. 269–70.

33  Anza's Diary (1775–6), in *Anza's California Expeditions*, vol. III: *The San Francisco Colony: Diaries of Anza, Font, and Eixarch, and Narratives by Palóu and Moraga*, trans. and ed. Herbert Eugene Bolton (Berkeley, 1930), pp. 105, 242–3 (Font's 'Short Diary'); *Anza's California Expeditions*, vol. IV: *Font's Complete Diary of the Second Anza Expedition*, trans. and ed. Bolton (Berkeley, 1930), pp. 244–5.

34  Guinn, *Historical and Biographical Record*, p. 33. The name derives from the feast day on 1–2 August that honours *Porciúncula*, the village near the little church of Our Lady of the Angels, where St Francis of Assisi was worshipping when he received God's blessing.

35  Dana W. Bartlett, *The Better City: A Sociological Study of a Modern City* (Los Angeles, 1907), p. 12; City of Los Angeles, Department of Public Works, *Los Angeles River Revitalization Master Plan* (Los Angeles, April 2007), I/2.

36  McCawley, *First Angelinos*, p. 202.

37  The Board of Water Commissioners was replaced by the Los Angeles Board of Water Commissioners in 1902, itself the precursor of the Board of Commissioners of the Department of Water and Power (1925).

38  J. B. Lippincott, 'William Mulholland – Engineer, Pioneer, Raconteur: Part 1. His Start in Life and His Service in the Los Angeles City Water Company', *Civil*

*Engineering*, XI/2 (February 1941), pp. 105–6; Margaret Leslie Davis, *Rivers in the Desert: William Mulholland and the Inventing of Los Angeles* (Chicago, 2001 [1993]), pp. 30, 258; Catherine Mulholland, *William Mulholland and the Rise of Los Angeles* (Berkeley, 2000), pp. 18, 24.

39 Élisée Reclus, *The Earth and its Inhabitants: North America*, vol. III, *The United States* (New York, 1893), p. 442.

40 The City's claim that it enjoyed absolute and sole 'pueblo right' to the water was eventually sustained: 'City Wins Point in Water Case', *Los Angeles Herald*, 14 November 1905; 'The False and True About Los Angeles Water Basin', *Los Angeles Herald*, 2 June 1907.

41 Harry J. Lelande, 'The Owen's River Aqueduct', in *Los Angeles, California: The City Beautiful, Report of the Municipal Art Commission for the City of Los Angeles, California* (Los Angeles, 1909), n.p.; John Walton, *Western Times and Water Wars: State Culture and Rebellion in California* (Berkeley, 1992), pp. 150–51, 167; Marc Reisner, *Cadillac Desert: The American West and Its Disappearing Water* (New York, 1986), pp. 57–86.

42 George Wharton James, *Through Ramona's Country* (Boston, MA, 1909), pp. 371–2.

43 Starr, 'Foreword', *Río LA*, p. 16.

44 FOVICKS (Friends of Vast Industrial Concrete Kafkaesque Structures), at http://seriss.com (accessed 16 March 2012).

45 Guinn, *Historical and Biographical Record*, pp. 126, 147.

46 Ibid., p. 266.

47 Charles Dudley Warner, *Our Italy* (New York, 1891), p. 15.

48 'Asks for Lease on River Bed', *LA Herald*, 28 April 1908.

49 'Los Angeles New Year's Flood', *Woody Guthrie, Library of Congress Recordings* (Alan Lomax, 1940), Disc 3 (Rounder Records, 1989).

50 Bartlett, *Better City*, pp. 32–4.

51 Charles Mulford Robinson, *Modern Civic Art, Or, The City Made Beautiful* (New York, 1904), pp. 54–6.

52 Charles Mulford Robinson, *The Improvement of Towns and Cities, Or, The Practical Basis of Civic Aesthetics* (New York, 1901), pp. 12–14; Robinson, *The City Beautiful* (suggestion) in *Los Angeles, California: The City Beautiful*, n.p.

53 Olmsted Brothers and Bartholomew and Associates, *Parks, Playgrounds and Beaches for the Los Angeles Region* (Los Angeles, 1930), pp. 38, 101–2, 113, 125–6. The 178-page report for the LA Chamber of Commerce, Citizen's Committee on Parks, Playgrounds and Beaches, is reproduced in facsimile in Greg Hise and William Deverell, *Eden by Design: The 1930 Olmsted-Bartholomew Plan for the Los Angeles Region* (Berkeley, 2000), pp. 65–283. References to the report indicate original pagination.

54 Olmsted and Bartholomew, *Parks, Playgrounds and Beaches*, p. 125.

55 Hise and Deverell, *Eden by Design*, pp. 268–9.

56 Cecilia Rasmussen, 'Flood of '38 Forever Altered the Southland Landscape', LA *Times*, 23 January 2005; 'Reptile Farm Gave L.A. a Wild Time', LA *Times*, 3 August 1997.

57 Emanuel Levy, *All About Oscar: The History and Politics of the Academy Awards* (New York, 2003), p. 18; LA *Times*, 4 March 1938; 'Catastrophe: Temperamental Fit', *Time*, XXXI/11 (14 March 1938).

58 Jared Orsi, *Hazardous Metropolis: Flooding and Urban Ecology in Los Angeles* (Berkeley, 2004), p. 119, Davis, *Ecology of Fear*, p. 67.

59 Gumprecht, LA *River*, p. 228.

60 Orsi, *Hazardous Metropolis*, p. 6.

61 Gumprecht, LA *River*, p. 224.

62 Federal Emergency Management Agency, *Flood Zone Bulletin* (November 1997), p. 1.

63 Brett Goldstone's 'Water with Rocks Gate' installation at South Atwater Village is a reminder of the river's power. Commissioned by North East Trees (NET) and dedicated on Earth Day 2001, it depicts the river rising to flood stage, then flowing around downtown high rises.

64 'In Search of the L.A. River', LA *Times*, 20 and 27 October 1985; 3, 7, 14, 21 and 28 November 1985; 8 December 1985; 23 and 30 January 1986. For another expedition account, see James Ricci, 'When They Look at the L.A. River, They See Green', LA *Times*, 20 August 2000.

65 'The Quality of Mersey is Not Strained' (a play on Portia's words in *The Merchant of Venice*), is the title of a folksong by Stan Kelly (*c.* 1961). Concerning a trip up the Manchester Ship Canal, it contains the sentiment: 'Now the quality of Mersey, boys, it isn't strained at all. It's full of shit and seaweed and it tastes like paraffin oil'. The phrase itself has a much longer pedigree. In 1870, an American journalist reported the Liverpudlian who, crossing the Mersey on the Woodside ferry, and noting the river's muddiness, reflected that Shakespeare got it right: 'the quality of *Mersey* is not strained': 'Editor's Drawer', *Harper's New Monthly Magazine*, 42 (CCXLVI) (December 1870), p. 158.

66 Dick Roraback, 'Up a Lazy River, Seeking the Source Your Explorer Follows in the Footsteps of Gaspar de Portola', LA *Times*, 20 October 1985; 'Exploring the L.A. River: Small Tales From Along Lario Trail', 31 October 1985; 'Bridging the Gap on the L.A. River With a Song in His Heart and a Yolk on His Shoe', 7 November 1985.

67 Dick Roraback, 'Scenes from the L.A. River: Exploring with Ants in his Pants', LA *Times*, 3 November 1985.

68 Gumprecht, LA *River*, p. 254.

69 American Rivers, *America's Most Endangered Rivers of 2002* (Washington, DC,

2002), p. 37; American Rivers, 'Los Angeles River', *North America's Most Endangered and Threatened Rivers of 1996* (Washington, DC, 1996), pp. 44–5. Industrialization along the LA River departed from historic norms. Industry used the Danube, Spree and Mersey to bring in raw materials and haul out finished products, while the water itself powered machinery and supplied industrial processes.

70 Robert Gottlieb, *Reinventing Los Angeles: Nature and Community in the Global City* (Cambridge, MA, 2007), pp. 163–7.

71 Judith Coburn, 'Whose River is it, Anyway?: More Concrete Versus More Nature', *LA Times*, 20 November 1994; Lewis MacAdams, 'Restoring the Los Angeles River: A Forty-year Art Project', *Whole Earth Review* (Spring 1995), p. 64; Friend, 'River of Angels', p. 46. For MacAdams's LA River poems, see *The River, Books One and Two* (Palo Alto, CA, 1998).

72 'Hope in Pasadena', press release, Ronald Feldman Fine Arts, New York, 1 May 1985, at www.feldmangallery.com (accessed 16 March 2012).

73 Sam Hall Kaplan, 'Artists Sketch Natural Look for Arroyo Seco', *LA Times*, 3 March 1985.

74 Robert Wood et al./Mersey Basin Campaign, 'Building a Healthier Economy Through a Cleaner Environment: Mid-Term Report', Manchester, November 1997, pp. 25, 30.

75 Price, 'Thirteen Ways of Seeing Nature in L.A.', p. 238.

76 'LA River', at http://councilcommittee.lacity.org (accessed 16 March 2012).

77 Eric Garcetti, quoted in Friend, 'River of Angels', p. 43.

78 Zack D. Freedman, 'Grounds for Renewal: The Revitalization of Compton Creek', University of California, Berkeley, Department of Landscape Architecture/Santa Monica Mountains Conservancy, 2003, p. 1.

79 Sam Hall Kaplan, 'Opening the Floodgates: Will the Latest Plan for the L.A. River Wash Away Past Failures?', *Los Angeles Downtown News*, 12 November 2004, at www.ladowntownnews.com (accessed 16 March 2012); Jessica Garrison, 'River Plan Rolls Along', *LA Times*, 4 November 2004.

80 Taylor Yard, a Southern Pacific Railroad freight-switching facility that encompasses three miles of riverfront, became inactive in 1985. Just north of downtown, this was probably where the Portolá expedition camped in early August 1769. In 2000, following a campaign initiated in 1992 by The Coalition for a State Park at Taylor Yard, consisting of some forty community groups put together by The River Project (which had secured legal protection against further industrial development), the Governor and the State Legislature approved $45 million to acquire a chunk of the site for Rio de Los Angeles State Park. Combining 'active' recreation ('groomed' facilities such as soccer fields and baseball diamonds), more naturalistic picnic

areas, habitat restoration, and educational and cultural facilities, Taylor Park (opened on 21 April 2007), exemplifies an urban riverside park's multiple benefits for a diverse constituency: Kaplan, 'Return of the River: Waterway's Past and Present Give Hope to a Vital Future', *LA Downtown News*, 24 January 2005; 'Taylor Yard History', at www.theriverproject.org (accessed 16 March 2012).

81  *Los Angeles River Revitalization Master Plan*, II, 1/6, 2/3; Reyes, 'Afterword: A Clear Future for the LA River', in Linton, *Down by the LA River*, pp. 293–4.

82  Mayor Antonio R. Villaraigosa, Preface, *Los Angeles River Revitalization Master Plan*. See also Robert Gottlieb and Andrea Misako Azuma, 'Bankside Los Angeles', in *Rivertown: Rethinking Urban Rivers*, ed. Paul Stanton Kibel (Cambridge, MA, 2007), pp. 23–46.

83  FOLAR, *State of the River II: The Fish Study* (Los Angeles, September 2008), p. 29.

84  *Los Angeles River Revitalization Master Plan*, 2/3, 3/11. Michael Amescua's 'Guardians of the River Gate' installation, which fronts onto the soft-bottomed stretch at Los Feliz (North Atwater), features a full set of historic river fauna. The visitor center at the Los Angeles River Center and Gardens, headquarters for FOLAR and other river improvement groups, houses a river museum with dioramas of flora and fauna and panels on river history and flooding.

85  Preface, City of Los Angeles, 'Los Angeles River Revitalization', Los Angeles River Project Office, Department of Public Works, Bureau of Engineering, 2008.

86  Price, 'Confluence Park, Los Angeles: Case Study'.

87  Jennifer Price, 'Paradise Reclaimed: A Field Guide to the L.A. River', *LA Weekly*, 10–16 August 2001; Christopher Reynolds, 'Where Shopping Carts Spawn', *LA Times*, 2 December 2003; Lewis MacAdams, 'D-Town Visions: Building a City the River Can be Proud of', Natural Resources Defense Council, Santa Monica, 2007.

88  Telephone conversation between Gumprecht and MacAdams (21 November 1997), quoted in Gumprecht, *LA River*, p. 298; Bettina Boxall, 'For L.A. River, a Vision Beyond the Concrete Environment', *LA Times*, 29 October 1989.

89  Coburn, 'Whose River Is It, Anyway?' The river has provided living space for generation of transients, from the tents of Chinese railroad workers in the 1870s to the unemployed of the 1930s.

90  Henry Savage, *River of the Carolinas: The Santee* (New York, 1956), p. 399.

91  Henry Van Dyke, *Little Rivers: A Book of Essays in Profitable Idleness* (New York, 1895), p. 12; Charles Lamb, 'Amicus Redivivus', in *The Last Essays of Elia: Being a Sequel to Essays Published Under That Name* (London, 1833), p. 134.

92  Blake Gumprecht, 'Who Killed the Los Angeles River?', in *Land of Sunshine: An Environmental History of Metropolitan Los Angeles*, p. 134.

93  P. Reyes, ed., Preface, *Los Angeles River Revitalization Master Plan*. Reyes chairs the Ad Hoc Committee on the Los Angeles River.

94  Scarlet Cheng, 'City's River a Flood of Inspiration: Two Exhibitions Capture the Gritty and Intriguing Stream that Bears Los Angeles' Name', LA *Times*, 8 March 2007.

95  Gary Snyder, 'Coming in to the Watershed: Biological and Cultural Diversity in the California Habitat', *Chicago Review*, XXXIX/3–4 (1993), p. 82.

96  Linton, *Down by the LA River*, p. 69.

97  Gumprecht, LA *River*, p. 245. There are additional unlined sections in Sepulveda Basin and the estuary. The unlined sections add up to nearly a quarter of the river: United States Environmental Protection Agency (EPA), Region IX, 'Special Case Evaluation Regarding Status of Los Angeles River, California, as a Traditional Navigable Water' (San Francisco, 1 July 2010), pp. 9–10.

98  Ellen Wohl, *Virtual Rivers: Lessons from the Mountain Rivers of the Colorado Front Range* (New Haven, CT, 2001), pp. 34–6, 167–72.

99  Edwin Corle, Foreword, *The Gila: River of the Southwest* (New York, 1951).

100  Ibid.

101  LeDuff, 'Los Angeles Journal; Los Angeles by Kayak'.

102  FOLAR, *State of the River II*, pp. 11–12, 19–20.

103  Elrick, LA *River*, p. 94.

104  William H. Brewer, *Up and Down California in 1860–1864: The Journal of William H. Brewer*, ed. F. P. Farquhar (New Haven, CT, 1930), p. 12.

105  'Rapanos et ux., et al. v. United States', U.S. Court of Appeals, Sixth Circuit (No. 04-1034), argued 21 February 2006, decided 19 June 2006, at http://laws.findlaw.com (accessed 16 March 2012).

106  EPA, 'Special Case Evaluation Regarding Status of Los Angeles River, California', cover letter, pp. 4–5, 9–10, 21, 23, 27–8, 34–5; Paul Quinlan, 'EPA Declares L.A. River "Navigable", Stretches Regulatory Reach', *New York Times*, 9 July 2010; Jean Guerrero, 'A River Really Runs Through It', *Wall Street Journal*, 31 July 2010. Set-piece canoe trips to demonstrate recreational potential date back to at least 1990: Jeff Meyers, 'Outdoors Streams of Consciousness: L.A. River Could Become Vital Source of Recreation', LA *Times*, 30 May 1990.

107  M. G. Lord, 'Memento Mori', in Anthony Hernández, *Everything* (Portland, OR, 2005), pp. 5–6; Judith Freeman, 'Rio Surreal; A Photographer Takes Exacting Aim at the L.A. River', LA *Times*, 17 October 2004.

108  'A Place in the Sun: Photographs of Los Angeles by John Humble', www.getty.edu and www.johnhumble.com (accessed 16 March 2012); *51 Miles of Concrete* was first displayed at the Jan Kesner Gallery, Hancock Park, Los Angeles, 27 October–1 December 2001.

109  Cynthia Dea, 'Stream of Views on L.A. River: Images Flow in a Skirball Display That Raises Issues About Nature and the City', LA *Times*, 17 August 2006; press release,

'L.A. River Reborn: Contemporary Photographs and Video Exhibition Finds Art in Infrastructure', Skirball Cultural Center, Los Angeles. The exhibit ran from 6 April to 3 September 2006: www.artscenecal.com (accessed 16 March 2012).

110 Hence 'Frogtown', as the area on the right-hand bank in the Glendale Narrows is known. See also Kimball L. Garrett, 'The Biota of the Los Angeles River: An Historical Overview and Current Analysis', in *The Biota of the Los Angeles River*, ed. Kimball L. Garrett (Los Angeles: Ornithology Department, Natural History Museum, Los Angeles County Foundation, 1993), pp. F1–F190.

111 Jonathan Spaulding, 'Reflections on "*L.A.: Light/ Motion/ Dreams*": Developing an Exhibition on the Natural and the Cultural', *Environmental History*, X/2 (April 2005), pp. 298, 306–7.

112 'Poured in Place', at http://douglashillphotography.com (accessed 16 March 2012); Douglas Hill, *Poured in Place: Every Bridge over the Los Angeles River* (Los Angeles, CA, 2008); Scarlet Cheng, 'City's River a Flood of Inspiration', LA *Times*, 8 March 2007. Hill's show was held at the Craig Krull Gallery, Santa Monica.

113 Jennifer McGregor, 'The Muhheakantuck in Focus', Wave Hill Glyndor Gallery (1 August–29 November 2009), pp. 14–15. The second sign refers to the US Airways Airbus that made a near-miraculous emergency landing (ditching) on the Hudson in mid-town Manhattan on 15 January 2009, minutes after take-off from LaGuardia, having struck a flock of Canada geese.

# Select Bibliography

## Danube

Asherson, Neil, and Sarah Hobson, eds, *Danube: River of Life* (Athens, 2002)

Baker, B. Granville, *The Danube with Pen and Pencil* (London, 1911)

Beattie, William, *The Danube: Its History, Scenery and Topography* (London, 1844)

Bigelow, Poultney, *Paddles and Politics down the Danube* (London, 1892)

Claridge, R. T., *A Guide Down the Danube* (London, 1837)

Fermor, Patrick Leigh, *A Time of Gifts: On Foot to Constantinople: From the Hook of Holland to the Middle Danube* (New York, 2005 [1977])

—, *Between the Woods and the Water: On Foot to Constantinople from the Hook of Holland: The Middle Danube to the Iron Gates* (New York, 2005 [1986])

Heidegger, Martin, *Hölderlin's Hymn 'The Ister'*, trans. William McNeill and Julia Davis (Bloomington, IN, 1996)

Hölderlin, Friedrich, *Poems and Fragments*, trans. Michael Hamburger (London, 2004)

Holzer, Anton, and Elisabeth Limbeck-Lilienau, eds, *Blue: Inventing the River Danube*, trans. Steven Grynwasser and Akos Doma (Salzburg, 2005)

Jerrold, Walter, *The Danube* (London, 1911)

Kohl, Johann Georg, *Austria, Vienna, Prague, Hungary, Bohemia, and the Danube* (London, 1843)

Lengyel, Emil, *The Danube* (London, 1940)

Magris, Claudio, *Danube: A Sentimental Journey from the Source to the Black Sea*, trans. Patrick Creagh (London, 1986)

Millet, Francis Davis, *The Danube from the Black Forest to the Black Sea* (New York, 1892)

Müller, Pohle, Andreas, *The Danube River Project* (Berlin, 2007)

Planché, James Robinson, *Descent of the Danube, from Ratisbon to Vienna, during the Autumn of 1827* (London, 1828)

Skene, F.M.F., *Wayfaring Sketches among the Greeks and Turks, and On the Shores of the Danube* (London, 1847)

## Spree

Carstens, Cornelia, et al., *Frauen an der Spree: Ein Spatziergang durch die Geschichte* (Berlin, 1999)

Conradt, Gerd, *An der Spree: Der Fluss, Die Menschen* (Berlin, 2007)

Fontane, Theodor, *Wanderungen durch die Mark Brandenburg, Vierter Band: Spreewald* (Munich, 1963 [1881])

Götze, Heinz, *398 Kilometer Spree: Von den Quellen in der Oberlausitz bis zur Mündung in Spandau* (Berlin, 1993)

Vollrath, Horst, and Bernd Lammel, *Wiedersehen am Strand der Spree: Ein Fluss und seine Geschichte* (Berlin, 1990)

## Po

Antonioni, Michelangelo, 'Concerning a Film about the River Po', in *Springtime in Italy: A Reader on Neo-realism*, ed. and trans. David Overbey (London, 1978), pp. 79–82

Bacchelli, Riccardo, *The Mill on the Po*, trans. Francis Frenaye (London, 1952 [1938])

—, *Nothing New Under the Sun*, trans. Stuart Hood (London, 1955 [1938])

Bey, Ismail Sirry, *Irrigation in the Valley of the River Po, Northern Italy: Being an Account of a Mission Undertaken in the Summer of 1899 for the Egyptian Government* (Cairo, 1902)

Borsa, Mario, *The Farm on the River Po*, trans. L. E. Marshall (London, 1931)

Braga, G., and S. Gervasoni, 'Evolution of the Po River: An Example of the Application of Historic Maps', in *Historical Change of Large Alluvial Rivers: Western Europe*, ed. G. E. Petts, H. Möller and A. L. Roux (New York, 1989), pp. 113–26

De Santis, Giuseppe, 'Towards an Italian Landscape', in *Springtime in Italy: A Reader in Neorealism*, ed. and trans. David Overbey (London, 1978), pp. 125–9

Guareschi, Giovanni, *The World of Don Camillo* (London, 1980)

Maffioli, Cesare S., *Out of Galileo: The Science of Waters, 1628–1718* (Rotterdam, 1994)

Mead, Elwood, *Irrigation in Northern Italy, Part 1* (Washington, DC, 1904)

Zavattini, Cesare, and Paul Strand, *Un Paese: Portrait of an Italian Village* (New York, 1997)

## Mersey

Allison, J. E., *The Mersey Estuary* (Liverpool, 1949)

Baines, Thomas, *History of the Commerce and Town of Liverpool, and of the Rise of*

*Manufacturing Industry in the Adjoining Counties* (Liverpool, 1852)

—, *Lancashire and Cheshire, Past and Present: A History and a Description of the Palatine Counties of Lancaster and Chester*, vol. I (London, 1868)

Blower, Benjamin, *The Mersey: Ancient and Modern* (Liverpool, 1878)

Greenwood, E. F., ed., *Ecology and Landscape Development: A History of the Mersey Basin: Proceedings of a Conference Held at Merseyside Maritime Museum, Liverpool, 5–6 July 1996* (Liverpool, 1999)

Palmer, William T., *The River Mersey* (London, 1944)

Scott, Dixon, *Liverpool* (London, 1907)

Wray, Ian, ed., *Mersey: The River that Changed the World* (Liverpool, 2007)

## Yukon

Berton, Pierre, *The Klondike Fever: The Life and Death of the Last Great Gold Rush* (New York, 1958)

—, *Drifting Home: A Family's Voyage of Discovery Down the Wild Yukon River* (Vancouver, 1973)

W. H. Dall, *The Narrative of W. H. Dall, Leader of the Expedition to Alaska in 1866–1868*, in *The Yukon Territory* (London, 1898)

Dawson, George M., *The Narrative of an Exploration Made in 1887 in the Yukon District*, in *The Yukon Territory* (London, 1898)

Edwards, William Seymour, *In to the Yukon* (Cincinnati, 1909 [1904])

Hildebrand, John, *Reading the River: A Voyage down the Yukon* (Boston, MA, 1988)

Hitchcock, Mary E., *Two Women in the Klondike: The Story of a Journey to the Gold-fields of Alaska* (New York, 1899)

Mathews, Richard K., *The Yukon* (New York, 1968)

McPhee, John, *Coming Into the Country* (New York, 1977)

Morse, Kathryn, *The Nature of Gold: An Environmental History of the Klondike Gold Rush* (Seattle, 2003)

Ogilvie, William, *Early Days on the Yukon and the Story of its Gold Finds* (London, 1913)

O'Neill, Dan, *A Land Gone Lonesome: An Inland Voyage Along the Yukon River* (New York, 2006)

Raymond, Charles W., *Report of a Reconnaissance of the Yukon River, Alaska Territory, July to September 1869* (Washington, DC, 1871)

Schwatka, Frederick, *Along Alaska's Great River* (New York, 1885)

—, *Exploring the Great Yukon* (New York, 1890)

Stuck, Hudson, *Voyages on the Yukon and Its Tributaries: A Narrative of Summer Travel in the Interior of Alaska* (New York, 1917)

Webb, Melody, *The Last Frontier: A History of the Yukon Basin of Canada and Alaska* (Albuquerque, NM, 1985)

Whymper, Frederick, *Travel and Adventure in the Territory of Alaska* (London, 1868)

Zagoskin, Lavrentii A., *Lieutenant Zagoskin's Travels in Russian America, 1842–1844: The First Ethnographic and Geographic Investigations in the Yukon and Kuskokwim Valleys of Alaska,* ed. Henry N. Michael (Toronto, 1967)

## Los Angeles River

Gumprecht, Blake, *The Los Angeles River: Its Life, Death, and Possible Re-birth* (Baltimore, MD, 1999)

Hise, Greg, and William Deverell, *Eden by Design: The 1930 Olmsted-Bartholomew Plan for the Los Angeles Region* (Berkeley, 2000)

Linton, Joe, *Down by the Los Angeles River: Friends of the Los Angeles River's Official Guide* (Berkeley, CA, 2005)

Morrison, Patt, and Mark Lamonica, *Río L.A.: Tales from the Los Angeles River* (Santa Monica, CA, 2001)

Price, Jennifer, 'Thirteen Ways of Seeing Nature in LA', in *Land of Sunshine: An Environmental History of Metropolitan Los Angeles*, ed. William Deverell and Greg Hise (Pittsburgh, PA, 2005), pp. 220–44

## General and Other Rivers

Ackroyd, Peter, *Thames: Sacred River* (London, 2007)

Anon., *Industrial Rivers of the United Kingdom, by Various Well-known Experts* (London, 1888)

Armstrong, Christopher, and Matthew Evenden and H. V. Nelles, *The River Returns: An Environmental History of the Bow* (Montreal, 2009)

Blackbourn, David, *The Conquest of Nature: Water, Landscape, and the Making of Modern Germany* (New York, 2006)

Cioc, Mark, *The Rhine: An Eco-biography, 1815–2000* (Seattle, 2002)

McCully, Patrick, *Silenced Rivers: The Ecology and Politics of Large Dams* (London, 2001)

Cusack, Tricia, *Riverscapes and National Identities* (Syracuse, NY, 2009)

Graves, John, *Goodbye to a River: A Narrative* (New York, 1960)

Mauch, Christof, and Thomas Zeller, ed., *Rivers in History: Perspectives on Waterways in Europe and North America* (Pittsburgh, PA, 2008)

Middleton, Nick, *Rivers: A Very Short Introduction* (Oxford, 2012)

Skinner, Constance Lindsay, 'Rivers and American Folk', Appendix to Carl Lamson
     Carmer, *The Hudson River* (New York, 1939), n.p.

Skrine, Henry, *A General Account of All Rivers of Note in Great Britain* (London, 1801)

Van Dyke, Henry, *Little Rivers: A Book of Essays in Profitable Idleness* (New York, 1895)

White, Richard, *The Organic Machine: The Remaking of the Columbia River* (New York,
     1995)

Wohl, Ellen E., *Virtual Rivers: Lessons from the Mountain Rivers of the Colorado Front
     Range* (New Haven, CT, 2001)

# Acknowledgements

My first and biggest debt is to the Leverhulme Trust for a twelve-month research fellowship that bought me the time I needed in 2008–09 to really get stuck into this project, and which financed research trips from Vienna to Los Angeles, including that most exotic of cruises – from Liverpool's Pier Head up the Mersey and Manchester Ship Canal to Salford Quays. I am also grateful to the Head of the School of Humanities at Bristol University, Roger Middleton, for arranging a six-month period of leave a few years later, following a period of time consuming management duties, that was crucial to the completion of the manuscript. And Bristol University's Arts Faculty Research Fund facilitated a final visit to Berlin. I would also like to thank the staff at various libraries, including the Austrian National Library (Österreichische Nationalbibliotek), the State Library in Berlin (Staatsbibliothek zu Berlin), the Berlin City Library (Berliner Stadtbibliothek), the New York Public Library and various Oxford University libraries; Ramona Marks of Friends of the Los Angeles River for giving me a tour; Giovanni Mazza, for taking me on a road trip along the Po (and Miriam Leonardi at Trattoria La Buca, Zibello, for cooking some of the finest food I have ever eaten); Michael Leaman at Reaktion for his patience and understanding; Martha Jay and Susannah Jayes, also at Reaktion; Pat and Barry Jones for putting me up on Merseyside; friends such as Harry, Richard and Tim for river talk; and my immediate family (Graziella, Giuliana and Ivana) for putting up with the grumpy state of distraction I always fall into when wrapping up a book. Not least, I am grateful to the various exhilarating rivers I swam in while working on this book.

# Photo Acknowledgements

The author and the publishers wish to express their thanks to the below sources of illustrative material and /or permission to reproduce it.

Photography © The Art Institute of Chicago: p. 153; Alaska State Library, Juneau: pp. 202, 205 top (Eric A. Hegg), 205 bottom (Case & Draper), 208 (Larss & Duclos), 209 (Amos Burg), 211 (Hamacher & Doody); Anchorage Museum of History and Arts, Library and Archives: p. 216 bottom; Austrian National Library: p. 65; Bodleian Library, Oxford: pp. 45, 48, 49 top, 206; © The Trustees of the British Museum: p. 120; Peter Coates: pp. 18, 42, 67, 87, 98, 101, 112, 128, 137, 163, 166, 173, 176, 254; Giuseppe Palmas Photographic Archive: p. 152; reproduced by permission of English Heritage: p. 165; Douglas Hill: p. 261; John Humble: pp. 235, 259; Alan T. Kohl: p. 55; Library of Congress, Washington, DC: pp. 52, 83, 84, 189, 231, 233 top, 237; Los Angeles Public Library: pp. 230, 236 (Akili-Casundria Ramsess), 232, 233 bottom, 245, 257 (Herald-Examiner Collection), 247, 248 (Bill Watson/Herald-Examiner Collection); Andreas Müller-Pohle: pp. 29, 30; NASA: p. 155; Rlichtefeld: p. 57; Salford Local History Library: p. 172; Science Photo Library: pp. 64 (MDA Information Systems), 121 (Royal Astronomical Society), 168 (NRSC Ltd), 199 (Dr Robert Spicier); Twice 24/Rinina25: p. 122; University of Alaska Fairbanks: pp. 212, 216 top (Frederick B. Drane Collection); John Urban Collection, Anchorage Museum of History & Art, Library and Archives: pp. 210, 215.

# Index